Broken Abacus?

*A More Accurate Gauge of
China's Economy*

AUTHORS
Daniel H. Rosen
Beibei Bao

FOREWORD
Carsten Holz

*A Report of the CSIS Freeman
Chair in China Studies*

September 2015

CSIS | CENTER FOR STRATEGIC & INTERNATIONAL STUDIES

ROWMAN &
LITTLEFIELD

Lanham • Boulder • New York • London

About CSIS

For over 50 years, the Center for Strategic and International Studies (CSIS) has worked to develop solutions to the world's greatest policy challenges. Today, CSIS scholars are providing strategic insights and bipartisan policy solutions to help decisionmakers chart a course toward a better world.

CSIS is a nonprofit organization headquartered in Washington, D.C. The Center's 220 full-time staff and large network of affiliated scholars conduct research and analysis and develop policy initiatives that look into the future and anticipate change.

Founded at the height of the Cold War by David M. Abshire and Admiral Arleigh Burke, CSIS was dedicated to finding ways to sustain American prominence and prosperity as a force for good in the world. Since 1962, CSIS has become one of the world's preeminent international institutions focused on defense and security; regional stability; and transnational challenges ranging from energy and climate to global health and economic integration.

Former U.S. senator Sam Nunn has chaired the CSIS Board of Trustees since 1999. Former deputy secretary of defense John J. Hamre became the Center's president and chief executive officer in 2000.

CSIS does not take specific policy positions; accordingly, all views expressed herein should be understood to be solely those of the author(s).

Center for Strategic & International Studies
1616 Rhode Island Avenue, NW
Washington, DC 20036
202-887-0200 | www.csis.org

Rowman & Littlefield
4501 Forbes Boulevard
Lanham, MD 20706
301-459-3366 | www.rowman.com

Contents

Foreword

No other nation in the world loves to keep track of things more than China does. Its history of official records is measured in thousands of years. Measurement was also central to the planned economy: planners needed accurate information from enterprises in order to design production and investment plans. In the reform period, measurement was soon needed for everything from determining the remuneration of managers of state-owned enterprises to deciding on the fate of provincial governors or setting monetary policy. More often than not, the measurement that was needed was a measure of output: in its most recent incarnation, value-added at the enterprise level, gross regional output at the provincial level, and gross domestic product (GDP) at the national level.

For more than two decades, GDP has been the centerpiece of national economic policy and the political psyche. The front page of the *People's Daily* would proudly proclaim the latest growth achievement. But given their prominence, these data have also repeatedly come under scrutiny.

In the Great Leap Forward, the data are known to have been falsified. Otherwise, Western researchers thought, the data were quite reliable. In the early 1990s, the World Bank felt that Chinese GDP was underestimated, but it soon abandoned its alternative calculations. Shortly thereafter, economic historian Angus Maddison claimed that Chinese GDP was overestimated. In the second half of the 1990s, China's National Bureau of Statistics (NBS) commissioner felt that there was a grave danger of falsification and brought to public attention the "wind of falsification and embellishment," which then triggered a campaign sanctioned by the Party Central Committee to end data falsification by reporting units and localities. It also triggered widespread domestic and foreign suspicion that China's GDP growth and China's GDP levels are overestimated.

This is where Daniel Rosen and Beibei Bao come in, providing an outsider's independent estimate of China's true economic size. In a heroic effort, they take apart the Chinese statistical system to reassess the choices the NBS makes. They do so armed with the tools of international statistical practices and an unprecedented understanding of the operations of China's statistical system.

Reading through their dissection and recompilation of Chinese data, it is hard not to become convinced that the authors are on to something. Their alternative calculations, accompanied by one robustness check after another, sector for sector of the economy, suggest that researchers outside the NBS have finally achieved what was previously deemed impossible: come up with a GDP figure for China that is likely a more accurate reflection of reality than the official figure. Their results are so solidly founded that they redefine the debate about China's national income accounting system and pose a direct challenge to business as usual.

The authors find a fair amount more GDP than proclaimed by the NBS. But does that additional GDP matter? We all know that China is big. At first sight, a bit more output may not seem a big deal, but once the authors delve into the possible implications, it quickly becomes apparent that this is no minor correction that one can easily ignore. From the sectoral analysis to the time series analysis, the amount of newly found GDP has some very serious implications that one would do well to take note of. I am also left with some hope that the authors' work may yet contribute to a quantum leap in China's national income accounting statistics, in terms both of the degree of transparency that the NBS will have to adopt in order to be able to engage with a challenge such as this and the actual GDP calculation methods that the NBS may choose to use in the future.

Carsten Holz
Hong Kong University of Science and Technology
Harvard University
March 19, 2015

Acknowledgments

The authors are grateful to a broad set of people, without whose counsel and enthusiasm this undertaking could not have been accomplished. First, a number of anonymous career statisticians at China's National Bureau of Statistics provided essential critique to our work. Internationally, Markus Rodlauer at the International Monetary Fund, Liu Xiaofan formerly of the World Bank, and Guo Jiemin at the U.S. Bureau of Economic Analysis provided valuable insights into the evolution of China's national accounts. A long line of respected academics have built the foundations on which this effort stands. We are most indebted to Carsten Holz at the Hong Kong University of Science and Technology, our principal adviser, whose unrivaled knowledge of Chinese statistics many times pointed us in the right direction. Zhang Jun at Fudan University shared important perspective on services and expenditure data. We have learned from discussions with Yao Yang, Huang Yiping, Xu Dianqing, Liu Shiguo, Ma Minnan, Scott Rozelle, Zhao Nan, Wang Yafei, and Wang Wensheng. In particular, in excellent work on China's input-output tables, Li Xiaoqin, formerly of the Conference Board, inspired elements of our methodological design. We are grateful to a number of non-Chinese China hands, including Stephen Green, Calla Weimer, Tom Orlik, and Andrew Polk, who offered useful views based on years of observation. Fan Dianhua, Li Tingzhen, and Cai Hongyu added to our understanding of specific industry conditions. Participants in a study group convened to shape our research approach, including (in alphabetical order) Nick Borst, David Dollar, Bob Goldberg, Nicholas Lardy, Wayne Morrison, Derek Scissors, Brad Setser, David Stockton, Kim Zieschang, and several of our colleagues at the Center for Strategic and International Studies (CSIS) mentioned below. Three of the scholars named above also served as final reviewers of our manuscript and offered additional commentary along with their endorsement.

A number of our Rhodium Group colleagues made important contributions. Excellent research work by Wang Yaqi, Cassie Gao, Dai Qi, and Anna Snyder helped manage a huge pool of data. Shashank Mohan, the firm's quantitative director, provided major early-stage inputs. Along the way, Thilo Hanemann and senior associate Jacob Funk Kirkegaard both provided advice and guidance. Jasper Hitchen, our superb in-house editor, made a complex text much easier to read.

Our collaborators at CSIS helped orient the study at inception by hosting our 2013 study group and at the finishing stage. We wish to thank Christopher Johnson, Matthew Goodman, and Michael Green in particular, as well as Dr. John Hamre for inviting us to collaborate with the Center on this significant endeavor. Grace Hearty and Nicole White provided great administrative support.

Last but not least, we thank our families, in particular Anna and Shaofeng, who endured our preoccupation with this study over the past two years and provided great encouragement. We dedicate this study to them.

Executive Summary

Skepticism has surrounded estimates of China's economic size throughout the post-1978 period, but it was obvious enough that the nation was growing fast, broadly, and had a long way to go to catch up to the advanced world. While a few economists made careers studying the nuances, business leaders and policymakers understood well enough what was happening. Today China has reached the point where the details are critical, and neither the magnitude of growth nor even the direction is obvious any more. Studies have examined China's annual growth rate in detail, but few addressed the accuracy of its nominal size, given the difficulty of that analysis. As the growth model assumptions that deflected many questions expire, previously deferred questions about China's economy—starting with the accuracy of its nominal GDP figures—must be resolved.

This study is an independent effort to reestimate China's economy in terms of gross domestic product (GDP), the most common measure used to compare national economies today. We rely on official data where there is a basis to be comfortable in doing so, and we document exhaustively the merits and pitfalls involved; we employ alternative data where necessary. We describe and follow China's stated methods for calculating national accounts wherever possible so that our results can better be compared to official figures.

Before undertaking that series of calculations and extrapolations in Chapter 3, we make our task—and the readers'—slightly easier by reviewing what GDP does and does not promise to measure so that misinformation about Chinese practices can be set aside at the beginning (Chapter 1). We also review past scholarly (or, often, semischolarly) debates about China's GDP practices to sort out which arguments are germane today and which are obsolete (Chapter 2). In the conclusion, written for non-technical readers (Chapter 4), we look at our findings through three distinct sets of eyes: those of economists in China, those of China's politicians, and those of foreign observers who—because they will be heavily impacted by the trajectory of China's economy—have an urgent interest and stake in this subject. We ease into this challenging study with a brief introduction following this Executive Summary.

Qualitative Findings

While our review of China's statistical system, economic history, and debates about measuring GDP may engross many readers, the busiest professionals will find a synopsis of our key findings most immediately valuable. The study provides a number of findings, qualitative and quantitative. Qualitatively, one of our key takeaways is that China has made great progress in modernizing GDP statistics and is not akin to the Soviet Union in national accounting terms. China's GDP methodologies are largely in line with international practice. Charges that China's estimates are sheer fabrications are misinformed. Chinese statisticians have worked earnestly to converge with international practices, and by and large have succeeded. GDP is an artificial construct for all economies, and in all cases there are imperfections in estimating it; China is no exception for having shortcomings. We conclude that suspicions about China's data arise from Beijing's choice to not make methods transparent and accessible, often going as far as to intentionally suppress information. At the same time, poor economic analysis of Chinese conditions, by both Chinese and foreign researchers, plays a part in this confusion.

In contrast to the general finding of improvement over time, we conclude that Chinese statistics and their transparency are still sometimes shaped by political interests. The latest illustration of that is Beijing's release of the five-year census results and related methodological improvements in December 2014. Based on China's National Bureau of Statistics (NBS) commitments to upgrade from the 1993 System of National Accounts (SNA) to the latest 2008 SNA, and our calculations of underestimation of GDP in 2008 both due to the archaic GDP production boundary and counting conventions as well as other factors, the revised 2013 GDP Beijing reported should have been larger. Instead a mere 3.4 percent upward revision was offered, following an unexplained last-minute three-day delay of the revisions release press conference. As the nation grows larger and more advanced, the level of expectations about its statistical practices naturally rises. The December 2014 release was an opportunity to demonstrate continued forward progress, and the NBS had made clear that practices would be improved. Yet what occurred instead suggested that political discomfort over the realities illuminated by better statistics can trump the benefits of transparency.

Key Quantitative Findings

Our most important results are quantitative because few studies have attempted such an independent reappraisal of China's nominal GDP. A comprehensive summary of our calculations is presented in Table ES.1, while a number of figures are used to describe our key findings below. Die-hard national accounting specialists and macroeconomists will find a multitude of quantitative results in the following chapters, but we believe seven are most noteworthy for experts and general China-interested readers alike:

1. **China is bigger, not smaller:** Our reassessment suggests that China's 2008 GDP was most likely 13.1 to 16.3 percent larger than official statistics indicated at the time. Beijing's reappraisal of 2008 GDP (released in Spring 2015) adjusted up the official number by less than 1 percent, leaving the bulk of activity we identified uncounted. Further, for general purposes, we believe it is reasonable to extrapolate those results to the current period as well, which leads us to the conclusion that China's 2013 GDP is more accurately stated at about $10.5 trillion, rather than the official $9.5

Table ES.1. A Reconstruction of China's 2008 GDP

Unit: RMB trillion

	Official	Recalculated	Recl./Official %
GDP*	**31.40**	**35.51**	**13.1%**
		36.53	**16.3%**
Primary Sector	*3.37*	*3.26*	*–3.2%*
Secondary Sector	*14.90*	*16.14*	*8.3%*
Industry	13.03	14.13	8.5%
Construction	1.87	2.01	7.3%
Tertiary Sector	*13.13*	*16.06*	*22.2%*
Transportation, Storage, and Postal Services	1.64	1.83	11.9%
Info Trans, Computer Services and Software	0.79	0.86	9.7%
Wholesale and Retail Trade	2.62	3.04	16.1%
Accommodation and Catering Services	0.66	0.70	5.7%
Finance	1.49	1.53	2.8%
Real Estate	1.47	3.43	132.8%
Education	0.89	0.87	–2.1%
Public Administration and Social Organizations	1.38	1.42	2.7%
Other Six Service subsectors	2.20	2.38	7.9%
Research and Development	*n/a*	*0.04* *1.07*	*n/a*

* The two values are derived from two scenarios of R&D inclusion's impact on GDP. The official data are not subject to 2013 census revisions.

Sources: NBS, authors' calculations.

trillion—a pattern likely to continue until NBS announces additional revisions. These results are illustrated in Figure ES.1.

2. **The service sector is most problematic:** We can rank the areas of the economy where the greatest adjustments are required, as illustrated in Figure ES.2. At the broadest sector level, the hard to count services cluster is unsurprisingly in greatest need of upward revision—22.2 percent in our estimate. The secondary sector, consisting of industry and construction, needs a smaller but important 8.3 percent revision. The primary sector, meanwhile, still requires a modest discounting by our reckoning. Last, we examined elements not even covered in China's official GDP, but which should be once practices are modernized—in particular the capitalization of research and development (R&D) investment (due to data limitations, the newly counted R&D value-added cannot be clearly divided between industrial and service activities, and hence we separated them from the other sectors, as shown in Table ES.1). China does not publish value-added data for R&D, but according to our calculations, officials are underestimating R&D value-added by $6.5 to $154 billion a year, though data do not permit us to specify a value within that wide range (Table ES.2).

Figure ES.1. Official versus Our Revised GDP Comparison
Unit: USD trillion

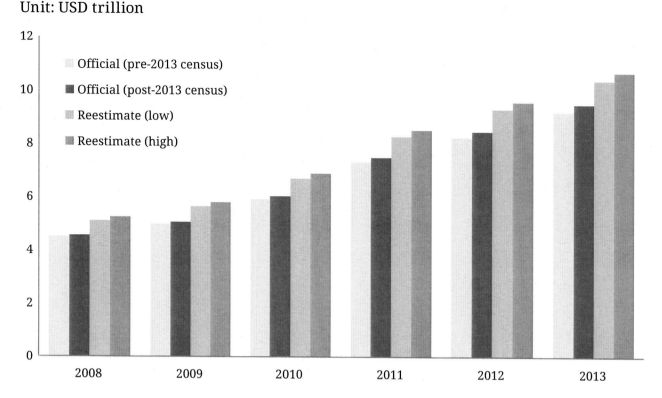

Sources: NBS, authors' calculations.

3. **Real estate is even more important than currently reflected:** The distribution of specific industrial underestimates taking place is striking. The largest revision, in real estate, is responsible for 38–48 percent of our total adjustment, suggesting that China's GDP growth has been even more dependent on a property boom than already understood (Figure ES.3). That output pattern also disproportionately benefits a minority of wealthier Chinese who are already widening the gap in income and wealth.

4. **Structural adjustment started earlier:** While problematic from a property sector and income distribution perspective, these results do come with a silver lining: the promising service sector overtook the industrial sector earlier than believed—in 2009, not 2012 as official data now suggest. This is a necessary indicator of a sustainable future, although not a sufficient one as long as it is overly dependent on real estate–related value. This earlier internal passing point was a key fact missing from the 2008–2013 policy debates. China was more like similarly developed countries than previously thought. It was, in this sense, more "normal." It also suggests that the end of the line for the old growth model arrived in the middle of the Hu Jintao era, rather than the beginning of the Xi Jinping era.

5. **A higher GDP denominator could change policy-relevant ratios:** Our calculations suggest that China's *output* value has been underestimated, not *input* costs: this has

Figure ES.2. A Breakdown of Marginal Revisions to 2008 Official GDP
Unit: USD billion

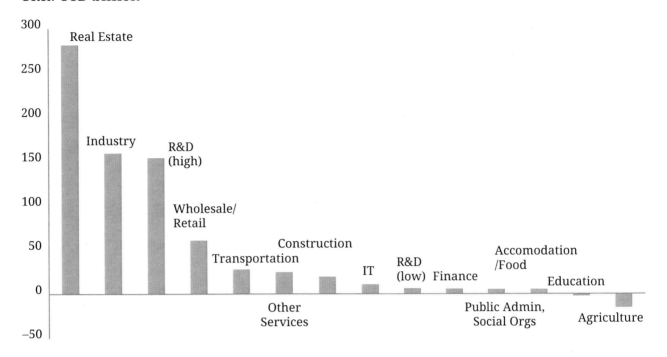

Sources: NBS, authors' calculations.

Table ES.2. Sectoral Adjustments' Impact on 2008 Headline GDP
Unit: RMB trillion

	Official Value-Added	Recalculated Value-Added	Revisions' Impact on Official Headline GDP
GDP*	31.40	35.51	13.1%
		36.53	16.3%
Primary Sector	3.37	3.26	−0.3%
Secondary Sector	14.90	16.14	4.0%
Tertiary Sector	13.13	16.06	9.3%
Research and Development	n/a	0.04	0.1%
		1.07	3.4%

* The two values are derived from two scenarios of R&D inclusion's impact on GDP. The official data are not subject to 2013 census revisions.
Sources: NBS, authors' calculations.

interesting implications for closely watched ratios used to gauge performance. With a higher GDP denominator and steady input numerator, the debt to GDP picture (or output per unit of capital invested) is slightly less dire. Gross output per worker is slightly higher, indicating a marginally better labor productivity. The energy intensity of GDP is slightly lower than previously observed. It is important, however, not to compare pre-revision intensities with post-revision estimates and mistake an artificially steep change for real progress. For instance, Beijing's carbon reduction

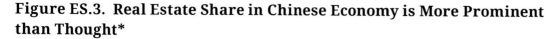

Figure ES.3. Real Estate Share in Chinese Economy is More Prominent than Thought*

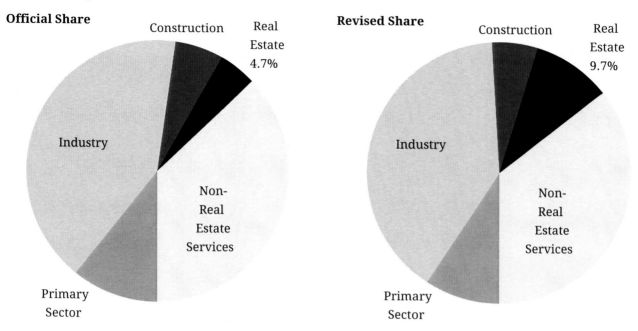

* This sectoral breakdown does not include impact of research and development capitalization, whose value is calculated using a different methodology from the rest. See details in Chapter 3.
Sources: NBS, authors' calculations.

goals, benchmarked against 2005 intensities, should be evaluated against a constant series, not a "broken" data set.

6. **China could be the world's largest national economy sooner than previously thought:** On the international policy side, the first and foremost quantitative question is whether China's economy is a Potemkin village of statistical artifice. We dismiss this line; China is as large or likely larger than officially stated. The most charged policy context in which this query arises is the discussion of whether and when China's nominal GDP could achieve the top spot globally. Our study suggests that the "global passing point" could arrive two to three years earlier as a result of the more advanced level of Chinese value-added, but the exact year depends on relative growth rates, inflation, and exchange rate outcomes in both China and abroad—especially in the United States. Our related insight is that it will be harder to wring higher growth out of the structure of today's more advanced Chinese economy in the years ahead.

7. **Knowledge-intensive industries are increasingly important:** A final headline observation is that high-skill, knowledge-intensive, and inherently international subsectors will account for a large and influential share of China's reported GDP growth in the years ahead. As noted earlier, value-added from R&D activity plays a key role in our upward revisions, especially in light of the latest international GDP practices. China's own restatements—announced in December 2014 and also in early

2015, right before the publication of this study—emphasized financial services value-added growth which we did not even count, for want of access to key information at the time. Both these market segments rely on professionals with a high degree of mobility—the choice to move to the most attractive opportunities internationally—and depend on free flows of information and ideas within and across China's borders. As will be discussed in Chapter 1, the rise of GDP as a standard yardstick for national economic performance was driven in part by popular demand for illumination as to the relative performance of different economic systems, and these advanced activities are the cutting edge of that contest today.

Overarching Observations and Caveats

The subsector-by-subsector calculations summarized above are an important contribution of this study. In addition, the study demonstrates that through a combination of historical context, attention to international practices, careful analysis of official data, and judicious selection of supplementary data it is possible to reduce the uncertainty about China to which many observers seem to be resigned. The study does not by any means resolve all arguments. It focuses on 2008 as the base year for reestimation due to data realities, and then makes bold assumptions about the applicability of those results to current conditions in drawing many conclusions. Many of the steps taken to test the value of Chinese output are debatable: wherever possible the study presents all reasonable approaches rather than simply a preferred strategy. We tackle some of the most important China economic questions of our time, despite the technical difficulties, and make our methods transparent to interested scholars and others with contrary opinions in order to restart discussion of these questions, rather than suggest we should have the last word.

Introduction: A $10 Trillion Question

Consider two facts about China: first, the consequences of China's size and performance for the rest of the world are increasingly great, and second, confidence about the accuracy and precision of standard measures of China's economic size and performance is low and diminishing further relative to expectations.[1] China is projected to overtake the United States as the world's largest economy in perhaps a decade; by some measures, such as purchasing power parity (PPP), it already has.[2] Yet, China's official economic data are thought to be incomplete and unreliable, and policymakers—as well as business leaders and other stakeholders worldwide—are left planning for the first peer competitor to rival the economic role of the United States in a century using suspect information. A virtual autarky three decades ago, China has grown rapidly, bulleting down the path of global economic integration to become a vital part of the international system. China's new heavyweight status affects welfare and security interests worldwide, and has reshaped the country's priorities in bilateral affairs and in interactions with global institutions. Therefore the time has come to reassess our understanding of China's concordance with international standards for measuring its economy, the reasons why observers are so skeptical, what a better estimation would suggest, and what the implications are. A brief review of China's economic progress is the starting point.

Growth and Statistics Since 1978

Since the start of economic reforms in 1978, China has delivered extraordinary growth by every measure. Growth was kick-started in the 1980s by decollectivizing agricultural production, allowing Chinese citizens to start private businesses, and opening up to foreign investment from Taiwan, Hong Kong, and other Asian economies in labor-intensive light manufacturing. After the Tiananmen crisis in 1989, Deng Xiaoping initiated another round of liberalization. Special Economic Zones were expanded to attract more foreign investment. In the mid-1990s price controls were lifted further, and many state-owned enterprises were privatized, modernized, or shut down. Accession to the World Trade

---

1. At lower-income levels, a nation's economic activity is limited to easily measured material goods and food production. At middle-income levels, a greater share of activity is composed, for instance, of relatively intangible services, which are inherently much harder to accurately measure. China has entered this stage.

2. IMF World Economic Outlook Database October 2014 Edition, http://www.imf.org/external/pubs/ft/weo/2014/02/weodata/index.aspx.

Organization (2001) was another milestone for the economy, introducing a standard template for domestic reform, helping to attract greater foreign direct investment, and facilitating China's deeper integration into global production networks. From the start of reform to the present, China reported roughly 10 percent average annual growth by traditional gross domestic product (GDP) measures, propelling it to the status of the world's second-largest economy, officially estimated today at $10.4 trillion. Much has been achieved, but with nearly 1.4 billion people and an average per capita GDP level of $7,600 in 2014 (compared to $54,600 in the United States), this economy has still further to go.

But this economic journey has proceeded hand in hand with concerns about data accuracy and validity, which are as old as China's economic boom. In fact, flawed statistics were an important part of the economic malaise of the 1970s that forced Beijing to change course and choose a path of economic reform. China's leaders radically misestimated their potential petroleum resources, forcing them to turn to foreign investment to achieve their goals. Earlier, during the Great Leap Forward (1958–1961), officials falsified agricultural output statistics on a massive scale in order to rationalize dedicating more resources to heavy industrial production—the key determinant in their career prospects at that moment. Overstated data for grain yields contributed to catastrophic famines with a death toll in the tens of millions.[3]

Since the end of Mao's social experiments and the beginning of Deng's reforms, the quality of statistics on Chinese economic activity has improved, though concerns remain and grow as China becomes a central player in the world economy. Some of the institutional factors that caused misreporting during the Great Leap Forward—such as incentives for local policymakers to over- or underreport economic activity—still exist. New factors add to the challenges of statistical accuracy, such as the growing importance of intangible service sector growth in China, which traditional accountants around the world struggle with estimating. Problems extend to all nodes of economic data: high-frequency data collected to track monthly activity and prices, national accounting figures such as GDP or balance of payments data, and the alternative indicators needed to assess the size and structure of activity outside standard statistical systems (for instance, in broad swaths of the rural economy).

These gaps and data quality problems produce uncertainties about China's GDP and other aggregate indicators. Moreover, with limited transparency and gaps in the explanation of methodologies the National Bureau of Statistics (NBS) uses to construct GDP figures, results cannot be reproduced and examined independently. This is likely to tempt political interference because leaders grade themselves, and one another, on whether they achieve the planned economic targets which they themselves keep score on. With imperfect information, independent analysts have estimated discrepancies from 1 to as high as

---

3. Chris Buckley, "Milder Accounts of Hardships Under Mao Arise as His Birthday Nears," *New York Times*, October 16, 2013, http://www.nytimes.com/2013/10/17/world/asia/advancing-a-milder-version-of-maos-calamities.html; Jisheng Yang, "China's Great Shame," *New York Times*, November 13, 2012, http://www.nytimes.com/2012/11/14/opinion/chinas-great-shame.html?_r=0.

7.9 percentage points between reported GDP and their private estimates for volatile periods, such as 1996 to 1999—allegations which define the prevailing cynicism right up until today.[4]

Today's Urgency for Better Economic Estimates

Despite these issues, China's statistical uncertainties were tolerable (to policymakers and business leaders, if not for independent economists and statisticians) until fairly recently, for two reasons. First, China's economy only became big enough to have truly global consequences in the past few years. Second, though the precision of data were questionable, the magnitude and direction of China's development were by and large indisputable—and that reality was more important than the details. In recent years both of these mitigating factors have changed.

Today China is more than big enough to matter, and, even more important, its economic trajectory is no longer obvious. For example, China has become central to global commodity prices. Between 1978 and 2000, China was able to achieve 9 to 10 percent annual economic growth without significantly straining domestic or international natural resource supplies because of significant improvements in the resource-intensity of the economy. State-owned enterprise reforms and price liberalization led to efficiency gains for the first time since 1949, while structural adjustment into less resource-intensive sectors lightened demand. But in 2003, after two decades of resource-intensity improvement, demand for energy and other commodities started growing *faster* than GDP. This upside surprise in Chinese consumption forced global prices for everything from oil to iron ore to become significantly higher between 2003 and 2008. Commodity markets were caught wrong-footed because of a failure to anticipate China's structural changes—due in large part to a paucity of quality Chinese economic and energy data. The global economy, not just China, paid a price for this demand shock. While this had great importance for foreign interests, the foremost consequences were felt by China itself.

With the structural drivers behind China's old growth model (demographic dividend and scale economies in traded labor-intensive manufacturing) running out of steam before replacement drivers (domestic demand and productivity growth) are locked in, the magnitude of China's growth is no longer a sure thing. The era in which rough approximations of China's economic production and demand were enough is over; henceforth, better statistical accuracy and transparency for the world's second-largest and fastest-growing major economy is not only desirable but essential.

The world *needs* a better abacus for China, and progress toward that end is the objective of this study.

---

4. Angus Maddison and Harry X. Wu, "China's Economic Performance: How Fast Has GDP Grown; How Big Is It Compared with the USA?," 2007, 5, http://www.ggdc.net/maddison/articles/China_Maddison_Wu_22_Feb_07.pdf.

1 | A Framework to Measure a Country's Economy

The task of this chapter is to unpack today's standard measure of a nation's economic size—its gross domestic product (GDP)—explain how it has evolved and why, and answer the important introductory question of whether China goes about national economic assessment the same way as other nations. An important starting point is that GDP, or any other estimation of activity, for that matter, is not an objective reality but rather a man-made, artificial construct, built to suit certain purposes rooted in the present moment. GDP was never built to measure environmental sustainability, and it simply does not. It does not reflect all of the work done in a society but only what is included within a chosen boundary. And it requires completely arbitrary computations of value-added to society from intangible activities that do not always add value, like financial speculation on junk bond markets. In the end, this study offers a detailed assessment and criticism of China's GDP estimates and processes. But it is important to understand that the system of national economic estimation itself, not just China's ability to comport with that system, is still evolving.

Why We Measure Determines *How* We Measure

Economic size is not an objective reality: all definitions of an economy are man-made. GDP itself has been called one of the "great inventions of the twentieth century."[1] What we choose to count and how we choose to value it in quantifying a national economy have changed radically over the past hundred years and continue to evolve today. Only a few decades ago, government expenditures were not counted in most estimates of national economic activity. Just as Premier Li Keqiang was reported to have said in the late 2000s (while as Liaoning province party secretary) that China's GDP data were "man-made" and unreliable, leaving him to depend on a more limited set of real economy indicators to manage growth, depression-era U.S. presidents struggled to steer policy "on the basis of such sketchy data as stock price indices, freight car loadings, and incomplete indices of industrial production."[2] Before getting too smug about our progress to date, it is worth considering that someday soon the current practice of not accounting for the depletion of

---

1. Richard T. Froyen, "GDP: One of the Great Inventions of the 20th Century," *Survey of Current Business* 80, no. 1 (January 2000): 6–8, https://www.bea.gov/scb/account_articles/general/0100od/maintext.htm.

2. Richard T. Froyen, *Macroeconomics: Theories and Policies* (Englewood Cliff, NJ: Prentice Hall, 2009), 13.

the natural environment might be considered barbaric and primitive. Current practice for valuing service sector activity in general is surprisingly arbitrary, raising questions about the GDP approach—designed to count tangible goods—in an era of service sector dominance.

Because economic size is "not a primary fact but an empirical construct,"[3] *how* we choose to measure it derives from *why* we are motivated to do so. Two powerful motives have shaped the approach to national accounting: one quite ancient and the other more modern. The older impulse is to aid the state in determining how much tax or production can be extracted to pursue sovereign goals, often for the imperative of making war. Today's measure of GDP was invented in the United States and Britain in the early days of World War II to determine how best to finance the war. That same necessity has been the crucible of economic policymaking and statistical measures throughout recorded history. The *Guanzi*—Chinese essays on statecraft published in the first century B.C. based on older records—included details on "using statistics to control state finances." The text advises rulers to conduct careful and comprehensive calculations of production activity in order to set appropriate monetary policy so that authorities can maximize the extraction of resources for war. Leaders are counseled that if they do not keep these summary national economic statistics secret, "those below will control the government on high."[4]

State finance has been the impetus for national accounting through millennia. In the Old Testament's Exodus 30:11–16, God stipulates that a census of Israel be carried out along with the collection of a per capita tax for the maintenance of religious facilities. The word *census* is Roman and comes from the survey and registration of resources available for military administration. Wherever records of government bureaucracy remain, efforts to count up economic activity for state purposes—especially martial—are in evidence.

In her *GDP: A Brief but Affectionate History*, Diane Coyle traces the roots of today's national economic measures, in a delightfully readable way, to seventeenth-century Britain. In the 1660s, Sir William Petty published articles proposing how to conduct an estimate of national economic wealth—both in terms of the stock of assets and annual flows of income—so that the nation's capacity to pay for fights abroad could be properly gauged.[5] Adam Smith's 1776 *The Wealth of Nations* advanced the effort to refine the measure of economies, principally by arguing for the separation of productive and unproductive activity. Smith's reasoning excluded activity that did not make a new material contribution to tangible output or add to the value of extant material goods like manufacturing. This

---

3. Attributed to Richard Stone, in Diane Coyle's *GDP: A Brief but Affectionate History* (Oxford: Princeton University Press, 2014), 24.

4. Zhong Guan, *Guanzi: Political, Economic, and Philosophical Essays from Early China—A Study and Translation*, trans. W. Allyn Rickett, vol. 2 (Princeton, NJ: Princeton University Press, ca. 1985–1998), XXII, 74, 71.2, 390.

5. Sir William Petty and John Graunt, *The Economic Writings of Sir William Petty*, vol. 1 (Cambridge University Press, 1899), 103–120, http://books.google.com/books?id=KNQoAAAAYAAJ&pg=PA100&lpg=PA100&dq =Verbum+Sapienti+william+petty&source=bl&ots=Eh-nhAsj1b&sig=8_Iz7s7v0qpb-J04pP3bwPJBApc&hl=en&sa =X&ei=10dmVNKjIfL_sASNlYLgAw&ved=0CFsQ6AEwCQ#v=onepage&q=Verbum%20Sapienti%20william%20 petty&f=false.

"boundary" excludes government services in the economy, including administrative and defense expenditure, as well as all other service activity by lawyers, doctors, teachers, financiers, and the more "frivolous" professions, as Smith describes them, such as entertainment.

The essence of Smith's argument for excluding materially "unproductive" activity from the measure of national activity continued to be relevant well into the twentieth century. The "material production system," or MPS, favored by the Soviet economies maintained this exclusion of service activity until the collapse of the Soviet Union. In China's case, it was formally used until 1993, and the legacy of that bias against counting intangibles continues to cast a long shadow over Chinese national accounts, as is explored at length in the following chapters.

While sophisticated perspectives on national economic measurement were evident in Britain more than 350 years ago, today's concept of GDP, standardized across countries, did not emerge until the 1940s. Several explanations have been offered for why there was not greater urgency for measurement until the mid-twentieth century. For one thing, economic growth was simply slower prior to the Industrial Revolution, and leaders and policymakers perceived less need to monitor performance on a continuous, real-time basis. The financial needs of the state, such as paying for wars, were seen as enduring and not in need of thorough rethinking. Moreover, the notion that the state could play an active role in smoothing out and optimizing economic activity, thus requiring a finely calibrated meter of activity, was still to come.

Beginning with the late industrial revolution, the complexity and resource needs of economies grew. Populations clustered in cities, and the predictable economic cycle tied to agrarian life gave way to more novel cycles of unfettered consumer demand and business investment, monetary behavior, and booms and busts. In tandem with those organic trends, concepts of economic statecraft and economics evolved. Alfred Marshall's 1890 *Principles of Economics* established the foundations we know today, recognizing services as a productive activity, introducing demand and supply balances to model prices in the marketplace, and describing the contest between producer and consumer surplus.

Marshall's framework pointed to a second and more modern motivation for national accounting: not so that the state could better extract resources from the people but so the people could evaluate the performance of the state. James Carville's famous reduction of the 1992 presidential campaign to three words—"the economy, stupid"—was the logical terminus of this reversal in motive. The need for statistics to evaluate the performance of government arose for two reasons. First, as Marshall had explored, the rules set by government would determine who won and who lost in the marketplace. Second, by the early 1930s, economists—most famously John Maynard Keynes—were arguing for the centrality of government in the economy, rather than the archaic conception of government as something that should not even be counted in national economic activity. Keynes and others viewed the government both as a supplier of public goods that would enhance general welfare, like education, and as a provider of countercyclical fiscal stimulus that should very much be counted in economic output. National economic statistics were required for officials to perform these functions and for voters to judge official performance.

We turn to the modern approach to measuring those performance statistics below. First, there is one more facet of the motivation for national accounting to lay out. While data indicators are a component of the contest of competence among political rivals and political parties within democratic nations today, they play a role internationally as well. Each nation makes tradeoffs—for instance, between liberty and equality—implicitly or explicitly, and these choices create different sets of winners and losers. Comparison of outcomes facilitates consciousness about the merits of these choices and whether citizens are being shortchanged by national performance. This comparison is useful, for example, in fine-tuning the set of policies generally shared among the market-oriented democracies, as demonstrated by debates in Italy, Germany, and Ireland about what level of taxation is justified or how much unemployment must be tolerated. Attempting to compare growth rates played an even more sensitive role in the twentieth century because of the Cold War struggle between the fundamental ideas of market capitalism and Soviet communism. Economists were motivated by the goal of comparing rival systems to understand their nature and potential for growth. Political leaders were fixed on the symbolic power of performance data to validate the superiority or inferiority of competing ideas.

The interest in cross-national comparisons, both among market nations and between them and nonmarket economies, amplified the need to refine the norms of economic measurement and standardize them internationally. The caucus of the Organisation for Economic Co-operation and Development (OECD) economies coalesced around GDP as their standard measure, while the communist bloc nations generally employed a measure of tangible output and value-added only. In addition, communist bloc nations tended to be secretive, and in some cases intentionally misleading, about economic information. Russia only switched to GDP in 1989, and China transitioned over the period from 1985 to 1993. With competing accounting systems, methodological differences sometimes became heated. We now know that an internal debate over the size of Cold War–era Russia divided government economists in Washington. The CIA's public history of these reviews noted a long-time Rand Corporation Fellow's final grades for the analysis (centered on gross national, rather than domestic, product [GNP]):

> In his category of "Validity and Accuracy," which he graded as little better than average, Wolf concluded that CIA overestimated the size of Soviet GNP—that is, in his view, it was no more than 30 percent of U.S. GNP compared with the geometric mean estimate of around 50 percent that the Agency claimed. Analysts persistently overestimated the Soviet economy's growth rate by "at least a couple of percentage points," and underestimated the military burden.[6]

---

6. James Noren, "CIA's Analysis of the Soviet Economy," in *Watching the Bear: Essays on CIA's Analysis of the Soviet Union*, ed. Gerald K. Haines and Robert E. Leggett (Langley, VA: Center for the Study of Intelligence, Central

The Agency's response was not to blame their analysts' judgment but rather the very concept of GNP:

> The disagreement was not over all the dismal things "we knew were going on," [but] the divergence was over whether "those things" were possible in an economy that was growing at an average of nearly 2 percent a year. The CIA argued that this was possible because GNP merely measured gross output without regard to use, quality, or contribution to welfare; it included, for example, the military production and raw quantities of wasteful output.[7]

This exchange underscores the extent to which debate over measuring economic activity had evolved: from early efforts to determine how much surplus there was for a state to extract from the population to pursue sovereign aims, to a focus on how well an economic system was serving the public interest, to a yardstick for geopolitical rivalry. Economic activity had progressed from a means to an end to the end in itself. Because measures of economic activity are contrived and inherently man-made—even within the framework of GDP—national accounting is inherently prone to disagreement over what to count, how to count it, how much is enough, and how to interpret the result. The disagreement did not end with the demise of the Soviet Union. With the adoption of GDP as its sole standard in 1993, China began a series of dramatic restatements of its economic size, including better counting of service sector activity for the first time. Those efforts continue today (as discussed in the following chapters). After a brief era of expectation that economic models were destined to converge following the Soviet collapse, epitomized by Francis Fukayama's *The End of History*, conflict over economic models resurfaced in the 2000s. China's commitment to full marketization along Western lines was called into question, while its growth rate suggested that its performance would eventually challenge the major economic incumbents, giving rise to the same fears that had accompanied the contest of systems in the Cold War. As before, concerns that reported GDP growth rates might be distorted for propaganda and other geopolitical purposes arose, and with them an urgency to refine the system of measurement and comparability so that such distortion would be less likely.

The System of National Accounts

Simon Kuznets and other experts at the U.S. Department of Commerce and the private National Bureau of Economic Research (NBER) led the production of the first set of national income accounts for the U.S. economy in 1934.[8] His accounts, covering the years 1929–1932, covered two of the three ways we measure national economic activity today: tallying

---

Intelligence Agency, 2003), https://www.cia.gov/library/center-for-the-study-of-intelligence/csi-publications/books-and-monographs/watching-the-bear-essays-on-cias-analysis-of-the-soviet-union/article02.html.

7. Douglas J. MacEachin, "The Tyrannical Numbers," in *CIA Assessments of the Soviet Union: The Record versus the Charges* (Washington, DC: Center for the Study of Intelligence, Central Intelligence Agency, 1996), https://www.cia.gov/library/center-for-the-study-of-intelligence/csi-publications/books-and-monographs/cia-assessments-of-the-soviet-union-the-record-versus-the-charges/tyran.html.

8. Simon Kuznets, "National Income, 1929–1932," in *National Income, 1929–1932* (Cambridge, MA: NBER, 1934), 1–12, http://www.nber.org/chapters/c2258.

incomes earned by labor, property owners, and businesses; and value produced by commercial activity. These are referred to as income-approach and production-approach accounts, respectively. His systematic coverage, which included government services, was an important foundation. By the mid-1930s, a number of nations were offering annual estimates, though most, like Kuznets, were focusing on *net national* activity (subtracting out asset depreciation and adding in output by national firms abroad rather than just *domestic*).[9, 10] As the revolution in thinking about the role of fiscal policy in price and income stability following Keynes's 1937 study *The General Theory* sank in, the remaining adaptations associated with a modern national accounting system came into focus, most clearly for the first time in a paper by James Meade and Richard Stone, with input from Keynes.[11] All three measures of activity, including expenditures, are laid out. Net national measures of the economy are employed rather than gross domestic, but that would be easily changed over time.[12]

A multilateral gathering to standardize national accounting internationally had ephemerally begun under League of Nations auspices in 1939, but the conflagration of WWII delayed the undertaking. Work immediately recommenced at the end of hostilities under the UN flag, with the Meade and Stone approach as the template. The resulting report in 1947, largely written by Stone, presented an official system under United Nations management—the first standardized international guidelines on national accounting, from which current guidelines are directly descended.

Driven by a desire to improve macroeconomic policymaking in tandem with the unfurling of the Marshall Plan for reconstruction and development assistance starting in 1951, a simplified and easy-to-use version of the UN guidelines was introduced (followed by three more amendments in the 1950s). Starting with the 1951 iteration, the title *system of national accounts*—or SNA for short—was introduced. The word *system* signifies that "SNA consists of a coherent, consistent, and integrated set of macroeconomic accounts, balance sheets, and tables based on a set of internationally agreed concepts, definitions, classifications, and accounting rules."[13] The 1953 SNA edition, under Richard Stone's authorship, specified four closely related sets of accounts under this system:

---

9. Frits Bos, "The History of National Accounting" (Central Bureau of Statistics of The Netherlands, 1992), 7–9, http://papers.ssrn.com/abstract=1032598.

10. Net national product was defined as the sum of the market value of all the commodities produced and all the direct services rendered during the year, minus the value of that part of the nation's stock of goods that was expended (both as raw materials and as capital equipment) in producing this total. The remainder constitutes the net product of the national economy during the year.

11. J. E. Meade and Richard Stone, "The Construction of Tables of National Income, Expenditure, Savings and Investment," *The Economic Journal* 51, no. 202/203 (June 1, 1941): 216–233.

12. In addition to the above efforts, many other intellectual developments during the 1930s and 1940s shaped the national accounts as we know them today. Notable among them were the development of the Input-Output framework by Wassily Leontief and Flow of Funds by Morris Copeland. For a good account of the historical development of national accounts, read *The Income of Nations*, by Paul Studenski, and *The Accounts of Nations*, edited by Zoltan Kenessey.

13. UNSD, *National Accounts: A Practical Introduction* (New York: United Nations, 2003), 1, http://unstats.un.org/unsd/publication/SeriesF/seriesF_85.pdf.

- National income and product accounts: accounts showing the total amount produced and the allocation of income and product arising from that production.

- Input-output tables: a set of tables identifying the sources of all inputs to production (intermediate goods, energy, labor) and tracking the allocation of all outputs, by industry.

- Flow-of-funds: accounts that summarize the aggregate stocks of financial assets and liabilities in the economy, with details of financial flows between debtor and creditor.

- Balance sheets: records of the beginning and ending values of assets and liabilities that institutional units hold during an accounting period.

GDP and other computations made to describe the state of economic activity depend on the raw materials collected in these tables, as organized into SNA. A series of revisions to the international SNA standards has sought to make these foundational data more complete, reliable, and uniform across nations. The 1953 report focused on defining the concepts for estimating national income—including what types of economic activities need to be included in the estimation of national income, the *production boundary*—and elaborating the methodologies for estimating each activity. A major revision came in 1968 with deeper integration of the four accounting frameworks to reflect technical progress and long-term planning aspirations and greater distinction among institutions (corporate and government), including financial, nonfinancial, and nonprofit. Reflecting the appetite for greater cross-country comparability, as discussed above, 1968 SNA laid foundations for the wider use of constant prices, allowing users to see past the differential rates of inflation that obscure real comparative performance.

The 1993 SNA revision further split up transactions into subcategories and stretched SNA accounts to make them relatable to a broader set of macroeconomic data available outside the system—for example, OECD *Guidelines on Foreign Direct Investment* and International Monetary Fund (IMF) manuals such as *Balance of Payments* and *Government Finance Statistics*. Definitions were elaborated in difficult areas—insurance transactions, financial intermediation services indirectly measured (FISIM), financial versus operating leasing, and the consumption of fixed capital. The importance of the digital economy was also incorporated into the accounts. Expenditures on software (negligible before the 1970s) were treated as a current cost in 1968 SNA. Starting from 1993 SNA, software expenditures—whether off-the-shelf or custom-built—were treated as capital formation. An important conceptual change made in the 1993 revision was to attribute a portion of government consumption to household sector final demand, rather than showing government as the final consumer of its own services such as health care and education.

The latest incarnation is 2008 SNA. The system's boundaries for what should be counted in economic output further evolved to reflect the increasing importance of innovation, intangibles, and international economic activity; after all, the period since the 1993 revision saw the rise of globalization. Where the 1993 SNA had made purchases of software a business investment in an asset, not just a current intermediate expense, 2008 SNA extended similar recognition to spending on research and development (R&D). Where 1993 made gold and similar precious item purchases an investment, given potential gains in value, 2008 extended similar treatment to original artworks like television shows. Implementing these changes led to a $560 billion upward restatement of U.S. GDP—a far from trivial change.[14]

It is important to remember that, since its conception, the managers of SNA have cautioned against the temptation to overrely on economic aggregates for guiding economic policymaking. For instance, 1968 SNA states that "for many purposes of both analysis and policy, however, it is not sufficient to work with aggregates alone; it is also necessary to look at many aspects of the economy in greater detail." The point is reemphasized in the 1993 report: "the System is primarily intended to provide disaggregated data to meet the needs of analysts and policymakers interested in the behavior of markets and the factors primarily responsible for major disequilibria such as inflation and unemployment." These caveats long anticipated the complaints about national accounting statistics frequently heard today: that it is an imperfect representation, that it neglects distributional outcomes like income inequality, and that it fails to value aspects of the environment such as air quality. SNA does not disparage these considerations; it is simply meant for different purposes.

It is also important to note that it is no easy task to implement the SNA framework. Full implementation requires national statistical agencies to produce an elaborate and technically complicated array of tables. A 2006 UN survey, almost 13 years after 1993 SNA, reported that conceptual compliance[15] with 1993 SNA was low: the national accounts of only 53 percent of developing countries were following the conceptual guidelines.[16] The IMF identifies a range of impediments to full implementation, most importantly capacity issues such as inadequate staffing, training, enforcement of reporting requirements, and difficulty capturing informal activity.[17] However, SNA is such a comprehensive framework that even nations with abundant staffing resources can fall short. It provides guidance on classifying economic flows that may differ from particular national classification systems, because the needs of national accounts users may not be in line with the international standards. For example, as required by SNA, U.S. National Income and Product Accounts (NIPA) "include estimates of value-added for the business sector and for corporations.

14. Gulab Singh, "2008 SNA—Main Changes from 1993 SNA" (presented at the Seminar on 2008 SNA Implementation, Addis Ababa, Ethiopia, April 11–15, 2011), http://unstats.un.org/unsd/nationalaccount /workshops/2011/addis/ECA-Pr6-ENG.PPT.

15. Based on UN National Accounts Questionnaire 1993 SNA (NAQ) and Conceptual Compliance Questionnaire (CQ) conducted by UNSD for monitoring the implementation of 1993 SNA. For detailed NAQ, see UNSD, *UN National Accounts Questionnaire 1993 SNA—Supporting Booklet* (New York: United Nations, 2011), http://unstats .un.org/unsd/pubs/questionnaires/Supporting%20Booklet%202010%20-%20English.pdf. For CQ, see UNSD, *Report of ISWGNA to the United Nations Statistical Commission—Thirty-Fifth Session* (New York: United Nations, March 2, 2004), 21, http://unstats.un.org/unsd/statcom/doc04/2004-10e.pdf.

16. Eurostat and UNSD, "Luxembourg Recommendations on Global Implementation and Outreach for the System of National Accounts" (presented at the International Conference on International Outreach and Coordination in National Accounts for Sustainable Growth and Development, Luxembourg, 2008), 4, http://ec .europa.eu/eurostat/documents/1001617/4433881/RECOMMENDATIONS-FINAL-1.pdf.

17. Ibid.

However, neither of these values matches the value-added of the corporate sector on an SNA basis. Specifically, the value-added of the NIPA business sector includes the value-added of unincorporated enterprises that are classified in the household sector and the value-added of state and local government enterprises (other than nontransit utilities) that are classified in the general government sector for the SNA-based estimates."[18]

The data requirements to implement the SNA framework are enormous. Data for national accounts are pulled from administrative records, statistical methods such as extrapolating survey results on the basis of a benchmark census, and estimation techniques improvised by national accounts bureaucracies. Each of these approaches presents challenges. Though coverage and reliability are usually higher in administrative records, like tax records, the coordination required between various government agencies to extract specific information for national accounts may reduce the timeliness of the data. Countries with less capable central governments have less ability to prevent misreporting for tax evasion motives. Survey methods overcome some administrative record deficiencies but require careful sampling design. A variety of estimation methods are used in compiling the national accounts, but they have their own problems. A common strategy, for instance, is using benchmark ratios, including in advanced economies such as the United States. According to the United Nations Statistics Division (UNSD), "Constant ratios of the most recent benchmark year—for instance, value-added/output ratios—are regularly used to extrapolate value-added of the current period given output," with the drawback, of course, that this assumes "that value-added/output ratios are not volatile, because it is assumed that technical change is slow, whereas of course such ratios are certainly not constant."[19]

Gross Domestic Product under SNA

Reservations about SNA notwithstanding, the most important statistic that emerges out of the national accounts is gross domestic product, or GDP. GDP captures the sum total of economic production (the "product" in GDP) within the economic territory of a country (the "domestic" in GDP; gross *national* product would also count production overseas by a nation's firms, minus production at home by foreign guest companies).[20] "Gross" indicates that *consumption* of fixed capital is not deducted from the economic production estimate—that is, it is not "net of depreciation," which would give us net domestic product, or NDP. Nor does it reflect environmental damage done by industrialization in the United States or China, which is outside the boundary of GDP, NDP, or even other figures that reflect depreciation of assets.[21] A slew of alternative calculations using these three variables also could be discussed, several of which have jockeyed for prominence over the past 60 years. As

---

18. Charles Ian Mead, Karin E. Moses, and Brent R. Moulton, "The NIPAs and the System of National Accounts," *Survey of Current Business* 84, no. 12 (December 2004): 17–32, http://www.bea.gov/scb/pdf/2004/12December/1204_NIPA&SNA.pdf.

19. UNSD, *A Practical Introduction*, 123.

20. This can be used in the context of a group of countries.

21. This is one reason to argue against the universal use of GDP as the standard measure of national accounting; it is not a China-specific issue.

"nationals" such as global corporations have dispersed so much economic activity beyond their home borders in the second half of the twentieth century, GNP grew less useful to many policymakers concerned with managing activity within their borders. GDP became progressively more universal for describing national activity and for international comparisons.

GDP under SNA can be estimated with three methods. In theory, all three should arrive at the same value, but in reality, they seldom do. Each is used in different ways and contexts, and each plays its own part in the full-blown national accounts system. First, one can measure the value of total *production* of goods and services. The important concept of *value-added* is critical here. To prevent double counting, intermediate input value is subtracted from the value of finished products before output is tallied. In short, GDP by production equals the sum of finished production value-added, which is:

$$\textit{The sum of output} - \textit{The sum of intermediate inputs}$$

The second approach is to measure GDP by the value of all *expenditures* in the economy, taking into account imports and exports. In this GDP by expenditure method, the national economy equals:

$$\textit{Household consumption} + \textit{Government consumption} + \textit{Gross capital formation} + \textit{Net exports}$$

Finally, a third approach is to count GDP as the sum of all *income* received by labor, capital, and government domestically, which delimits (in theory) how much can be bought and sold:

$$\textit{The sum of compensation to labor} + \textit{Mixed income} + \textit{Other taxes less subsidies}$$
$$\textit{on production} + \textit{Gross operating surplus}$$

$$\textit{Define as: Gross operating surplus} = \textit{Net operating surplus} + \textit{Consumption of fixed capital}$$

Most nations rely on more than one approach to complete their estimate of GDP, due to gaps in data or other weaknesses that make it impossible to do so based on a single formula. That is definitely the case with China, to which we now turn.

Is China Concordant with the SNA Framework?

Is China's national accounting framework an outlier from the international SNA standard? Judging from the vitriol often directed at Beijing's statistics, one would think so. But given the preceding discussion, China's harshest critics may be applying a mistaken set of expectations. In the next section, we compare China against the reality of the SNA framework and find that it is by and large compliant, with exceptions. China currently applies nonstandard industry classifications[22] (counting activity at the *enterprise* level, rather than the

---

22. NBS, "China's 2002 SNA—Basic Structure," October 13, 2010, http://www.stats.gov.cn/ztjc/tjzdgg/hsyjh1/yjhxsjlh/qt/201010/t20101013_69208.html.

suggested *establishment* level) and uses different prices for production value calculations (*purchasers* prices, as opposed to the suggested *basic prices* received by producers—the latter being less likely to incorporate transport costs and other charges that should not be represented in a specific product's cost). However, these divergences are not, by and large, atypical, even for advanced economies, and the pace of convergence for China with SNA norms, rather than the divergences, is the more notable point—at least up until recently.

CHINA'S PRACTICES

Under Russia's tutelage, China employed a Material Product System (MPS) starting in 1952 to compile national accounts and would utilize that system for the next 40 years (ironically, until a few years after it was abandoned in Russia).[23] MPS was developed by the USSR in the 1920s, and the first detailed Soviet national accounts based on it were published for 1923–1924—long before Meade and Stone in the United Kingdom and Kuznets in the United States attempted such an exercise. Like SNA, MPS aspired to be a "complete, consistent and interrelated set of accounts, balances, and tables together with the definition of the corresponding concepts and methodological explanations which describe the functioning and development of the economy."[24] Unlike SNA, the MPS excluded most services from the definition of economic production and only considered new value that was created in material goods production. That bias about what constitutes "production" is shared by premodern antecedents going back to Adam Smith.

China received technical assistance from Soviet statisticians to not only implement the MPS but also to design the data collection machinery required for its implementation.[25] From early on, Chinese statistical development encountered setbacks. During the Great Leap Forward (1958–1959), the compilation of most MPS tables was banned on the pretext that "they were trivial or overloaded with details."[26] During the Cultural Revolution (1966–1976), statistical offices were shut down, and statisticians were sent to work in the fields. Statistical work gradually recovered after that politically turbulent period, but it did so slowly, and with the disadvantage of a lost decade of observation.

From that point until 1985, Chinese statisticians focused on improving the implementation of the 1950s-vintage MPS, even while policy reform emphasized movement toward Western market models. In 1985, NBS started to transition from the MPS to SNA, demonstrating an awareness of the need for a different approach to economic measurement even before the fall of the Soviet Union. Annual production-approach GDP estimates by industry were issued from 1985, annual GDP by expenditure from 1989, and quarterly GDP by

23. Xianchun Xu, "The Establishment, Reform, and Development of China's System of National Accounts," *Review of Income & Wealth* 55, no. S1 (July 2, 2009): 442–465, http://www.roiw.org/2009/2009-33.pdf.

24. Janos Árvay, "The Material Product System (MPS): A Retrospective," in *The Accounts of Nations*, ed. Zoltan Kenessey (Washington, DC: IOS Press, 1994), 219.

25. François Lequiller and Derek Blades, *Understanding National Accounts* (Paris: OECD, 2014), 337, http://www.oecd.org/std/UNA-2014.pdf.

26. Xu, "The Establishment, Reform, and Development," 444.

industry from 1992.[27] However, these were mostly estimated by translating data collected using the MPS system rather than by designing a separate data collection system for SNA.[28]

In 1993, NBS formally abandoned the MPS in favor of SNA. The national accounts were woefully inadequate at that juncture, but there have been major revisions since then. Statistical capabilities in 1993 were good at collecting detailed information on centrally planned material outputs such as steel, cement, and grain but were almost nonexistent for gauging nonmaterial outputs such as services or judging quality considerations. The first *Tertiary Sector Census* for services activity was conducted from 1993 to 1994 for the years of 1991 and 1992, resulting in an initial major revision of services value-added in the post-MPS era: an upward revision of 8.7 percent to 1993 GDP, on top of substantial adjustments to tertiary value-added for 1991–1993.[29] In 1997, China launched the first national agricultural census with 1996 as the measurement year, which did not entail significant revisions to agricultural value-added but wound up cutting output of certain commodities by a wide margin.[30] From 2004 onward, Beijing began conducting a general economic census every five years, a practice in line with other major countries.[31] The census, initially scheduled for 2003 as the measurement year, was delayed until 2004 due to the SARS epidemic. When it was published in 2005, it delivered a whopping 16.8 percent upward revision to 2004 GDP.[32] The second full economic census looked at 2008 and was conducted in 2009, as originally planned (for years ending in 3 and 8). It led to a smaller, but not inconsequential, 4.4 percent upward revision to 2008 GDP, most of which came, again, from revisions in the tertiary sector.[33] The third economic census of 2013 activity produced an initial 3.4 percent upward revision to 2013 GDP, which was reported in December 2014, though full details were held back then. As explored in depth in this study, we believe that adjustment does not fully reflect the present underestimation of China's economy.[34] All along there has been annual fine-tuning of industry classifications, data coverage, and methodologies to bring

27. Ibid., 447.

28. Lequiller and Blades, *Understanding*, 367.

29. NBS, "Statistical Bulletin of First *Tertiary Sector Economic Census*," November 21, 2001, http://www.stats.gov.cn/tjsj/tjgb/scpcgb/qgscpcgb/200203/t20020331_30469.html; Carsten A. Holz, "China's Statistical System in Transition: Challenges, Data Problems, and Institutional Innovations," *Review of Income and Wealth* 50, no. 3 (2004): 381–409. Holz came to a different estimate for this revision—9.99 percent—from his reading of follow-up adjustments NBS later made.

30. NBS, *China Statistical Yearbook* 1997 (Beijing: China Statistics Press, 2012), http://www.stats.gov.cn/tjsj/ndsj/information/nj97/ml97.htm; NBS, *China Statistical Yearbook* 1998 (Beijing: China Statistics Press, 2012), http://www.stats.gov.cn/tjsj/ndsj/information/nj98n/index98.htm; NBS, *China Statistical Yearbook* 1999 (Beijing: China Statistics Press, 2012), http://www.stats.gov.cn/yearbook/indexC.htm. In particular, the gross output value of animal husbandry was revised downward by 15 percent and meat output by 22 percent. The scale of downward adjustment was self-calculated based on official statistics.

31. Xu, "Establishment, Reform, and Development," 455. The first economic census had 2004 as the measurement year but was mostly conducted in 2005. The census combined the previous industrial and tertiary sector censuses as well as basic unit census but excluded the primary sector, which had its own census as mentioned just now. This design remains the same today.

32. Carsten A. Holz, "China's 2004 *Economic Census* and 2006 Benchmark Revision of GDP Statistics: More Questions than Answers?," *China Quarterly*, no. 193 (March 1, 2008): 150–163, http://ihome.ust.hk/~socholz/CQ-Holz-EconomicCensus04-13July07.pdf.

33. OECD, *OECD Economic Surveys: China 2010*, vol. 2010 (Paris: Organisation for Economic Co-operation and Development, 2010), 20, http://www.oecd-ilibrary.org/content/book/eco_surveys-chn-2010-en.

34. NBS, "Announcement on Revisions to 2013 Gross Domestic Product," December 19, 2014, http://www.stats.gov.cn/tjsj/zxfb/201412/t20141219_655915.html.

Chinese statistics more in line with international practices. NBS has worked with various international organizations (for example, the OECD and IMF)[35] and foreign statistical agencies (especially those of Japan, the United States, and Canada)[36] to improve the quality of its statistical output.

Today, China relies on a combination of two of the three GDP estimation approaches to gauge its economic size: the production approach and the income approach. Confusion is aggravated here by odd Chinese terminology. China sometimes refers to GDP calculations as "production accounting" (*shengchan hesuan*), or simply production-based GDP, because either the production or the income approach is from a production perspective, as opposed to the expenditure approach, which focuses on final use,[37] even though its approach to counting annual GDP actually employs a hybrid of production and income approaches. For primary-sector activity (such as farming) both production and income measures are made, but the production value is definitive. For secondary subsectors (mining, manufacturing, utilities, and construction), both production and income are measured, but since 2005, the income-approach estimates have been the principal basis for final estimates. For tertiary (services) subsectors, the same as secondary subsectors, the income approach is primarily used. All in all, the income approach has dominated China's GDP calculations since the first economic census, but Beijing still occasionally refers to this as "production accounting" and has failed to update the methodological change in official materials, including even the annual *China Statistical Yearbook*.[38] Expenditure basis estimates are presented as well, but with a discrepancy: the income/production-approach figures are the authoritative ones.[39]

Beneath these three broad categories of primary, secondary, and tertiary sectors, NBS publishes nominal value-added data for 19 high-level subsectors such as "mining," "manufacturing," and "real estate" annually,[40] and publishes monthly *value-added growth* in

35. For OECD, see OECD, "13th NBS-OECD Workshop on National Accounts," November 19, 2009, http://www.oecd.org/std/na/13thnbs-oecdworkshoponnationalaccounts30november-4december2009haikouchina.htm. For IMF, see NBS, "Agenda for International Symposium on Reforms, Achievements, and Challenges: China and Its Partners in Statistical Cooperation," May 11, 2014, http://www.stats.gov.cn/english/specialtopics/intsymposium/200410/t20041026_52280.html.

36. For Canada, see NBS, "Mr. Ma Jiantang Met with Mr. Morrison, Assistant Chief Statistician of Canada," September 29, 2014, http://www.stats.gov.cn/english/InternationalCooperation/201409/t20140929_617084.html.

37. Xianchun Xu, "Accurately Understand China's Economic Statistics," *Economic Research Journal*, no. 5 (2010): 26, http://www.usc.cuhk.edu.hk/PaperCollection/webmanager/wkfiles/7903_1_paper.pdf.

38. NBS, "Industry: Explanatory Notes on Main Statistical Indicators," in *2009 China Statistical Yearbook* (Beijing: China Statistics Press, 2009), http://www.stats.gov.cn/tjsj/ndsj/2009/indexch.htm.

39. NBS, *2012 China Statistical Yearbook* (Beijing: China Statistics Press, 2012), http://www.stats.gov.cn/tjsj/ndsj/2012/indexch.htm. There exists a small difference between the two figures. For example, in 2011, China's GDP by the production/income approach was RMB 47.3 trillion versus RMB 46.6 trillion by the expenditure approach. In all official releases and major media headlines, the production-income hybrid GDP number is cited.

40. According to China's economic industrial classification in use in 2008, under the high-level primary, secondary, and tertiary sectors, there are 20 subsectors, of which NBS only counts and publishes data on value-added for 19 in both census and noncensus years. The one left out is "International Organizations": it is included in China's industrial classification but is not part of China's GDP accounting. It has only one industry that is also called "International Organizations" at the further disaggregated 95-industry level, but the data for that are also not published. In alignment with China's actual national accounts practice, in this study we do not consider this category as part of Chinese GDP (in China's case, its value is minimal anyway). Hence, when talking about classification, we include international organizations, but when talking about values, we exclude it, because data for that are unavailable. The 2008 *Economic Census* did not cover the subsector of international

inflation adjusted (real) terms for 39 industries at the further disaggregated 95-industry level (for example, "manufacture of paper and paper products").[41] Note that these data on value-added *growth* rates do not provide researchers with access to crucial figures for the actual *amount of value-added* in renminbi terms, nor do these value-added growth data cover the primary and tertiary industries. These are big gaps. Further, the 1984 industrial classifications have been revised three times, bringing them closer to international classification norms but creating inconsistencies in the time series data in the process.[42]

IMF FRAMEWORKS FOR COMPARISON

In its annual *Article IV Consultation Staff Report* on China, the IMF includes a review of statistical issues. The 2014 edition notes that China compiles and disseminates annual and quarterly GDP statistics using the production approach, which the IMF refers to as "activity" and "volume" measures, based on SNA (1993), as well as annual expenditure basis numbers.[43] While the quarterly part was correct, the report does not observe that Beijing is actually using a production-income hybrid approach as its definitive measure for the annual figure. The report states that "the techniques for deriving volume measures of GDP are not sound and need to be improved."[44] The report notes that expenditure-approach numbers are not published using constant prices, only current prices (obscuring the true inflation impact on growth), and not on a quarterly basis in nominal terms. The IMF recognizes, as we do, that monthly industrial production data adjusted for inflation (chain-linked time series) are not available (only *growth* in value-added, not amounts) and that revisions fail to fully update past series. Labor market data are particularly lacking. Capacity problems, such as measuring the size of the growing private sector, are noted.

These comments correctly identify where China falls short of the ideal but may be misleading in terms of how concordant China is with SNA practices relative to other nations. In Chapter 2, we examine the principal complaints about China's methods more closely, and in Chapter 3, we construct an independent reestimate. For introductory purposes. consider that the IMF offers a Data Quality Assessment Framework (DQAF)[45] as a

organizations: NBS, "Statistical Bulletin of Second National *Economic Census*," December 25, 2009, http://www .stats.gov.cn/tjsj/tjgb/jjpcgb/qgjpgb/201407/t20140731_590163.html.

Non-census-year national accounts do not include international organizations: NBS, 中国非经济普查年度*GDP核算方法* (2010年修订版) (*Methods of Annual GDP Estimates of Non-Economic Census Year in China, 2010 Ed.*), 2010, 9, http://www.ytboc.gov.cn/article_show.aspx?id=2121.

41. In 2011, China's NBS updated the "Classification of National Economic Industries" based on its 2002 version (GB/T 4754-2002). The changes included mergers and separations of several industries at the previous 95-industry level, and the resulting number of industries became 96. But because the 2011 version (GB/T 4754-2011) was not enforced until the 2013 *Economic Census*, we made a decision to continue using the 2002 version in our study so all the data points in the past decade would be consistent and comparable.

42. Carsten Holz, "Chinese Statistics: Output Data" (Working Paper No. 473, Stanford Center for International Development [SCID], 2013), 5, http://scid.stanford.edu/publicationsprofile/2561.

43. IMF, *People's Republic of China: 2014 Article IV Consultation-Staff Report*, July 30, 2014, 13, http://www .imf.org/external/pubs/ft/scr/2014/cr14235.pdf.

44. Ibid.

45. IMF, "DSBB—Data Quality Assessment Framework (DQAF) for National Accounts Statistics," May 2012, http://dsbb.imf.org/Pages/DQRS/DQAF.aspx. The IMF DQAF is a premier framework for national statistical data quality assessment. IMF DQAF allows countries to diagnostically assess the quality of their national accounting data by comparing country statistical practices with internationally accepted standards.

guide to improve GDP estimates. The Fund framework has prerequisites for quality data assessment, including institutional, financial, and staffing capacity, and then points to five criteria:

1. Assurances of integrity (legal foundation and transparency)

2. Methodological soundness (compliance with international standards)

3. Accuracy and reliability (quality of data and statistical methods)

4. Serviceability (timeliness, consistency, and revision practice)

5. Data accessibility (data and methodology availability)

China has institutional weaknesses, including lack of staffing (in particular high-quality statistical personnel), inadequate legal and political mechanisms to ensure integrity, data quality concerns, serviceability problems (such as the patchy revisions the IMF points to), and data accessibility gaps that are huge. However, progress toward methodological soundness and compliance with international standards has been consistent as well (at least until recently, when, as discussed further below, Beijing appeared to slow progress on GDP methodology). Over the 22 years since switching from MPS to SNA, China's NBS has largely come into alignment with 1993 SNA. Xu Xianchun, NBS deputy chief, provided a useful comparison of Chinese and international SNA practices, laying out 12 differences with the 1993 SNA ideal, but noting the extent to which these shortfalls are common among other economies, including advanced economies.[46] Some of these issues could have an impact on China's GDP calculation; others affect only the composition, not the aggregate value.

The 1993 SNA recommends inclusion of illegal economic activities; this is one of several "production boundary" issues. China does not do so, but neither do most nations, including the United States, Canada, and Japan. A few countries attempt to reflect activities such as prostitution. Where this has been studied, full inclusion of illegal activity might add 2 percent to nominal GDP. Other boundary issues are whether to include purchases of valuables, such as gold or works of art, as investments in assets rather than consumption or expenses. As noted above, most other nations are taking their time to make these adjustments.[47] Likewise, China is still in the process of crediting business acquisitions of software as investment (as specified in 1993 SNA) and debating whether to treat research and development expenditures as investment as specified under 2008 SNA (Table 1.1).

Government production, or value-added, is computed with a contrived formula that adds depreciation of government-owned assets like highways to annual compensation of

46. Xianchun Xu, "Some Differences in GDP Measurements between China's Practice and 1993 SNA Guideline," *China Economic Review* 19, no. 3 (September 2008): 480–488, http://www.sciencedirect.com/science /article/pii/S1043951X08000047.

47. Charles Aspden, "Implementation of the 2008 SNA in the OECD," October 2008, http://www.oecd.org/std /na/41514291.ppt; Jennifer Ribarsky, "OECD Survey on Intellectual Property Products" (Geneva, May 7, 2014), http://www.unece.org/fileadmin/DAM/stats/documents/ece/ces/ge.20/2014/3._OECD_IPP_presentation.pptx.

Table 1.1. 2008 SNA Conversion: Advanced Economies

Time of Conversion	Country
December 2009	Australia
October 2012	Canada
July 2013	United States
March 2014	Israel, South Korea, Netherlands
May 2014	France, Singapore
June 2014	United Kingdom
September 2014	The remaining EU countries, Iceland, Norway, Switzerland
November 2014	New Zealand

Sources: Various state statistical authorities, OECD, IMF.

public sector employees. China departs from SNA practice by computing that depreciation value using the original cost of building these assets, notably in public sectors such as government services, rather than SNA-recommended current replacement cost. Given rising costs in past years, the current replacement cost might well generate a much larger value for annual government value-added. Therefore, this practice understates GDP, though by how much is unclear. Finally, most countries, including in the OECD, do not follow SNA's prescriptions for dealing with the value of FISIM. These methods are highly controversial. Beijing employs its own idiosyncratic approach to apportioning a measure of FISIM between intermediate services and final consumption, making it a component of GDP. We return to some of these SNA-divergences that affect the GDP estimate in the following chapters; in the case of FISIM, we rely on alternative, non-FISIM approaches to the financial subsector because the source data are simply not available for us to attempt to second-guess China using a FISIM approach to measuring services with no explicit charges (shortly before the publication of this study, China systematically updated its reported financial services value-added with respect to the expanded industrial coverage in the latest 2011 industrial classification, which we address in great detail in Chapter 3).

Xu noted that other areas where the Chinese fall short on 1993 SNA compliance had no impact on GDP, only on the attribution of activity *among* sectors or industries.[48] For instance, 1993 SNA recommends that if an enterprise conducts multiple industrial activities in somewhat equal measure, it can be separated into two establishments for data reporting purposes, but all businesses in China, including conglomerates, with only few exceptions, have their total value-added counted as part of a single industry in their principal activity (*zhuying yewu*), the activity that contributes the most value-added to the enterprise.[49] While this does not change total GDP, it changes the breakdown of GDP into constituent activity.

---

48. Ibid.

49. The exception is that if a single corporate unit is engaged in secondary and tertiary activities simultaneously, and if both activities are in comparable measure, then the statisticians may conduct extra work to split the total value-added. But if the different activities all belong to the secondary or the tertiary sector, then the value-added generated will be counted toward the subsector or industry of the principal activity. This was garnered from our interactions with NBS.

That makes it a concern for structural policy analysis. We go into these issues more deeply in Chapter 2. As a related matter, the definitions of gross output, intermediate input, and value-added specified under SNA, which depend on the splitting of reported activity by a firm as noted above when it has multiple activities, cannot be applied in China. Again, this does not change total GDP, but it does distort the mix of activity and can indirectly contribute to double counting and underreporting. China uses other practices that affect which industries are credited with how much value-added but also do not impact the aggregate GDP number, such as using producers' and buyers' prices rather than basic prices to calculate an entity's value-added output, as noted earlier.

The bottom line is that China's departures from SNA are finite, are not atypical, often reflect good-faith efforts to improve practice from a rather low base, and in many cases do not impact aggregate GDP. China's statistical system has many problems, but the basic design of national accounts is not one of them.

A Still Evolving System

China, SNA, and even the reliance on GDP as the standard for international comparison are not standing still. As noted, the world is in the process of adapting to 2008 SNA, the latest update to best-practice standards in national accounting. China has internal manuals to reflect its concordance with SNA. "Chinese 2002 SNA" has been the formal domestic system for 13 years, defining China's implementation of 1993 SNA. Beijing originally intended to replace this with a "Chinese 2014 SNA" manual in late 2014 or early 2015 that would define China's upgrade to 2008 SNA, but as of mid-2015 it appears this was deferred at the last-minute.[50]

In 2014 China conducted its third economic census, for the measurement year 2013, which it planned to conduct in combination with a transition to 2008 SNA.[51] A transition would mean eliminating some of the nonconformities to 1993 SNA discussed above, continuing the pattern of convergence with international standards. These next-generation steps would include counting R&D as investment (gross fixed capital formation) rather than as consumption of intermediates; counting imputed rent more accurately; augmenting the measure of household consumption to count goods and services paid for by government but enjoyed by households, like education; counting land rights transfer earnings as farmers' income; and the inclusion of stock options as employee compensation. As with past idiosyncrasies, some of these changes would add to the value of GDP, while others would just change its composition. As detailed in the chapters ahead, the bulk of that transition appears to have been deferred, at the last moment, for reasons that are unclear, calling into question the mix of political and technical motives at work in China's statistical evolution.

---

50. NBS, "Reform of National Accounts System is Ongoing," November 18, 2013, http://www.stats.gov.cn/tjgz/tjdt/201311/t20131118_463817.html.
51. Ibid.

It is not a contradiction to say that China is aligned with international GDP practices, while at the same time current measures are insufficient. In Chapter 2, we examine the problems that arise in execution, and in Chapter 3, we attempt to construct a better estimate. Being *generally* concordant is not a comfort to Beijing, or policymakers around the world whose economies could be impacted by China's uncertainties. Beijing is upgrading its participation in other statistics regimes as well. China has participated in the IMF's General Data Dissemination System (GDDS) since 2002, and, as of November 2014, has committed to subscribe to a parallel, higher standard known as the Special Data Dissemination Standard (SDDS).[52] All members of the G20 (other than Saudi Arabia) are SDDS participants, so it was fitting that China join.[53] We explore this evolution in greater detail in Chapter 2. Now that China has begun this undertaking, one can expect to hear discussion of its progression to the SDDS-*Plus* club, which would introduce nine additional areas of data upgrading.[54]

Finally, serious discussion around the limits of GDP as the singularly most important metric with which to gauge national progress has come and gone since the birth of national accounts in the 1930s. Simon Kuznets was insistent that factors that made no contribution to human welfare should not be counted in the same figures that captured things that did: spending on offensive weapons and nuclear bombs, for instance, would not have been counted if he had had his way. GDP measures output, not welfare: it was not built to. Diane Coyle lays out three lines of complaint with GDP as the key metric today: first, the complexity of today's economy, especially the radical improvements in quality and the role of globalization, are woefully under-reflected in GDP; second, the explosion of services in advanced economies relative to tangible goods, and many services that are essential to our way of life, that have no price and that we have come to expect to be free—like Google, Wikipedia, and Facebook—are virtually impossible to capture in GDP with the same confidence that steel output is measured; and finally, the depletion of our natural environment, likewise, is largely ignored in GDP.[55] These are profound considerations. To some extent we are struggling to measure China's economy using an antiquated system designed to value tangible products at a time when intangible products and value are booming and nonmaterial considerations like sustainability and quality of life are coming to a head. Coyle concludes that for the time being we do not have any better metric, and certainly not one ready to be embraced across a broad spectrum of nations, or by China.[56]

---

52. IMF, "DSBB—SDDS Subscribing Countries," http://dsbb.imf.org/pages/sdds/NSDPPages.aspx.

53. Ted Truman, "More Transparency Needed: Making Official Holdings More Open" (Peterson Institute for International Economics, June 2014), http://www.iie.com/publications/papers/truman201406.pdf.

54. These are, from the SDDS-Plus online site, "sectoral balance sheets; quarterly general government operations; general government gross debt; other financial corporations surveys; financial soundness indicators; debt securities; participation in the Coordinated Portfolio Investment Survey (CPIS); participation in the Coordinated Direct Investment Survey (CDIS); and participation in the Currency Composition of Official Foreign Exchange Reserves (COFER) database."

55. Coyle, *Affectionate History*, 122–135.

56. Ibid., 135–140.

2 | A Diagnosis of China's GDP Data

In Chapter 1, we reviewed the process of China transitioning from the Material Product System (MPS) to the System of National Accounts (SNA), and discussed the changes that China has made to its framework since 1992. In essence, the guiding principles in China's national accounts system are aligned with those recommended in 1993 SNA; however, due to institutional deficiencies—many common among former centrally planned economies—like limited source data and weak implementation, Chinese official statistics have persistently been clouded by misgivings and criticism.

In this chapter we review debate over the last two decades on the quality of China's statistical output, classify the main lines of concern, and select the points of contention that remain relevant to today's evaluation; we then move into a three-part analysis of the quality of Chinese national accounts data. First, we focus on irregularities in China's data reporting practices and why it is necessary to separate time series and "snapshot" data issues. Second, we address statistical terms with Chinese characteristics—that is, terms defined differently or in a confusing way that leads to misunderstanding. This is a step toward separating "fake" China data problems from the genuine ones and providing an analytical framework. Third, we turn to the institutional basis of some data problems, beginning with a dissection of China's statistical hierarchy—how the central and local authorities work together, and where they split up the tasks.

Throughout the past two decades, particularly from the mid-1990s to the mid-2000s, a prominent group of scholars and economists have used their own models to cross-check Chinese data and found discrepancies with many official claims. Thomas Rawski, prominently, put together a national income measure in 2001 and concluded that China's official statistics contained major exaggerations of real output growth beginning in 1998 and that cumulative gross domestic product (GDP) growth between 1997 and 2001 was no more than half of official claims and possibly much smaller, even negative.[1] In 2002, Rawski, a professor of economics and history at the University of Pittsburgh, reiterated that China's official growth claims for 1998 and 1999 were totally divorced from reality and that actual growth amounted to a maximum of about 2 percent annually for those years, possibly much less.

---

1. Thomas G. Rawski, "What Is Happening to China's GDP Statistics?," *China Economic Review* 12, no. 4 (2001): 349, http://www.sciencedirect.com/science/article/pii/S1043951X01000621.

Beginning in 2000, he said, China's economic performance improved substantially, though still at rates lower than official claims.[2] Likewise, F. Gerard Adams at the University of Pennsylvania argued from the mid-1990s that, based on an energy consumption–growth model, China's expansion was much lower than shown in official statistics.[3]

Harry X. Wu, a long-time China statistics watcher at Japan's Hitotsubashi University, said in one of his latest studies that, based on his weighted-index model, China had overreported GDP growth rates in the reform era. Wu calculated 1978–2012 average growth to be 7.2 percent, compared with China's official claim of 9.8 percent.[4] In an earlier analysis, Wu and Angus Maddison, a late economist who specialized in cross-country GDP accounting comparisons, argued that Chinese official numbers were "subjected to a smoothing procedure to disguise a significant slowdown of output growth between 1996 and 1998."[5] In a more recent example of skepticism toward China's official numbers, former Standard Chartered Bank Greater China research head Stephen Green calculated the economy's growth rate in 2011 and 2012 at 7.2 percent and 5.5 percent, respectively, based on tangible indicators such as cement and steel production, electricity usage, and Kentucky Fried Chicken restaurant sales.[6]

Because nominal economic size and pace of expansion are closely related, scholars' criticism also concerns nominal measurements of China's national accounts. In a study released in 1994, the World Bank significantly revised up China's 1992 nominal GDP by 34.3 percent, of which 11.8 percent was from output scope adjustment and 18.3 from price reevaluation. In 1992 China had not yet fully transitioned to the SNA and was using an MPS-SNA hybrid to measure the economy.[7] As explained in Chapter 1, the Soviet-style MPS was not designed to capture output in services and considered material goods production only, so it missed a significant portion of intangible activity. In explaining its adjustments, the World Bank listed three sources of upward revision: making China more internationally consistent, expanding China's national account coverage, and improving price data (Table 2.1). The Bank continued to suggest alternative numbers until it accepted China's official revisions in 1999, following a request by National Bureau of Statistics (NBS) in 1998 and an early 1999 inspection visit.

Maddison also doubted the robustness of Chinese data on a constant price basis. In a 2006 study he calculated his own series of Chinese nominal data based on the 1990

2. Thomas G. Rawski, "Measuring China's Recent GDP Growth: Where Do We Stand?," *Jingjixue* (*China Economic Quarterly*) 2, no. 1 (October 2002): 2, http://www.pitt.edu/~tgrawski/papers2002/measuring.pdf.

3. F. Gerard Adams and YiMin Chen, "Skepticism about Chinese GDP Growth—the Chinese GDP Elasticity of Energy Consumption," *Journal of Economic & Social Measurement* 22, no. 4 (December 1996): 237, http://iospress.metapress.com/content/n3247ph670410231/.

4. Benjamin Robertson, "Mainland China Growth Rates Don't Add up," *South China Morning Post*, July 14, 2014, http://www.scmp.com/business/economy/article/1553600/mainland-china-growth-rates-dont-add.

5. Maddison and Wu, "China's Economic Performance," 15.

6. Robertson, "Don't Add up."

7. Qiang Li, "中国国民经济核算体系的建立、变化和完善 (The Establishment, Development, Improvement of China's System of National Accounts)," NBS, October 2001, http://www.stats.gov.cn/ztjc/tjzdgg/hsyjh1/yjhxsjlh/hsll/200911/t20091130_69113.html.

Table 2.1. World Bank's Corrections to China's 1992 GDP

Adjustment Item	Impact on GDP
Treatment Consistency Adjustment	*+1.6%*
Self-produced, self-used grains	+0.8%
Additions to inventories	−1.6%
Enterprises' welfare services to employees	+1.6%
Government subsidies to cover enterprise losses	+0.8%
Scope Adjustment	*+11.8%*
Grain output	+0.9%
Vegetable output	+2.3%
Rural industrial output	+0.6%
Rural service sector consumption	+6.5%
Housing services (scope adjustment)	+1.5%
Valuation Adjustment	*+18.3%*
Housing services (price adjustment)	+1.5%
Other services with distorted prices	+16.6%
Total Compounded Adjustment*	**+34.3%**

*The total adjustment combines a +13.4% revision for reporting difficulties and an
   additional (compounded) +18.3% revision for nonmarket pricing.
Sources: World Bank (1994),[8] Xu Xianchun (1999).[9]

international Geary-Khamis dollar.[10] He found that Chinese GDP had been systemically underreported in the pre-1990 period and overstated in the post-1990 period. Maddison's revised 2003 Chinese GDP was 20 percent lower than official claims, and thus his revised per capita GDP was smaller, too.[11]

NBS also revised up headline GDP several times in the ongoing post-1992 effort to align with SNA practices. As noted in Chapter 1, the most consequential revisions occurred after the 2004, 2008, and 2013 economic censuses. NBS revised up 2004 GDP by 16.8 percent after the 2004 census, 2008 GDP by 4.4 percent after the 2008 equivalent, and 2013 GDP by 3.4 percent just this year. Each time the biggest changes came from the service sector, the long-time black hole in China's national accounts due to the legacy of the MPS era. These restatements, despite being the result of NBS efforts to improve accuracy, led to renewed doubts about China's national accounts data, partly because Beijing did not fully restate

8. World Bank, *China GNP per Capita* (World Bank, December 15, 1994), 8–25, http://www-wds.worldbank.org/external/default/WDSContentServer/WDSP/IB/1994/12/15/000009265_3961007061544/Rendered/PDF/multi0page.pdf.

9. Xianchun Xu, "World Bank Adjusted China's Official GDP," *Economic Research Journal*, no. 6 (1999): 52–58, http://lib.cnki.net/cjfd/JJYJ906.006.html.

10. The Geary-Khamis dollar is commonly known as the international dollar and is often used for comparison of value terms across countries. It has the same purchasing power parity that the U.S. dollar had in the United States in a given year (in this case, in 1990).

11. Angus Maddison, "Do Official Statistics Exaggerate China's GDP Growth? A Reply to Carsten Holz," *Review of Income and Wealth* 52, no. 1 (2006): 122, http://onlinelibrary.wiley.com/doi/10.1111/j.1475-4991.2006.00178.x/abstract.

past data to comport with the new information and methodological improvements. That has left problematic breaks in the series beyond the most recent years that were retrospectively revised. For example, after the first economic census, NBS amended data back to 1993, when China fully converted to the SNA; after the second census, the revision only traced back to 2005, despite important conceptual and methodological changes. Likewise, NBS only revised historical data back to 2009 following the 2013 *Economic Census* (except for systemic changes in certain industries' classification and the financial subsector's boundary setting, which were too fundamental to ignore for previous years). This tendency results in major gaps in the juncture years of 1993, 2005, and 2009, rendering data beginning in those years technically incomparable with previous years and reducing the utility of Chinese statistics.

NBS has communicated a desire to better clean up historical data retrospectively. However, as a weak agency in China's system, NBS lacks budget and staff. In China, young professionals looking for government jobs take a public service officer examination and fill in their preferred institutions, which they are assigned based on performance and preferences. A major application motive is job perks (or it was before the current antigraft campaign). Because NBS is not a profit-generating agency and cannot furnish lucrative perks for staff, it has trouble attracting top talent. For this reason NBS's institutional capabilities are limited. The Bureau has a limited ability to overcome these constraints in China's bureaucratic system, where bargaining power is often contingent on financial strength and political clout.

While NBS has professional statisticians who are dedicated to improving fundamental data practices, bureaucrats who simply want to muddle through or use their job as a stepping-stone to a better position are not in short supply either, especially at the local levels. As one senior NBS official told us frankly, statisticians' sense of the importance of time series was "not very strong," and the entire national accounts office at NBS headquarters had roughly 30-odd staff—notably small compared with advanced economy counterparts. Japan, for instance, with an economy roughly half the size of China's, reported 50 Department of National Accounts staff in 2012 and specifically noted that this team was smaller than other countries.[12] In the same year, National Economic Accounts section staff under the Bureau of Economic Analysis (BEA)—the U.S. equivalent of NBS—numbered 151, of which 144 were full-time employees.[13] The gap in the quantity of professional national accounts statisticians between China and the other major economies is stark. These staffing shortages lead to an inadequate explanation for changes. The practice of making data comparable before and after major framework changes is a common challenge shared by transition economies like China: Beijing's failure to document many necessary and useful decisions has often overshadowed the laudable effort to improve data quality.

---

12. IMF, "DSBB–SDDS Japan National Accounts," September 21, 2012, http://dsbb.imf.org/Pages/SDDS/DQAFBase.aspx?ctycode=JPN&catcode=NAG00.
13. U.S. Department of Commerce, "Economic and Statistical Analysis Budget: Budget Estimates for Fiscal Year 2013," February 2012, 27, http://www.bea.gov/about/pdf/ESA_FY2013_CongressionaJustificationFINAL.pdf.

Another cluster of China statistical specialists argue that, based on many years of assessment, there is little evidence of systematic data distortion and that official numbers are largely reliable. Carsten Holz, a China economist at Hong Kong University of Science and Technology, is an important figure in this camp. Having examined Chinese data over the decades at a more granular level than almost any foreign researcher, Holz concluded in a November 2013 paper that "there is no clear evidence of data falsification."[14] On the one hand, Holz acknowledged abundant reasons for suspicion, including opaque and complicated data compilation systems, frequent statistical benchmark and definitional changes, and the withholding of key economic indicators that outside researchers could use to cross-check official data. On the other hand, after smoothing out the data gaps in official numbers and applying methods such as Benford's Law[15] to check for systemic anomalies, Holz concluded that evidence of systemically falsified data is simply lacking. Other career China economists, including veteran professor Dwight Perkins, come to broadly similar conclusions, and in any case find as many or more problems with alternative estimates as they do with NBS series. In a 2007 paper forecasting China's economic growth, Perkins coauthors with the same Thomas Rawski known for his late-1990s doubts, and they found that "the figures compiled by NBS provide the best available picture of long-term trends in China's economy."[16]

The intensity of debate over the quality of Chinese statistics has waned in recent years, in part because there was little new to be said and in part because overblown past theories that data distortions were masking an imminent collapse had proven so completely wrong. Iacob Koch-Weser of the U.S.-China Economic and Security Review Commission observed that Chinese economists have not debated this complex subject at length since the early 2000s.[17] The decline in the intensity and depth of discussion also reflects the loss of several key protagonists, including Angus Maddison and F. Gerard Adams. As the Xi administration implements a more comprehensive reform program to transition the growth model, we sense that domestic attention to work in the field of Chinese statistics is on the rise again.

---

14. Carsten A. Holz, "The Quality of China's GDP Statistics" (Working Paper No. 487, Stanford Center for International Development [SCID], 2013), 28, http://scid.stanford.edu/publicationsprofile/2681.

15. Ibid., 23. Benford's Law, also called the "first digit law," states that the frequency distribution of first digits in many—but not all—real-world data is not distributed uniformly but according to the widths of gridlines on a logarithmic scale: the first digit "1" occurs with 30.1 percent frequency, the first digit "2" with 17.6 percent frequency, and so on, with continuously declining frequencies all the way to the first digit "9" (4.6 percent).

16. Dwight H. Perkins and Thomas G. Rawski, "Appendix to 'Forecasting China's Economic Growth over the Next Two Decades,'" in *China's Great Economic Transformation*, ed. Loren Brandt and Thomas G. Rawski (Cambridge: Cambridge University Press, 2008), 3–4, http://scholar.harvard.edu/files/dperkins/files/chapter20appendix.pdf.

17. Iacob N. Koch-Weser, *The Reliability of China's Economic Data: An Analysis of National Output*, Staff Research Report (U.S.-China Economic and Security Review Commission, January 28, 2013), 7, http://www.uscc.gov/sites/default/files/Research/TheReliabilityofChina%27sEconomicData.pdf.

Time Series Data versus Snapshot Data

Throughout our research we found much of scholarly suspicions about China's national accounts concentrated on breaks in time series data. Such frustration, fueled by China's own failure in effectively communicating its practices for interested researchers to parse, is reasonable. However, the preponderance of suspicions about data breaks has diverted attention from the many improvements in the quality and comprehensiveness of point-in-time data along the way, which we call "snapshot" data. Over the years, improvements in the latter have gone barely noticed and even induced frustration because of poor explanations of their rationale in the context of China's continuing efforts to revise its national accounts framework. Not all of these changes, significant or incremental, were made clear to China data watchers. Beijing's weak record of disclosing the steps and logic of policy-making in general applies to their statistical work, too.

Sober analysis of Chinese data quality requires a careful review of both current data and reliable historical figures. Among the literature we surveyed, in-depth study of current data is scarce; industry-by-industry revisions like the World Bank did for China's GDP in 1992 have not been conducted since, except for the work of a few career China economists in subsectors such as industry and agriculture and some expenditure components like household final consumption. Because academic investigations into point-in-time "snapshot" data are limited, we are missing half of the picture on Chinese data quality. It is unreasonable to judge the overall value of Chinese data based simply on time series data breaks, that major institutional failing notwithstanding. Best-effort statistics of current data are just as important as time series for analyzing production capability and growth potential. The gaps in time series data exist precisely because China, unlike many other developing economies, has not stood still using consistent yet outdated methods, but has revised its approach to national income accounting repeatedly since 1992.

CHINA'S INTERNATIONAL REPORTING PRACTICES

As a participant in the International Monetary Fund's (IMF) General Data Dissemination System (GDDS),[18] China is committed to improving statistical systems using the Fund's standards and reporting its conceptual data system frameworks for the real, fiscal, financial, and external sectors. Based on these disclosures, outside researchers can evaluate the soundness of China's system (as with other participants) using the Data Quality Assessment Framework (DQAF), a related IMF framework for assessing national statistical quality. The DQAF allows countries to diagnostically assess the quality of their national accounting

---

18. In November 2014, President Xi Jinping announced China's intention to subscribe to the IMF's Special Data Dissemination Standard (SDDS), which is a set of more rigorous publication requirements. Some government agencies such as the State Administration of Foreign Exchange (SAFE) already started publishing data in accordance with SDDS; but because of technical preparation and IMF assessment on many other fronts, China has not yet officially graduated into the higher bracket. The SDDS is one level above the GDDS, so if China officially subscribes to the SDDS before the publication of this book, then China would be a "former participant" in the GDDS.

data by comparing their statistical practices with internationally accepted standards.[19] In our three-part analysis of Chinese data in this chapter, we use the DQAF's measurement dimensions as a guiding standard. In addition to the "prerequisites" of a legal and institutional environment supportive of statistical monitoring, and necessary commensurate resources like staffing and budget, these include assurances of integrity, methodological soundness, accuracy and reliability, serviceability, and accessibility.[20]

As a subscriber to the GDDS, China voluntarily committed to using the IMF framework to guide its statistical development and to comply with basic international standards in data compilation, calculation, and publication. Using the DQAF, we conclude that, with limited exceptions, China's description of its system of national accounts is well aligned with 1993 SNA recommendations, and its data are comparable to other countries' based on a more or less concordant framework. Just as other countries selectively adopt 1993 SNA standards to suit their own conditions and needs, China's national accounting system has idiosyncratic features. However, because Chinese authorities have frequently revised statistical practices rather than maintaining older methodologies, these anomalies and inconsistencies have drawn far greater attention and scrutiny for their possible connection to time series data breaks.

A number of examples illustrate how improvements in China's reporting practices have, ironically, fueled criticism. Opaque Chinese practices often contribute to the problem, but in retrospect, critics are often too quick to reach negative conclusions. Taking criticisms based on an overreading of what good practice by GDDS members means *off the table* is a first step toward identifying which problems *do* require more attention.

International analysts often rely on the GDDS reporting as an authoritative resource, but irregular Chinese reporting practices can lead to inconsistencies between the definitive Chinese language version of the latest national accounting systems and the English language GDDS records. This can mislead researchers outside China on the current state of Chinese practice.

As laid out in Chapter 1, three interrelated methods are used to assess GDP, at each nation's discretion: the production approach, the income approach, and the expenditure approach. Understanding which of these is used as the *preferred* approach is the first step to evaluating a country's GDP accounting system. As a former centrally planned economy, China has a long history of reliance on the production approach, fueling controversy over the last decade. The production approach demands a massive volume of statistical collection, especially "input and output data industry by industry," which is seen as unrealistic for China to deliver given its limited bureaucratic resources in statistics.[21] BEA came to the

---

19. IMF, "DQAF."

20. Ibid.

21. Ximing Yue, "中国国内生产总值估算改革之我见 (My Perspective on Reform of China's GDP Accounting Method)" (Chinese Academy of Social Sciences, 2003), http://www.stats.gov.cn/ztjc/tjzdgg/zggmjjhstx/200305 /t20030527_38607.html.

same conclusion, finding that "measuring production was significantly more difficult than measuring income."[22] In its current framework, the United States derives GDP from final expenditures, while also reporting the sum of all income as gross domestic income, or GDI, and using production-approach data to produce tables for analysis of the industrial composition of the U.S. economy.[23] These are secondary tools when it comes to official GDP, for which BEA considers expenditure component data more reliable than other approaches.[24]

In China's case, because the production approach to GDP gives more weight to the final gross *output* than the income and the expenditure approaches do, it is thought to create a perverse incentive for local governments and enterprises to distort and overreport production to achieve local growth performance targets. Many scholars have therefore argued that China should stop relying predominantly on the production approach and turn to the income approach or, even better, the expenditure approach to GDP—as the United States, Canada, Japan, and many other advanced economies do.[25] The choice of calculation approach is thus presumed to encourage both macro-level data quality problems and—quite likely—real overproduction.

But what *is* China's "preferred" approach? In the GDDS database, last updated May 23, 2012, China's methodology chapter section on "Concepts and Definitions" states:

> Gross domestic product (GDP) and value-added by kind of activity (19 subsectors) at current market prices are published. For these estimates, the value-added of agriculture and industry is estimated by the production approach (gross output minus intermediate consumption), while the value-added for other kinds of activity is estimated by the income approach (sum of the components of value-added).[26]

According to this explanation, it seems that for agriculture and other primary sector activities, and for the industrial subsector (mining, manufacturing, utilities), government applies the production approach, while for the construction subsector (also part of the

---

22. Steven J. Landefeld, Eugene P. Seskin, and Barbara M. Fraumeni, "Taking the Pulse of the Economy: Measuring GDP," *The Journal of Economic Perspectives* 22, no. 2 (April 1, 2008): 195, http://www.bea.gov/about /pdf/jep_spring2008.pdf.

23. U.S. Bureau of Economic Analysis, "Measuring the Economy: A Primer on GDP and the National Income and Product Accounts," October 2014, 3–4, 11, http://www.bea.gov/national/pdf/nipa_primer.pdf.

24. U.S. Bureau of Economic Analysis, "Concepts and Methods of the U.S. National Income and Product Accounts," November 2014, 2–11, http://www.bea.gov/national/pdf/chapters1-4.pdf.

25. Yue, "Reform"; IMF, "SDDS Subscribing Countries." According to IMF and the EU commission, the expenditure approach is a dominant accounting method for many developed economies such as the United States, Canada, Japan, Germany, Iceland, and Sweden. But a lot of advance economies use the production approach simultaneously, such as Belgium, Singapore, Switzerland, and Australia. In particular, GDP in Korea is "compiled primarily taking the production approach, because production data are more accurate and more readily available than those for expenditures and incomes." The same is true in Austria, Finland, Italy, and Luxembourg. Some countries balance or take the average of GDP estimates across three approaches, such as the United Kingdom and Australia. Therefore, most developed countries rely more on either expenditure or hybrid approaches. Most developing countries that have subscribed to SDDS, like Turkey, Brazil, and Egypt, still use the production approach as the dominant GDP accounting method.

26. IMF, "DSBB—GDDS China, People's Republic National Accounts," May 23, 2012, http://dsbb.imf.org /pages/gdds/DQAFViewPage.aspx?ctycode=CHN&catcode=NAG00&Type=CF.

secondary sector) and the tertiary sector, NBS relies on the income approach. This is not correct.

Chinese language public records make clear that NBS began to shift its preferred calculation method for industrial activity from the production approach to the income approach starting in 2004, the first economic census year. During that economic census, for industrial enterprises "above the designated threshold" (Textbox 2.1), a simple arithmetic mean of production- and income-approach measures was used to calculate final value-added. For smaller firms, including enterprises "below the designated threshold," entities that follow administrative unit rather than enterprise accounting rules, and industrial production units that were classified into nonindustrial categories, value-added was calculated with the income approach. For self-employed businesses, production-approach data remained preferred.[27] For the 2008 *Economic Census*, NBS adopted the income approach as the preferred calculation method for *all* industrial activities. In noncensus years post-2008 (between the every-five-year censuses), NBS has emphasized the income approach in calculations. This transition was undertaken to reduce the data collection challenges facing China's statistical authorities, reduce the aforementioned "water content" (overstatement distortion) in output reporting, and better capture the nature of China's evolving economy.

In up-to-date Chinese language versions of accounting methodologies, NBS makes clear that except for the primary sector (farming, forestry, animal husbandry, fisheries, and agricultural services),[28] where the production approach remains dominant, GDP estimates derived from the income approach are final (this change has been picked up by some non-Chinese scholars, such as Carsten Holz, and noted in their work).[29] The latest revision to China's *Methods of Annual GDP Estimates of Non-Economic Census Year in China* (*Zhongguo fei jingji pucha niandu guonei shengchan zongzhi [GDP] hesuan fangfa*) released in 2010 states that for industrial, construction and all kinds of service activities, value-added will be calculated by both the production and income approaches, and the latter used as the benchmark (Textbox 2.2).[30]

For the primary sector, NBS uses both production and income approaches to calculate value-added but takes the former for final GDP purposes. China's agricultural sector is

---

27. NBS, 中国经济普查年度国内生产总值核算方法 (*Methods of Annual GDP Estimates of Economic Census Year in China*) (Beijing: China Statistics Press, 2006), 15, 25, http://www.cdstats.chengdu.gov.cn/uploadfiles/022504 /中国经济普查年度国内生产总值核算方法.pdf.

28. NBS, *Methods of Non-Economic Census Year, 2010 Ed.*, 15–127; NBS, "Classification of Tertiary Sector," January 14, 2013, http://www.stats.gov.cn/tjsj/tjbz/201301/t20130114_8675.html; NBS, "NBS Explains 2013 GDP Revisions," December 19, 2014, http://www.stats.gov.cn/tjsj/sjjd/201412/t20141219_655923.html. In the 2010 version of the noncensus-year national accounts manual, agricultural services were counted as part of the primary sector. However, in the 2012 update, agricultural services were assigned to the tertiary sector, a change that was later reflected in the 2013 *Economic Census*. However, because our measurement year is 2008 and the 2012 reclassification has not been included in any formal national accounts manual, in this study we followed the pre-2012 revision classification.

29. Holz, "Quality," 13.

30. NBS, *Methods of Non-Economic Census Year, 2010 Ed.*, 17–127.

Textbox 2.1. China's Classification of Industrial Enterprises in National Accounts

Starting in 1998, China's industrial enterprises have been divided into two categories for statistical purposes according to their revenue size (as well as ownership, in the now outdated classification prior to 2007). The threshold for the types is designated by the state, which has been evolving over the years as China's economy expands. Enterprises above that revenue threshold are called *"guimo yishang gongye qiye,"* whereas those below the threshold are *"guimo yixia gongye qiye."*

Data for enterprises above the threshold are collected on a more regular basis and in a more systemic and reliable manner. Their operating statistics are published by NBS in not only economic census years but in noncensus years as well. This is not the case for enterprises below the threshold, whose data are only collected extensively and published systemically in census years, while extrapolated from sample surveys and the last census's results in years between the two censuses. Due to these differences in the data compilation and publication processes, China economist Carsten Holz—an advisor to this study—dubs the first group "DRIEs"—directly reporting industrial enterprises.[1] For consistency purposes, we adopted the acronym. For enterprises below the threshold, we call them non-DRIEs or non-DRIE enterprises (to differentiate from self-employed businesses, which are also part of the non-DRIE group but are not enterprises).

The designated threshold for DRIEs has been revised several times, a fact that caused confusion about Chinese data, which we discuss at length in the following sections. From 1998 to 2006, DRIEs included all state-owned enterprises (SOEs) in the industrial subsector, as well as non-SOEs with "principal business revenue" no smaller than RMB 5 million.[2] In 2007, NBS revised that definition to "all industrial enterprises with principal business revenue no smaller than RMB 5 million," regardless of ownership type. In 2011, the revenue threshold was raised to RMB 20 million.[3]

The concept of "enterprise above the designated threshold" was not invented until 1998. Prior to that year, the DRIEs were not defined with a quantitative threshold but included all independently accounted industrial enterprises at or above the township level.[4] Since 1998, a quantitative threshold has been used to differentiate DRIEs from smaller enterprises.

---

1. Holz, "Quality," 6.

2. Principal business is defined as the enterprise's most important production activity. Because the basic accounting units in China's national accounts system is enterprise, rather than the recommended establishment, as noted in Chapter 1, the industry of principal business is usually what the enterprise's total value-added is assigned to.

3. NBS, "常见问题解答: 工业统计 (Frequently Asked Questions: Industrial Statistics)," July 14, 2014, http://www.stats.gov.cn/tjzs/cjwtjd/201311/t20131105_455942.html.

4. For the definition of "industrial enterprises at or above the township level," refer to NBS, "Structural Adjustment of Industrial Economy," November 6, 2008, http://www.stats.gov.cn/ztjc/ztfx/jnggkf30n/200811/t20081106_65695.html.

Textbox 2.2. An Institutional Change to Industrial Enterprise Accounting

In 2009, NBS introduced an important change to industrial accounting in order to obtain more accurate data on value-added ratios in different industries under the income approach. The value-added ratio, an important efficiency indicator for production activity, is calculated as Industrial Value-Added (IVA) divided by Industrial Gross Output Value (GOV).

The change was to establish a cost-and-expense survey mechanism (*chengben feiyong diaocha*) that covers about 100,000 DRIEs, including all large and medium-sized DRIEs and some small DRIEs. NBS, along with local authorities, would survey these 100,000 DRIEs to compute each enterprise's IVA and IVA/GOV ratio, then impute their respective industry's IVA/GOV ratio, based on enterprise-level data.[1]

In calculating each DRIE's IVA, the authorities would also compute its IVA composition under the income approach. Therefore, based on enterprise information in each industry, the statisticians could impute the income-approach composition for all surveyed DRIEs at the industry level, with each income-approach component as a share of GOV. Then, with each industry's total DRIE GOV, they can compute the value of each income-approach IVA component for all the DRIEs at the industry level, as well as their relationships. Finally, combining the results with non-DRIE IVA derived from sample surveys and census-based extrapolations, the authorities can obtain the value-added for the entire industrial subsector.[2]

This institutional change was put into use after the 2008 *Economic Census*. It allows authorities access to more timely and reliable data on IVA/GOV ratios at the industry level. Previously, the ratios they used to extrapolate noncensus-year or monthly IVA data were often outdated or derived from the production approach. The reform marks the expansion of NBS's use of the income approach in not only national accounts but also gradually in regular industrial accounting as part of the broad efforts to enhance Chinese data quality.

---

1. NBS, "FAQs: Industrial Statistics."
2. NBS, *Methods of Non-Economic Census Year, 2010 Ed.*, 19.

dominated by small-scale operators and informal service operations like freelance harvesters, with many self-employed businesses and individuals (*getihu*), and small workshops, according to the second agricultural census conducted in 2007 for reference year 2006.[31]

---

31. NBS, "第二次全国农业普查主要数据公报 (第二号) (Statistical Bulletin of Second National *Agricultural Census*)," February 22, 2008, http://www.stats.gov.cn/tjsj/tjgb/nypcgb/qgnypcgb/200802/t20080222_30462.html. According to the second *Agricultural Census* for 2006, for example, only 5 percent of all agricultural tractors are large and medium-sized tractors. The rest are all small tractors. This does not count those off-record rural households without agricultural machinery.

With these types of operations representing the majority of producers in the sector, it makes sense to rely on the production approach. It would be challenging for self-employed farmers to calculate income components themselves, such as fixed asset depreciation. The production approach, which subtracts intermediate inputs from the final gross output to calculate GDP, seems a more sensible option.

Despite China's up-to-date national accounts manual, the GDDS listing remains inaccurate and uncorrected, continuing to mislead readers not conversant with NBS's highly technical Chinese language manuals. The primary responsibility to update metadata when changes in statistical practice take place, at least once a year, stands with Beijing.[32] Inasmuch as the GDDS system is meant to provide a vehicle for the IMF to "guide member countries in the dissemination to the public of comprehensively, timely, accessible, and reliable economic, financial, and sociodemographic statistics," one can ask whether the Fund is proactive enough on this front as well.[33] That said, failure to duly report on methodological practices is a more modest shortcoming than calculating GDP based on China's flawed methods. Although there is reason to suspect that not all local statistical bureaus have fully converted their GDP calculation methods, even 10 years after NBS launched the transition, wholesale indictment of the statistics on this ground is clearly misplaced.

In November 2014 President Xi Jinping announced that China would upgrade from the GDDS to the higher standard maintained by the IMF Data Standard Initiative, the Special Data Dissemination System (SDDS), as described in Chapter 1. The Fund also dispatched a mission to Beijing to assess the proposed subscription. The higher standard of reporting and explanation should in principle be good for international confidence in China's national accounting and thus good for China's ability to transcend its reputation for data laxity. However, as the GDDS experiences described above illustrate, commitments without conscientious follow-through quickly become counterproductive. But the confusion over how China's national accounting works is not solely a matter of more timely translation of Chinese language materials. Inconsistent statements in different official Chinese materials make the work of analyzing China's data challenging for native economists, too, not just foreign observers.

DOMESTIC PUBLICATIONS ON CHINA'S NATIONAL ACCOUNTS

The inaccuracies in China's English publication of its GDP accounting methods are not simply due to a language issue or a time lag in updates but result from larger shortcomings in information disclosure practices. Although we conclude above that China's 2002 system of national accounts is *generally* consistent with 1993 SNA and that the data produced under that system compare favorably internationally *by and large,* we are also cognizant of numerous discrepancies and ambiguities in Chinese official statements. Some of these problems concern the form of data publication, while others concern the substance. Both fuel misgivings about Chinese data, and it is important to examine each separately.

---

32. IMF, "DSBB—What Is the General Data Dissemination System (GDDS)?," http://dsbb.imf.org/Pages/GDDS/WhatIsGDDS.aspx#features.

33. Ibid.

Combing through Chinese methodology documents, one encounters ambiguities that seem to serve little purpose other than to make it difficult for scholars to replicate and stress-test the official methods independently. These gaps in methodological clarity mean that if independent analysts do manage to come up with alternative results, officials can blame unrevealed differences in formulation, rather than simple errors in calculation on their part or intentional "cooking the books" to explain why the final numbers do not match. That is precisely the reason why Perkins and Rawski noted in the appendix of their 2007 essay that the independent scholars' methods in coming up with alternative numbers are rarely subject to verification and possible rejection—because what the standards are is unclear.

This was also an enormous challenge that we encountered when trying to come up with an independent measure of China's economic size (see Chapter 3). Some researchers, including us, are left replicating China's official methodology wherever possible and making reasonable assumptions aligned with official *principles* found in statistical manuals otherwise. In addition to these ambiguities, black boxes, and missing ingredients in statements of official methodology, we also discern instances where the claimed official methods seem not to match actual practice. This sows confusion and uncertainty and misleads even the most sophisticated domestic scholars, let alone economists with limited Chinese language skills. Some of our efforts to untangle this confusion are described below.

A first example of divergence in stated methodologies in official documents is that while NBS switched its preferred GDP calculation method for industries from the production approach to the income approach following the 2004 *Economic Census*, the bureaucracy still said through 2012 in the annual statistical yearbook that the calculation was based on the production approach.[34] It is hard for outside scholars to decide which statement is true, because published NBS data in these years were insufficient to support the bottom-up calculation for *either* the production approach *or* the income approach. It remains unclear if statisticians, especially at local levels, were *still* not applying the income approach for industrial GDP almost a decade after the transition was decreed on paper, or whether NBS fully converted and simply failed to update the description in the yearbook—which would be a curious oversight.

In interviews, statistical officials invariably suggest the latter. A senior official with direct experience said China made the de facto transition to the income approach for the industrial subsector but did not remove the line that stated that "IVA [industrial value-added] in this yearbook was calculated by the production approach" until 2013, for the 2012 yearbook.[35] Even assuming that the central-level NBS had been employing the income approach throughout the 2004–2012 period, we remain skeptical of local bureaus' practices in this era.

There are cases where we have a clearer idea of whether, and to what extent, officials actually do deviate from official statements. For example, the NBS 2010 accounting manual

---

34. NBS, "Industrial Subsector: Explanatory Notes on Main Statistical Indicators," in *2011 China Statistical Yearbook* (Beijing: China Statistics Press, 2011), http://www.stats.gov.cn/tjsj/ndsj/2011/indexch.htm.
35. NBS, interview by authors; NBS, *2012 Statistical Yearbook*.

for GDP in noncensus years says that for income-approach GDP, authorities will collect raw data on the four components of the formula—labor remuneration, net taxes on production, fixed asset depreciation, and operating surplus—and add them up. For depreciation, the manual says NBS collects data on "cumulative depreciation" directly reported by DRIEs (directly reporting industrial enterprises) that participate in the cost-and-expense survey and subtracts the previous year's cumulative depreciation from the current year's to obtain a value for the current year's depreciation, which would then be counted as part of income-approach GDP.[36] A similar methodological statement has also appeared in the sections for banks, securities firms, administrative units, and private not-for-profit organizations. However, in theory, the net incremental depreciation between two consecutive years does not equal current-year depreciation; the latter is one of four components of the income-approach GDP equation while the former is not. In a nutshell:

$$\text{Cumulative depreciation this year} = \text{Cumulative depreciation last year} + \text{Current-year (new) depreciation} - \text{Value of the asset that has been scrapped this year} + \text{Revaluation}$$

This subtle difference between two consecutive years' cumulative differential and the latter year's current-year depreciation can easily perplex even accounting staffers at reporting enterprises—so much so that in a 2013 training PowerPoint prepared by Beijing's government statisticians, mistaking current-year depreciation for the cumulative differential was listed as one of the most frequent errors.[37] Hence, although China's 2010 noncensus-year manual, which incorporated 2008 census changes as a guide for the noncensus years following that census, claims industrial enterprises' current-year depreciation is calculated as the difference between two years' cumulative depreciation, we doubt that is the case in practice. On the other hand, if the statisticians did what is stated in the manual it would be an even worse mistake. What has compounded the problem here is that in China's *Economic Census Year GDP Accounting Manual* (2006), an older guidebook that summarized the methodology for the first economic census, the value of industrial enterprises' fixed asset depreciation for the year was correctly put as equal to the single item of "current-year depreciation."[38]

That interesting change in the methodology begs questions. Table 2.2 summarizes the gap between DRIEs' current-year and cumulative depreciation: as the pattern goes, the former, which does not consider the scrapping of assets, is almost *always* larger, indicating the two are not interchangeable in either conceptual or quantitative terms. In 2012, the last

---

36. NBS, *Methods of Non-Economic Census Year, 2010 Ed.*, 23. In the census-year accounting manual, depreciation data for enterprises above the designated size should come directly from the self-reported "current-year depreciation" data. However, such data points are missing in both the original databases and the final yearbook. We are unclear as to why NBS did not release these data points that year; if they did not collect it, it is unclear how they calculated the aggregate.

37. NBS (Beijing) Daxing District Survey Team, Statistical Bureau of Beijing's Daxing District, *Training on Surveyed Units' Annual and Regular Reporting of Basic Conditions*, December 2013, 37, 41–42.

38. NBS, *Methods of Economic Census Year*, 29–30.

Table 2.2. Gap between DRIEs' Current-Year and Cumulative Depreciation Data

Unit: RMB trillion

	Current-Year Depreciation (A)	Cumulative Depreciation	YoY Change in Cumulative Depreciation (B)	A–B
1998	0.32	1.99		
1999	0.36	2.25	0.26	0.11
2000	0.40	2.58	0.34	0.06
2001	0.45	2.96	0.38	0.07
2002	0.49	3.31	0.34	0.15
2003	0.59	3.73	0.43	0.16
2004	0.75	4.36	0.63	0.12
2005	0.95	5.03	0.67	0.28
2006	1.13	5.89	0.86	0.27
2007	1.36	6.96	1.07	0.29
2008	n/a	8.71	1.74	n/a
2009	n/a	9.89	1.18	n/a
2010	n/a	12.35	2.47	n/a
2011	2.73	15.73	3.38	(0.65)
2012	3.06	17.79	2.06	1.00

Sources: NBS, CEIC, authors' calculations.

year for which data is available, the difference between current-year and cumulative depreciation was as large as RMB 1 trillion, nearly 2 percent of annual GDP.

The likely deviation between official claims and actual practice reinforces concerns that Beijing manipulates current-year depreciation data (the easiest factor to use as a residual adjustment item) for political purposes by smoothing gaps in time series data. Accounting for depreciation is arcane and difficult to second guess, and the fact that authorities are not straightforward about methodologies aggravates suspicion. However, we do not leave these insinuations at that; we attempt to further stress-test them on our own.

With the help of two Chinese enterprise databases containing a vast array of data reported directly by hundreds of thousands of enterprises for various accounting purposes, we are able to calculate an alternative series on DRIE depreciation.[39] Here we use 2008, the year of China's second economic census, to illustrate the discrepancies between enterprise-level data and the official aggregate. Despite the economic volatility brought about by the global financial crisis, 2008 is considered to have been a solid year for data reliability and accuracy thanks to the census. Due to database limitations, we focus on cumulative depreciation here, aligned with the equation in the 2010 manual; data on straightforward current-year depreciation was, unfortunately, not available.

---

39. 中国工业企业数据库 (China Industrial Enterprise Database), 1998–2009. Note that although the database contained source enterprise data from 1998 to 2009, data in 2008 and 2009 were incomplete. We supplemented the 2008 data sets with a more complete set of data from the 2008 *Economic Census* database—which we will introduce in greater detail in Chapter 3—but we were unable to do that to the 2009 data entries.

China's 2006 census-year manual, as noted previously, states that the government collects current-year depreciation data directly from both large and small industrial enterprises as well as production units.[40] For the second census for 2008, it was unclear whether NBS relied on current-year data or the differential of cumulative data to calculate GDP because the technical manual was not made public. We can, however, guess the 2008 method from the 2010 vintage, which was assembled to reflect the latest changes brought about by that second census. Starting in 2008, the data entry for "current-year depreciation" disappeared in the industrial enterprise database (NBS resumed reporting the figure in 2011 after the three-year suspension[41]). There is no transparent explanation for that and we were unable to compute current-year depreciation directly. We had to go with cumulative depreciation and see whether the result comports with the official story.

According to NBS, 2008 cumulative depreciation less that of 2007 is RMB 1.74 trillion, which is, by definition in the 2010 manual, the value of fixed asset depreciation for DRIEs that year. However, our bottom-up calculation suggested a somewhat different result: RMB 1.56 trillion, which appears more reasonable compared with the official value of current-year depreciation of RMB 1.36 trillion for 2007 and historical patterns. In other words, the official depreciation value was larger than our estimate by RMB 180 billion.

What does this say about China's statistical system? It means that when China does make official current-year depreciation readings available, we end up with two inherently different calculation formulas which have both appeared in official manuals and three sets of industrial depreciation data: official current-year values, the differential based on changes in official cumulative data, and the differential apparent in independently calculated cumulative data series such as ours. And this is before even considering the data gaps for depreciation in smaller industrial enterprises and for *all service enterprises*. Such inconsistencies exist not only between the raw source databases and final official publications but also among different final official publications. One explanation for these discrepancies that seems realistic is that China's statistical authorities do not, in practice, strictly follow their accounting manuals. Or perhaps they applied different rules at different times and did not bother—or have the confidence or the time—to bring their numbers into concordance with one another and fully explain them to superiors and independent researchers.

A third and more general example of confusion arising from China's data reporting regime lies in a complicated sequence of "three readings" of annual GDP. By design, China publishes an initial reading of annual GDP around January 20 of the following year, an initial result known as the *chubu hesuan*, which is based on quarterly GDP accounting.[42] As fuller annual figures from localities are compiled, NBS publishes a first revision, known as

---

40. NBS, *Methods of Economic Census Year*, 29–30.

41. The exact reason for the suspension was unclear, but our guess was that NBS suspended the publication while it internally revamped its data reporting system to prepare for the 2008 census and the kickoff of the cost-and-expense survey in 2009, and resumed reporting after things became streamlined. But there is a lack of direct evidence supporting that view.

42. NBS, "2012 年国内生产总值初步核算情况 (Statistical Bulletin of 2012 GDP: Initial Result)," January 19, 2013, http://www.stats.gov.cn/tjsj/zxfb/201301/t20130119_12931.html.

the *chubu heshi*, by the end of September of that following year (e.g., September 2013 for full year 2012 revised GDP) in the statistical yearbook for the measurement year.[43] After further examining the data and integrating new materials that emerge after the first revision, such as final fiscal numbers, NBS publishes a second and final revision of GDP by the end of January of the following year (e.g., January 2014 for *final* 2012 numbers), known as the *zuizhong heshi*.[44] A key publication channel for the final revision is the statistical yearbook for the year following the year in question. Thus, *final* GDP for 2012 was officially published in the 2013 *China Statistical Yearbook,* which was released in September 2014. After that, authorities generally do not revise GDP numbers unless and until a future five-year economic census applies an accounting framework change and therefore requires a restatement of past values to provide a consistent time series.[45] But, alas, when making those postcensus restatements of past-year values to concord with new accounting boundaries and principles, Beijing rarely revises the *full* past time series data on the grounds that available resources are simply inadequate. Typically only the past five years of data will be restated—starting in the first year after the previous economic census. This results in fragmented time series, trend lines, and data patterns, and a reason to doubt the accuracy of just about any historical chart stretching back across one of these many break points.

To make matters still more confusing to the public, NBS traditionally does not provide an explanation of the adjustments made in its two revisions. Such explanatory notes—for instance, as provided without fail by the U.S. BEA with each and every GDP revision—are one of the most valuable exercises in international statistical work.[46] The knowledge that such detail *must* be provided imposes better discipline on statisticians, forces realism on political authorities about the need to allocate sufficient resources to GDP accounting, and creates business opportunities for investors able to operate with more sophisticated models based on more reliable data.

In today's China, NBS simply reports revisions in nominal and real (inflation adjusted) terms, without clarifying the reasons for adjustments (Table 2.3). This leaves

---

43. NBS, "国家统计局关于 2012 年国内生产总值初步核实的公告 (Statistical Bulletin of 2012 GDP: First Revision)," http://www.gov.cn/zwgk/2013-09/02/content_2479754.htm.

44. NBS, "国家统计局关于 2012 年国内生产总值最终核实的公告 (Statistical Bulletin of 2012 GDP: Final Revision)," http://www.stats.gov.cn/tjsj/zxfb/201401/t20140108_496941.html. Note that these are the conventions in noncensus years. In economic census years, China would usually take the census result as the final revised numbers and do not publish the two regular revisions following the initial release. The first reading of census-revised results would usually be published in December the year following the measurement year. For example, the 2013 census result was first published in December 2014.

45. In the case of 2012, the final GDP numbers were revised again after the 2013 *Economic Census,* which led to a 2.8 percent *upward* revision to the 2012 headline GDP. That headline adjustment, along with renewed figures for select subsectors, was quietly published in February 2015.

46. Dennis J. Fixler, Ryan Greenaway-McGrevy, and Bruce T. Grimm, "The Revisions to GDP, GDI, and Their Major Components," *Survey of Current Business* 94, no. 8 (August 2014): 3; U.S. Bureau of Economic Analysis, "News Release: Gross Domestic Product: Third Quarter 2014," October 30, 2014, 3, http://www.bea.gov /newsreleases/national/gdp/2014/pdf/gdp3q14_adv.pdf. BEA initially prepares an advanced annual estimate (January in the following year), which is followed by three revisions—a second estimate (February), a third estimate (March), and a fourth estimate (late July, also known as the annual NIPA revision). The fourth estimate (i.e., the third revision) is not revised until the next comprehensive NIPA revision, which occurs about every five years. In addition to the releases, data sources, key assumptions, analysis of estimates, and methodological and statistical changes will all be posted on the website in the monthly *Survey of Current Business.*

Table 2.3. China's Initial and Two Revised GDP Estimates—A 2012 Example

	Nominal GDP Level (RMB billion)				Real GDP Growth (%)			
	Initial Estimate	First Revision	Final Revision	Total Adjustment	Initial Estimate	First Revision	Final Revision	Total Adjustment
Gross Domestic Product	**51,932**	**51,894**	**51,947**	**14.8**	**7.8**	**7.7**	**7.7**	**(0.1)**
Primary Sector	5,238	5,237	5,237	(0.3)	4.5	4.5	4.5	0.0
Secondary Sector	23,532	23,516	23,516	(15.7)	8.1	7.9	7.9	(0.2)
Industry	19,986	19,967	19,967	(18.9)	7.9	7.7	7.7	(0.2)
Construction	3,546	3,549	3,549	3.2	9.3	9.3	9.3	0.0
Tertiary Sector	23,163	23,141	23,193	30.8	8.1	8.1	8.1	0.0
Transportation, Storage, and Postal Services	2,496	2,496	2,466	(30.0)	7.0	7.0	6.8	(0.2)
Wholesale and Retail Trade	5,025	4,939	4,939	(85.2)	11.9	10.4	10.4	(1.5)
Accommodation and Catering Services	1,043	1,046	1,046	3.0	7.8	8.0	8.0	0.2
Finance	2,860	2,872	2,872	12.2	9.9	10.0	10.0	0.1
Real Estate	2,901	2,901	2,936	35.5	3.8	3.8	4.1	0.3
Other Services	8,838	8,886	8,933	95.3	7.3	7.9	7.9	0.6

Sources: NBS,[47] authors' calculations.

47. NBS, "2012 GDP Initial Result"; NBS, "2012 GDP First Revision"; NBS, "2012 GDP Final Revision."

observers in the dark about what motivated those changes. Thin reporting with only superficial methodological explanation fuels suspicions about validity, undermining the extensive efforts made to advance national accounting practices to date—which is a shame. The lack of due process in the control of China's national accounting, we conclude, does no good for China's authorities, the credibility of the nation with intelligent business people at home and abroad, or long-term economic power and wealth.

CONCEPTUAL AND QUANTITATIVE BREAKS IN TIME SERIES DATA

In working with any statistics, researchers need data series to follow consistent definitions, standardized collection and computation processes, and regular publications with a minimum level of explanation so that do-it-yourself fixes can be made if authorities do not have time to do them. This is critical for analysts interested not just in current patterns but in long-term trends and relative performance. Unfortunately, that need is often unmet in the case of Chinese statistics.

Since China transitioned to the 1993 SNA-based national accounts system more than 20 years ago, statistical authorities have made numerous adjustments and improvements to the framework, ranging from the coverage of GDP calculation, to industrial classifications, to methodologies for specific accounting items. As a result of NBS's inability to maintain historical data comparability through these changes, scholars face a forest of data fragmented by definitions, methodologies, and classifications over the course of more than six decades. Researchers are left to their own devices in the effort to make them consistent for research purposes. As previously described, sometimes changes took place so frequently and in such minute ways, with so little documentation, that even China's most sophisticated statistical officials are unable to completely recall what changes were made.[48] While change was inevitable, and, in fact, essential, from a primitive starting point of marketization and statistical competence, the reluctance to catalogue and report this evolution, for the sake of independent fact-checking as well as internal coherence, was not foreordained— and it is certainly not justifiable today.

Some data breaks are more problematic than others, and while they are generally less egregious as the system advances, they continue to impede modernization. Many have been cited widely to substantiate concerns about China's data framework. Holz shows that following China's first economic census for 2004, a significant statistical gap occurred.[49] In the *2005 Statistical Yearbook*, the table summarizing data for DRIEs indicates that 219,463 enterprises were covered, with a total IVA of RMB 5.48 trillion at current price.[50] Holz argues, and we agree, that these data were collected prior to

---

48. NBS, interview by authors, 2013–2014.
49. Carsten A. Holz, "Chinese Statistics: Classification Systems and Data Sources" (SSRN Scholarly Paper, Social Science Research Network, 2013), 12, http://papers.ssrn.com/abstract=2202532.
50. NBS, *2005 China Statistical Yearbook* (Beijing: China Statistics Press, 2005), http://www.stats.gov.cn/tjsj /ndsj/2005/indexch.htm.

the 2004 census through conventional annual accounting methods, because by the time of this yearbook's publication, the 2004 census was not yet completed. Two years later in the 2007 *Statistical Yearbook*, NBS for the first time reported key industrial enterprise data *predating* the current year, going back to 1998, based on the census work and retrospective revisions. As Holz noticed, although NBS revised the number of enterprises from 219,463 to 276,474 for 2004—the group of DRIEs was expanded as a result of the fuller coverage generated by the 2004 census—and the gross output value (GOV) was revised up 7.7 percent, the IVA of the enlarged set of enterprises *remained the same!*

This is logically impossible. As the number of qualified enterprises increased—because the economic census *was* "capturing" previously missed business entities—the size of IVA should have risen, too. Even if NBS found overlapped reporting from the same enterprise during the census or reclassified them, which may result in a bigger count for the number of enterprises but leave the IVA unchanged, that cannot explain why the GOV was restated but the IVA was not. What makes the 2004 number look even more dubious is that when data on the number of enterprises and IVA are traced back year by year from 1998 to 2006, only the 2004 data show a divergence between original and postcensus reporting (Table 2.4).

Although the data comparison shows there was only one year out of nine when the data were inconsistent on this point, the anomaly set off alarm bells over the reliability and overall quality of China's reporting on myriad other data that were detrimental to public confidence.

A textbook illustration of the data breaks in China's official reporting is the classification and publication of China's industrial enterprise data. Coming from an industry-heavy command economy, the most important data China reported for its industrial subsector prior to the 1993 transition was GOV, known in Chinese as *gongye zongchanzhi*. Beginning in 1993, NBS began publishing data on IVA,[51] *gongye zengjiazhi*, in compliance with the requirements of 1993 SNA. However, an examination of IVA data and industrial GDP exposes serious problems: by China's definition, the IVA published in the yearbooks only covers value-added from DRIEs, for which the definition evolved significantly over time—as thoroughly explained in Textbox 2.1—without a backward revision to past-year statistics.

---

51. NBS, "Statistical Bulletin of 1992 National Economy and Social Development," February 18, 1993, http://www.stats.gov.cn/tjsj/tjgb/ndtjgb/qgndtjgb/200203/t20020331_30006.html. In 1992, the last year before NBS fully converted to the SNA framework, there was also a data point for the value of DRIE IVA. However, it is never included in NBS's systematic publication of the series starting from 1993. Neither was it revised following the 2004 census, as other data points were (the CEIC database records the first observation year for this data series as 1993 as well). For the purpose of this study, we do not consider DRIE IVA prior to 1993. Carsten Holz has extrapolated such data series prior to 1992; see the details in his explanations for Figure 3 in Holz, "Quality," 41.

Table 2.4. 2004 Census Restated Enterprise Number, But Not Their Value-Added

Unit: Number, RMB trillion

	Number of DRIEs (Original)*	Number of DRIEs (Post-2004 Census)†	DRIE Value-Added (Original)	DRIE Value-Added (Post-2004 Census)
1998	165,080	165,080	1.94	1.94
1999	162,033	162,033	2.16	2.16
2000	162,885	162,885	2.54	2.54
2001	171,256	171,256	2.83	2.83
2002	181,557	181,557	3.30	3.30
2003	196,222	196,222	4.20	4.20
2004	**219,463**	**276,474**	**5.48**	**5.48**
2005	271,835	271,835	7.22	7.22
2006	301,961	301,961	9.11	9.11

* Annual data are from each year's NBS *Statistical Yearbook*. For example, 2004 data are from Yearbook 2005.
† 1998–2006 data are from NBS *Statistical Yearbook* 2007, Table 14-4.
Source: NBS.

Until China suspended the series in 2008, the data were fragmented by different threshold definitions and values and were never consistently adjusted through the 15 years of publication. NBS would note in each year's statistical yearbook which definition it used to calculate the current year's aggregate data, but the burden of rendering the series consistent was left to outsiders—who possessed inadequate information to do so.

Deeper flaws with the data emerge when one compares IVA from the DRIEs—essentially, the GDP value of these firms—to IVA of *all* industrial enterprises and nonenterprise production units such as self-employed business. The ratio of DRIEs' IVA to all IVA started climbing in the late 1990s and wound up, impossibly, at *more than 100 percent of total IVA* in 2007.

From 1998, the first year NBS instituted a quantitative threshold for the DRIEs, through 2006, the ratio of IVA over industrial GDP rose steadily from less than 60 percent to an unrealistic 99.7 percent. In 2004, China's first economic census year, the DRIE share of GOV of the entire industry was a touch below 91 percent. In the second census for 2008, that share rose to 93 percent. Because IVA is GOV less intermediate inputs and value-added taxes, assuming there is no major disruption in input costs or taxes, the two should move in tandem.[52] Under IMF's GDDS reporting regime, NBS states that GOV "can be compared with the value-added" from the national accounts.[53] The two are both value measures for the production process, but they focus on different stages: GOV concerns the production process, while the IVA is all about the newly created value.

---

52. NBS, *Methods of Non-Economic Census Year, 2010 Ed.*, 19–20.
53. IMF, "GDDS China."

Table 2.5. DRIE Value-Added Exceeded Total Industrial GDP in 2007

Unit: RMB trillion

	DRIE Value-Added	Industrial GDP	DRIE VA/Industrial GDP Ratio
1993	1.28	1.42	90.5%
1994	1.47	1.95	75.5%
1995	1.54	2.50	61.9%
1996	1.80	2.94	61.2%
1997	1.98	3.29	60.3%
1998	1.94	3.40	57.1%
1999	2.16	3.59	60.1%
2000	2.54	4.00	63.4%
2001	2.83	4.36	65.0%
2002	3.30	4.74	69.6%
2003	4.20	5.49	76.4%
2004	5.48	6.52	84.0%
2005	7.22	7.72	93.5%
2006	9.11	9.13	99.7%
2007	**11.70**	**11.05**	**105.9%**
2008	n/a	13.03	n/a
2009	n/a	13.52	n/a
2010	n/a	16.07	n/a
2011	n/a	18.85	n/a
2012	n/a	19.97	n/a
2013	n/a	21.07	n/a

Sources: NBS, CEIC, authors' calculations.

In other words, if in GOV terms the DRIEs, whose definition remained unchanged from 1998 through 2006, accounted for 91 to 93 percent of total industrial enterprises between the two censuses, it is virtually impossible that in IVA terms the DRIEs accounted for nearly 100 percent of total enterprises in 2006. This is not just an empirical observation; we applied statistical tests to confirm it. Based on our model and the databases containing enterprise-level raw statistics, in 90 percent of industries in China's industrial subsector, the greater enterprise revenue is, the less IVA per unit of GOV is observed (discussed further in Chapter 3 in terms of reestimating IVA for all types of industrial entities).[54] That means if DRIEs accounted for 91 to 93 percent of total industrial enterprises' GOV, their IVA share should be lower, not higher. Holz shares this view, noting that the 2006 reported DRIE share of IVA—99.7 percent—seemed "far too high" given that in the previous year, that ratio was 93 percent.[55]

But the 2006 story is still not the *most* glaring anomaly. In China's official reporting, the 2007 DRIE share of value-added exceeded that of all industrial enterprises combined,

---

54. Minna Ma, interview by authors, November 2013. Our finding is endorsed by Ms. Ma, dean of the Statistics School at Jilin University of Finance and Economics.

55. Holz, "Classification Systems," 9.

accounting for 105.9 percent of the total, a logically impossible result (Table 2.5). Although NBS revised the definition for the DRIEs in 2007, that did not change the fact that they constituted a *subgroup* of industrial enterprises that cannot be bigger than the whole. This befuddled even the most agile China watchers. Writing in January 2013, Holz noted those logically impossible values "question the quality of either the DRIE data or the quality of the NIPA (national accounts) data" but did not offer an alternative estimate.[56] In another publication later that year, he added that the discrepancy "points at severe difficulties of NBS in measuring IVA even at a degree of up to, perhaps, +/–20 percent accuracy."[57]

The answer may lie in simple bureaucratic discord. As with other data breaks in China's official reporting, the divergence here was primarily due to NBS's fragmented bureaucratic structure and the lack of interdivision collaboration. Industrial statistics, including DRIE IVA data, are compiled and calculated by the Industrial Statistical Department at NBS headquarters, while the GDP aggregates are handled by the National Economic Accounts Department.[58] People knowledgeable about the internal division of work suggest that the national accounts department has qualms with source data from the industrial department and thus uses alternative data, such as value-added tax, to revise enterprise data before putting them into use. These two NBS departments *both* calculate value-added data for industrial enterprises, large and small, and for self-employed businesses, but only the national accounts department's whole-industry results—in the form of industrial GDP—and industrial statistical departments' DRIE IVA data were published prior to the 2008 suspension of the latter. Although the source data that the national accounts department uses come from the industrial enterprise database *supervised by the industrial statistical department*, it is not taken at face value but is put through significant downward revisions before inclusion in GDP accounting. In Chapter 3 we explore this further in technical detail.

This division of labor sheds light on accusations of industrial data value inflation as a basis to reject Chinese GDP data: industrial statistics and their use as an element of GDP are handled by different divisions, and final numbers are not calculated based on exactly the same set of source statistics. These problems are ongoing. Until NBS brings data from all of its divisions in line with one another and publishes all series in a transparent and replicable manner, doubts over backstage operations and reliability will remain.

Unfortunately, Beijing has taken an opposite strategy to transparency in recent years. Starting in 2008, NBS discontinued the release of DRIE IVA data, seemingly to avoid a reoccurrence of the embarrassing results that suggested bureaucratic fragmentation. The official line explaining why publication of the data was dropped was that "IVA for enterprises above the designated threshold is a basic and procedural variable, based on

---

56. Ibid., 9–10.
57. Holz, "Output Data," 41.
58. NBS, "国家统计机构设置 (NBS Organizational Chart)," http://www.stats.gov.cn/zjtj/gjtjj/jgsz/.

imputations, in the process of calculating GDP," implying that there is little strategic value in publishing this intermediate data series separately.[59] The statement is not factually wrong, but it is antithetical to a culture of statistical self-assurance and openness, and it ignores the need to address public doubts. NBS claimed that to make up for discontinuing DRIE IVA data, it now includes value-added data for the complete group of industrial enterprises in the annual GDP release, but it is essentially the same concept as industrial GDP, and NBS combined the publication of "total IVA" and "industrial GDP."[60] Embarrassment is avoided with the consolidated publication, but scholars have no way of knowing the share of IVA attributed to the DRIEs.

In similar form to the suspension of DRIE IVA data publication in 2008, in 2013, NBS stopped publishing 2012 annual GOV data for DRIEs. Again, there was no explanation—though one imagines there has to be a reason, because any NBS department that wants to remove an existing data series from the statistical yearbook must justify the change to decisionmakers. Our guess is that NBS did not want outside researchers to use DRIEs' GOV data to infer IVA by multiplying certain value-added ratios—a method widely used by researchers to construct IVA data in the absence of official figures. We hypothesize that NBS fears that scholars would utilize GOV data, in lieu of IVA figures, to arrive at conclusions that would contradict some other official statistics. Perkins and Rawski noted in 2007 that many, if not most, China data specialists would agree that when Chinese statistics reflected poorly on the real economy, the government would not typically resort to massive falsification, except during the 1958–1960 period; instead, they would simply decide to stop publishing the data.[61]

The cases of IVA and GOV are only two examples of the irregularities in China's publication regime of national accounts data. While one may argue that removing the flawed data is a sign of progress in China's data system per se, the poor explanatory work on that front has significantly drained the government's credibility, and as Holz noted, it is not a promising solution to the problem.[62] In the following two sections, we explore other problems and sources of public suspicion one level deeper, with regards to specific concepts, calculation methods, and the bureaucratic structure of China's statistical system. Those problems present both symbolic and substantial concerns over the validity of Chinese data. We offer our judgment on workarounds where possible.

Because China has yet to straighten out various aspects of its data system, it was unable to meet the requirements for graduation to the SDDS after more than a decade of GDDS participation. As discussed in Chapter 1, with China gradually opening its capital account and continuing further integration of the domestic economy with international markets, it has announced plans to make that move. After all, China was one of only two G20 countries (along with Saudi Arabia) not advanced to the SDDS.

---

59. NBS, "FAQs: Industrial Statistics."
60. NBS, "2013 年国内生产总值初步核算情况 (Statistical Bulletin of 2013 GDP: Initial Result)," January 21, 2014, http://www.stats.gov.cn/tjsj/zxfb/201401/t20140121_502731.html.
61. Perkins and Rawski, "Appendix," 2.
62. Holz, "Output Data," 41.

Due to the higher threshold for entrants, the IMF calls the adherence to the SDDS a test of "good statistical citizenship."[63] While IMF staff find China's data broadly adequate for surveillance purposes, they are also clear that the "techniques for deriving volume measures of GDP are not sound and need to be improved."[64]

External pressure for China to make a commitment to improving its data publication practices has mounted. Advanced economies involved in strategically important relationships with China have worked to convince Beijing of a mutual interest in adherence to higher standards and dissemination of essential data to the public. On November 15, 2014, President Xi Jinping announced at the G20 Summit in Brisbane that China intended to adopt the SDDS commitments, marking a milestone in the history of Chinese statistics and signaling a fundamental change in the government's attitude toward a sound data system. Although the SDDS is no longer the highest tier in the IMF's Data Standards Initiatives—the organization created an SDDS-Plus in 2012 to further raise the bar on data transparency, and nine countries have made a formal commitment as of 2014[65]—the fact that China is converging with international statistical norms and institutions must be acknowledged as a significant achievement for a country with a relatively short history of modern national accounting.

Statistical Terms with Chinese Characteristics

Policymakers with the fate of the nation on their shoulders and business leaders with their reputations, money, and employee welfare on the line depend on valid economic signals to steer their course. Often, they turn to heuristics, anecdotal indications or proxies, when they do not have confidence in more systematic measures. A common criticism of China's GDP data is that it is inconsistent with cross-checks against alternative high-frequency data, for which values, trends over time, or both, often diverge. Comparison with proxy data to test for quality and consistency is a standard academic and professional research practice internationally and naturally are of interest given the problematic data compilation and calculation processes described above. However, these exercises must be treated with extra caution in China, not only because the economic structure has been evolving so rapidly, making data correlations unstable over time, but also because changes to definitions and coverage of data variables are poorly documented—especially in English—and are insufficiently understood. The potential for bad choices in picking cross-checking metrics is high in China and has given rise to a variety of errors.

REAL PROBLEMS, FAKE PROBLEMS

A well-known case of using alternatives to evaluate China's economic growth concerns Premier Li Keqiang himself when he was serving as Communist Party chief of Liaoning

---

63. IMF, "Factsheet–IMF Standards for Data Dissemination," November 17, 2014, http://www.imf.org/external/np/exr/facts/data.htm.

64. IMF, *China: 2014 Article IV*, 13.

65. IMF, "Press Release: IMF Launches the Special Data Dissemination Standard Plus," November 18, 2014, http://www.imf.org/external/np/sec/pr/2014/pr14523.htm.

Figure 2.1. Keqiang Index versus Real GDP Growth
Unit: Percentage

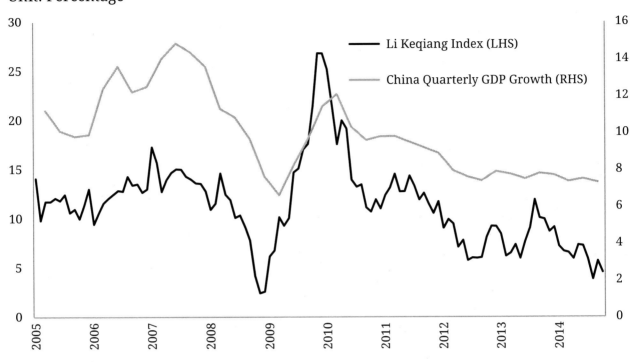

Sources: NBS, CEIC, Bloomberg, authors' calculations.

Province from 2004 to 2007. In a private dinner with the American ambassador reported in an embassy cable that was subsequently leaked, Li said he regarded official GDP statistics to be "man-made" and unreliable and for "reference" only. He was quoted as saying he depended on data from electricity consumption, rail cargo volume, and bank lending statistics, from which he felt he could get a "relatively accurate" picture of growth.[66]

The *Economist* magazine created a "Keqiang Index" to explore the movement of Li's three preferred indicators relative to announced headline growth rates. Applying this cross-check to the period 2005–2014 produced an estimate of growth consistent with reported official growth (a little *higher*—about 1.5 percentage points—than it in fact was, over that period of time, suggesting official understatement not exaggeration) but with considerably greater volatility (Figure 2.1). Smoothing out indications of performance outside of policymakers' comfort zone, rather than distorting the long-term economic trends, would seem to be the pattern. It is therefore far more pronounced in periods of economic turbulence, such as the global financial crisis. As the magazine said:

---

66. WikiLeaks, "Fifth Generation Star Li Keqiang Discusses Domestic Challenges, Trade Relations with Ambassador," March 15, 2007, https://wikileaks.org/cable/2007/03/07BEIJING1760.html.

Electricity consumption and cargo traffic both shrank in the final months of 2008 and in early 2009, implying that China's economy suffered more grievously than the official figures allow. A loan surge in 2009 presaged the rapid recovery that followed.[67]

That the premier looked to such proxies to guide his work in Liaoning lends credence to efforts by independent economists who have taken a similar approach over past decades. But as will be evident, these anecdotal approaches are just, at best, useful for discerning general patterns and in many cases fail to resolve the big questions. Obviously, a rough estimate based on a couple of metrics offers no substitute to systematic national accounts.

The most famous example of an independent economist using Premier Li's style of spot-checks on selected data to critique official GDP is a series of commentaries by Thomas Rawski arguing that Beijing papered over a deep contraction in growth during the years of the Asian Financial Crisis in the late 1990s. Rawski observed that while GDP growth declined from 9.3 percent in 1997 to 7.8 percent in 1998 and then to 7.1 percent for 1999 before rebounding in 2000,[68] more tangible proxies for economic performance showed a more severe downturn. For example, he noted that China's energy use contracted 6.4 percent and 7.8 percent in 1998 and 1999, respectively, which he did not believe could be explained by a rapid growth in energy efficiency, because "it's not a hallmark of China's economy."[69] He also made sensible inferences from comments by some Chinese economic insiders, such as economist Wu Jinglian, who talked about China's economic downturn starting in 1997, despite official figures asserting a sanguine picture.[70] Some of Rawski's suggestions for a "starting point" from which to establish a better gauge of actual growth in these years, notably growth in civil aviation passenger miles flown, seem like weak choices in retrospect, especially as a basis to argue that actual growth was at most 2.2 percent. In fact, Rawski himself acknowledged that his alternative figures for China's GDP growth, from –2 to +2 percent for 1998 in comparison with the official +7.8 percent, and from –2.5 to +2 percent for 1999 compared with the *then* official +7.1 percent, "represents little more than guesses" and "are not firmly grounded in empirical data."[71]

But argument by anecdote works both ways. If the energy use patterns Rawski pointed to were hard to square with steady growth above 7 percent, then the strong and externally verifiable Chinese import growth data for these years, pointed out by economist Nick Lardy, were hard to square with talk of collapsing growth as presented by Rawski.[72]

---

67. "Keqiang Ker-Ching," *The Economist*, December 9, 2010, http://www.economist.com/node/17681868.

68. The 1999 growth was later revised to 7.6 percent by NBS after the first economic census for 2004. NBS confirmed with us that they applied a formula to revise GDP growth from 1993 through 2004 after that census. They did not revise it for 1998 because they too believed the statistic was unreliable. This is among the most direct evidence of NBS acknowledging that the original 1998 growth rate was inaccurate.

69. Rawski, "What Is Happening," 348.

70. Ibid., 351.

71. Ibid., 352–353.

72. Nicholas R. Lardy, "Evaluating Economic Indicators in Post-WTO China," *Issues & Studies* 38, no. 4 (March 2003): 251–254, http://www.airitilibrary.com/Publication/alDetailedMesh?DocID=10132511-200303-38-4%2639-1-249-268-a.

Commentators who played it safe and split the difference between the brave-faced official numbers and Rawski's deep skepticism seem, with hindsight, to have been closest to the mark.[73]

Anecdotal evidence—whether Rawski's energy use or Premier Li's cargo freight—is also subject to infinite argument as to whether special circumstances are distorting the readings. In one Chinese rebuttal to Rawski, Chinese economist Ren Ruo'en offered examples of cases where energy use proxies would have offered misleading conclusions in other economies, including Japan, South Korea, Germany, Britain, and the United States.[74] To be clear, Rawski never suggested that a handful of metrics for real economy activity could provide a sufficiently accurate or precise gauge of overall economic activity the way well-run national accounting is meant to. He was simply pointing out very problematic patterns in Chinese data patterns, with constructive motives in mind. In fact, as noted in footnote 68, the fact that NBS revised GDP growth rates for all the years from 1993 to 2004, except 1998, after the first economic census, already demonstrated that Beijing believed 1998's statistics were inaccurate. Prior to that revision, the growth rate for 1998 was 7.8 percent and 7.1 percent for 1999, as Rawski noted in his 2001 paper; later, however, the 1998 rate remained unchanged, and the 1999 growth was revised up to 7.6 percent. At least for the year 1998, Rawski's qualitative assessment was indirectly recognized by Chinese authorities. Besides, the influence of Rawski's work on a whole generation of Chinese and foreign analysts has been great, and the impact of his short commentaries in setting the agenda for debate was profound.

However, the nuanced debate over interpreting China's growth performance lost its subtlety and—to a great extent—its value once it was picked up by a wider audience, especially of foreign non-GDP specialists who already harbored dark views of Chinese economic policy. Where Rawski's arguments were precise, authors such as Gordon Chang, with his 2001 *The Coming Collapse of China*, extrapolated these economic debates into a picture of impending ruin. Conservative pundits in Washington fit Rawski's late-1990s concerns into stories with titles such as "China's Economic Façade" and suggested that China was still contracting well into the 2000s, which was blatantly incorrect.[75] Right through the present day, one hears superficial invocations of Rawski's 14-year-old data observations as though they prove that current statistics are made up.

In contrast, throughout the intervening years, independent researchers working more systematically have made important contributions to the statistical system. Two Chinese professors based in Shanghai, Zhang Jun of Fudan University and Zhu Tian of the China Europe International Business School (CEIBS), have, for example, made arguments much

---

73. "The Art of Chinese Massage," *Economist*, May 21, 2009, http://www.economist.com/node/13692907.

74. Ruoen Ren, "中国 GDP 统计水分有多大—评两个估计中国 GDP 数据研究的若干方法问题 (How Inflated Is China's GDP Statistics: A Comment on Methodological Problems with Two Assessments on Chinese GDP Data)," *China Economic Quarterly*, no. 4 (2002): 4, http://ceqc.ccer.edu.cn/publish_contributions/download?file=/public/system /publish/648/020103.pdf.

75. Arthur Waldron, "China's Economic Facade," *Washington Post*, March 21, 2002, http://www.taiwandc .org/wp-2002-01.htm.

bolder and more provocative than the now stale 1990s debate. Through analysis of urban and rural consumption expenditures, they assembled alternative estimates using official data and formulas and concluded that household and government consumption accounts for more than 60 percent of GDP, rather than the official estimate just below 50 percent.[76] In a separate writing focused on China's hefty investment, the authors critically reproduced NBS's methodology for calculating gross fixed capital formation (GFCF) and postulated that the Bureau is using this investment measure as a residual variable in expenditure-based GDP, rather than actually deriving it from source data. These economists' objective is to make expenditure-based GDP results robust and consistent with the income-production approach, while remaining entirely separate. Zhu and Zhang argued that Beijing is only developing the income-production side numbers from scratch and then using them as a guide to fill out the expenditure-side numbers and make them align—in sharp contravention to the procedures outlined in the official national accounts manual.[77] In our discussions with Zhang, he noted that officials appeared to be holding back from challenging these conclusions.

In Chapter 3, we also attempt to replicate NBS methods and formulas to recalculate China's economic size, based on a combination of income and production approaches. Before doing that, it is necessary to understand a few more nuances of China's national account concepts and methods to ensure that we focus attention on real problems with the accounting rather than red herrings.

TWO EXAMPLES

Analysts know that multiple data series exist related to various components of GDP and that, while using several might be useful for getting a more complete picture of economic activity, one must take care to identify the appropriate measures when making a proper calculation of GDP. This is not just a concern for China; it is universal. Problems can occur when series that are useful for short-term purposes get comingled with the official numbers that go into GDP calculation, and when proxies selected based on an understanding of a past economic model are over-relied upon to gauge a rapidly restructuring economy. Examples from recent years concern household consumption and business investment in expenditure-approach GDP. The problems arise both from misidentification of the appropriate series and idiosyncrasies in China's definitions.

First, while the proper input to expenditure-based GDP for consumption is *household final consumption expenditures*, researchers frequently look at the alternate *total retail sales of consumer goods* (RSCG or "retail sales") because it is released in a more timely fashion and is more germane for some purposes. The statistic is published monthly by NBS, and reports gross consumption by tracking retail-level sales of consumer durables

76. Jun Zhang and Tian Zhu, "Re-Estimating China's Underestimated Consumption" (Working Paper, Social Science Research Network, 2013), 1, http://papers.ssrn.com/abstract=2330698.

77. Tian Zhu and Jun Zhang, "中国投资率高估之谜 (The Myth of China's High Investment Ratio)," *Financial Times Chinese*, August 6, 2014, http://www.ftchinese.com/story/001057593?full=y.

(e.g., appliances) and nondurables (e.g., toothpaste) to both individuals and institutions, including government offices, army units, and schools, ostensibly for final use (not resale or for production), plus revenue from catering services.[78]

RSCG is related to the "C" component of expenditure-side GDP and correlates closely most of the time, but it is not the same. Because RSCG is available monthly, it is often used as a leading indicator of quarterly consumption growth in expenditure-based GDP. The proper series used for quarterly GDP, actual consumption by households ascertained through direct surveys and extrapolation, is released only four times a year, with a lag. When it is released, it is grouped with government consumption as "final consumption expenditure"; in addition, only the contribution and share of the headline GDP growth rate from that combined indicator are published, rather than the nominal increment. Through various techniques for direct observation of retail activity, analysts can watch trends even second by second in today's Internet-based economy and are loath to wait three months for what can be *more or less* observed in real time.

For directional guidance on consumption growth, retail sales are useful, but important differences make it unsound to substitute one for the other. Alas, this happens often. For instance, in early 2009, quarterly GDP growth was reported at 6.1 percent (later revised to 6.2 percent), down from 9.8 percent at the end of 2008, despite retail sales and total fixed asset investment reported *up*, at 15.9 percent and 28.8 percent year on year in real terms, respectively.[79] This sparked a round of charges that household statistics were not genuine, given that government-issued vouchers were being issued to bolster demand.[80] Analysts turning to the RSCG data encountered the long list of distinctions between that series and household consumption, and some reacted as though those differences were an attempt to distort the picture, rather than simply a difference in focus.

For example, the RSCG measure captures not just domestic households but non-Chinese residents living in China, institutions at various levels of governments that shop retail (imagine local governments buying through Staples in the United States), as well as social organizations, corporations, military units, and schools. It omits most services purchases by households, an increasingly prominent component of family budgets. Therefore, by nature, RSCG better mirrors the commodity portion of the society's *total* final consumption expenditure than it does for the "C" component—households' total consumption of commodities and services. Some mistakenly think the RSCG statistic must incorporate wholesale business despite the definition indicating otherwise. On one hand, their suspicion is not groundless. As demonstrated earlier, Beijing does not appear to always abide by the official line in economic accounting. On the other hand, in the case of RSCG, Beijing adopts a more rigorous Internet-based, direct-reporting approach in data collection and

78. NBS, "社会消费品零售总额 (Total Retail Sales of Consumer Goods)," October 2013, http://www.stats.gov.cn /tjzs/tjbk/nsbzb/201310/P020140226567121458913.pdf.

79. Xianchun Xu, "Accurately Understand," 21, 26.

80. Gordon G. Chang, "Another Chinese Fib: 6.1% Growth," *Forbes*, April 22, 2009, http://www.forbes.com /2009/04/21/china-economic-statistics-growth-opinions-columnists-wen-jiabao.html.

scrutinizes collected information to ensure the numbers are restricted to retail goods sold *not* for resale and production purposes (otherwise it will include wholesale). Such practices have satisfied Chinese economists such as Li Xunlei at Haitong Securities and Huang Yiping at Peking University that the statistic is largely sound[81] and concords with the official definition.[82] As noted previously, the two concepts—the "C" component in the expenditure-based GDP and RSCG—are quite different.[83] While in normal times they both respond to demand conditions, and the correlation between them is high (0.9), at volatile moments when households pull back and countercyclical fiscal efforts kick in, they are bound to diverge.[84]

The practice of combining these series in a manner that risks confusing the veracity of the GDP picture remains common. In a recent column, Yukon Huang of the Carnegie Endowment for International Peace asked, "How can one reconcile retail sales that were growing at 15 to 20 percent a year for decades with GDP numbers that suggest lackluster growth in personal consumption? This raises suspicion that something is amiss, quite possibly that consumption is seriously understated."[85] There are indeed problems with the household survey, but the difference between retail sales and expenditures growth should not be taken as evidence of GDP mismeasurement, or even underestimating consumption in favor of investment in GDP composition, as Huang concludes. First, over the last decade and a half, RSCG growth was about 13 percent, rather than 15 to 20 percent, as Huang suggested—much closer to household consumption's nominal growth over the period, which was roughly 11 percent. Over just the last decade, RSCG and household consumption growth would be 16.1 and 13.7 percent, respectively, the difference only slightly greater than in the longer timeframe (Figure 2.2). Second, after accounting for the conceptual differences, legitimate countercyclical policy impacts on RSCG over household consumption, and acknowledged room for improvement in coverage (especially for services), the gap is largely explained. NBS Deputy Xu Xianchun published an essay clarifying most of this, subsequently discussed in Western media in 2009.[86]

Analyzing Chinese consumption performance is not easy. For urban households, there is no monthly series and only one consumption data series published quarterly: "urban resident consumption expenditure per capita" (*chengzhen jumin renjun xiaofeixing zhichu*).

81. Xunlei Li, "A Major Misjudgment on Chinese Economy: Investment Overstatement and Consumption Understatement," *Forbes China*, June 4, 2012, http://www.forbeschina.com/review/201206/0017247_3.shtml.

82. Yiping Huang, "China's Economic Rebalancing Already Underway," *East Asia Forum*, February 12, 2012, http://www.eastasiaforum.org/2012/02/12/china-s-economic-rebalancing-already-underway/.

83. NBS, "Retail Sales"; Xu, "Accurately Understand," 22.

84. There are other important differences as well. RSCG includes sales of construction materials to urban and rural residents for housing, but in the expenditure approach, this spending is counted as investment. RSCG does not cover household consumption of self-produced products, including home-grown food. In addition to not capturing most regular consumer services, RSCG misses implicit services such as imputed rent for owner-occupied housing and indirectly measured activities like financial intermediation.

85. Yukon Huang, "China's Misleading Economic Indicators," *Financial Times: The A-List*, August 29, 2014, http://blogs.ft.com/the-a-list/2014/08/29/chinas-misleading-economic-indicators/.

86. Andrew Batson, "China Downplays Retail Sales Data," *Wall Street Journal*, May 14, 2009, http://blogs.wsj.com/chinarealtime/2009/05/14/china-downplays-retail-sales-data/.

Figure 2.2. Nominal Growth for Household Consumption and Retail Sales
Unit: Percentage

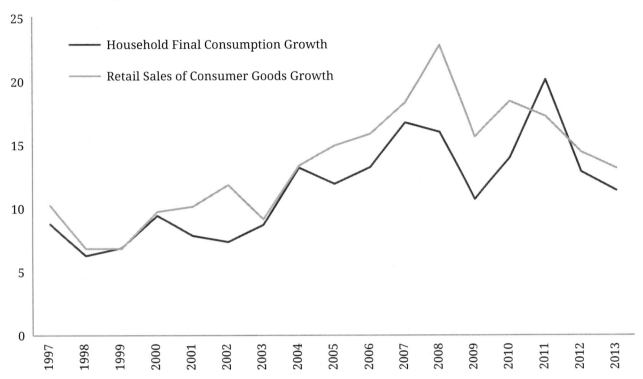

Sources: NBS, CEIC, authors' calculations.

Eight categories are covered, including food, clothing, residence, household facility and services, transportation, medical, recreation, and other. The *residence* item is important and potentially confusing: unlike annual household final consumption in the national accounts and GDP, the quarterly reports cover "explicit expenditures" only and *do not include* "implicit expenditures," including imputed rents for owner-occupied housing.[87] The remainder of the coverage is the same, including explicit expenditures such as market rents, property management fees, maintenance costs, and housing utility expenses. Zhang Jun and Zhu Tian from Shanghai, in an exercise to quantify the portion of underreported household consumption in China, added up the per-capita household consumption expenditure data on residence in 2009 and compared it with the aggregate variable in national accounts. They found the discrepancy between the two was about 2 percent of that year's annual GDP. Further, they moved on to recalculate the value-added generated by imputed rents that was missing from the official GDP, and their reestimates raised that year's expenditure-based GDP by 9.2 percent.[88] For measures of rural private consumption, the minutia required to replicate stated official practices are even more complicated.

87. NBS, "常见问题解答: 住户调查 (Frequently Asked Questions: Household Surveys)," August 29, 2013, http://www.stats.gov.cn/tjzs/cjwtjd/201308/t20130829_74325.html. More specific explanations of China's household survey and categories of consumption expenditure can be found in Xu, "Accurately Understand," 22, 29.

88. Zhang and Zhu, "Underestimated Consumption," 5–6, 12–13.

The largest component of China's expenditure GDP—*gross capital formation*, which is primarily *gross fixed capital formation*, or GFCF—presents a similar situation. Because China only publishes GDP-compatible GFCF figures in nominal terms in its final annual releases (and inflation-adjusted contribution and share of GDP growth quarterly), researchers are left using *fixed asset investment* (FAI) as a monthly proxy, and trouble ensues. In general international use, FAI is the value of aggregate fixed asset construction and acquisition investment in an accounting period, plus related expenses incurred in those activities. As a GDP component, GFCF measures what has been created in the measurement period and counts the net change in fixed and intangible assets in the period arising from investment. Even though GFCF counts both tangible and intangible, while FAI does not, FAI tends to be significantly larger because the same asset can be sold twice in a measurement period, for instance, and the value of transactions can be multiplied relative to the growth in the stock of assets (1.7 times greater in 2013, in fact). But again, because FAI is available monthly, while GFCF is not, it is watched more frequently, raising the chance that the two series are comingled.

On the intangible asset front, Zhang Jun examined provincial-level data from Shanghai on FAI and GFCF and found the relationship between the two inverse to the general national pattern, concluding it was partly due to Shanghai's intangible capital formation outpacing the national level.[89] Although the way China compiles intangible assets investment data for GDP purposes is opaque and controversial, its GFCF does cover part of this activity, whereas FAI records physical asset investment only. For all these reasons, NBS officials stress that GFCF and FAI must be carefully distinguished.[90]

In a late 2013 announcement of the plan to converge with 2008 SNA, NBS committed to improving its GFCF national accounts coverage, of which the most important change will be counting research and development expenditure as fixed capital formation instead of intermediate inputs.[91] However, that plan appears to be postponed indefinitely. Beijing did not revise the accounting method for R&D expenses in its latest 2013 *Economic Census* as originally scheduled, and acknowledged using the 1993 SNA-based methods for the latest 2014 GDP accounting (though not until some time after the initial economic census release). This indicates that the economic census also did not adopt the latest SNA standards. The change of heart to not include R&D investment in fixed capital formation—and to not comport with the latest SNA in the census—has still not been explicitly addressed as of this writing.

It remains unclear to us why NBS—and central officials above NBS's ranking—chose to delay the convergence they had planned. One of our hypotheses is that Beijing did not want a revision bigger than the 2004 and 2008 censuses to create further suspicion of their data work. A smaller restatement, they may have thought, would help demonstrate solid progress in improving data quality. This is what NBS said in its official explanatory note following

89. Jun Zhang, interview by authors, November 2014.
90. Xu, "Accurately Understand," 23, 30.
91. NBS, "Reform of National Accounts System."

Figure 2.3. Gap between Fixed Asset Investment and GFCF Widens
Unit: RMB Trillion

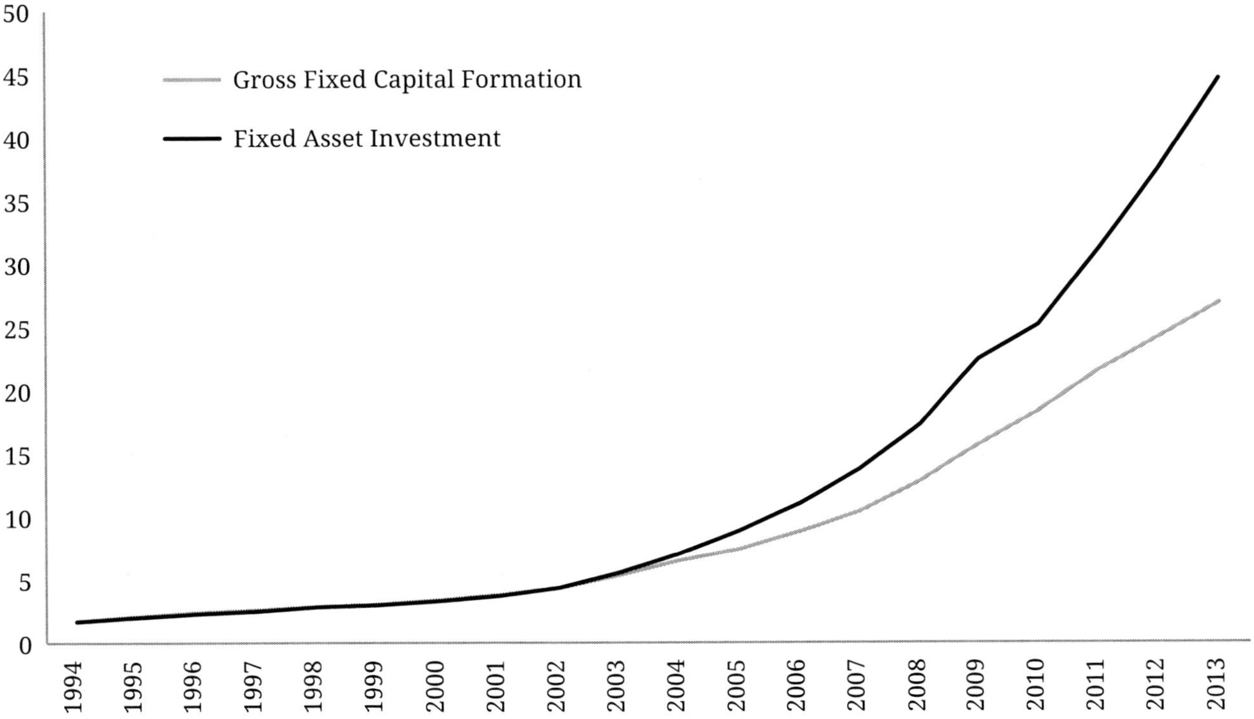

Sources: NBS, CEIC, authors' calculations.

the census revisions.[92] Another hypothesis is that in understating the revision, Beijing leaves itself some maneuvering room in managing growth expectations down the road.

Over the years the expanding gap between FAI and GFCF (Figure 2.3) has attracted attention from Chinese researchers as well, not just foreigners. As mentioned above, Zhu and Zhang attempted to reconstruct China's whole GFCF series based on NBS models and official source data and wound up concluding that final published numbers are likely downwardly adjusted to eliminate an embarrassing gap between expenditure- and hybrid production–based GDP.[93] In essence, that GFCF is used as a residual, adjustment factor rather than being calculated properly. This is a bold statement.

Using alternative measures, Beijing could get two vastly different GDP numbers from production income– and expenditure-based approaches. Because China derives official GDP from a combination of income and production approaches, it might adjust GFCF to bring the expenditure-based GDP down to within a reasonable margin around the production-based result. For 2012, Zhu and Zhang calculated GFCF data at 64 percent above the official reported levels but only *slightly* higher than FAI. They argue that NBS

92. Ibid.
93. Zhu and Zhang, "(Myth)."

Figure 2.4. China's GDP by Income/Production versus GDP by Expenditure, 2004–2013*

Unit: RMB Trillion

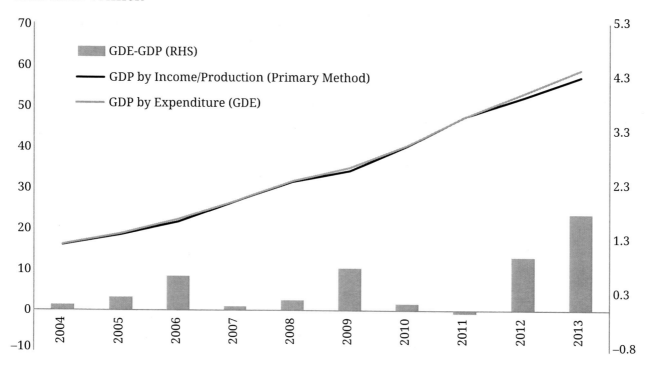

* 2009–2013 numbers are prior to 2013 *Economic Census* revisions.
Sources: NBS, CEIC, authors' calculations.

discounted FAI by 20 to 40 percent to obtain GFCF data in line with the hybrid production-approach GDP minus total final consumption and net exports.[94]

Although NBS has not responded to Zhu and Zhang, a larger gap than officially acknowledged is noted in other independent work. Further, when explaining why China does not publish expenditure-based GDP growth numbers, Yue Ximing, a renowned finance professor at Beijing's Renmin University, concluded that the production/expenditure-approach gap is too wide to permit publication of expenditure-based results until the margin between the two can be narrowed to a "tolerable level."[95] But Yue claimed the methods and source data for the two approaches are independent from each other. Wu You, a senior national accounts officer at NBS said in a 2011 presentation that source data and materials for the expenditure approach were lacking and discrepancies still existed between expenditure-based and production-based GDP.[96] However, according to China's final official releases, the gap between the two GDP measurements was minimal, so it is reasonable to infer that NBS has conducted certain adjustments prior to the announcement (Figure 2.4).

---

94. Ibid.
95. Yue, "Reform."
96. You Wu, "China Expenditure-Based GDP Accounting" (Shenzhen, April 25, 2011), 31, http://unstats.un.org/unsd/economic_stat/China/GDPFE/2.%20China.ppt.

As economists who have worked with national accounts data know, especially when working with developing economies, getting *one* good measure of GDP using a single approach is hard enough. Running all three frameworks and expecting them to match up well in a developing nation is unrealistic. China makes clear that it prefers a hybrid production approach and has acknowledged expenditure data problems. The work by Chinese economists discussed above demonstrates just how serious those problems could be. It also makes clear why there are so many private misgivings about China's official data. If state statisticians are manipulating GFCF expenditure data to avoid questions about concordance with other approaches, then conditions have a long way to go.

Institutional Arrangements and Constraints

China's central and local governments began to account GDP and gross regional product (GRP) separately in 1985. During the first decade or so, GDP was actually greater than GRP by a modest margin, around 5 percent. In 2002, that pattern reversed. The gap between the sum of provincial output and the national aggregate has been expanding—to as much as 11 percent in 2012—and has become a major source of suspicion about the quality of Chinese data. Noticing this reversed trend, Iacob N. Koch-Weser, a policy analyst at the U.S.-China Economic and Security Review Commission (USCC), argued that Beijing may have "automatically" adjusted provincial figures downward since 2002, based on the assumption that local numbers are too high.[97] Looking more closely at individual sectors, Koch-Weser discovered some interesting facts: under the hybrid production approach, the overshooting of provincial data has primarily come from the secondary sector (Table 2.6). And under the expenditure approach, the major culprit is gross capital formation, an expenditure component that is highly correlated to industrial output.[98] That provided us some perspective on the quality of Chinese sector data and helped us make assumptions about the reasons underlying the statistical discrepancies, both of which facilitated our recalculation work in Chapter 3.

In advanced economies where a central agency has full control over national accounts work, the sum of state or province GDPs should equal the national total.[99] In other economies where national and local authorities share the responsibility of calculating economic output, the central-local divergence has been seen, too, but is not as egregious as in China. For example, in Japan, which employs a central-local GDP accounting structure similar to China's, the sum of all Japanese prefectures' GDP surpassed the national aggregate by 5 percent in 2011, while in China, the discrepancy was nearly 10 percent (Table 2.7). China's

---

97. Koch-Weser, *Reliability*, 30.

98. Ibid., 31; Tongxin Guo, "关于我国服务业统计和占比的有关问题 (Problems Regarding China's Service Sector Statistics and Economic Share)," NBS, June 17, 2010, http://www.stats.gov.cn/ztjc/ztfx/grdd/201006/t20100617_59066.html.

99. John E. Broda and Robert P. Tate, "Comprehensive Revision of Gross Domestic Product by State: Advance Statistics for 2013 and Revised Statistics for 1997–2012," *Survey of Current Business* 94, no. 7 (July 2014): 2, http://www.bea.gov/scb/pdf/2014/07%20July/0714_gdp_by_%20state.pdf.

Table 2.6. Chinese Provincial GDP Do Not Add Up

Unit: RMB trillion

	Total GDP*			Primary Sector			Secondary Sector			Tertiary Sector		
	National	Provincial	Gap[†]	National	Provincial	Gap	National	Provincial	Gap	National	Provincial	Gap
1990	1.87	1.85	-0.9%	0.51	0.51	0.1%	0.77	0.78	0.9%	0.59	0.56	-4.1%
1991	2.18	2.13	-2.4%	0.53	0.53	-0.9%	0.91	0.90	-0.9%	0.73	0.69	-6.2%
1992	2.69	2.60	-3.3%	0.59	0.58	-1.5%	1.17	1.16	-1.2%	0.94	0.86	-7.9%
1993	3.53	3.43	-2.9%	0.70	0.68	-2.0%	1.65	1.62	-1.6%	1.19	1.13	-5.2%
1994	4.82	4.56	-5.4%	0.96	0.92	-3.7%	2.24	2.14	-4.7%	1.62	1.50	-7.5%
1995	6.08	5.76	-5.2%	1.21	1.18	-2.7%	2.87	2.63	-8.2%	2.00	1.95	-2.4%
1996	7.12	6.81	-4.3%	1.40	1.37	-2.4%	3.38	3.10	-8.3%	2.33	2.34	0.4%
1997	7.90	7.68	-2.8%	1.44	1.45	0.1%	3.75	3.50	-6.8%	2.70	2.74	1.4%
1998	8.44	8.30	-1.7%	1.48	1.48	-0.1%	3.90	3.75	-4.0%	3.06	3.07	0.4%
1999	8.97	8.86	-1.2%	1.48	1.46	-1.3%	4.10	3.98	-3.0%	3.39	3.42	0.9%
2000	9.92	9.87	-0.5%	1.49	1.48	-0.8%	4.56	4.44	-2.4%	3.87	3.94	1.7%
2001	10.97	10.88	-0.8%	1.58	1.55	-1.8%	4.95	4.86	-1.9%	4.44	4.46	0.6%
2002	12.03	12.08	0.4%	1.65	1.62	-2.1%	5.39	5.40	0.2%	4.99	5.05	1.3%
2003	13.58	13.95	2.7%	1.74	1.71	-1.4%	6.24	6.49	4.0%	5.60	5.74	2.5%
2004	15.99	16.79	5.0%	2.14	2.08	-3.1%	7.39	8.01	8.4%	6.46	6.70	3.7%
2005	18.49	19.92	7.7%	2.24	2.27	1.3%	8.76	9.74	11.2%	7.49	7.91	5.6%
2006	21.63	23.28	7.6%	2.40	2.41	0.4%	10.37	11.59	11.7%	8.86	9.28	4.8%
2007	26.58	27.97	5.2%	2.86	2.86	-0.1%	12.58	13.89	10.4%	11.14	11.22	0.8%
2008	31.40	33.33	6.1%	3.37	3.35	-0.6%	14.90	16.72	12.2%	13.13	13.26	0.9%
2009	34.09	36.53	7.2%	3.52	3.52	0.0%	15.76	17.99	14.1%	14.80	15.02	1.4%
2010	40.15	43.70	8.8%	4.05	4.05	0.0%	18.74	22.01	17.4%	17.36	17.64	1.6%
2011	47.31	52.14	10.2%	4.75	4.74	-0.1%	22.04	26.38	19.7%	20.52	21.02	2.4%
2012	51.95	57.66	11.0%	5.24	5.24	0.0%	23.52	28.56	21.5%	23.19	23.85	2.8%
2013	56.88	63.00	10.8%	5.70	5.70	0.0%	24.97	30.68	22.9%	26.22	26.63	1.6%

* Data are not subject to 2013 *Economic Census* revisions.

[†] The gap—for all four columns—is calculated as the differential between provincial sum and national gross as a percentage of the latter.

Sources: NBS, CEIC, authors' calculations.

Table 2.7. Japan's Sum of Prefecture GDP Exceeds National Aggregate*

Unit: JPY trillion

	Prefecture GDP Sum	National Aggregate	Differential	Differential (% of National GDP)
2001	520.8	501.7	19.1	3.8%
2002	516.6	498.0	18.6	3.7%
2003	517.6	501.9	15.7	3.1%
2004	523.6	502.8	20.8	4.1%
2005	525.9	505.3	20.6	4.1%
2006	532.5	509.1	23.4	4.6%
2007	535.7	513.0	22.7	4.4%
2008	512.8	489.5	23.2	4.7%
2009	492.0	473.9	18.1	3.8%
2010	496.5	480.1	16.4	3.4%
2011	*497.4*	*473.3*	*24.1*	*5.1%*
Decade's Average				4.1%

* All data are fiscal-year values; prefectures' calendar-year data are unavailable.
Sources: Cabinet Office of Japan, authors' calculations.

nominal discrepancy that year was larger than the GDP of Shandong province. Chinese Web users joked that local statisticians added an extra province to China's map through GDP accounting.[100]

This divergence has emboldened China data skeptics. The counterpoint is that central authorities are well aware of this phenomenon and have worked to address it. Commentators taking Beijing to task for this pattern disregard a number of less nefarious, well-understood explanations for the pattern. But first, understanding the reasons for this divergence requires a little more familiarity with the statistical bureaucracy.

BUREAUCRATIC STRUCTURES: CENTER VERSUS LOCAL

In calculating GDP, NBS does not simply add up subnational reports but compiles data independently and makes its own calculations. The central-local discordance is therefore not compelling evidence that national figures are unreliable. This layered accounting structure in China's national accounts system, *fenji hesuan*, was officially acknowledged as early as 2004, when provincial numbers surpassed the precensus national GDP by RMB 2.6 trillion, and the implied growth rate of the former outpaced the latter by nearly 4 percentage points.[101] To address these doubts, then NBS head Li Deshui said national-level GDP

---

100. Changyan Ma, "地方 GDP 连续 4 年比全国多出'一个经济大省'" (Sum of Regional GDP Exceeds National GDP by 'One Large Economic Province' for Four Consecutive Years)," *China Economy News*, February 5, 2013, http://www.ce.cn/xwzx/gnsz/gdxw/201302/05/t20130205_24094700.shtml.
101. NBS, 2005 *Statistical Yearbook*.

was independently accounted according to international norms and not simply summed from provincial figures and then somehow deflated. He said some of the source data for national-level accounting came from the surveys conducted by NBS headquarters' directly supervised "survey teams," or *diaocha dadui*.[102] This was to minimize local governments' intervention in both the data compilation and accounting process. Local government heads were not happy to be accused of statistical incompetence and/or dishonesty, as Li implied.

According to public records and our interviews with NBS, survey teams are responsible for agricultural, household, and price data work, and they report directly to NBS headquarters. Survey team heads are appointed by the head of NBS, unlike local government data chiefs who are named by provincial leaders. Survey team financing is controlled by NBS headquarters as well. The survey teams are vertically administered by NBS headquarters in Beijing and held accountable for their survey results. In certain cases, local governments can task them with assignments and share the agricultural and household data the survey teams collect, but local governments have no administrative authority.[103]

The way NBS and local governments' statistical bureaucracies are structured is typical of the Chinese scheme of governance on many other fronts: a unitary system consisting of *tiao-tiao* and *kuai-kuai* authorities. *Tiao-tiao* lines of authority tie each unit vertically to superior organs of power at the Center, whereas *kuai-kuai* lines of authority tie them horizontally to local powers.[104] The NBS headquarters and its directly supervised survey teams stationed at the local level present a *tiao-tiao* line of authority, while NBS, local government statistical departments, and non-NBS statistical authorities such as the central bank and General Administration of Customs constitute a *kuai-kuai* line of authority. Different divisions in this interlocked system have their own roles, as well as shared responsibilities. For example, NBS headquarters and its directly supervised survey teams are in charge of data collection for national accounts,[105] industrial accounting for enterprises below the designated size, consumer prices, and agricultural output.[106] Local government statistical bureaus, meanwhile, are responsible for local GRP accounting, as well as industrial accounting for enterprises above the threshold, local population, economic, and certain service sector surveys.[107]

102. Jianping Zhang and Qianjiang Gu, "Regional GDP Exceeded National GDP by 3.9%," *Sina News*, March 7, 2005, http://finance.sina.com.cn/g/20050307/18281409949.shtml.

103. NBS, "国家统计局调查总队主要职责 (Main Responsibilities of NBS Survey Teams)," http://www.stats.gov.cn/zjtj/gjtjj/dczd/201310/t20131031_450534.html.

104. Kenneth G. Lieberthal and David M. Lampton, eds., *Bureaucracy, Politics, and Decision Making in Post-Mao China* (Berkeley: University of California Press, 1992), 286, http://publishing.cdlib.org/ucpressebooks/view?docId=ft0k40035t&chunk.id=d0e9310&toc.id=d0e9196&brand=ucpress.

105. The system of national accounts includes the gross domestic product account, input-output table, flows of funds account, national balance statement, and national accounts, consistent with international norms.

106. NBS, "(Survey Teams)"; NBS, "国民经济核算司: 服务业统计司 (Department of National Accounts: Office of Tertiary Sector Statistics)," July 25, 2008, http://www.stats.gov.cn/zjtj/gjtjj/jgsz/xzdw/200109/t20010907_52314.html.

107. Shanghai Bureau of Statistics, "上海市统计局主要职能 (Shanghai Bureau of Statistics: Main Responsibilities and Organizational Chart)," http://www.stats-sh.gov.cn/frontinfo/staticPageView.xhtml?para=shtjj.

The capabilities of NBS and local government statistical bureaus vary greatly. Within NBS's vertical *tiao-tiao* system, there is an official head count of 1,299 staff, including 358 at formal Bureau posts (*xingzheng bianzhi*) and 941 at NBS-affiliated administrative or enterprise posts (*shiye bianzhi*). The former type of posts includes various NBS departments such as national accounts department; the latter type consists of the census center, the NBS research institute, and China Economic Climate Monitoring Center, and so forth. NBS's *tiao-tiao* system also includes all the directly supervised survey teams and a publishing house—but neither of these is included in the official head count. NBS survey teams in the provinces and other subnational jurisdictions are administered similarly to regular public service officers, and they include an additional 19,600 staff. At local levels, regional government statistical bureaus list another 76,000 staff, but these only include official, full-time posts above the county level.[108] Many local statisticians do not have advanced education or training in statistics. NBS directly supervised survey teams sometimes share staff with local government bureaus, a common phenomenon known as "one personnel team, two offices" (*yitao banzi, liangkuai paizi*), although there is little evidence of local governments interfering in NBS survey team operations.

That said, the number of NBS professional staff assigned to data collection, collation, and analysis is clearly incapable of handling the full task for the world's most populous nation, especially given that China didn't fully leverage an online system to reduce the onerous burden of collecting hard copy data materials until recently. As was noted earlier in the chapter, NBS headquarters has 30-something staff responsible for the entire country's national GDP accounting work, while the head count at the U.S. BEA's National Economic Accounts section was 151, of which 144 were full-time employees.[109] In Brazil, another large developing country, the number of staff reported in charge of their national accounts at the Brazilian Institute of Geography and Statistics (IBGE), the national statistical office, is 55, while in Indonesia, the number was even bigger at 120 individuals. At the end of 2014, NBS head Ma Jiantang announced a plan to accelerate the unification of national and local GDP accounting in 2015, and to officially kick off the integrated GDP accounting regime in 2016.[110] If implemented well, the responsibilities of accounting local data would be consolidated into the hands of NBS, which could help to significantly improve the quality of data, at least technically. But that mandate will also require NBS—and, more importantly, central agencies above NBS's ranking—to properly staff, finance, and legally and politically empower the mission. Otherwise, the reform may fall off the rails, just like what we saw with NBS's 2013 commitment to adapt to the current SNA.

POLITICAL DISTORTIONS

Generally speaking, data produced by the NBS *tiao-tiao* system is more reliable than local-level statistics. Through its directly administered survey network, NBS compiles data on

---

108. NBS, *China's Main Statistical Concepts: Standards and Methodology* (China Statistics Press, 2013), 7–9.

109. U.S. Department of Commerce, "Budget."

110. Economic Observer, "Highlights of NBS's 2015 Policies: National Accounts System Reform," *Economic Observer*, March 1, 2015, http://finance.sina.com.cn/china/bwdt/20150301/003521615466.shtml.

urban and rural household income, consumer prices, producers' prices, home sales data, agricultural output, and industrial enterprise data for cross-checking and use in adjusting final national-level GDP. In addition to the data it compiles, NBS relies on data from tax authorities and volume indicators, such as crude steel output and electricity consumption, to assess the value numbers.[111] According to NBS officials, headquarters uses a composite index of more than 450 indicators, in volume terms, to cross-check value data because on that extensive scale, the aggregate of volume variables would be quite reliable and hard to falsify. An underlying assumption in this cross-checking exercise is that in a short period of time, a comprehensive group of volume indicators cannot grow at a pace that is too different from the real-term GDP.[112] Unfortunately, what exactly these 400-odd cross-checking indicators are does not have an easy answer. In China's industry economy statistical yearbook, there is a list of more than one hundred main industrial products which are likely included in that cross-checking framework, but that constitutes only one-quarter of what one would need to conclude that NBS is entering a new era of transparency.

This analysis of the *tiao-tiao* and *kuai-kuai* systems is not to say that the data produced by the centralized regime are the best they could be. The motives and opportunities for distortion that existed in the past still remain. Under China's political system, economic plans approved by the National People's Congress (NPC) are legally binding, including all the targets laid out,[113] though in some regions, that hard constraint on growth has been relaxed to a soft goal in a pilot effort to explore better economic governance models.[114] In the majority of regions that still follow the old order to meet legally binding goals they committed to the NPC, delivering results at all costs is a political mandate; leaders are otherwise obligated to make a formal explanation for failures. Falling short of targets is an embarrassment and opens the door for political rivals. Those consequences constitute a strong incentive for many central and local authorities to meet the growth targets no matter what.

Besides inherent political motivations, there are public pressures. According to China's official explanations in the GDDS framework under the IMF, annual preliminary estimates of GDP are shown to the State Council before they are released to the rest of the government and the general public.[115] This preliminary reading, released around January 20 for the preceding year's GDP, generally has the greatest market impact and is seen as politically sensitive; release of the two subsequent revisions usually occurs with little fanfare. There are concerns that central authorities sometimes alter NBS's final numbers for political purposes. While there is no direct evidence to prove this occurs, there is strong indirect

---

111. NBS, interview by authors; NBS, *Methods of Non-Economic Census Year, 2010 Ed.*
112. NBS, interview by authors, June 2014.
113. Deshui Li, "国民经济指标和经济形势分析方法 (National Accounts Indicators and Methods in Analyzing Economic Performance)," Government website, *NPC*, (June 2014), http://www.npc.gov.cn/npc/xinwen/2004-06/25/content_1383237.htm.
114. Yining Li, "China's New Normal," *Beijing News*, November 18, 2014, http://epaper.bjnews.com.cn/html/2014-11/18/content_546560.htm?div=-1.
115. IMF, "DSBB—GDDS China."

evidence—including in the December 2014 preview of 2013 census revisions—of alteration of NBS results to accommodate political considerations.

Evidence of local government data falsification is, by contrast, abundant. In 2004, NBS head Li Deshui described the tendency for each successively lower level of government to deliver above-average growth results relative to provincial-level targets.[116] Officials intentionally falsified data to qualify them for higher positions, leaving behind the burden of distorted indicators that their successors had to perpetuate in order to avoid appearing incompetent. A full 10 years after Li's comments, Beijing is still trying to reform the bureaucratic evaluation system to stop incentivizing such behavior and consolidate national accounting responsibility under NBS.

Current reforms aimed at removing incentives to manipulate data and opening the way to greater transparency are significant for reducing political distortions of statistics—especially at the local level. At the November 2013 Third Plenum of the Central Committee, policymakers decreed that China needed a better statistical system and data to enhance policy effectiveness. Overhauling the system of national accounts would not be sufficient. Beijing would need to redesign the bureaucratic evaluation system and end the dominance of GDP growth targeting as an objective. By the end of 2013, more than 1,100 counties out of 2,787 in China had affirmed their commitment to moving away from the GDP-based evaluation system.[117] By August 2014, more provinces, including Fujian, Shanxi, Ningxia, and Hebei, had officially joined the club to adjust their bureaucratic evaluation system by downplaying or scrapping GDP evaluation. At the same time they committed to upgrading environmental and social welfare indicators in an effort to reshape incentives and improve data accuracy.[118] In January 2015, Shanghai, the most affluent Chinese city, ditched a growth target for the first time in its annual government work report previewing the policy priorities for 2015, becoming the first major region that took that step.[119]

In September 2014, NBS unveiled a new accounting regime to shift local focus from GDP. It listed over 40 indicators, including consumption, urbanization, debt-to-fiscal revenue ratio, research and development spending, and pollution, to be published by local authorities regularly—a step forward, yet still a long way from the ultimate goal of a transparent, consistent system of GDP accounts.[120]

---

116. Zhang and Gu, "Regional GDP Exceeded National."

117. People's Daily, "全国 1100 多个县明确不考核 GDP (More than 1,100 Counties Confirmed No Evaluation for GDP Achievement)," *People's Daily*, December 12, 2013, http://news.sohu.com/20131212/n391655136.shtml.

118. "70 余县市已取消 GDP 考核 中国正告别'唯 GDP 论'时代 (China Is Bidding Farewell to GDP-only Era: More than 70 Cities and Counties Scrapped GDP-Based Evaluation)," Xinhua, August 13, 2014, http://news.xinhuanet.com /fortune/2014-08/13/c_126863583.htm; Ruowei Sheng, "Amended Local Cadre Evaluation System: Moving Away from GDP Evaluation," *People's Daily*, December 12, 2013, sec. 4, http://paper.people.com.cn/rmrb/html/2013-12 /12/nw.D110000renmrb_e20131212_7-04.htm.

119. Financial Times, "Shanghai First Major Chinese Region to Ditch GDP Growth Target," *Financial Times*, January 26, 2015, http://www.ft.com/intl/cms/s/0/2c822efc-a51d-11e4-bf11-00144feab7de.html#axzz3Q69XH79l.

120. "New Accounting Regime Ends 'GDP Supremacy,'" Xinhua, September 22, 2014, http://news.xinhuanet .com/english/china/2014-09/22/c_133663180.htm.

SYSTEMIC AND TECHNICAL CONSTRAINTS

Technical constraints are at least as significant as political motivations in undermining Chinese data credibility. In an unusually high-profile October 2013 action, NBS exposed a scandal in Henglan, a small town in the southern province of Guangdong found to have exaggerated local industrial gross output by nearly 75 percent. When inspecting enterprises reported by Henglan as "above the designated threshold," auditors found that a large share were below the revenue threshold, or had discontinued operations, relocated, or canceled their registration.[121] In total, the township had reported 249 enterprises above the threshold, or DRIEs. Inspectors found the data of 248 were misreported—by the government, not by the enterprises themselves. For observers of China's data system, there are at least three takeaways from this case.

First, source data at the lowest level of China's data pyramid are prone to rampant distortion, with unpredictable quantitative and even directional effects on final aggregate statistics. Disciplining such behavior is limited by constraints in staffing and budgets at local-level statistical bureaus, a long-time institutional problem. Local data offices are left with few options other than forging data, cooking their books in an effort to meet requirements on short notice.[122] This reality is particularly onerous before China began transitioning to a nationwide direct-reporting system in 2012, which removed or reduced requirements for paper-based data collection in most places. This, to some extent, alleviated the reporting burden, freeing up resources for local staff to enhance data quality.

Second, the flawed design of the national accounting system results in double-counting. A major culprit is that China uses the *enterprise*, rather than the recommended *establishment*, as the basic unit for national accounts, as previously noted. This practice remains in place today despite many other changes Beijing has undertaken over the past two decades to converge with the SNA ideal, and changes are not expected. The rationalization for that is that Chinese enterprises are not sophisticated enough to account for their operations of different production units. In practice, official output is reduced in localities where enterprises have real operations but are not domiciled. In GDP-obsessed China, officials want credit for as much activity as possible. Hence, for cross-jurisdictional enterprises, governments in multiple locations both claim value-added. This is especially rampant in geographically expansive subsectors such as construction, which we will discuss at length in the section on the double-reporting phenomenon in Chapter 3. NBS has made some effort to resolve this problem, migrating from domicile location-based accounting to an operation

121. NBS, "关于中山市横栏镇在统计上弄虚作假及整改情况的通报 (Audit Report on Statistical Fraud and Rectification in Henglan Township, Zhongshan City)," June 14, 2013, http://www.stats.gov.cn/tjfw/bgt/201310/t20131029_449705.html.

122. Tao Xiao, "关于加强当前农村统计工作的几点建议 (Suggestions on Strengthening Current Rural Statistical Work)," People.com.cn, January 9, 2008, http://www.people.com.cn/GB/43063/107687/107724/107988/6755399.html; Hunan Provincial Bureau of Statistics, "提高统计数据质量 应从六个方面着手 (Six Ways to Improve Quality of Statistics)," Government website, *Statistical Information of Hunan* (January 2, 2008), http://www.hntj.gov.cn/fzyd/zfxd/200910/t20091012_69884.htm.

location-based approach for construction enterprises,[123] but double counting will persist until the general accounting unit problem is resolved.

A third takeaway from Henglan is that, thanks to the online direct-reporting system NBS established nationwide in February 2012, higher officials are better able to identify irregularities. When reporting was only on paper and central databases were lacking, such discoveries were rare. The expansion of the direct-reporting system was one of NBS's "Four Major Programs" to enhance Chinese statistics. This effort to reduce technical and systemic flaws in the system and better support policymaking included a renewed catalog of businesses, an integrated questionnaire for enterprises, and modern data collection and processing software, as well as the online reporting system.[124] As with most bureaucratic innovations, these efforts received little attention compared to the national-provincial GDP gap, but its implications are far more important and far-reaching.

Developing countries like China grapple with a variety of statistical problems—and all the more so when they are growing rapidly and constantly altering the legal and political obligations of firms and individuals to report on economic activity. In this chapter, we attempted to separate real problems affecting the reliability of China's official, national GDP statistics from a number of issues that are less concerning or no longer as concerning as they once were. A clear taxonomy of factors muddying China's statistical waters today can help us more confidently attempt to produce an adjusted assessment in Chapter 3. There are copious competing imperatives facing officials concerned with the reaction of an unsophisticated population to self-styled independent pundits empowered to debate the state of China's macro-economy.

Councilor Guan Zhong admonished Duke Huan Qi in China's Spring and Autumn period 2,700 years ago that *if one does not keep statistics secret, those below will control the government on high.*[125] But Guan Zhong could not have imagined the complexity and wealth of today's China. China's leaders are coming to realize that the only thing more dangerous than making statistics public is trying to keep them secret.

---

123. NBS, "关于统计调查对象所在地认定问题的批复 (Reply to Question on Recognizing the Location of Target Entity for Statistical Surveys)," May 20, 2003, http://www.stats.gov.cn/statsinfo/auto2072/201311/t20131104_454934.html.

124. NBS, "统计四大工程 (The Four Major Statistical Programs)," 2012, http://www.stats.gov.cn/tjzs/tjbk/nsbzs/201310/P020131031498585803980.pdf.

125. Guan, *Guanzi*, 390.

3 | A Better Abacus?

It is obvious that China's economy has grown rapidly: virtually all observers have been dazzled by the visible evidence of expansion over the reform era. None, however, have been confident in the accuracy of growth estimates. The world's most populous nation was booming; a nuanced measure of that development would have been desirable, but it self-evidently was not *necessary*. In fact, by opening the door to more research on the *quality* of growth, better data might well have reduced the sheer *quantity* that the Communist Party delivered—long understood by virtue of the party's plain to see promotion criteria to be the principal objective of economic policy. There were perpetual complaints about data quality from some quarters, such as when provincial economic output statistics surpassed the national aggregate or China's trade numbers did not match trade partner records, but these seldom tempered the multibillion-dollar trade and investment flows that swelled by the decade.

This era of resignation toward statistical accuracy is largely over: Chinese policy and business decisionmakers and their foreign counterparts all have a mounting, urgent need for better estimates of economic activity. But the development of independent contributions to better national accounting is still deeply hampered. While Beijing has *generally* converged toward alignment with international norms since the 1990s, as reviewed in the previous chapter, both specific shortcomings and institutional weaknesses afflict the National Bureau of Statistics (NBS) and the political context in which it operates. NBS controls the data needed to measure the economy and intentionally withholds much of it from outside scholars. This permits NBS, when it wishes, to forcefully defend against independent suspicions about data quality: no one else has a comprehensive set of figures, permission to see them, or the right to collect alternatives on their own dime.[1] When NBS officials want to refute their critics, they can do so easily.[2] When independent researchers are consigned to parsing a few select proxies like electricity or freight loads to double-check a complicated, multitrillion-dollar economy, they are bound to reach debatable conclusions.

---

1. There are anecdotal product survey aspects of China's economy not generally available to the public. For instance, consultancies track most industries for investors and marketing managers. A few commercial offerings purport to offer national statistical coverage using independent data sourcing—notably the *China Beige Book,* in operation since 2012 (see http://www.chinabeigebook.com/index.php). These statistics and methodologies are not public and thus cannot be fully assessed. It is unclear whether such survey products utilize legally acceptable information collection practices.

2. Xu, "Accurately Understand," 22.

Scholars nonetheless make contributions. In our view the most effective outside work has started by reproducing the framework used by NBS, based on enterprise-, industry-, and subsector-level data, and explored methodological problems from within. Numerous economists adopt this approach in their analysis of Chinese data. Zhang Jun and Zhu Tian point out that China's household consumption had been underestimated because imputed rent for home owner-occupiers is not properly factored in, while still following the broad NBS approaches.[3] Carsten Holz was able to construct a consistently defined series for China's monthly industrial output data for the period from 1980 to 2012, while the official version is severely fragmented by breaks in methodology.[4] Renmin University economist Nie Huihua and colleagues looked at enterprise-level data through the comprehensive Chinese Industrial Enterprise Database, NBS's foundation for constructing national-level gross output, and produced a thoughtful assessment of fundamental data flaws and how they affect higher-level analysis.[5]

In this chapter we too set out to improve upon the standard reported gross domestic product (GDP) estimates from NBS by working from *within* the NBS framework. For all sectors and industries, we start our recalculation by replicating official practices for constructing value-added using officially sourced enterprise- and industry-level data and the methodologies documented in NBS manuals. We then compare the results from our calculations to official statistics and identify inconsistencies. Those discrepancies are either resolved based on further investigation or described as problems.

Where this bottom-up approach is not possible, we employ alternative methods. For example, enterprise-level data are limited for service sector firms: bottom-up recalculation using official data and methods produces a value of only 70 percent of the officially reported number. In this case we use a carefully designed cross-country comparison approach to explore the size of two of China's biggest service subsectors, as well as a variety of domestic volume and value proxies for a few other tertiary subsectors and industries. In other cases we compare the existing framework to changes planned for the transition to the 2008 *System of National Accounts* (SNA) and reflect an "adjusted GDP boundary" in our reestimation. In those cases, because the transition is forthcoming and adjusted-basis enterprise-level data are nonexistent, we must base our model on alternative publicly available statistics, as well as official documents pertaining to NBS's intentions and preparations to upgrade the Chinese SNA.

The reestimation of China's GDP in this chapter is organized as follows. First, we explain our adjustments to secondary sector activity—for mining and quarrying; manufacturing; production and supply of electricity, water, and gas; and construction. Second, we turn to the tertiary (service) sector, starting with an assessment of the literature to date

---

3. Zhang and Zhu, "Underestimated Consumption," 7–8.

4. Carsten A. Holz, "Monthly Industrial Output in China 1980–2012" (Working Paper No. 487, Stanford Center for International Development (SCID), 2013), 17, http://siepr.stanford.edu/publicationsprofile/2559.

5. Huihua Nie, Ting Jiang, and Rudai Yang, "中国工业企业数据库的使用现状和潜在问题 (Chinese Industrial Enterprise Database: Current Use and Potential Problems)," *Journal of World Economy*, no. 5 (May 2012): 143, http://www.cnki.com.cn/Article/CJFDTOTAL-SJJJ201205011.htm.

and offering revised estimates for major services. We then describe how we factor in two national account items that NBS proposed incorporating in its transition to 2008 SNA: upgraded accounting for homeowners' imputed rent that was previously based on current construction costs and capitalization of research and development (R&D) expenses that were previously not included in final value-added (a change to the production boundary of GDP newly introduced by 2008 SNA). Among all the methodological, conceptual, and categorical changes that China would adopt in its transition, embodied in a new 2014 Chinese SNA framework (a process expected to take four to five years, according to some estimates),[6] these two would most immediately and significantly alter China's GDP size if implemented (as Chinese statisticians indicated to us privately, an expectation now unrealized).[7] Third and finally, we present our assessment of primary sector output data—principally grain, meat, and fishery production.

Choice of Measurement Year and Other Basics

Before going forward, it should be noted that the recalculations of the nominal size of China's economy in this chapter are for the year 2008 rather than for an extended period, as often seen in other statistical analysis of China. There are a several reasons for this choice.

First, as stated in Chapter 2, China's statistical authorities are more capable of improving data compilation and calculation quality for current and future terms than retroactively revising for past terms. Similar to other formerly planned economies, China's data series are littered with conceptual gaps and methodological breaks following major changes to the system, even when those changes were important steps forward. Making pre- and post-change data conceptually and quantitatively comparable may be inherently difficult, but reducing the fragmentation in these series that frustrates researchers and public policy is not a hopeless cause, and we hope our undertaking makes a contribution.

Second, among the target years we considered, 2008 appeared to offer the best available data. With the second economic census, 2008 saw the collection of more comprehensive industrial, construction, and basic service benchmark statistics than noncensus years. In addition, China conducted a benchmark national input-output survey for the previous year, 2007—such surveys are conducted in years ending in 2 and 7, but the 2012 results are not yet available. A comprehensive 2006 national agricultural census was conducted mainly in 2007. The proximity of these national surveys to our 2008 base year benefitted our analysis, not least because China's five-year economic censuses do not cover the primary sector

---

6. Menggen Chen, "2008 SNA 实施与国家统计发展战略 (Implementation of 2008 SNA and National Strategy for the Development of Statistics)," *Statistical Research*, no. 3 (March 2012): 18, http://tjyj.stats.gov.cn/CN/abstract/abstract4063.shtml.

7. NBS, "Reform of National Accounts System," interview by authors, 2014, Beijing.

and we needed a basis from which to establish values for that sector.[8] Other year choices either lacked the benefits of using economic census data—which can greatly affect assessment because the 2009–2013 period relied heavily on 2008 statistics for current-year extrapolations—or were simply of much lower quality, as the 2004 census was. Third, as pointed out in Chapter 2, 2007 was the last year NBS published industrial value-added (IVA) for industrial enterprises above the threshold—the so-called DRIEs—industry by industry. Because our recalculations for China's GDP are also at the industry level, in some cases when the enterprise-level data are lacking, we rely on earlier years' official data to extrapolate statistics for 2008 and then compare our results to the official version in order to find inconsistencies in the data and assumptions. Using 2008 as the measurement year minimized compounding errors in our extrapolation approach, because 2008 was the year after NBS suspended the release of official IVA data.

Given the considerations above, we decided to go with the year 2008 and use NBS's published census year and noncensus year national accounting manuals as the primary technical guidance for our recalculations. The census year manual—as introduced in Chapter 2 —called the *GDP Accounting Methods for Economic Census Year in China* (中国普查年度国内生产总值核算方法), was published in 2006, based on the rich data collected for the 2004 census, and it was intended to enhance the transparency of China's national accounting work. In 2006, NBS also compiled a set of methods for noncensus years. While similar, the noncensus-year manual bases many calculations on statistics and ratios coming out of the census, because the source data for noncensus years are not as comprehensive as for census years. That creates a chance for us to examine how government statisticians use census-year data and ratios to extrapolate numbers for years without the luxury of census results.

In 2009, following the second economic census, NBS composed an updated set of methodologies for census-year national accounting. This included changes in the way value-added was calculated in the industrial, construction, financial, and military subsectors, as well as for self-employed businesses. Unfortunately, the technical manual summarizing the changes in the 2008 census was not published; instead, NBS published a 2010 revision of the noncensus-year methodology that said the manual was revised based on the first version and included the 2008 changes to "link the methodologies for noncensus and census years consistently."[9] In light of the official explanation, we believe the 2010 noncensus-year manual correctly reflects the technical methods in use for the 2008 accounting. That, in combination with the 2004 manual, constitutes proper official guidance for our attempts to reproduce their approach. Materials that also feed into our conceptual

---

8. It should be noted that excluding agricultural activities from economic census is not a Chinese idiosyncrasy. According to a 2006 survey conducted by the United Nations Statistics Division of national practices in economic censuses, two out of three countries conducting economic censuses do not include units from agriculture and public administration. UNSD, *Economic Census: Challenges and Good Practices: A Technical Report* (New York: United Nations, October 2010), 11, http://unstats.un.org/unsd/economic_stat/Economic _Census/Economic%20Census%20TR.pdf.

9. NBS, *Methods of Non-Economic Census Year, 2010 Ed.*, 2.

framework include regular or ad hoc methodological notes put out by NBS on specific concepts or surveys, essays by senior national statisticians, and well-grounded analyses by peer scholars.

When it comes down to the micro-foundation of our analysis, a primary source is two databases handled by NBS. One is the Chinese Industrial Enterprise Database (中国工业企业数据库), which includes enterprise-level data from all the state-owned industrial enterprises and non-state-owned industrial enterprises above the threshold from 1998 to 2009. The other database includes virtually all industrial and service enterprise data collected during the 2008 *Economic Census* regardless of the size of the enterprise's principal business revenue. However, in that survey the basic survey unit is enterprise, not establishment—an important difference that has implications for ultimate data accuracy and interpretations, as noted in Chapters 1 and 2. This will be revisited in greater detail for its impact on certain Chinese sectors in the sections to come. Access to the databases for our project was handled by an associate in mainland China who is authorized to access them, with permission from the associate's institution. Some scholars have pointed out flaws in these databases, including ineffective samples (enterprises that lack essential information or demonstrate explicitly erroneous information), unclear identification for specific enterprises, and institutional enforcement flaws that have caused implausible outcomes (such as what we described in Chapter 2: that the sum of DRIEs' IVA exceeded the economic output of the entire industry). Despite all these problems, the 2008 *Economic Census* database and the industrial enterprise database are still China's two most comprehensive databases, containing the largest collections of enterprise-level data, and they are seen as an indispensable foundation for industry-level analysis.[10] We have employed various measures to clean up these databases before aggregating them, and the explanations for those measures are described in the following sections.

This study is the first attempt by outside scholars to comprehensively evaluate China's nominal GDP data—encompassing the primary, secondary, and tertiary sectors—through the lens of the officials' own databases, calculation, and extrapolation approaches, supplemented by alternative methods where necessary. We hope these efforts bring a better understanding of China's statistical system and the latest methodological choices within reach of interested outside observers.

Secondary Sector

As introduced in Chapter 1, the official preferred approach to GDP accounting in China is a combination of income and production methods, unlike the United States, which prefers the expenditure approach. Prior to China's first economic census in 2005, with 2004 as the measurement year, Beijing used the production approach to account for primary and secondary sectors, excluding construction. For the rest of the economy NBS applied an

---

10. Nie, Jiang, and Yang, "(Chinese Industrial Enterprise Database)," 144.

income approach.[11] But following the 2004 and 2008 censuses, NBS introduced fundamental changes to the national accounts system.

INDUSTRY

Using the conventional production approach to measure the industrial economy created a number of problems, ranging from local governments and large enterprises overreporting output in order to outrank their peers, to double counting of business entities operating in multiple regions. Using the 2004 *Economic Census* as an opportunity to revamp the system, NBS calculated two versions of IVA for the first time, by production and income approaches, respectively, and took the simple average as the final IVA estimate for DRIEs. The results from the two approaches were not made public, but the outcome from the production approach was said to be bigger than from the income approach, confirming the widespread perception that data on intermediate inputs in China were insufficient and the production approach–based value-added had likely been overstated.

In the years following, NBS gradually shifted toward the income approach and converted fully after the 2008 *Economic Census*. Following the 2008 census, NBS officially revised the accounting methods for noncensus years, dictating that the income approach would be the benchmark approach for all industrial entities going forward.[12] However, NBS said during our 2014 meetings that neither all localities nor all sectors had fully transitioned; the transition is still ongoing. Therefore, judging from both top-level methodological mandate and local practice, China's approach to accounting for industrial activity today remains a hybrid. This shapes the conceptual foundation for our own design of recalculation formulas.

Directly Reporting Industrial Enterprises

China's secondary sector consists of four subsectors: mining; manufacturing; supply and production of electricity, gas, and water; and construction. Under China's publication conventions, the first three are grouped as "Industry," which is the focus of this section. The Industry category includes 39 industries, grouped according to China's Classification of National Economic Industries (GB/T 4754-2002), now in its third revision as of 2011.[13] According to the NBS noncensus-year methodology manual, the formulas to account for value-added in the 39 industries are the same.

---

11. Xianchun Xu, "中国国民经济核算的新特点 (New Characteristics of China's System of National Accounts)" (OECD, 2006), 5, 11, http://www.oecd.org/std/na/37601130.doc.

12. NBS, *Methods of Non-Economic Census Year, 2010 Ed.*, 19.

13. China's classification of national industries is largely aligned with the United Nations' *International Standard Industrial Classification of All Economic Activities*, Rev. 3 and Rev. 4. But there are moderate differences that we assume reflect the particular nature of China's economy. The 2011 revision of industrial classification was not put into use until the 2013 *Economic Census*, almost three years after its publication.

For directly reporting industrial enterprises (DRIEs), the production- and income-approach formulas are as follows:[14]

1. Industrial value-added = Gross industrial output − Intermediate inputs

2. Gross industrial output = Industrial Gross Output Value (GOV) + Value-added tax (VAT) payable

3. Intermediate inputs = Gross industrial output − Income-approach value-added[15]

4. Income-approach value-added = Labor remuneration + Net production taxes + Fixed asset depreciation + Operating surplus

The fact that intermediate inputs are extrapolated from GOV less income-approach value-added indicates that the income approach is of higher importance. Holz argues that GOV is almost identical to sales revenue and that the latter is a reliable data point because businesses compute it for their own operating purposes. GOV approximately equals sales revenue plus net additions to inventories, and the difference between GOV and sales revenue is on the order of one percent. Net inventory change is also a regular accounting entry and generally reliable. Thus GOV is inherently better quality than other national accounts data such as value-added—items which exist solely for national accounting purposes and must be computed separately from day-to-day company accounting, adding to firms' onerous accounting burden and the risk of slipshod submissions.[16] Hence, in all but a few cases, when our recalculations required GOV data we used statistics reported by enterprises to the authorities through the databases.

For several reasons our reestimates generally used the 2008 *Economic Census* database rather than the regular industrial enterprise database. First, the coverage of the census database is more comprehensive and not limited to industrial enterprises. Because our recalculations cover service enterprises as well, we think the *Economic Census* database helps maintain the highest level of comparability in terms of data sources. Second, as briefly described in Chapter 2, the industrial enterprise database is missing important data entries for 2008, including wage and depreciation data. Because these data points were essential to our recalculations, we had to rely on the *Economic Census* database for them. Third, looking at the Industry category alone, the *Economic Census* database seems to perform better when using GOV data as a barometer for the completeness of source data. According to our count, the *Economic Census* database covers 419,429 industrial enterprises, while the industrial enterprise database recorded about 8,000 fewer.

---

14. NBS, *Methods of Non-Economic Census Year, 2010 Ed.*, 19–20.
15. NBS, interview by authors, June 2014. According to NBS, the intermediate inputs are calculated based on the income-approach value-added, rather than being summed by different input items.
16. Holz, "Quality," 11, 32.

Of the 419,429 enterprises recorded by the *Economic Census* database, 412,750 were DRIEs according to the definition at the time: principal business revenue of at least RMB 5 million. In comparison, the number of DRIEs as published by NBS in the 2008 census yearbook was 426,113, exceeding our total by 13,363, or about 3 percent. To make sure we had the most complete data on hand, we compared individual enterprise entries between the two databases and were able to supplement the census database with entries from the 2008 industrial enterprise database that were missing from the census database. The consolidated database we wound up with contained 417,416 DRIEs, still about 2 percent smaller than NBS's published number in the census yearbook but probably the most comprehensive assembled by outside scholars.

As for the remaining difference in the number of DRIEs, one reason for the discrepancy was our own adjustments to clean up the data. That mainly involved eliminating data entries by enterprises that did not meet DRIE requirements, contained obvious accounting errors, or were missing essential information that we could not extrapolate ourselves based on alternative information provided by firms. For example, in the "Mining and Washing of Coal" industry, NBS said in both the economic census release and the regular statistical yearbook that DRIEs numbered 9,212. In the *Economic Census* database, the number of DRIEs recorded for this industry was also 9,212. However, some of the documented DRIEs did not actually meet DRIE requirements. To be more specific, 16 of the 9,212 recorded DRIEs were state-owned enterprises with principal business revenue of less than RMB 5 million, and another 208 were nonstate enterprises below the revenue threshold, mostly wholly private firms. In our own computations we eliminated these unqualified entities, as well as those that lacked essential statistical information or demonstrated explicit accounting errors, such as having a fixed asset value of less than zero or negative accumulated depreciation. Viewing the quality of official data through this lens, we believe the number of DRIEs recorded in the final economic census release and the statistical yearbook did *not* accurately reflect the size of the group in China, indicative of the flaws in the official procedures for managing the databases.

However, this marginal error in the number of DRIEs did not appear to significantly affect our calculations in value terms. According to our estimates, the extra 2 percent of DRIEs in the official accounts contributed only modestly to aggregate GOV and IVA. Some in that bunch, as have been demonstrated, were not actual DRIEs; some, even if they passed the revenue threshold, were small DRIEs that did not affect the result of our model in any statistically meaningful way. The sum of GOV for the 417,416 DRIEs in our consolidated database, for example, was RMB 50.53 trillion. In the 2008 *Economic Census Yearbook*, NBS put the sum at RMB 50.73 trillion. In the regular statistical yearbook, the sum was RMB 50.75 trillion, less than half a percentage point bigger than ours. Calculating the average GOV per DRIE for that extra 2 percent DRIEs in the official accounts, each would generate about RMB 23 million of GOV in 2008 and less in value-added terms. Because that extra 2 percent of DRIEs was so insignificant in value terms, we believe it had no impact on the comparability of our recalculations with official 2008 value-added claims.

Table 3.1. Discrepancies in Enterprise Numbers

Unit: Number of enterprises, percentage

2008	Number of DRIEs			
	Economic Census Yearbook (A)	Consolidated Database (B)	Difference (A) – (B)	Percentage Difference as a % of (A)
Mining/Processing of Nonferrous Metal Ores	2,539	1,211	1,328	52.3%
Smelting and Pressing of Nonferrous Metals	8,200	6,749	1,451	17.7%
Manufacture of Communication Equipment, Computers, and Other Electronic Equipment	14,347	13,099	1,248	8.7%
Manufacture of Artwork/Other Manufacturing	7,692	6,984	708	9.2%
Industry	426,113	417,416	8,697	2.0%

Sources: NBS, consolidated database, authors' calculations.

Among all the real DRIEs recorded in the *Economic Census* database, not all entities reported all the variables required in the official formulas to calculate value-added. For those short of the most indispensable information, such as GOV and costs of the principal business, we could not help but drop them (this group of entities overlapped with those that did not meet the DRIE threshold and included slightly more than 10,000 enterprises, consistent with the gap in the number of DRIEs between our database and official reporting). For those that had GOV or principal business cost information but lacked data on less essential items, such as wages, we used the method of equal proportion to extrapolate the missing variable. For example, if 10 percent of DRIEs in a specific industry lacked labor remuneration data, we would assume the ratio of labor remuneration to GOV for this group was equal to the median value of that ratio for the remaining 90 percent of DRIEs in that industry. After all, GOV (almost identical to sales revenue) is a fundamental business indicator for enterprises; using it as the base to extrapolate missing variables that are components in creating it is a rational assumption. If strictly confining one's selection of DRIEs to those that reported all the required data, almost half of the 417,416 DRIEs we have in the consolidated database would drop out, a result that would undermine any attempts to replicate the official methodology and draw a comparison between the results.

After eliminating problematic entities in the database and filling in the missing numbers for the remaining DRIEs, four industries still looked dubious to us. For those four industries the officially reported number of DRIEs surpassed what was recorded in our consolidated database by about 17 percent on the whole, ranging from 8.7 to 52.3 percent per industry. Definitive explanations for that gap are lacking. We cannot be sure whether the differences were caused by careless inclusion of non-DRIEs, eliminating ineffective entities, additional entities to the database that were not included in our version of the collection, or a combination of these and perhaps other factors (Table 3.1).[17] The scale of the missing DRIEs in these four industries in our database accounted for more than half of the combined difference in the number of DRIEs between ours and the official result. As said, in value terms, these DRIEs appear much less significant than in numerical terms, and it is possible that the *Economic Census* database was not exactly the same as the one NBS used to compile the *Economic Census Yearbook*.[18] Future use of the database and assessment of Chinese industrial data should keep that finding in mind.

A Bottom-Up Approach We devised our recalculation formulas for DRIEs based on the official instructions in NBS manuals and the availability of data in the *Economic Census* database. In a nutshell, the equations below reveal the inherent connection between NBS's production- and income-approach methods and allow us to compute alternative values on DRIEs' IVA using available but incomplete numbers from the database:[19]

1. DRIEs' value-added = GOV – Intermediate inputs + VAT payable

2. Intermediate inputs = Costs of goods sold × Ratio of gross output to sales[20] – Labor remuneration – Taxes in administrative expenses – Taxes for principal business – Fixed asset depreciation + Income from subsidies[21]

3. Labor remuneration = Wage payable + Employee benefits payable + Pension insurance + Housing provident fund + Unemployment insurance

4. Net taxes on production = Taxes for principal business + VAT payable + Taxes in administrative expenses – Income from subsidies[22]

---

17. We also tested the possibility of repeat reporting by the same enterprise, in light of the known problem of enterprises being recorded multiple times in the official system due to name changes or ownership reforms. The problem did not appear to be significant in the *Economic Census* database. Some enterprises reported their GOV as 0 (a couple of tobacco manufacturers among them), which is implausible but not a significant number.

18. Nie, Jiang, and Yang, "(Chinese Industrial Enterprise Database)," 144. For the regular industrial enterprise database, Nie et al. said there are several versions, but each is only modestly different from the others. For the *Economic Census* database, we believe it is also possible that there are several versions in the market for academic and policy research use.

19. We devised the formulas based on official methodology, technical explanations in the two NBS manuals, and available data in the databases. After several rounds of comparisons between ours and the official aggregate numbers and revisions, we decided upon the final formulas above. For further explanations, please refer to the NBS manuals.

20. The product here is "costs of goods produced," a cost variable conceptually equivalent with intermediate inputs and GOV. The latter two both focus on gross production rather than just sales.

21. An underlying assumption in our formulas is that an enterprise's operating surplus—one of the four components in the income-approach IVA formula—is equal to the enterprise's GOV less total costs for production.

22. The *Economic Census* database does not include the entry "taxes for principal business," but NBS published the industry-level data on "taxes for principal business and surcharges" for all 39 industries. So we used the industrial-level ratio of such taxes and surcharges to the principal business revenue to extrapolate the principal business taxes and surcharges for each enterprise. This extrapolation is not necessary for our DRIE recalculations here but will be used for our later reestimation of non-DRIE IVA.

5. Fixed asset depreciation = Original value of fixed assets × 7 percent[23]

6. Operating surplus = Operating profits + Income from subsidies[24]

The results of our recalculations for industrial value-added for DRIEs in the 39 industries are shown in Table 3.2. Because NBS ceased publishing IVA for DRIEs after 2007, we are unable to compare our DRIE IVA reestimates directly with the official reporting. However, we conducted such a comparison between our version of DRIE GOV and the official version.

The reestimates above were calculated directly from the data in our consolidated database, based on the methodologies and assumptions described above. We then applied our methodology to the three years prior to the 2008 *Economic Census*, from 2005 to 2007; used the source data in the industrial enterprise database to recalculate DRIE IVA; and compared the results to the official version for each year (Table 3.3).[25] Our DRIE IVA reestimates for 2005 to 2007 were about 2 to 4 percent below official claims, a result that validates the comparability of our 2008 recalculations to the official figures.[26] We did not trace back further than 2005 because major methodological changes during the 2004 *Economic Census* and the lack of essential data in the 2004 industrial enterprise database significantly reduced the reference value of doing so.

Table 3.3 shows that without further manipulation to straighten out the source data, our recalculated value-added for DRIEs—identical to their contribution to GDP—is 6.1 percent bigger than officially reported value-added for the 39 industries. Because our reestimates were not subject to manipulation at the aggregate level, it is likely that the official DRIE IVA numbers have been adjusted down. In fact, as noted in Chapter 2, the ratio of official DRIE IVA to official industrial GDP rose to an implausibly high level in 2006

23. NBS, "国民经济核算 (Explanation of Terms: National Accounts)," October 29, 2013, http://www.stats.gov.cn/tjsj/zbjs/201310/t20131029_449553.html. Ideally, current year fixed asset depreciation should be calculated based on the current value of fixed assets. However, due to the backwardness of asset accounting in China, requesting that all entities adopt this approach is unrealistic. Entities unable to track their depreciation based on fixed assets' current value do so on a cost basis. The depreciation ratio of 7 percent was the median value of enterprise-level depreciation ratios from 2005 to 2007, when NBS still published data on "current year depreciation" (neither the *Economic Census* database nor the industrial enterprise database included that data point for 2008). The ratio was calculated as current year depreciation divided by the original value of fixed assets. When we applied this approach to calculating the current year depreciation for 2008, the result we got, RMB 1.68 trillion, was quite close to the officially published, RMB 1.74 trillion. Therefore, we believe our assumptions and the formula were reasonable.

24. Tonglu Zhao, "增加值核算方法 (Methods of Value-Added Accounting)," NBS National Accounts Department, 2012, 2. Zhao said an enterprise's operating surplus is basically equal to its operating profits plus income from subsidies, less bonuses paid to labor from the profit portion (which is different from labor remuneration). Because the database does not include a data entry on bonuses paid out of operating profit, we assumed it was negligible for industrial enterprises in 2008, an assumption that is largely justified in the context of the external negative shocks that year (the global financial crisis).

25. Note that the definition for DRIEs changed in 2007; we applied different definitions in 2005–2006 and 2007 accordingly.

26. It should be noted that the source data for 2005–2007 recalculations were from the industrial enterprise database instead of the census database. Also, our methodology is based on the official methodology adopted during the 2008 *Economic Census*, so it is likely somewhat different from the official methodology used in 2005–2007.

Table 3.2. A Recalculation of Value-Added for DRIEs

Unit: RMB billion

2008	GOV (Official)	GOV (recl.)	IVA (recl.)
Mining and Washing of Coal	1,462.6	1,553.1	841.1
Extraction of Petroleum and Natural Gas	1,061.6	1,078.2	627.6
Mining/Processing of Ferrous Metal Ore	376.1	388.8	165.2
Mining/Processing of Nonferrous Metal Ores	272.8	115.8	46.3
Mining/Processing of Nonmetal Ores	186.9	188.5	78.1
Mining of Other Ores	1.0	1.0	0.4
Processing of Food from Ag Products	2,391.7	2,413.9	455.6
Manufacture of Foods	771.7	776.4	257.8
Manufacture of Beverages	625.0	630.4	285.1
Manufacture of Tobacco	448.9	458.2	396.9
Manufacture of Textile	2,139.3	2,148.3	548.0
Manufacture of Textile Wearing Apparel, Footware, and Caps	943.6	949.2	311.4
Manufacture of Leather, Fur, Feather, and Related Products	587.1	588.7	180.5
Processing of Timber, Manufacture of Wood, Bamboo, Rattan, Palm, and Straw Products	480.4	486.0	130.8
Manufacture of Furniture	307.3	308.0	91.2
Manufacture of Paper and Paper Products	787.4	790.7	221.1
Printing, Reproduction of Recording Media	268.5	269.8	98.0
Manufacture of Articles for Culture, Education, and Sports Activities	249.8	250.4	76.7
Processing of Petroleum, Coking, Processing of Nuclear Fuel	2,262.9	2,284.7	189.1
Manufacture of Raw Chemical Materials and Chemical Products	3,395.5	3,428.6	908.8
Manufacture of Medicines	787.5	790.1	378.7
Manufacture of Chemical Fibers	397.0	397.1	67.2
Manufacture of Rubber	422.9	423.6	111.0
Manufacture of Plastics	989.7	991.2	262.8
Manufacture of Nonmetallic Mineral Products	2,094.3	2,105.2	654.0
Smelting and Pressing of Ferrous Metals	4,472.8	4,565.7	742.8
Smelting and Pressing of Nonferrous Metals	2,094.9	1,791.0	303.1
Manufacture of Metal Products	1,503.0	1,511.3	379.5
Manufacture of General Purpose Machinery	2,468.8	2,484.7	714.3
Manufacture of Special Purpose Machinery	1,452.1	1,407.8	389.4
Manufacture of Transport Equipment	3,339.5	3,417.6	915.0
Manufacture of Electrical Machinery/Equipment	3,042.9	3,049.0	801.6
Manufacture of Communication Equipment, Computers, and Other Electronic Equipment	4,390.3	4,273.8	867.4
Manufacture of Measuring Instruments/ Machinery for Cultural Activity/Office Work	498.4	498.3	141.9
Manufacture of Artwork/Other Manufacturing	408.9	372.4	93.8
Recycling and Disposal of Waste	113.8	114.6	19.5
Production/Supply of Electric/Heat Power	2,989.7	2,985.1	968.2

(continued)

Table 3.2. (*continued*)

Unit: RMB billion

2008	GOV (Official)	GOV (recl.)	IVA (recl.)
Production and Supply of Gas	150.7	151.4	35.2
Production and Supply of Water	91.3	91.7	66.2
Total	**50,728.5**	**50,530.2**	**13,821.2**

Sources: NBS, consolidated database, authors' calculations.

Table 3.3. A Comparison of Official and Recalculated Industrial Value-Added

Unit: RMB trillion, percentage

	DRIE IVA (Official)	DRIE IVA (recl.)	Indus. GDP (Official)	% of Recl. to Official DRIE IVA	Official % of DRIE IVA to Indus. GDP	Recl. % of DRIE IVA to Indus. GDP
2004	5.48	n/a	6.52	n/a	84.0%	n/a
2005	7.22	7.02	7.72	97.3%	93.5%	90.9%
2006	9.11	8.72	9.13	95.7%	99.7%	95.5%
2007	11.70	11.33	11.05	96.8%	105.9%	102.5%
2008	n/a	13.82	13.03	n/a	n/a	106.1%
2009	n/a	n/a	13.52	n/a	n/a	n/a

Sources: NBS, consolidated database, authors' calculations.

and 2007. That was evidence that prior to the GDP release, which the national accounts department is responsible for, IVA was already adjusted down to keep the result aligned with headline GDP. This was confirmed during our meetings with NBS. The national accounts department at NBS suspected that source industrial data, which the industrial accounts department is responsible for, were overreported. Releasing these statistics without adjusting was not an option, but the industrial department lacked the capability to conduct adjustments on its own. Hence, the national accounts department began requesting raw data from their industrial department colleagues and conducting adjustments themselves. This has become convention.

Therefore, if we were to accept the unadjusted aggregate IVA derived from our database calculation, we would risk overstating actual output. NBS reminded us of this fact during our interviews with them: we agreed. Aware that NBS employs alternative data to refine enterprise IVA statistics—such as taxes, electricity use, and production volumes—we felt it was essential to have such cross-checking steps ourselves. However, NBS adjustment methods are not public, and the alternative data they have for benchmarking are much more abundant than what is available to us as general researchers. We had to find our own way.

A Value-Added Tax Approach Using tax data to adjust our aggregate numbers was the first option we considered. In a recent publication, Carsten Holz had contemplated using Chinese VAT payable data to cross-check the IVA data. VAT payable data for industries are available beginning in 1995. According to China's regulations, the VAT rate is 17 percent for most entities and individuals, with exemptions and lower rates applied in a few areas such as utility providers and fertilizer.[27] When examining past series of IVA and VAT payable data—only available for DRIEs—Holz noticed that the ratio of VAT payable to IVA, after peaking at 14.6 percent in 1998, declined continuously through 2007 to 11.7 percent, the last year DRIE IVA data were available (Table 3.4).[28] That lasting decline was accompanied by news reports of enterprises exploiting the multilayer VAT ratio structure to evade taxes.[29]

Holz posited that if VAT payable statistics were reliable and the ratio of VAT payable to IVA remained constant from 1998 through 2007, then the 2007 IVA number should have been recalculated based on the 1998 ratio. That computation would reduce total 2007 DRIE IVA share below 90 percent from the previously implausible 105.9 percent.[30] We then tested official VAT payable data using our consolidated database and found the gap between the official claim on tax data and the sum of VAT payable statistics from the database was almost nonexistent, meaning there was virtually no official "adjustment" to the tax data that enterprises reported.[31] This validated Holz's hypothesis that, assuming the VAT payable data are correct—as officials did—one can extrapolate IVA with current VAT payable statistics and historical tax ratios. We follow this approach is the sections ahead.

Holz's second hypothesis—that the ratio of VAT payable to IVA remained constant from 1998 to 2007—is largely reasonable because the highest-tier VAT rate in China has been 17 percent over those years, with the portion of industrial enterprises that qualify for a lower VAT rate being modest. Thus, the continuous decline in the actual VAT payable share of IVA was supported by neither empirical nor statistical evidence.

Building upon Holz's hypotheses, we extrapolated 2008 DRIE IVA, using the actual 1998 VAT payable ratio and arrived at RMB 12.15 trillion. The share of DRIEs in official industrial GDP fell to 93.3 percent, approximately the 2005 level in official accounts and well below the implausible 2006 and 2007 levels.

Most importantly, these calculations allowed us to cross-check our bottom-up reestimates. The newly calculated DRIE IVA based on the 1998 ratio is 12 percent smaller than our previous reestimate, consistent with what three senior NBS officials told us; the extent

---

27. China taxes certain types of activity at lower rates of 13 percent, 11 percent, 6 percent, or 0 percent; some other low VAT rates are applied in special cases. Industrial subsectors, utility- and agriculture-related industries are qualified for a lower rate, for example, but most are in the regular 17 percent bracket.

28. According to our calculations, the VAT/IVA ratio actually peaked in 1995 at 15.1 percent, compared to 14.6 percent in 1996.

29. Yejun Wang and Lizhao Sun, "7月起增值税合并部分税率 调后仍存7档 (Adjustments to Simplify VAT Rates from July; Seven Tax Brackets Remain)," *Beijing Business Today*, June 19, 2014, http://www.bbtnews.com.cn/news /2014-06/19000000138117.shtml.

30. Holz, "Quality," 11.

31. In 2008, for example, our database showed DRIEs' total VAT payable was RMB 1.78 trillion, while NBS put it at RMB 1.77 trillion.

Table 3.4. Industrial VAT Ratio on Decline since the Late 1990s

Unit: RMB trillion

	DRIE VAT Payable	*DRIE VA*	*VAT Ratio*
1995	0.23	1.54	15.1%
1996	0.25	1.80	13.7%
1997	0.28	1.98	14.0%
1998	**0.28**	**1.94**	**14.6%**
1999	0.31	2.16	14.4%
2000	0.37	2.54	14.5%
2001	0.40	2.83	14.2%
2002	0.45	3.30	13.6%
2003	0.55	4.20	13.1%
2004	0.69	5.48	12.6%
2005	0.85	7.22	11.8%
2006	1.07	9.11	11.8%
2007	1.37	11.70	11.7%

Sources: NBS, authors' calculations.

of their downward revision to the aggregate raw industrial data was at least 10 percent, but no more than 15 percent for GDP calculations.[32] NBS confirmed to us that they use industry-by-industry VAT data as a check on each industry's value-added. Unfortunately, those by-industry tax data are not public, so we can only rely on the overall industrial VAT data to assess the level of total IVA.

We then expanded the extrapolation for DRIE IVA from 1995 (the earliest year of available VAT payable data) to 2013. Interestingly, assuming the 1998 ratio of 14.6 percent remained constant throughout the period, the share of extrapolated DRIE to industrial GDP, starting in 2010, would again rise to an implausibly high ratio above 95 percent (Figure 3.1). So while the VAT payable ratio adjustment produces a more reasonable growth track for DRIE share of industrial GDP in the early 2000s, the overshoot problem emerges again in 2010.

In GOV terms, DRIEs usually account for between 85 and 95 percent of an industry's output. For reasons explained in Chapter 2, IVA share should be the same or lower, because smaller enterprises with shorter production chains usually have a higher IVA share of GOV; we will demonstrate this statistically in the next section. So what caused the overshooting?

There are a couple of plausible explanations: the actual VAT share could have been higher in those years than the 1998 level of 14.6 percent; actual industrial GDP could have been higher than official claims; or VAT payable could have been overreported.

---

32. NBS, interview by authors, 2014.

Figure 3.1. Official and Recalculated DRIE Share of Industrial GDP
Unit: Percentage

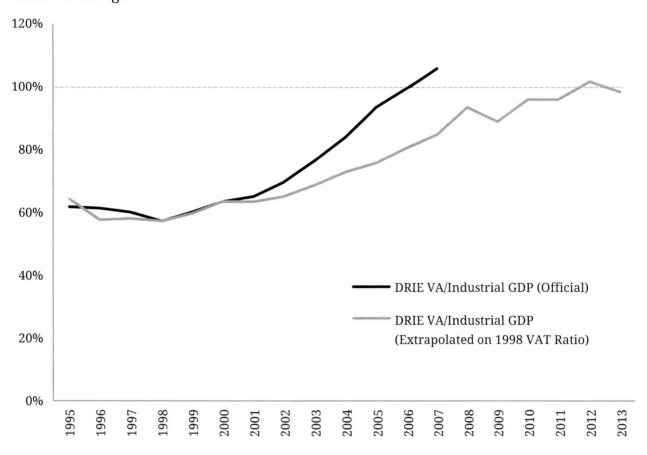

Sources: NBS, authors' calculations.

Regarding the first scenario, looking at the macro-level trend of VAT as a share of national GDP, we find that the national VAT share fell slightly in recent years, from 5.7 percent in 2008 to 5.4 percent in 2009 and then to 5.1 percent in 2013, which coincided with growth in the service share of the economy.[33] To be sure, peculiar patterns in certain industries could disrupt the overall trend, and tax data are not perfect. But given the macro patterns, the fact that tax data are often the most reliable of Chinese statistics, and the aforementioned examination of source VAT data we conducted through our database, we lean toward the second scenario: that industrial GDP was higher than the officially reported figures. In other words, we believe the "plate" was too small for the "cake," and we need to change the size of the plate. We explore how to make that happen in great detail in the next section.

---

33. In China, most service industries only paid income taxes and not VATs until 2011, when pilot tax policy reforms kicked in. For more information, see Shanghai Municipal Office, "交通运输业和部分现代服务业营业税改征增值税试点实施办法解读 (Interpretation on Implementation of VAT Pilot Program for Transportation and Other Selected Tertiary Subsectors)," http://www.csj.sh.gov.cn/pub/ssxc/zlzy/zcgll/zzskw/nszn/201112/t20111219_388791.html.

Table 3.5. Extrapolated DRIE Value-Added Under Two VAT Ratio Scenarios

Unit: RMB trillion, percentage

	Industrial GDP	VA (Official)	VA (98 Ratio)	VA (95-01 Ratio)	VA/Indus. GDP (Official)	VA/Indus. GDP (98 Ratio)	VA/Indus. GDP (95-01 Ratio)
1995	2.5	1.5	1.6	1.6	61.9%	64.2%	65.1%
1996	2.9	1.8	1.7	1.7	61.2%	57.8%	58.6%
1997	3.3	2.0	1.9	1.9	60.3%	58.1%	58.9%
1998	3.4	1.9	1.9	2.0	57.1%	57.1%	57.9%
1999	3.6	2.2	2.1	2.2	60.1%	59.5%	60.3%
2000	4.0	2.5	2.5	2.6	63.4%	63.2%	64.1%
2001	4.4	2.8	2.8	2.8	65.0%	63.3%	64.2%
2002	4.7	3.3	3.1	3.1	69.6%	64.8%	65.7%
2003	5.5	4.2	3.8	3.8	76.4%	68.6%	69.5%
2004	6.5	5.5	4.7	4.8	84.0%	72.8%	73.8%
2005	7.7	7.2	5.9	5.9	93.5%	75.8%	76.8%
2006	9.1	9.1	7.4	7.5	99.7%	80.6%	81.7%
2007	11.1	11.7	9.4	9.5	105.9%	84.8%	86.0%
2008	**13.0**	**n/a**	**12.2**	**12.3**	**n/a**	**93.3%**	**94.6%**
2009	13.5	n/a	12.0	12.2	n/a	88.8%	90.1%
2010	16.1	n/a	15.4	15.6	n/a	96.1%	97.4%
2011	18.8	n/a	18.1	18.3	n/a	95.9%	97.2%
2012	20.0	n/a	20.3	20.6	n/a	101.7%	103.1%
2013	21.1	n/a	20.7	21.0	n/a	98.2%	99.6%

Sources: NBS, authors' calculations.

One last observation we have made for this VAT approach is that the data from our extrapolation and official claims on the share of DRIE IVA of industrial GDP were basically in alignment with each other from 1995 through 2001 but have tracked less closely since 2002, as demonstrated in Figure 3.1. That gives us reason to believe that the VAT payable documented by officials from 1995 to 2001 were basically equal to what the taxpayers should have paid given the value-added they created. But beginning in 2002, the problem of tax evasion worsened, and the amount of DRIE IVA suggested by the official tax data increasingly deviated.

In light of this finding, we decided to use the average of the actual VAT payable ratios from 1995 to 2001 as the final adjuster to extrapolate DRIE IVA from 2002 to 2013, instead of using the single 1998 ratio (Table 3.5). The recalculated DRIE IVA based on the average VAT payable ratio is RMB 12.32 trillion, slightly above the previous estimate because the VAT ratio dropped from the 1998 ratio of 14.6 percent to 14.4 percent. This new reestimate is also 11 percent smaller than our bottom-up recalculation and in line with NBS's apparent downward revisions. The other problems we have identified, such as the post-2010 overshooting in the industrial GDP share of DRIEs, still exist.

A Value-Added Ratio Approach In the previous two sections, we analyzed the value of DRIE data and explored using VAT data to extrapolate industrial value-added. Now we will navigate a third and final approach to recalculate DRIE IVA for 2008, which will combine cross-checking officially published industry-by-industry numbers and results from our bottom-up approach.

The key factor in this method is the IVA/GOV ratio: how much new value is created in gross output over time. In the income approach to calculating GDP value-added consists of labor remuneration, operating surplus, net taxes on production, and fixed asset depreciation. Under the production-approach value-added is equal to gross output value less intermediate inputs. For any industry, the ratio of IVA to GOV should remain fairly stable over a short time period barring a shock that alters value-added per unit of gross output, such as a financial crisis, technological revolution, or tax policy change. To confirm these relationships we calculated the IVA/GOV ratio for industries with data available from 1993 to 2007.[34] We found that the fluctuation for most industries' IVA/GOV ratio over these years was low (Table 3.6).

For all but a few industries, the IVA/GOV ratio fluctuated within +/–10 percent of the period mean.[35] Encouraged, we set out to extrapolate a 2008 IVA/GOV ratio for 37 industries—36 with long time-series data from 1993 to 2007, and the industry "processing of food from agricultural products" with only 2003–2007 data available—which featured a three-year average of 2005–2007 IVA/GOV ratios. After obtaining the results, we multiplied the ratios by their respective GOV from the consolidated database to extrapolate IVA for 2008. For two industries lacking IVA/GOV ratio data, we used the results of our bottom-up approach instead.

The aggregate IVA for DRIEs calculated this way is RMB 14.63 trillion, exceeding official industrial GDP by a significant margin. A credible explanation is that the global financial crisis acted as an external shock and fundamentally re-engineered the relationship between IVA and GOV for some industries. Hence, simply taking the average of 2005–2007 ratios as a proxy for the 2008 ratio would have overestimated the actual IVA level. To address that problem, we drew a back-to-back comparison between the average 2005–2007 IVA/GOV ratio and the 2008 IVA/GOV ratio calculated from our bottom-up approach based on 2008 source data that had internalized the impact of the financial shock.

Interestingly, for 13 out of the 37 industries, the differential between our extrapolated 2008 IVA/GOV ratio and the three-year average ratio exceeded the +/–10 percentage range. Using such divergent results would make our results incomparable with official results. Therefore we decided to use our bottom-up reestimates for those 13 industries, in addition to substituting IVA for the 2 industries that lacked 2005–2007 IVA/GOV ratios, before recalculating aggregate value-added for the 39 secondary sector industries (Table 3.7). Under

---

34. 1993–2007 source data were incomplete for 3 of 39 industries: recycling and waste disposal, artwork manufacture and other manufacturing, and food processing from agricultural products.

35. As a rule of thumb, coefficient of variation (i.e., standard deviation/mean) less than or equal to 10 percent of the sample mean indicates low volatility.

Table 3.6. Coefficient of Variation of IVA to GOV Ratios*

Unit: Percentage

	CV 02-07	CV 93-07
Production/Supply of Electric/Heat Power	24.6	17.5
Mining/Processing of Nonferrous Metal Ores	12.6	9.9
Processing of Petroleum, Coking, Processing of Nuclear Fuel	12.6	16.7
Production and Supply of Gas	8.9	51.9
Mining of Other Ores	8.7	15.8
Manufacture of Chemical Fibers	6.5	15.6
Manufacture of Textile Wearing Apparel, Footware, and Caps	6.1	9.7
Extraction of Petroleum and Natural Gas	5.3	10.1
Mining/Processing of Nonmetal Ores	5.0	10.2
Manufacture of Tobacco	5.0	9.6
Manufacture of Leather, Fur, Feather, and Related Products	4.8	8.3
Mining/Processing of Ferrous Metal Ore	4.5	8.2
Processing of Timber, Manufacture of Wood, Bamboo, Ratan, Palm, and Straw Products	4.4	10.5
Manufacture of Foods	4.0	9.3
Mining and Washing of Coal	3.9	5.3
Manufacture of Measuring Instruments/ Machinery for Cultural Activity/Office Work	3.8	9.3
Manufacture of Special Purpose Machinery	3.6	4.4
Manufacture of Communication Equipment, Computers, and Other Electronic Equipment	3.3	7.9
Manufacture of Transport Equipment	3.2	3.6
Manufacture of Textile	2.8	7.8
Manufacture of Rubber	2.6	5.6
Manufacture of Plastics	2.3	7.6
Manufacture of Beverages	2.2	5.7
Smelting and Pressing of Ferrous Metals	2.2	6.8
Manufacture of Furniture	1.9	6.0
Manufacture of Raw Chemical Materials and Chemical Products	1.9	5.0
Printing, Production of Recording Media	1.8	4.6
Manufacture of Nonmetallic Mineral Products	1.6	7.5
Smelting and Pressing of Nonferrous Metals	1.6	7.7
Production and Supply of Water	1.6	3.8
Manufacture of Metal Products	1.6	6.7
Manufacture of Articles for Culture, Education, and Sports Activities	1.2	6.1
Manufacture of Medicines	1.1	8.3
Manufacture of General Purpose Machinery	1.1	3.6
Manufacture of Electrical Machinery/Equipment	0.8	4.8
Manufacture of Paper and Paper Products	0.7	4.9
Recycling and Disposal of Waste	n/a	n/a
Manufacture of Artwork/Other Manufacturing	n/a	n/a
Processing of Food from Ag Products	n/a	n/a

* Coefficient of variation (CV) by definition equals the ratio of standard deviation to mean. The industries are ranked according to the CV of their value-added ratios over the period of 2002 to 2007.

Sources: NBS, CEIC, authors' calculations.

Table 3.7. Extrapolation of DRIE Value-Added—A Value-Added Ratio Approach

Unit: Percentage, RMB billion

2008	DRIE VA/GOV % (Bottom-Up Estimates)	DRIE VA/GOV % (Official 2005–2007 Avg)	DRIE VA* (Consolidated Estimates)
Mining and Washing of Coal	54.2%	50.4%	737.52
Extraction of Petroleum and Natural Gas	**58.2%**	**77.3%**	**627.57**
Mining/Processing of Ferrous Metal Ore	42.5%	43.0%	161.77
Mining/Processing of Nonferrous Metal Ores	40.0%	40.2%	109.62
Mining/Processing of Nonmetal Ores	41.4%	37.2%	69.60
Mining of Other Ores	**37.5%**	**32.0%**	**0.38**
Processing of Food from Ag Products	**18.9%**	**26.4%**	**455.65**
Manufacture of Foods	33.2%	30.9%	238.44
Manufacture of Beverages	**45.2%**	**37.2%**	**285.08**
Manufacture of Tobacco	**86.6%**	**74.6%**	**396.93**
Manufacture of Textile	25.5%	25.9%	553.92
Manufacture of Textile Wearing Apparel, Footware, and Caps	32.8%	29.4%	277.15
Manufacture of Leather, Fur, Feather, and Related Products	30.7%	28.1%	164.91
Processing of Timber, Manufacture of Wood, Bamboo, Rattan, Palm, and Straw Products	26.9%	28.5%	136.81
Manufacture of Furniture	29.6%	26.7%	82.19
Manufacture of Paper and Paper Products	28.0%	27.5%	216.90
Printing, Reproduction of Recording Media	36.3%	32.5%	87.22
Manufacture of Articles for Culture, Education and Sports Activities	**30.6%**	**26.2%**	**76.67**
Processing of Petroleum, Coking, Processing of Nuclear Fuel	**8.3%**	**16.4%**	**189.05**
Manufacture of Raw Chemical Materials and Chemical Products	26.5%	26.9%	912.70
Manufacture of Medicines	**47.9%**	**36.0%**	**378.71**
Manufacture of Chemical Fibers	**16.9%**	**19.0%**	**67.21**
Manufacture of Rubber	26.2%	27.0%	114.13
Manufacture of Plastics	26.5%	25.9%	255.91
Manufacture of Nonmetallic Mineral Products	31.1%	31.0%	648.51
Smelting and Pressing of Ferrous Metals	**16.3%**	**27.1%**	**742.80**
Smelting and Pressing of Nonferrous Metals	**16.9%**	**24.6%**	**303.09**
Manufacture of Metal Products	25.1%	26.1%	391.88
Manufacture of General Purpose Machinery	28.7%	27.8%	685.98
Manufacture of Special Purpose Machinery	27.7%	28.5%	413.69
Manufacture of Transport Equipment	26.8%	24.8%	826.76
Manufacture of Electrical Machinery/Equipment	26.3%	25.4%	774.28
Manufacture of Communication Equipment, Computers, and Other Electronic Equipment	20.3%	20.9%	919.30

(continued)

Table 3.7. (*continued*)

Unit: Percentage, RMB billion

2008	DRIE VA/GOV % (Bottom-Up Estimates)	DRIE VA/GOV % (Official 2005–2007 Avg)	DRIE VA* (Consolidated Estimates)
Manufacture of Measuring Instruments/ Machinery for Cultural Activity/Office Work	28.5%	26.9%	134.11
Manufacture of Artwork/Other Manufacturing	25.2%	n/a	93.79
Recycling and Disposal of Waste	17.0%	n/a	19.46
Production/Supply of Electric/Heat Power	32.4%	32.5%	977.97
Production and Supply of Gas	**23.3%**	**27.8%**	**35.20**
Production and Supply of Water	**72.2%**	**45.1%**	**66.23**
Total			**13,629.08**

* Value-added for the 13 highlighted industrial segments are substituted with bottom-up estimates due to an overly large gap between the two imputed value-added ratios.

Sources: NBS, CEIC, consolidated database, authors' calculations.

this approach, recalculated aggregate IVA is RMB 13.6 trillion—still beyond the official industrial GDP but below the first estimate.

From the three approaches above, we extrapolated reestimates for DRIEs' IVA in 2008 in the range of RMB 12.32 trillion to RMB 13.82 trillion. We find the extrapolations based on VAT payable data most credible because they effectively offset some distortions in the raw enterprise data. In the following section, we turn to the non-DRIE enterprises, and address the earlier question of how to resize the industrial GDP plate to properly hold the DRIE cake.

Nondirectly Reporting Industrial Entities

Non-directly reporting industrial entities (non-DRIEs) are an uncertainty, even in official reports. Non-DRIEs cover industrial enterprises below the revenue threshold and self-employed businesses—entities whose data are often unreliable. For industrial accounting in the 2004 census, NBS compiled data not only from DRIEs, non-DRIE enterprises, and self-employed businesses, but also from administrative entities in industrial subsectors and industrial production units that were categorized into nonindustrial subsectors. For simplicity, in 2008, NBS narrowed down the coverage to include only DRIEs and non-DRIEs as we defined previously (Textbox 3.1).[36]

---

36. NBS, interview by authors, 2014. From 2008 onward, it is not completely clear to us what subsectors the industrial administrative units were classified under, possibly "Public Administration and Social Organization" in the tertiary sector. For industrial production units, because the value-added they generated was insignificant compared to the principal business they are affiliated with, the units were generally classified into the principal businesses' industry.

> **Textbox 3.1. Different Treatment of Nonenterprise Entities in China's Two Censuses**
>
> To illustrate challenges in categorizing and accounting for enterprises and production units in China, consider the example of a steel producer running a supermarket in its compound. In the 2004 census, NBS would separate the value-added the supermarket created from the steel producer's main business—steelmaking—and classify it into the tertiary sector; in the 2008 census, they discontinued that practice and instead grouped all an enterprise's value-added together and classified it into the steelmaking industry segment. In cases where the side business is significant enough and belongs to an utterly different industry, NBS would make an effort to calculate value-added separately. But such cases were rare, and in 2005, NBS found that separating them had only minimal impact on headline GDP and industrial composition. We also do not think including side businesses in the enterprises' principal business would affect the aggregate output in a significant way. Holz estimated that side business activities account for no more than 5 percent of total activity. This change in NBS's industrial classification between the 2004 and 2008 censuses was noted in Chapter 2.

In 2008, non-DRIEs included industrial firms whose principal business revenue was less than RMB 5 million, and individuals and households licensed to engage in self-employed industrial operations. The first time China systematically published data on self-employed businesses was after the 2004 *Economic Census*. According to then-director of the national economic census Lin Xianyu, for self-employed businesses, NBS first thoroughly surveyed administrative information, such as locations and business heads, and then selected representative businesses to survey economic conditions.[37] It turned out that NBS's select group of self-employed businesses was quite big: as many as 23 million were selected for the sample survey—of which 22 million were officially licensed—of a possible 39.2 million businesses, according to the 2004 *Economic Census Yearbook*.[38]

Despite the large pool of samples, NBS officials recall that the data quality for self-employed businesses in 2004 was not satisfactory, precisely because of the huge amounts of source data that challenged NBS capabilities to identify and correct abnormalities.[39] Having learned a lesson from the 2004 census, NBS turned to the tax authorities during the 2008 census. With tax records, widely believed to represent the best statistics in China, NBS was able to extrapolate the value-added in a more reliable way. The scale of their survey

---

37. Xinhua News, "国家统计局副局长林贤郁谈首次经济普查 (NBS Deputy Chief Lin Xianyu on First Economic Census)," China.com.cn, October 21, 2004, http://www.china.com.cn/chinese/PI-c/685957.htm.

38. NBS, *2004 China Economic Census Yearbook* (Beijing: China Statistics Press, 2006), http://www.stats.gov.cn/tjsj/pcsj/jjpc/1jp/indexch.htm. Zheng Liu, "全国首次经济普查: 依法接受普查 不作处罚依据 (*First National Economic Census*: Participation Is Mandatory, While Statistics Will Remain Confidential)," *Xinhua News*, December 31, 2004, http://news.xinhuanet.com/fortune/2004-12/31/content_2401788.htm.

39. NBS, interview by authors, 2014.

Table 3.8. China's Self-Employed Businesses (SEB) Blossomed

Unit: Million

	# of Total SEBs*	# of Licensed SEBs	# of Employed Individuals[†]	Avg # of Employed Individuals per SEB (person)[‡]
2004	39.22	21.87	94.22	2.40
2008	50.55	28.74	81.95	2.85

*NBS did not publish data on the number of total SEBs in 2008; the statistic is our own calculation based on the official statement of the number of sampled SEBs and the sampling ratio.

[†] The 2008 statistic refers to the number of licensed SEB individuals.

[‡] Lacking total employment data, the 2008 value is extrapolated from that of licensed SEBs.

Sources: NBS, authors' calculations.

was comparable to that of the 2004 census. According to NBS Chief Ma Jiantang, NBS conducted a full survey of 28.7 million licensed self-employed businesses in the second census, accounting for 57 percent of the total number (Table 3.8).[40]

Because NBS was able to leverage economic data obtained from the tax bureau to calculate value-added in the 2008 census, their survey of non-DRIE businesses focused on administrative information. That shift in focus reduced the room for distortions by these firms but also caused a notable reduction in the data entries NBS eventually published on self-employed businesses.

In the 2008 *Economic Census Yearbook*, there are only two data entries on self-employed businesses: the number of licensed business units and the number of licensed individuals engaged in such business. The two entries are broken down by subsector and by province. In comparison, the 2004 version had eight entries, which included the number of total self-employed businesses, the number of licensed businesses, the number of employed workers, operating revenue, operating expenses, compensation to employees, taxes and fees paid, and the original value of fixed assets.[41]

A Regression Equation Approach Without 2008 survey or tax value data for self-employed businesses and lacking non-DRIE data in our database, it was impossible for us to perform a bottom-up recalculation to reestimate the value-added for non-DRIEs. So we took an indirect approach first suggested to us by Carsten Holz. As an adviser to our study, Holz proposed that smaller industrial enterprises generally have higher IVA/GOV

40. NBS, "马建堂局长在第二次全国经济普查工作座谈会暨总结表彰会上的讲话 (NBS Chief Ma Jiantang on *Second National Economic Census*)," http://www.stats.gov.cn/tjsj/pcsj/jjpc/2jp/html/xu.htm; NBS, "第二次全国经济普查主要数据公报 (Statistical Bulletin of Second National *Economic Census*)," December 25, 2009, http://www.stats.gov.cn/tjsj/tjgb/jjpcgb/qgjpgb/201407/t20140731_590163.html.

41. NBS, *2008 China Economic Census Yearbook* (Beijing: China Statistics Press, 2010); NBS, 2004 *Census Yearbook*.

ratios than larger ones, thanks to their shorter production chains. Given our access to DRIEs' data, Holz suggested that we test that possibility using the two enterprise databases. We scanned the data and confirmed the hypothesis: the bigger the enterprise revenue, the lower the IVA/GOV ratio. This trend held for DRIEs in all industries except for petroleum and natural gas extraction, ferrous metal mining and dressing, and tobacco manufacturing.

Based on this finding and our previous recalculation work on DRIEs, we came up with the following approach to reestimate value-added for non-DRIE enterprises (source data for self-employed businesses was not available, unfortunately):

1. Use enterprise data in our consolidated database to compute a linear regression equation for each of the 39 industries:

$$\mathbf{Y} = a + b \times \mathbf{X}$$

where X is DRIEs' principal business revenue, and Y is DRIEs' IVA/GOV ratio.

2. Make an assumption that in the same industry, the regression coefficient beta ("b") is the same for DRIEs and non-DRIEs. Here, the unit for the coefficient is percentage, which describes the incremental change in an enterprise's IVA/GOV ratio for every additional RMB 100 million of principal business revenue.

3. For each industry, because we already have principal business revenue data for each individual DRIE, we added them up and deducted the sum from the industry's total enterprise principal business revenue (data are available in the 2008 *Economic Census Yearbook*). The differential we came up with was principal business revenue for all non-DRIE enterprises combined in that industry.

4. Because we also had data on the number of non-DRIE enterprises from the 2008 *Economic Census Yearbook*, we computed the average revenue for a non-DRIE enterprise, industry by industry. After we obtained those statistics, we went on to calculate the differential between DRIEs' and non-DRIE enterprises' average revenues, which would become the variable X in the aforementioned regression equation.

5. Integrate a second equation into the model:

$$\textit{Non-DRIE enterprises' average } \frac{IVA}{GOV} \textit{ ratio} = \textit{DRIEs' average } \frac{IVA}{GOV} \textit{ ratio} -$$

$$\textit{Revenue differential from the previous step} \times b$$

The implication of this is that the differential between DRIEs' and non-DRIEs' IVA/GOV ratios can be computed by multiplying the differential in their revenue size to the previously calculated regression coefficient b.

6. Finally, we took the average IVA/GOV ratio of non-DRIEs from the last step to multiply the GOV of non-DRIEs; the latter was calculated by subtracting DRIEs' GOV from all the enterprises' GOV in the same industry.

The third and last equation in our model to compute non-DRIE enterprises' IVA is:

$$\text{Non-DRIE enterprises' IVA} = \text{Non-DRIE enterperises' average } \frac{IVA}{GOV} \text{ ratio}$$

$$\times \text{Non-DRIE enterprises' } \frac{IVA}{GOA}$$

Through this method, our recalculated value-added for non-DRIE enterprises in 2008 is RMB 1.2 trillion. The details are shown in Table 3.9.

Table 3.9. A Value-Added Ratio Regression Method for Non-DRIE VA Recalculation

2008	Avg IVA/GVIO % of DRIEs*	Regression Coefficient b	Avg IVA/GVIO % of Non-DRIEs	Recl. IVA of Non-DRIEs[†] (RMB billion)
Mining and Washing of Coal	61.3%	−0.01	63.1%	54.67
Extraction of Petroleum and Natural Gas	58.9%	0.00	55.8%	1.46
Mining/Processing of Ferrous Metal Ore	36.7%	0.00	36.5%	18.38
Mining/Processing of Nonferrous Metal Ores	44.6%	0.00	44.6%	9.73
Mining/Processing of Nonmetal Ores	40.8%	−0.03	42.0%	41.20
Mining of Other Ores	38.4%	−0.21	45.8%	0.82
Processing of Food from Ag Products	24.0%	−0.02	25.7%	53.83
Manufacture of Foods	31.9%	−0.01	32.5%	24.38
Manufacture of Beverages	40.8%	0.00	40.8%	23.39
Manufacture of Tobacco	84.8%	0.00	73.3%	0.23
Manufacture of Textile	25.8%	−0.01	26.5%	53.65
Manufacture of Textile Wearing Apparel, Footware, and Caps	33.2%	−0.02	34.4%	48.76
Manufacture of Leather, Fur, Feather, and Related Products	30.6%	−0.01	31.4%	19.05
Processing of Timber, Manufacture of Wood, Bamboo, Rattan, Palm, and Straw Products	28.5%	−0.03	29.6%	37.12
Manufacture of Furniture	30.5%	−0.02	31.5%	20.55
Manufacture of Paper and Paper Products	25.8%	0.00	26.2%	22.76
Printing, Reproduction of Recording Media	32.8%	0.00	32.8%	29.78
Manufacture of Articles for Culture, Education, and Sports Activities	31.9%	−0.02	32.1%	11.32

Table 3.9. (continued)

2008	Avg IVA/GVIO % of DRIEs*	Regression Coefficient b	Avg IVA/GVIO % of Non-DRIEs	Recl. IVA of Non-DRIEs† (RMB billion)
Processing of Petroleum, Coking, Processing of Nuclear Fuel	23.8%	−0.01	37.1%	5.76
Manufacture of Raw Chemical Materials and Chemical Products	27.5%	−0.01	29.2%	47.02
Manufacture of Medicines	40.8%	0.00	42.8%	8.58
Manufacture of Chemical Fibers	19.2%	−0.01	20.8%	1.53
Manufacture of Rubber	30.1%	−0.01	30.8%	11.41
Manufacture of Plastics	27.1%	−0.02	27.9%	50.58
Manufacture of Nonmetallic Mineral Products	32.5%	−0.02	33.1%	144.21
Smelting and Pressing of Ferrous Metals	18.1%	−0.01	28.1%	11.65
Smelting and Pressing of Nonferrous Metals	19.5%	−0.01	22.4%	9.37
Manufacture of Metal Products	27.9%	−0.02	28.5%	68.58
Manufacture of General Purpose Machinery	29.2%	−0.01	30.3%	99.20
Manufacture of Special Purpose Machinery	32.6%	−0.02	34.0%	53.84
Manufacture of Transport Equipment	30.8%	−0.01	36.1%	49.45
Manufacture of Electrical Machinery/Equipment	28.3%	−0.01	30.8%	47.03
Manufacture of Communication Equipment, Computers, and Other Electronic Equipment	31.3%	−0.02	37.9%	26.88
Manufacture of Measuring Instruments/ Machinery for Cultural Activity/Office Work	36.2%	−0.02	38.6%	14.09
Manufacture of Artwork/Other Manufacturing	31.9%	−0.03	32.6%	28.19
Recycling and Disposal of Waste	21.1%	−0.02	21.1%	3.69
Production/Supply of Electric/Heat Power	43.7%	−0.02	43.7%	24.01
Production and Supply of Gas	38.1%	−0.03	38.1%	3.04
Production and Supply of Water	82.1%	−0.01	82.1%	19.09
Total				**1,198.27**

* Refers to median value.

† Enterprises only, excluding self-employed businesses.

Sources: NBS, consolidated database, authors' calculations.

A Provincial Data Approach As noted above, while the regression equation approach offers a quantitative means to get the value-added of non-DRIE enterprises, the result does not include value-added from self-employed businesses. Lacking source data in value terms for those businesses, we are unable to apply any of the methods we have used to recalculate their size.

NBS stopped publishing national-level DRIE IVA in 2008. But what about the provincial level? Although the provincial-level data are not compiled by NBS headquarters but by local statistical authorities, they are an available reference point for comparing our extrapolated non-DRIE enterprise data. From there it is possible to compute the differential between their total reported non-DRIE IVA and the estimate of IVA for non-DRIE enterprises, *excluding the self-employed businesses* that we calculated ourselves, to see if the implied level of self-employed business IVA in those provincial numbers makes sense.

From the annual provincial statistical communiques for 2008, we were able to put together total and DRIE IVA data for most provinces.[42] We then deducted their DRIE IVA from the total IVA to obtain the implied value for non-DRIE IVA, covering both non-DRIE enterprises and self-employed businesses (Table 3.10). For the 10 of 31 provinces that lacked either DRIE IVA or total IVA data, our treatment was as follows:

1. For two provinces that did not report their DRIE IVA in 2008—Qinghai and Chongqing—we used their DRIE IVA in 2007 to extrapolate the 2008 statistics based on the average growth of their DRIE VAT payable and total industrial GDP in 2008.

2. For eight provinces missing total IVA for 2008—Liaoning, Jilin, Heilongjiang, Jiangsu, Shandong, Hubei, Shaanxi, and Ningxia—we used industrial GDP as a substitute. In theory, industrial GDP is equal to the sum of DRIE IVA and non-DRIE IVA. That was our underlying assumption. But as with national data, provincial industrial GDP does not equal the sum of DRIE IVA and non-DRIE IVA, which is clear from provinces that provide both industrial GDP and total IVA data. The two sets of statistics are produced by different offices in local statistical bureaucracies, and industrial GDP is adjusted from original industrial data; this is not unexpected. Having said that, industrial GDP is the best available proxy we had in lieu of total IVA. For the purpose of this study, we treated the discrepancy between the official provincial industrial GDP and total industrial value-added as negligible.

3. We made additional adjustments for Liaoning and Shandong. In official accounts, both provinces reported DRIE IVA bigger than their industrial GDP by tens of billions of RMB, implausible because DRIE IVA is a component of industrial GDP. We first calculated aggregate non-DRIE IVA for the 31 provinces without adjusting for Liaoning and Shandong data, and then we used neighboring province data to extrapolate values for the non-DRIE economy.

---

42. Mainland China consists of 22 provinces, four directly administered municipalities and five autonomous regions. All these are provincial-level administrative authorities. For the purpose of this study, we refer to them using the undifferentiated term *provinces*. For example, we would say mainland China has 31 provinces.

Table 3.10. Provincial Data on China's Non-DRIE Economy

Unit: RMB billion

2008	Non-DRIE IVA	Notes*
Beijing	4.2	
Tianjin	1.3	
Hebei	185.7	
Shanxi	41.0	
Inner Mongolia	34.8	
Liaoning	58.3	A2 (−24.4)
Jilin	19.7	A2
Heilongjiang	42.2	A2
Shanghai	13.5	
Jiangsu	51.2	A2
Zhejiang	227.7	
Anhui	22.9	
Fujian	61.6	
Jiangxi	44.3	
Shandong	352.1	A2 (−82.4)
Henan	224.1	
Hubei	54.9	A2
Hunan	70.9	
Guangdong	198.1	
Guangxi	65.1	
Hainan	2.4	
Chongqing	36.0	A1
Sichuan	13.3	
Guizhou	19.1	
Yunnan	25.3	
Tibet	0.3	
Shaanxi	28.7	A2
Gansu	8.7	
Qinghai	0.9	A1
Ningxia	2.2	A2
Xinjiang	6.3	
Total†	**1,917**	**1,400**

* A1 denotes the provinces lacking DRIE IVA data for 2008 that underwent the first adjustment we noted above; A2 denotes the provinces treated with the second type of adjustment for missing total IVA data. The negative numbers in parentheses indicate the size of non-DRIE economy in Liaoning and Shandong prior to the adjustments for their data based on nearby provinces' conditions.

† If unadjusted for the negative values for Liaoning and Shandong, the result would be RMB 1,400 billion.

Sources: Annual provincial data reports, NBS, authors' calculations.

In line with NBS's practice of benchmarking dubious provincial data against nearby provinces' conditions to see if the select province was an outlier, we assumed that the share of non-DRIE economy in the two provinces was equal to the average level in nearby provinces. For Liaoning, we picked Heilongjiang and Jilin as proxies, where shares of non-DRIE activity in 2008 were 11 percent and 7.3 percent, respectively, putting the share for Liaoning at 9.15 percent. For Shandong, we chose Hebei and Henan.[43] The share of non-DRIE activity reported in official data for Hebei and Henan were 22.6 percent and 21.7 percent, respectively, so we set Shandong at 22.2 percent.

Using this provincial data approach, we were able to get an official reading for national non-DRIE value-added of RMB 1.92 trillion, or RMB 1.4 trillion if not adjusting for the implausible but officially implied non-DRIE figures for Liaoning and Shandong. If taking the former result, the differential between it and our regression approach reestimate for non-DRIE enterprises is RMB 720 billion, which can be taken to represent the size of self-employed business value-added. Concerned about the quality of provincial data, we took our recalculations back to the national level for a cross examination.

A Labor Productivity Approach Our third approach to estimating the size of China's non-DRIEs was inspired by an NBS practice from the 2008 *Economic Census*. According to NBS's Xu, when redefining labor remuneration and operating surplus shares in value-added created by self-employed businesses, the Bureau refers to the shares of same-industry, similar-scale enterprises as benchmarks.[44] From NBS's perspective, self-employed businesses—unincorporated production units as defined under the SNA framework—appear to share important statistical characteristics with incorporated entities (enterprises) at similar size. Unfortunately, we do not have access to full non-DRIE data and are unable to break down what NBS published in the yearbook by enterprise size. But for the purpose of this approach, we can make a reasonable assumption that employees at self-employed businesses and non-DRIE enterprises are comparable in terms of their capability to generate value.

In 2008, according to economic census data, non-DRIE enterprises had 21.5 employees on average, whereas licensed self-employed businesses averaged 2.9. Assuming a reasonable degree of labor mobility between non-DRIE enterprises and self-employed businesses in similar industries, wages should be comparable. As a corollary, value-added per worker—measured by their wages—should be comparable, too. Based on these assumptions and our IVA reestimate for non-DRIE enterprises from the regression equation approach, we extrapolated the value-added created by licensed self-employed businesses in 2008 to be RMB 530 billion. Adding this statistic to the regression-based IVA for non-DRIE enterprises suggests China's total non-DRIE IVA in 2008 was RMB 1.73 trillion (Table 3.11).

---

43. We did not pick Shandong's other two neighboring provinces for benchmarking because Jiangsu has a much more export-oriented economy than Shandong, and Anhui's industrial GDP was much smaller than Shandong's, diminishing their comparability.

44. Xianchun Xu, "当前我国收入分配研究中的若干问题 (Several Issues on the Study of China's National Income Distribution)," *Comparative Studies*, December 1, 2011, http://magazine.caixin.com/2011-12-14/100337967.html.

Table 3.11. Recalculation of Non-DRIE VA—A Labor Productivity Approach I

Unit: RMB billion, million persons

2008	Value
Non-DRIE Value-Added	**1,728.5**
VA for Non-DRIE Enterprises (Regression Method)	1,198.3
VA for Self-Employed Indus. Businesses	*530.3*
# of Employees at Non-DRIE Enterprises*	31.7
# of Licensed Individuals in Self-Employed Indus. Businesses	14.0

* 2008 annual average.
Sources: NBS, authors' calculations.

Another set of comprehensive data on self-employed businesses that allowed us to examine the validity of our labor productivity approach came from China's 2004 *Economic Census*. That data series is in some ways more useful than the 2008 version because the 2004 value data let us test the assumption we made in the first step: value-added per worker in 2008 was equal between non-DRIE enterprises and self-employed businesses.

Lacking ideal data points for value-added in 2004, we took a gross output approach. We compared the gross output per capita for non-DRIE enterprises with sales revenue per capita for self-employed workers. For self-employed workers sales revenue is essentially their gross output, according to the NBS manual for the 2004 census.[45] The comparison was quite interesting; in 2004, self-employed workers were 13 percent more productive than their counterparts in non-DRIE enterprises. We applied this finding to our reestimates in the first step—assuming the productivity gap between the two types of entities remained constant between the two censuses—which lifted the recalculated value-added for self-employed businesses. The revised value added is RMB 600 billion, 70 billion more than the first estimate. The total non-DRIE IVA correspondingly rose to RMB 1.8 trillion (Table 3.12).

However, this approach is still incomplete because 2008 self-employed business data did not include unlicensed businesses. It is unclear how much value-added this group of businesses has created. The only measure we can extrapolate from the official accounts is what we laid out in the beginning of this non-DRIE section: there were estimated to be about 22 million licensed businesses that year. Beyond that, there was no reliable method for us to extrapolate any other statistic associated with the group. Yet despite the huge number of such entities that existed, the total value-added of these informal businesses is not likely to be large compared with the size of China's overall industrial economy.

Now we need to consolidate our reestimates. To maximize the accuracy and comprehensiveness of our final estimate for non-DRIEs, we decided to take the average of the modified provincial data approach and the two labor productivity approaches. That way we include

---

45. NBS, *Methods of Economic Census Year*, 26.

Table 3.12. Recalculation of Non-DRIE VA—A Labor Productivity Approach II

Unit: RMB billion, million persons

2008	Value
Non-DRIE Value-Added	**1,798.1**
VA for Non-DRIE Enterprises (Regression Method)	1,198.3
VA for Self-Employed Indus. Businesses	*599.9*
2004 Data for Imputation	
GOV for Non-DRIE Enterprises	2,059.4
VAT Payable % for Industrial Enterprises*	12.61%
Gross Industrial Output for Non-DRIE Enterprises	2,319.1
# of Employees at Non-DRIE Enterprises[†]	26.8
Gross Output Per Capita for Non-DRIE Enterprises (RMB)	86,475
Sales Revenue for Self-Employed Indus. Businesses[‡]	2,509.9
# of Individuals in SEBs	25.7
Gross Output Per Capita in SEBs (RMB)	97,822
% of SEB Labor Productivity to Non-DRIE Enterprises	1.13

* This was the ratio paid by DRIEs, and we assumed it was equal to what the non-DRIE enterprises paid, as data for the latter were lacking.
[†] 2004 annual average.
[‡] Equivalent to their gross output value.
Sources: NBS, authors' calculations.

Table 3.13. Summary of Industrial Revisions

Unit: RMB trillion

2008	Official VA (A)	Revised VA (B)	B/A Ratio	Recalculation Method
Industry	**13.03**	**14.13**	**8.5%**	
DRIEs		12.32		VAT Payable % Method (1995–2001 avg %)
Non-DRIEs		1.81		Average of three estimates*
		1.73		Labor productivity approach I
		1.80		Labor productivity approach II
		1.92		Modified provincial data approach

* "Average" denotes the arithmetic mean of the estimates from the three approaches.
Sources: NBS, CEIC, authors' calculations.

the most entities in our coverage and reduce the possibility of overstating output; our consistent bias in this study is on the conservative side. The consolidated result, RMB 1.81 trillion, is, we believe, the most reasonable estimate of the level of 2008 non-DRIE value-added in China. This represents a 12.8 percent non-DRIE share in the entire industrial economy.

Combining this non-DRIE statistic with our most credible DRIE reestimate—derived from the VAT payable approach—gives us aggregate value-added of RMB 14.13 trillion for the secondary sector of the Chinese economy, 8.5 percent higher than the official figure NBS ultimately reported for 2008 (Table 3.13). This upward revision alone would add about 3.5 percent to official nominal GDP for 2008.

CONSTRUCTION

The construction subsector, which accounted for 12.6 percent of official industrial GDP and about 6 percent of headline GDP in 2008, receives less attention than the industrial economy from a production perspective. Viewed through the expenditure accounting lens, however, construction has been a leading driver of China's economic growth throughout the last two decades, given its close relationship to infrastructure and real estate activities. In our research and recalculation of data for this subsector, we identified a number of statistical issues little addressed in the existing literature. We flag these in addition to providing three value-added reestimates.

According to China's 2002 industry classification (in use until the 2013 *Economic Census*) the construction subsector consists of four industries: building and civil engineering, which includes house building and civil engineering; construction installation; construction decoration; and other construction. Of the four, the first industry is predominant and accounted for 83.4 percent of the entire construction subsector's gross output value in 2008, according to official statistics.[46] Construction activities for housing, rail, roads, ports, pipelines, and hydro facilities are all categorized into this industry.[47]

A second way to break down the construction subsector is by enterprise qualifications. The construction subsector has a concept equivalent to DRIE called "independent-accounting construction enterprises with construction-enterprise qualifications"—that is, construction enterprises meeting certain Chinese standards that also have an independent accounting system. For simplicity we call them "qualified construction enterprises" (QCEs) in this study. In non-economic census years, only QCEs are required to report their conditions to the government. National accounting in noncensus years is conducted based on the current-year information for QCEs and certain ratios between QCEs and non-QCEs derived from the last economic census.[48]

Within the construction subsector, enterprises are also broken down by their nature of business: general contractors (*zong chengbao qiye*), professional contractors (*zhuanye chengbao qiye*), and labor subcontractors (*laowu fenbao qiye*), with QCEs present in each set; non-QCEs are generally not differentiated by business nature but referred to as a whole. This is made clear both in NBS manuals and the *Economic Census Yearbook*. Interestingly, when we tried to compute the three contractor types' respective share of QCE gross output value and value-added, we found that although labor subcontractors contributed about 1 percent of total construction gross output in 2008, none of them were categorized as QCE in terms of their

---

46. NBS, 2008 *Census Yearbook*.
47. It is interesting to note that preparatory work for those construction activities, such as land clearance and equipment setup, are not in industry 1 but grouped with "other construction" (industry 4).
48. NBS, *Methods of Non-Economic Census Year, 2010 Ed.*, 30.

Table 3.14. Breakdown of Construction Enterprises by Nature of Business

Unit: RMB billion

2008	# of Enterprises	GOV	VA	VA/GOV %
QCEs (Official)	71,095	6,203.7	1,248.9	20.1%
General Contractors	38,212	5,423		
Professional Contractors	32,883	781		
Labor Subcontractors (Implied)	0	0		
Labor Subcontractors (Official)	6,837	66.5		
QCEs (recl.)	77,932	6,270.2		
Non-QCEs (Offical)	111,527	604.3		
Total	**189,459**	**6,874.4**	**1,874.3**	**27.3%**

Sources: NBS, authors' calculations.

contribution to the officially reported number of QCEs and QCE GOV. In other words, official accounts suggested that in 2008 all the labor subcontractors were non-QCEs (Table 3.14).

However, these findings directly contradict other official records. In the 2008 *Economic Census Yearbook*, NBS explicitly indicated that labor subcontractors were not part of the non-QCEs group but failed to clarify whether the 6,837 subcontractors were categorized as QCEs. In the 2009 and 2010 yearbooks—which recorded pre- and postcensus 2008 values, respectively—NBS implicitly excluded labor subcontractors from QCEs, suggesting there were zero labor subcontractors classified as QCE in 2008, as shown in Table 3.14. It is unclear to us why NBS would exclude labor subcontractors from two mutually exclusive categories that, together with self-employed construction businesses, constitute the entire construction sector.[49] NBS said in its post-2008 census manual that construction enterprises are either QCEs or non-QCEs.[50] In our recalculation, we treat labor subcontractors as QCEs despite the absence of NBS yearbook validation. This is an important hypothesis embedded in the estimates that follow and is, in fact, supported by definitions in the NBS manual and by local authorities.[51]

A Bottom-Up Approach According to the NBS manual, construction value-added is calculated by both production and income approaches starting from the 2004 *Economic Census*,

---

49. According to the NBS noncensus-year manual, the accounting scope for the construction subsector also includes construction production units that are affiliated with different subsectors. But, as we previously argued, in China's national accounts practice, value-added for such production units is not separated from the principal activity they are affiliated with. Also, because NBS does not differentiate "construction value-added" and "construction enterprises' value-added," we use these two terms interchangeably in the study, too. The value-added generated by self-employed businesses in this subsector is presumably quite small.

50. NBS, *Methods of Non-Economic Census Year, 2010 Ed.*, 25.

51. Dongguan Bureau of Statistics, "Statistical Bulletin of First National *Economic Census*: Dongguan," January 26, 2006, http://tjj.dg.gov.cn/website/web2/showArticle.jsp?ArticleId=924&pageNo=4&maindoc=924&columnId=4002&parentcolumnId=4000; Muyang County Bureau of Statistics, "Survey Results on Construction Enterprises in Muyang County," September 29, 2014, http://www.shuyang.gov.cn/shuyangtjj/infodetail/?infoid=dda98751-732b-414e-9046-56b560e714c0&categoryNum=006.

with the latter's result taken as the final figure.[52] We therefore constructed our recalculation approach as we did for DRIEs, working from the QCE data in the *Economic Census* database to recalculate value-added.[53]

Our income-approach formulas, based on the official formula in the NBS manual and the availability of data in the database, are as follows:

1. Construction value-added = Fixed asset depreciation + Labor remuneration + Net taxes on production + Operating surplus

2. Fixed asset depreciation = Current-year fixed asset depreciation

3. Labor remuneration = Wage payable + Employee benefits payable + Public − Accumulated housing fund and subsidies + Unemployment premium

4. Net taxes on production = Taxes in administrative expenses + Taxes and extra charges on project settlement accounts

5. Operating surplus = Income from project settlement accounts

6. Income from project settlement accounts = (Revenue − Costs − Taxes and extra charges) on project settlement accounts

Applying this approach, we calculated value-added for QCEs in 2008 at RMB 1.65 trillion, 32 percent higher than the RMB 1.25 trillion NBS published in the 2010 *Statistical Yearbook*—which included QCEs only—after census revisions. Because enterprise data in our database were classified by industry (building and civil engineering, construction installation, etc.), rather than by the nature of their business (general contractors, professional contractors, etc.), it was technically impossible for us to separate labor subcontractors out from general and professional contractors. Also, because NBS did not clarify how much value-added the subcontractors created, we were unable to obtain a precise, separate value-added number for them.

However, a document issued by the municipal government of Longyan in Fujian province shed some light on the subject. That document, released in 2012 for statistical training purposes, reported that the value-added share of GOV for labor subcontractors ranged between 40 and 60 percent.[54] Taking 50 percent as a national average, according to NBS data, labor subcontractors created RMB 33.25 billion in value-added in 2008. But adding this to the denominator—VA for the yearbook-defined QCEs plus VA for the newly calculated labor subcontractors[55]—barely changed the bottom-up reestimate. Our recalculated value-added for QCEs is still 28.5 percent higher than the modified official figure.[56]

---

52. NBS, *2013 China Statistical Yearbook* (Beijing: China Statistics Press, 2013).

53. The industrial enterprise database does not include construction enterprise data.

54. Longyan Municipal Bureau of Statistics, "建筑业统计基本知识 (Basics on Construction Statistics)," 2012, 6, http://lytjj.longyan.gov.cn/wsbs/bgxz/201207/P020120723386338403286.doc.

55. An implied assumption here is that NBS should have included labor subcontractors as QCEs, but they did not. We adjusted their accounting scope in order to make the base for two estimates comparable.

56. With the addition of labor subcontractors' VA, the revised official figure would be RMB 1.28 trillion in 2008, including QCEs.

Table 3.15. Extrapolated Construction VA under Three Scenarios

Unit: RMB trillion

2008	Gross Output Value	Assumed VA % for Non-QCEs	Total Construction Value-Added
Official	6.87		1.87
Scenario 1		20.1%	1.81
Scenario 2		93.2%	2.21
Scenario 3		27.3%	1.81
Avg of Scenario 2,3			2.01

Sources: NBS, authors' calculations.

For the rest of the construction subsector, lacking sufficient source data to conduct such recalculations, we had to rely on other official statistics for our reestimate. The first option that came to mind was the value-added ratio approach, similar to what we deployed for DRIEs. With NBS statistics on GOV and VA for both the entire construction subsector and QCEs, we were able to compute the officially implied VA/GOV ratio for QCEs, non-QCEs, and average construction enterprises.

According to official accounts, the VA/GOV ratio for QCEs in 2008 was 20.1 percent and for non-QCEs was 93.2 percent—a shockingly wide spread in performance by the two sets. For reference, the Longyan government document puts the value-added ratio for labor subcontractors between 40 and 60 percent, between 30 and 35 percent for house building and civil engineering enterprises, and usually 40 percent for construction installation and decoration enterprises. In particular, the Longyan government noted that all these percentages were based on the assumption that the enterprises were profitable; if they were in the red, ratios would be lower.[57] None of these reference cases helps us to untangle why the value-added ratio for non-QCEs implied in NBS data was that high. We concluded it would be unwise to use that ratio alone in our final reestimates.

Based on our recalculation for QCEs, we tweaked the official numbers under different value-added ratio scenarios. In scenario one, we assumed non-QCEs had the same value-added ratio as QCEs (20.1 percent); in scenario two, we assumed the officially implied (and likely implausible) value-added ratio for non-QCEs was correct (93.2 percent); and in scenario three, we used the construction sector's average value-added ratio (27.3 percent) as a substitute for that of non-QCEs. The extrapolation results are shown in Table 3.15.

Whether based on our source data, official NBS figures, or the Longyan government instructions, non-QCEs invariably demonstrated a higher value-added ratio than QCEs. Knowing that, we decided to take the average of the results under scenarios two and three as our final estimate for this bottom-up approach. With that figure, RMB 2 trillion, we were able to take NBS yearbook-defined QCEs, labor subcontractors, and non-QCEs into account,

---

57. Longyan Municipal Bureau of Statistics, "(Construction Statistics)," 6.

Table 3.16. 2008 Economic Census Revisions: Construction Subsector

Unit: RMB trillion

	Precensus*	2008 Census†	Postcensus‡	Postcensus Revision
Construction VA	1.71	n/a	1.87	9.8%
QCE VA	1.19	n/a	1.25	4.8%
QCE GOV	6.20	6.20	6.20	0%

* Data are from the 2009 statistical yearbook. Unlike in noncensus years, the yearbook for census years (such as the 2009 yearbook for census year 2008) records the initial GDP reading, *chubu hesuan*, instead of the first GDP revision, *chubu heshi*.

† Data are from 2008 *Economic Census* yearbook.

‡ Data are from 2010 yearbook.

Sources: NBS, authors' calculations.

and incorporate the latter's higher value-added ratios. This reestimate is also 7.3 percent higher than NBS's postcensus claim.

To some this upward revision may seem counterintuitive, because the double reporting issue in China's construction sector is notoriously widespread. Double reporting results when an enterprise's value-added is counted twice, by different governments. In the next section we delve into the institutional causes for that phenomenon. Here it is worth noting that NBS actually revised up construction value-added by a wide margin after the 2008 *Economic Census*, wider for non-QCEs than for QCEs (Table 3.16). That suggests to us that double reporting is not the biggest problem in this sector.

A Ratio Extrapolation Approach In addition to the value-added ratios for different types of construction enterprises, the Longyan government document offered other useful information. In its instructions for calculating construction value-added, it provided two additional reference ratios relevant to our study:[58]

1. Wage payable should constitute about 30 percent of gross output value (be cautious not to miss wages for temporary workers and employees at nonqualified construction enterprises).

2. Taxes and extra charges on project settlement accounts are 3 to 5 percent of gross output value.

Using the wage payable data calculated from our database, publicly available information, and our bottom-up reestimate, we extrapolated the entire construction subsector's GOV. That figure was implausible, merely half of the official claim. There are a few explanations for that, including that the Longyan-suggested ratio of 30 percent was too high. We do not know whether enterprises paid their employees that much and then underreported wage data to the authorities or if the authorities did not capture those enterprises at all.

---

58. Ibid.

Because we made an assumption in our extrapolation that non-QCEs wages are comparable to QCEs, we likely overestimated the wage share. In China, construction bosses routinely exploit labor and underpay salaries.

With these realities in mind, we were only able to get a reestimate for construction value-added comparable to our bottom-up recalculation when we lowered the wage payable share to 15 to 16 percent of gross output value, half the level the Longyan government suggested. For reference, looking at QCE data only, wage payable accounted for 14.2 percent of gross output value. In light of that, we set the wage payable ratio at 15 percent of gross output value and extrapolated the construction value-added at RMB 1.93 trillion (Table 3.17). However, we did not include this calculation as one of our final reestimates, because the officially specified ratio did not apply and the one we decided upon could not be sufficiently justified.

As for the second reference ratio the Longyan government offered, we extrapolated two sets of data based on 3 and 5 percent tax and surcharge ratios, respectively (Table 3.18).

From this approach we derived two figures: RMB 2.33 trillion based on the 3 percent ratio and RMB 1.4 trillion based on the 5 percent ratio. In 2008, the business income tax ratio for construction enterprises was set at 3 percent.[59] It was impossible to calculate the exact tax and surcharge share for all construction enterprises, because there are many cases in which the tax ratio was lowered for certain enterprises, surcharges were levied, or enterprises evaded tax obligations. For the purpose of this approach, we took the average of these two, RMB 1.86 trillion, as the final reestimate for the approach.

Finally, we returned to the various construction-industry value-added ratios the Longyan document suggested. Because the 2008 *Economic Census Yearbook* provided detailed gross output value data for house building, civil engineering, construction installation, decoration enterprises, and labor subcontractors and other construction enterprises, we applied the suggested ratios and obtained a VA reestimate for the entire construction sector of RMB 2.7 trillion.[60]

Of the four reestimates we made above, we assigned the highest credibility to the first one, which was based on the bottom-up approach, and the third, which was derived from tax data. As noted earlier, tax statistics often represent the highest-quality Chinese data. But because the tax-derived figure also relied on bottom-up statistics, simply averaging them does not help reduce inherent uncertainties (though the two were 8 percentage points

---

59. State Council, "中华人民共和国国务院令第 540 号—中华人民共和国营业税暂行条例 (Decree of the State Council of the People's Republic of China [No.540]—Interim Regulations of the People's Republic of China on Business Tax)" (Gov.cn, November 14, 2008), http://www.gov.cn/zwgk/2008-11/14/content_1149510.htm.
60. For our extrapolation here, we applied the VA ratio of 32.5 percent to house building enterprises, the 40 percent ratio to decoration enterprises in both QCEs and non-QCEs, and the ratio 50 percent ratio to the rest.

Table 3.17. Extrapolation of Construction Value-Added Based on Wage Data

Unit: RMB trillion

2008	QCE Wage Payable	QCE GOV	Construction GOV	Construction VA
Bottom-Up Estimate	0.89	6.20	6.87	2.01
Wage Payable % Approach	0.89	5.94	6.59	1.93

Sources: NBS, consolidated database, Longyan government (2012), authors' calculations.

Table 3.18. Extrapolation of Construction VA Based on Tax and Surcharge Data

Unit: RMB billion

2008	QCE Taxes and Surchages	QCE GOV	Construction GOV	Construction VA
Bottom-Up Estimate	216	6,204	6,874	2,011
3% Scenario	216	7,189	7,966	2,331
5% Scenario	216	4,313	4,780	1,398
Average of Two Scenarios				*1,865*

Sources: NBS, consolidated database, Longyan government (2012), authors' calculations.

different), and we decided to settle on the most credible first reestimate—RMB 2.0 trillion—for our final restatement of production.

An important question remains: what institutional incentives cause double reporting or, conversely, understatement? On top of the institutional factors explained at length in Chapter 2 and the industrial section, there is a particular idiosyncrasy in China's accounting methods for construction activity. According to the NBS national accounts manual, when calculating regional GDP, one should abide by the "location of operation principle," which means no matter where the entities are registered (or where the upper-level entities they are affiliated with are registered), the value-added from activities should be counted in the place where it took place.[61] This is in alignment with how gross domestic product is defined—essentially the aggregate value-added of all "resident institutional units." However, in regular accounting for the construction sector, Chinese entities still follow a "location of registration principle": no matter where the entities operate, their value-added will be counted toward the region where they are registered, incorporated, or affiliated with a parent entity.[62]

---

61. NBS, *Methods of Non-Economic Census Year, 2010 Ed.*, 142.

62. Longyan Municipal Bureau of Statistics, "有关建筑业统计的基础知识 (Basic Concepts on Construction Statistics)," November 26, 2013, http://www.stats-fj.gov.cn/gzcy/zxft/fthz/zxft_707/.

As of this writing, most construction data in China are still collected under the registration location regime, due to limitations faced by state statisticians.[63] Needless to say, competition for higher GDP rankings between regions immeasurably worsens the problem, because governments in multiple locations want to include value-added on their books. To address this, in economic census years NBS calculates an alternative construction VA value based solely on location of operation.[64] For example, in calculating Beijing contractors' value-added, NBS should deduct activity outside Beijing while adding in activity by contractors' from outside Beijing carried out in the capital. One can imagine the difficulty. In noncensus years, NBS does not attempt an adjustment to "purify" the value of "local" construction and other economic activities. These problems affect provincial GDP counts, but should not necessarily change national aggregates.

These loopholes encourage governments and enterprises to manipulate data, an urgent issue for Beijing to resolve. Central authorities must strengthen cross-regional accounting. NBS said in its 12th five-year plan (2011–2015) that it wanted to change the registration location-based accounting for the construction subsector to an operation-based regime.[65] This effort has long been impeded by local governments seeking to preserve their GDP bases and reform is not assured.

Forthcoming revisions to the *Chinese System of National Accounts* (which NBS pledged to complete in late 2014/early 2015 to replace the 2002 version, but has postponed) may create a window for institutional change, but the new system will bring new problems as well. If the activity of locally registered construction enterprises outside their hometowns cannot be counted where they are incorporated, home governments may try to prevent them from going out.

Since the 2013 Party Third Plenum, Beijing has publicly downplayed GDP as the measure of local success, acknowledging that such a fixation distorts local politics and fuels resource misallocation. Most provincial governments lowered their 2015 GDP growth targets.[66] Shanghai did not mention any GDP target for the first time in its 2015 policy preview.[67]

---

63. Jiaying Ma, Ping Zhang, and Ting Peng, "按经营地原则进行建筑业增加值核算初探 (Calculating Value-Added for Construction Subsector Based on Location of Operation)," Xinjiang Bazhou Bureau of Statistics, April 3, 2006, http://tjj.xjbz.gov.cn/older/html/zhtj/tjfx/200643104934.htm.

64. NBS, *Methods of Non-Economic Census Year, 2010 Ed.*, 142. The latter data are the jurisdiction of NBS's fixed asset investment statistics department.

65. NBS, "国家统计局关于印发'十二五'时期统计发展和改革规划纲要的通知 (NBS Notice on Strengthening Statistics Work in 12th Five Year Plan)," April 7, 2011, http://www.stats.gov.cn/statsinfo/auto2072/201310/t20131029_449672.html.

66. Min Liang, "多省将下调 2015 年 GDP 预期 (Several Provinces to Lower 2015 GDP Target)," *Sina News*, January 8, 2015, http://finance.sina.com.cn/china/20150108/141121253505.shtml.

67. Gabriel Wildau, "Shanghai First Major Chinese Region to Ditch GDP Growth Target," *Financial Times*, January 26, 2015, http://www.ft.com/intl/cms/s/0/2c822efc-a51d-11e4-bf11-00144feab7de.html#axzz3QO9zeFFM.

Tertiary Sector

Because China's statistical regime evolved from the Material Product System (MPS), which was created to measure tangible output only, China has historically struggled to measure tertiary activity. After transitioning to the SNA in 1993, China undertook a first *Tertiary Sector Census* for 1991 and 1992, lasting through 1994. The census identified significant understatement in tertiary industries and resulted in 24.6 and 33.2 percent upward revisions for 1991 and 1992. This lifted the tertiary share of GDP to 34.3 percent in 1992, 6.1 percentage points higher than previously reported.[68]

Despite these revisions, statistical authorities were far from solving fundamental problems. China still lacked a tertiary surveying regime. The initial framework for a professional tertiary sector national accounts system was not established until 2007, and a supplementary sample survey regime did not take shape until 2011.[69] Between the first *Tertiary Sector Census* and China's first national economic census in 2005 (for reference year 2004), China's service statistics were flimsy. After the first economic census, China revised overall GDP up by 16.8 percent—92.6 percent of which came from tertiary restatements. After the second economic census for 2008, out of 4.4 percent revision to the headline aggregate, 81.1 percent came from tertiary adjustments. And again, after the third economic census for 2013, services accounted for 71.4 percent of the total 3.4 percent upward GDP revision. The most significant upward service revisions were in wholesale and retail trade, transportation, storage and postal services, information transformation, computer services and software, accommodation and catering services, and real estate.

CHALLENGES IN SERVICE ACCOUNTING

Concerns about China's service numbers persist today. The general view is that services VA remains undercounted; we subscribe to this view. Many factors distort the data—mostly downward—and here we look at six major ones.

Unaligned Data Accounting Purposes

First, in national services accounting NBS relies on subsector regulators. However some subsectors do not have a direct regulator, including wholesale and retail trade, accommodation and catering services, real estate, residential care and repair services, and certain

---

68. NBS, "Statistical Bulletin of First *Tertiary Sector Economic Census*."

69. NBS, "国务院办公厅转发统计局关于加强和完善服务业统计工作意见的通知 (Forwarded by the State Council General Office: NBS Notice on Strengthening and Improving Statistical Work Concerning the Service Sector)" (General Office of the State Council of PRC, September 26, 2011), http://www.gov.cn/zwgk/2011-09/26/content_1956569 .htm; NBS, "部分服务业抽样调查统计报表制度 (Sample Survey Methods for Selected Tertiary Subsectors)," May 6, 2011, http://www.stats.gov.cn/statsinfo/auto2073/201310/t20131031_450584.html. According to the State Council's definition for *service sector* in the 2007 framework document, the coverage of China's service sector is the same as that of the tertiary sector, which includes 14 subsectors and 46 industries under the Chinese 2002 industrial classifications (the 15th subsector, *international organizations*, is not statistically accounted, so it is excluded in many government documents concerning statistics). Consequently, in this study, we use *tertiary sector* and *service sector* interchangeably.

transportation services and storage business.[70] NBS has difficulty collecting reliable and accurate information for these. Before a Service Accounting Department was formed in April 2010, presumably the best they could do was collect as much data as possible in national economic censuses and retrospectively revise data in noncensus years.[71] Even data on subsectors *with* clear regulators are challenging for national accounts purposes. As implied in 2007 State Council guidelines calling upon provinces and ministries to coordinate statistical work with NBS, the data that regulators collect are for regulatory purposes, not for national accounts. This lack of coordinated statistical practice results in accounting failures. As an Asian Development Bank paper pointed out, "Data that could be useful for the national accounts statisticians may be available in the accounts of the service corporations, but the regulatory agencies do not require them to submit information. Alternatively, the information may be submitted to the regulatory agencies, but it is not subsequently sent on to NBS."[72]

These problems cannot be solved until the central government aligns service subsector regulator practices with national accounting requirements and establishes a professional service survey system that allows NBS to conduct quality checks. The former remains a problem today: missing or flawed basic national accounts data for tertiary statistics posed a huge challenge in our recalculation effort. Most published information on the tertiary subsectors covers regulatory matters, such as transport turnover and securities transactions; these are useful for testing value-added data, but they are not substitutes. The NBS service accounting system is improving. In 2007, NBS said they had established "regular" survey regimes for retail trade, accommodation, and catering services, and were expanding to transportation, real estate, and a dozen other subsectors, followed by their creation of an internal service accounting office three years after. In May 2011, they established a modern sample survey regime for 11 industries without supervising regulators that have expanded significantly in recent years, including business and leasing services; residential care (such as nursing care, hairdressing, and funeral services) and repair services; computer services; storage; and loading, unloading, and other transportation services.[73] This is conducted by NBS's directly administered survey teams for quality control.[74]

High Concentration of Small Entities

Another major reason for distorted tertiary sector data is the high concentration of small enterprises and unincorporated entities, or self-employed businesses. According to the

---

70. NBS, "(NBS Notice on Service Sector)."
71. NBS, "奋进中的中国统计: 我国服务业统计工作成就和展望 (China's Statistical Work in Evolution: Achievements and Prospects on China's Tertiary Sector Statistical Work)," *China Information*, October 22, 2010, http://www.stats.gov.cn/ztjc/zthd/sjtjr/zgtjfz/201010/t20101022_71160.
72. Bishnu Pant and Blades Derek, *Measurement of Services Sector Statistics in the People's Republic of China: How Can They Be Improved?* (Asian Development Bank, November 20, 2007), 9, http://www.adb.org/publications/measurement-services-sector-statistics-peoples-republic-china-how-can-they-be-improved. In the original text, the authors used the quoted line to describe the conditions for "financial" corporations, but because what they said is applicable for all the other service sectors with a regulatory agency, we modified the sentence to refer to "service" corporations.
73. NBS, "(Sample Survey Methods for Selected Tertiary Subsectors)."
74. NBS, "(Survey Teams)."

second economic census, of nearly 30 million licensed self-employed businesses in 2008, 91 percent were in tertiary sectors; of more than 80 million individuals working in such licensed businesses, 80 percent were working in services. This means that the unincorporated businesses in service subsectors are both more concentrated and smaller than those in industry and construction, thus even harder for NBS officials to measure.

State-owned and large enterprise data are considered more accurate because these firms are more closely monitored by supervising regulatory agencies and tax authorities. Plus, as businesses grow bigger, the need for better accounting increases, contributing positively to national accounts data.

This view is shared by NBS, as indicated by a note explaining how they conduct national accounting for services in noncensus years. Three general methods were outlined by author Guo Tongxin for three sets of subsectors, depending on basic data quality. The first and best-counted group includes state-owned and state-controlled enterprises in transportation, storage, and postal services; large wholesale/retail and accommodation/catering businesses; and financial and property development corporations. This bundle of entities "has a better statistical foundation and rather comprehensive (accounting) coverage, whose detailed financial information is accessible." The second group is subsectors that have a regulatory agency, such as telecom, information transmission, education, health care, public administration, and the social organization subsector. The second group's detailed financial data are accessible, too, because regulatory agencies collect data for regulatory purposes but are less complete than the first group's because regulatory agencies are not fully capturing all the activities in their subsectors, especially for smaller and emerging players. For this second group, NBS relies mainly on ratio extrapolation, with ratios derived from the most recent economic census. Current-year data used for extrapolation comes from regulatory agency records. The final group includes subsectors and industries filled with small shops and unincorporated businesses, which generally lack statistically capable regulatory agencies. These include nonstate entities in transportation, property management, real estate agency and leasing, and residential care and repair services. For these NBS resorts to tax data, their own sample survey data, and wage data to extrapolate VA.[75]

In short, the more small and unincorporated entities in a subsector, the more extrapolation is required. Due to the opacity of official extrapolation methods, it is hard for scholars to assess the quality of these practices, feeding into suspicions and doubts. Our recalculation models indicate that there are indeed reasons for concern.

Stronger Relationships to Consumption, Not to Investment

A third factor is also related to the size of many tertiary enterprises, but from an expenditure perspective. According to NBS's Guo, China's tertiary sector output more closely correlates with consumption expenditures, while secondary sector activity is more associated with investment. In China's 2007 *Input-Output Tables*, every 1 percent increase in

---

75. Guo, "(Tertiary: Measurement and Share)."

investment generates 0.47 percent additional secondary sector value-added and 0.18 percent new tertiary VA. Each 1 percent increase in consumption lifts secondary VA by 0.25 percent and tertiary VA by 0.59 percent.[76]

The consumption-intensity of services is related to underreporting of its activity. First, many of the statistics gauging tertiary activity, especially for smaller firms, depend on *fapiao*, or invoices, which are notorious for massive falsifications because they are used to evade taxes.[77] Selling goods and services without invoices or understating actual revenue in invoices reduces taxable income; conversely, industrial enterprises have an incentive to get revenue and cost records right because they are taxed based on value-added (China's tax system is explained in greater detail in the next section). Because service sector data frequently rely on a corrupted invoicing system, they are often distorted. When we applied the bottom-up recalculation method used for secondary industries to service industries, we obtained VA results for the wholesale/retail subsector only 76 percent of official figures, and accommodation/catering services amounted to less than half of official values—an extraordinary finding that illuminates the scope of basic data collection problems. These stark differences between official values and our recalculations means NBS is unlikely to merely use a bottom-up value-added computation for certain tertiary subsectors, as they claim. They likely resort to other value and volume measures as proxies to extrapolate final figures. This is what we resort to for certain subsectors.

An Enterprise-Based Value-Added Distribution

A fourth factor, that China's GDP is enterprise- rather than establishment-based as recommended in 1993 SNA, was introduced in the previous secondary sector section, but it has tertiary implications as well. Under China's conventions, no matter how diverse most enterprises' activities, their VA is solely attributed to their principal business. According to NBS, there are exceptions for enterprises engaged in secondary and tertiary activity simultaneously where the two sides of operations are comparable.[78] But this proves difficult in reality, and NBS has largely discontinued splitting enterprise VA since its sole attempt to do so in the 2004 *Economic Census*. NBS does not strictly separate different business segments' VA from one another; its usual practice is what the Asian Development Bank called the "factory approach," whereby the entire VA of the enterprise is assigned to the single activity (*zhuying yewu*) that makes the largest contribution to VA.[79]

This problem is unlikely to be solved in the short term. In our interactions with NBS, statisticians argued that because enterprises themselves are unlikely to separate VA from their different activities, it was impossible for the Bureau to do so.

---

76. Ibid.

77. David Barboza, "Coin of Realm in China Graft: Phony Receipts," *New York Times*, August 3, 2013, http://www.nytimes.com/2013/08/04/business/global/coin-of-realm-in-china-graft-phony-receipts.html ?pagewanted=all&_r=1&.

78. NBS interview by authors, June 2014.

79. Pant and Derek, *Measurement of Services*, 7.

China's large corporations, whether state-owned or private, typically engage in multiple activities, so these idiosyncrasies in basic accounting create several problems. First, enterprises misclassify VA from services to industrial activity (or intermediate inputs) to reduce their tax bills, shrinking the national tax base. Taxing services on a value-added basis, like industry, would reduce that tendency. A pilot transition from an income- to a value-added-based regime began in 2011 in a few service industries and expanded geographically to include more industry segments in the following years. Because industrial enterprises cannot obtain tax deductions for service purchases, they prefer to source services internally, impeding both service sector development and more precise accounting.[80]

A second problem is the "headquarters" effect. The headquarters of companies operating in multiple regions often provide "management" services to branches, such as accounting, auditing and legal advice, market research, and advertising. The VA of headquarters' services should be accounted separately as if the headquarters were a standalone establishment; otherwise, because those internal services were free of charge, the VA of headquarters' services can be negative after deducting compensation of employees and other costs from its zero revenue.[81] Both of these problems reduce the reported level and share of service activity in China, and they will do so until NBS shifts from enterprise-based accounting to an establishment basis.

Location of Registration versus Location of Operation

As with construction above, according to 2007 State Council guidelines service activities should be counted in the region where they are performed, rather than where firms are registered.[82] However statisticians presently find it prohibitively difficult to ascertain where and how activities actually occur when they are distributed beyond the domicile of a parent firm. With large numbers of small and unincorporated entities, getting an accurate assessment of service sector activity is harder than for the secondary sector.

Emerging New Activities

The last factor is the rapidly evolving nature of China's missing service activity, which is accelerated by economic liberalization, regulatory reform, and a policy emphasis on lifting the service share of the economy. NBS's Guo Tongxin acknowledged that as new service activities emerge and firms diversify, the existing service accounting regime is increasingly inadequate. Guo said NBS had undertaken a series of measures since the 2004 census to improve accuracy, resulting in a smaller revision to tertiary value-added after the 2008 census. Guo argues that this indicates that China's tertiary statistical work had improved.[83]

In our view, progress is not so clear. A smaller upward revision in a single census year is not proof of regime improvement. Because the 2004 census is generally believed to have

80. Guo, "(Tertiary: Measurement and Share)."
81. Pant and Derek, *Measurement of Services*, 6–7.
82. NBS, "(NBS Notice on Service Sector)."
83. Guo, "(Tertiary: Measurement and Share)."

Textbox 3.2. Changes in Production Scope for Financial Subsector

For the financial subsector, the 2002 and 2011 versions of the industrial classification system both include four industries. But the 2011 version—which first appeared in NBS's release of 2013 *Economic Census* results and was used for revising 2013 GDP data—contained more nuanced and reclassified industry segments as well as more detailed explanations for each, reflecting both the evolving nature of Chinese economic activities and Beijing's conscious convergence with the updated United Nations guidelines, known as the fourth revision to the *International Standard Industrial Classification of All Economic Activities* (ISIC Rev. 4).

Expansion of the accounting boundary for the subsector (and a few other obscure methodological changes) resulted in a 22.8 percent upward revision to financial value-added after the 2013 *Economic Census*, which alone accounted for 40 percent of the total census adjustment, the single largest source of change. Also, because the expansion in scope is considered a systemic methodological change that is too significant to ignore for pre-2009 years, Beijing retrospectively revised financial value-added back to 1978, extending far beyond the regular five-year revision period for the economic census. Such bold changes demonstrate Beijing's ambition to improve national accounts, but some argue that the latest classification still does not cover all the new financial activities that it should have.

For instance, in the 2002 version the banking industry covers activities of the central bank, commercial banks, and policy banks; this is replaced with a new, broader industry called "monetary and financial services" in the 2011 publication. The new industry includes not only conventional banking activities, but also lending activities by nonbank financial institutions such as financial leasing companies, finance companies, pawnshops, micro credit companies, and rural cooperative funds. Some of these appeared in the 2002 version, but under the vague category of "Other Financial Activities." There are dozens more items in the 2011 version that were not included in the 2002 version under the financial subsector, and it seems unlikely that activities not specified in the national industrial classification are captured by lower-level statisticians.[1] In addition, as comprehensive as the 2011 classification is, some activities—like offshore financing activities conducted within the borders of China—are still not listed.

---

1. NBS, "国民经济行业分类 (GB/T 4754-2002) (Industrial Classification of National Economy 2002)," 2002; NBS, "国民经济行业分类 (GB/T 4754-2011) (Industrial Classification of National Economy 2011)," 2011, http://www.stats.gov.cn/tjsj/tjbz/hyflbz/; Guoxiang Xu and Xinji Liu, "我国金融业分类及其季度增加值计算研究 (Research on Financial Subsector Classification and Calculation Methods of Quarterly Financial Value-Added)," *Statistical Research* 29, no. 10 (October 2012): 8–9, http://tjyj.stats.gov.cn/CN/abstract/abstract4181.shtml. In this study we adopt the 2002 version because the 2011 version was not yet invented in 2008.

still understated service VA, and with more new activity emerging between the two censuses constantly, the second correction should likely have been *bigger,* not *smaller.* Some at NBS observe that emerging service activities are so new and hard to comprehend from a national accounts perspective that they are simply not reflected in the economic census for 2008, and even the latest census for 2013 under the renewed classification framework. This is supported by a side-by-side comparison of 2002 and 2011 versions of China's industrial classification system and close scrutiny of the latter (Textbox 3.2).

As Beijing is further liberalizing regulation of market activities and promoting a "decisive" role for market forces, new activities are bound to emerge more rapidly. The challenge for NBS and other statistical authorities is to assess the nature of those activities, classify them in the national accounts framework, and institutionalize the inclusion of further new items. Otherwise, the fast-restructuring economy will render the existing framework more and more divorced from reality.

CONVENTIONAL ARGUMENTS FOR SERVICE REESTIMATES

Both technical issues and apparent paradoxes prompt economists to search for better services counting strategies. For instance, despite the world's second largest economy, China's service share of GDP is abnormally low. The Asian Development Bank points out that China's 2004 tertiary share (40.4 percent prior to the 2013 census revision; 41.2 percent after) was not only lower than the Organisation for Economic Co-operation and Development (OECD) averages in the 60 to 75 percent range but also well below India, Malaysia, Singapore, and Thailand.[84] Services only officially surpassed the secondary share in 2012 (Table 3.19), to reach 45.5 percent.

Many wonder how the service share in China could be so modest in a country where service businesses and consumption activities have been booming for two decades. The obvious answer is that as much as services boomed, heavy industry, infrastructure, and property investment boomed far more: China does not so much have a modest amount of services as an inordinate amount of industrial activity.

A few economists have pursued alternative strategies to second-guess the volume of services value-added, such as using other countries' data to indirectly estimate China's activity. Qian Yingyi—then an economics professor at the University of California, Berkeley and now dean of Tsinghua University's economics school—and his colleague Bai Chong'en from Tsinghua benchmarked China's service share of GDP against India's for 2002 and found the Chinese share was 16.4 percentage points below the Indian level. Their reason for selecting India as a comparator was that it had development conditions similar to China's but much stronger statistical work, a helpful legacy of British colonialism. The authors were surprised to find the biggest gaps in service shares were in wholesale/retail and catering, followed by transportation and storage, and government organizations. They

---

84. Pant and Derek, *Measurement of Services,* 1.

Table 3.19. China's GDP by Sector 2003–2014*

Unit: Percentage

	Primary	Secondary	Tertiary
2003	12.4	45.5	42.1
2004	13.0	45.8	41.2
2005	11.7	46.9	41.4
2006	10.7	47.4	41.9
2007	10.4	46.7	42.9
2008	10.3	46.8	42.9
2009	9.9	45.7	44.4
2010	9.6	46.2	44.2
2011	9.5	46.1	44.3
2012	*9.5*	*45.0*	*45.5*
2013	9.4	43.7	46.9
2014	9.2	42.6	48.2

* All numbers are post-2013 *Economic Census* revisions.
Sources: NBS, CEIC, authors' calculations.

felt "it was hard to imagine" China being behind India in the service share of these subsectors, given China's overall economic and infrastructure conditions.

As a way to roughly estimate China's "correct" service share, Qian assumed China's combined GDP shares for wholesale/retail, catering, and transportation/storage were equal to India's, when official numbers showed China 9.3 percent points behind. They casually concluded that no difference could explain why China was behind India in terms of these service shares; that implied China's "correct" service share should be 43.3 percent compared with India's 51 percent.[85]

Less than a month after Qian made that comment, NBS published 2004 census revisions in which the wholesale/retail/catering and transportation/storage subsectors underwent heavy upward adjustment. Combined with real estate revision, the three groups accounted for about 70 percent of total tertiary revisions derived from the 2004 census. The two economists concluded that their previous assumption was proved correct by the official restatements and that China's service shares should not have been much smaller than India's corresponding shares because the two were both "large developing economies."[86]

However, their conclusion was flawed. The economists neglected to observe Indian underinvestment in industrial activity as the source of their "strong" service sector share. In 2004, prior to the 2013 census revision, China's tertiary sector accounted for 40.4 percent of GDP

85. Yingyi Qian, "关于经济增长模式 (Economic Growth Models)," Presented at the Caijing Magazine Annual Conference—2006: Forecasts and Strategies, Sina News, 2005, http://finance.sina.com.cn/roll/20051213/14362194762.shtml.

86. Chong'en Bai, "A Cross-Country Comparison of GDP," People.com.cn, January 1, 2006, http://finance.people.com.cn/GB/1045/3993507.html.

and India's 53 percent, but China's secondary sector was 46.2 percent of the overall economy, while India's was merely 28 percent. Simply put, the *share* of any sector depends not just on its own value but also that of the rest of the economy; it is a relative measure. China's service economy was not smaller than India's in absolute terms, but because China's industrial economy was *much* bigger than India's, it weighed down the share of the service economy.

Qian and Bai were not the only ones trying to second-guess China's tertiary GDP. In a 2013 report for the Institute of National Accounts at Beijing Normal University, Li Xin drew a regression between the GDP per capita level and the tertiary share of GDP in 2011 for more than 180 countries. She found that based on China's GDP per capita for that year, the tertiary share of GDP should be 52 to 58 percent, versus an official estimate of 43.4 percent (absent the 2013 census revision). Li classified the world into six country groups by income level and computed a world average: China's 2011 service share of GDP was below *all* groups and vastly below the world average of 70.9 percent. She concluded that China's service GDP was "undoubtedly underestimated," because China's service sector is obviously stronger than low-income countries such as Zimbabwe and the Philippines, which she based on tourist experiences on the ground because Chinese statisticians lacked sound tax data to do proper extrapolations.[87]

The regression strategy for extrapolating China's service share was cleverly designed. We found useful elements from this exercise to apply in our recalculations. However, Li's conclusions are also deeply flawed.

First, a country's tertiary share of GDP is not solely related to its economic development level; instead, it reflects factor endowment, industrial structure, and development models. Within the group of high-income OECD countries, the 2008 tertiary share of GDP ranged from 53.6 percent in Norway to 84.5 percent in Luxembourg. Expanding the group to all high-income countries, the range widens, from a single-digit percentage to more than 80 percent.[88] The conclusion that China's tertiary share of GDP "should" be higher just because certain subsectors are more developed than in other countries is unfounded.

Second, for economies with aggregate size close to China's—the other of the world's largest economies in 2013[89]—secondary sector share of GDP is invariably smaller than China's. Among the top 10 economies, the Russian Federation's was the second highest, with secondary sector at 36.3 percent of GDP, 7.4 percentage points lower than China's, while reporting a tertiary sector share of 59.8 percent, nearly 12.9 percentage points higher than in China. All other top economies reported a secondary sector share in the 20-percent range, and none of them had China's characteristics: a large overall economy (including a

87. Xin Li, "GDP Share of Tertiary Sector," in *2013 National Accounts Report*, ed. Institute of National Accounts (Beijing: Beijing Normal University, 2013), 292–293.

88. World Bank, 2014 World Development Indicators, http://databank.worldbank.org/data/views/reports/tableview.aspx#.

89. World Bank, "Gross Domestic Product 2013" (World Bank, December 16, 2014), http://databank.worldbank.org/data/download/GDP.pdf. The other nine largest economies in 2013 were the United States, Japan, Germany, France, the United Kingdom, Brazil, Italy, the Russian Federation, and India, according to the World Bank.

Table 3.20. Economic Structure of Some Developing Economies in 2008*

Unit: Percentage

| | Primary | Secondary | | | | Tertiary | | | |
		Total	Mining, Mfg, Utilities	Mfg	Construction	Total	W/R, A/C†	Transp, Strg, Postal	Other
Philippines	13.24	32.88	27.45	22.81	5.43	53.88	17.05	7.11	29.72
Thailand	10.12	39.63	36.87	30.86	2.76	50.24	17.47	7.27	25.51
Egypt	13.22	37.91	33.61	16.25	4.30	48.87	14.71	10.80	23.35
Belarus	9.96	44.60	34.74	30.08	9.86	45.44	13.70	8.23	23.52
Malaysia	10.07	45.55	42.78	24.80	2.77	44.38	14.98	6.10	23.31
Vietnam	20.41	37.08	31.16	18.58	5.92	42.51	16.42	4.23	21.86
China	**10.73**	**47.45**	**41.48**	**32.65**	**5.97**	**41.82**	**10.44**	**5.21**	**26.17**
Indonesia	14.48	48.06	39.58	27.81	8.48	37.46	13.97	6.31	17.18

* China's 2008 data are not subject to 2013 census revisions to ensure comparability with other countries' from the UN database.

† Wholesale/retail and accommodation/catering services.

Sources: UN National Accounts Main Aggregates Database, authors' calculations.

large services economy in absolute terms) and an enormous secondary sector that proportionally represses the service share. The Asian Development Bank paper and others argue that because China's service share of GDP has been growing, faster growth is likely to continue and make China's economy look more like that of developed economies in the future, characterized by a high service sector share.[90]

Our final observation on tertiary statistics is related to developing economies whose tertiary shares were higher than or close to China's. In Malaysia and Thailand—the two economies the Asian Development Bank paper cited—the scale of their tertiary shares above China's in 2008, was, interestingly, approximately equal to the scale of their secondary share below China's. For Thailand, its service share was 8.4 percentage points above China, and its secondary sector was 7.8 percentage points lower. In Malaysia's case, the two ratios were 2.6 percentage points higher in tertiary and 2 percentage points lower in secondary (Table 3.20). This again demonstrates our earlier point about broad cross-country comparisons: that deducing China's tertiary share simply based on its overall economic size and development level is not supported by empirical data. This is not to say we think China's tertiary level and share are accurately reflected in NBS data, but the underlying logic the scholars used to conclude there was a tertiary understatement does not stand up to empirical tests.

China's oversized industrial economy, whether viewed through official data or independent estimates, is a misleading factor when scholars apply a broad-brush cross-country comparison approach that treats the entire tertiary sector as a whole. More useful alternative estimates can be undertaken at the subsector level. Unlike the secondary sector, tertiary subsectors are vastly different from one another by nature, scale, and recent developments. We used three methodologies to examine data and compute alternative value-added for China's service subsectors. Our first methodology, involving five different recalculation approaches, is to employ value and volume measures to extrapolate 2008 VA for the eight largest service subsectors, and then to expand our estimates to the six remaining subsectors. Our second approach is a subsector-level cross-country comparison for wholesale/retail and accommodation/catering services, with two estimates for each based on market exchange rates and purchasing power parity. We applied a third method for rental activity in the real estate subsector only, which centers on shifting from the official current VA calculation for rent based on current construction costs to a new method proposed by NBS in late 2013 (but not yet employed) that relies on market rental data. We evaluated estimates from these different approaches and produced a composite reestimate of VA for China's service sector using our best judgment.[91]

THE DOMESTIC VARIABLE APPROACHES

For the tertiary sector, we applied the same principle that guided our recalculations for the secondary sector—namely, computing alternative estimates by reproducing official

90. Pant and Derek, *Measurement of Services*, 1–2.
91. NBS, "Reform of National Accounts System."

Table 3.21. Eight Service Subsectors Selected for Recalculations

Unit: RMB billion

2008	GDP	% of GDP	% of Tertiary GDP
Tertiary Sector	**13,134.0**	**41.8%**	**100.0%**
Sum of Eight Selected Subsectors	*10,929.5*	*34.8%*	*83.2%*
Transport, Storage, and Postal Services	**1,636.3**	**5.2%**	**12.5%**
Information Transmission, Computer Services, and Software	**786.0**	**2.5%**	**6.0%**
Wholesale and Retail Trade	**2,618.2**	**8.3%**	**19.9%**
Accommodation and Catering Services	**661.6**	**2.1%**	**5.0%**
Finance	**1,486.3**	**4.7%**	**11.3%**
Real Estate	**1,473.9**	**4.7%**	**11.2%**
Leasing and Business Services	560.8	1.8%	4.3%
Scientific Research, Technical Services, and Geological Prospecting	399.3	1.3%	3.0%
Management of Water Conservancy, Environment, and Public Facilities	126.6	0.4%	1.0%
Services to Households and Other Services	462.8	1.5%	3.5%
Education	**888.8**	**2.8%**	**6.8%**
Health, Social Securities, and Welfare	462.9	1.5%	3.5%
Culture, Sports, and Entertainment	192.2	0.6%	1.5%
Public Administration and Social Organizations	**1,378.4**	**4.4%**	**10.5%**

Sources: NBS, authors' calculations.

methods and then comparing the differential and assessing problems from within the official framework. However, constrained by the insufficiency of national accounts data and small entities' figures in the *Economic Census* database, we were unable to reproduce the official methodology for all 14 service subsectors. For the purpose of this study, we started with the top eight subsectors that contributed the most value-added to China's tertiary GDP in 2008, totaling about 83 percent according to the second economic census (Table 3.21). After we obtained what we believed to be the most reasonable alternative VA for these eight subsectors, we assumed the differential by which official tertiary VA of those subsectors varied from our recalculation was the same as the differential in the remaining six subsectors for which we had no separate estimates (accounting for 17 percent of official service VA in 2008). Through this extrapolation, we recalculate 2008 VA for all service activity.

A Bottom-Up Approach For the bottom-up approach for service subsectors, we leveraged the same strategy we used for the secondary sector. According to the NBS national accounts manual renewed in 2010, the officially preferred approach to count service VA is the income approach, from which we draw our recalculation formulas, paired with basic data from the *Economic Census* database:

1. Service value-added = Operating income[92] + Current-year depreciation[93] + Net taxes on production + Labor remuneration

2. Net taxes on production = Principal business taxes and surcharges + Amount of net taxes on production in operating, administrative, and financial fees[94]

3. Labor remuneration = Wage and employee benefits payable ÷ Share of that payable to labor Remuneration at administrative accounting–based entities

Applying this set of formulas to our cleaned-up databases, we were able to compute industry-level VA for all subsectors except education, public administration and social organizations, and finance. Basic data for these subsectors are extremely spotty in the database. When aggregated, the recalculated education VA is RMB 126 billion versus the official claim of RMB 890 billion. This is most likely caused by the evolving nature of China's education service conditions. Previously, education service providers mainly relied on government grants, but an expanding portion of the subsector is increasingly living on the prices they charge for their services.[95] The basic data the Ministry of Education (MOE) is able to collect through its own system is increasingly divorced from actual circumstances. A more reliable reference in this regard is the *China Educational Finance Statistics Yearbook* (*zhongguo jiaoyu jingfei tongji nianjian*), jointly compiled by MOE and NBS.[96]

According to government records, MOE's financial statistics covered all educational establishments except for those provided by the Party schools, military schools, and Communist Youth League schools.[97] Educational services by these entities are categorized as "other unspecified educational services" under China's industrial classification 2002. Through the *2008 Economic Census Yearbook*, we were able to compute the revenue ratio between "other educational services" and the entire educational subsector, which was about 5 percent. It should be noted that the "other education services" in the national industrial classification and the yearbook also include vocational and special education, so we assumed the educational services provided by the military, the Party, and the Youth League accounted for one-third of that 5 percent. With that newly calculated extrapolation ratio, we computed labor remuneration for the entire educational subsector—based on the ratio of wage and employee benefits to labor remuneration for educational workers in the

---

92. Ideally, this item should be "operating surplus," which is equal to operating income minus "investment income," minus "income from changes in fair value," plus the amount of operating surplus in operating, administrative, and financial fees. However, none of those variables, except for "operating income," existed in the 2008 *Economic Census* database, mostly because "operating surplus" is a national accounts concept that enterprises do not compute for their own operational purposes. Lacking the basic data to do our own computation, here we take "operating income" as a substitute for "operating surplus."

93. Current year depreciation for a specific subsector is computed based on the database-included entities' median ratio of depreciation/original value of fixed assets and the original value of total fixed assets for the entire subsector.

94. For the ratios used to calculate the amount of net taxes on production in each subsector's operating, administrative, and financial fees, see NBS, *Methods of Non-Economic Census Year, 2010 Ed.*, 137.

95. Pant and Derek, *Measurement of Services*, 1–2.

96. Ibid, 6.

97. Yumiao Zeng, "服务行业增加值核算试行方法 (Pilot Implementation of Methods for Service Sector Value-Added Estimates)" (Zhejiang Jinhua Municipal Statistics Information Network, November 22, 2004), http://www.jhstats.gov.cn/shownews.aspx?id=1556.

Table 3.22. Revision of China's 2008 Educational VA

Unit: RMB billion

Item	Value
Educational VA (Official)	888.8
Total Education Revenue	1,231.8
Rev. of Regular Edu. Institutions	1,171.6
Rev. of Other Edu. Services	60.2
Labor Remuneration	740.3
Wage and Employee Benefits	557.3
Educational VA (Recl.)	*943.7*

Sources: Ministry of Education, NBS, authors' calculations.

2008 Economic Census Yearbook—and used the relative ratios among the four income-approach components in the *2007 Input Output Tables* (operating surplus, fixed asset depreciation, labor remuneration, and net taxes on production) to obtain a 2008 education value-added of RMB 943.7 billion, 6 percent higher than the official figure (Table 3.22).

For public administration and social organizations, the formula and the extrapolation approaches above did not apply, so we were unable to compute an alternative value through this method. Financial subsector enterprise data was missing for unexplained reasons. Odder still, these enterprise data are missing from the economic census yearbook, too, which only lists the statistics for financial entities implementing administrative accounting rules.[98] Lacking other basic national accounts data for this bottom-up approach, we had no choice but to adopt a quasi-official estimate jointly produced by two People's Bank of China (PBoC) statisticians and a finance professor. Their estimates for banking,[99] securities, and insurance were better than none. According to their estimates, of the RMB 1.49 trillion of financial VA in 2008, banking and other financial services contributed RMB 1.18 trillion, securities RMB 98.7 billion, and insurance RMB 205.8 billion.[100] Although we suspect the activities conducted by unconventional financial entities were undercounted—especially those missing from the 2002 national industrial classification and newly added to the 2011 classification—we did not have sufficient bottom-up empirical evidence to quantify the underestimated portion, a long-time black hole even in official statisticians' accounting book.

The knowledge gap for China's financial subsector activities was narrowed with the 2013 census revisions, which suggested a one-fifth upward revision. These novel adjustments were not available in time for inclusion in our recount. However, directionally they are consistent with our conclusion that newer, more advanced service activities are undercounted in China. Using the bottom-up reestimation approach, recalculated VA for

---

   98. NBS, *2008 Census Yearbook*.

   99. For the purpose of their study, the authors grouped "other financial services" with banking services.

   100. Jianchao Zhao, Chunping Zhao, and Zhenjiang Peng, "金融业对经济增长贡献的测算及中美两国比较 (Measuring Contribution of Financial Subsector to Economic Growth and A Comparison between China and the United States)," *Financial Regulation Research*, no. 4 (2014): 76–78.

Table 3.23. Bottom-Up Calculations for Tertiary VA

Unit: RMB billion

2008	VA (Official)	VA (recl.)	Recl./Official %
Transport, Storage, and Postal Services	1,636.3	1,478.8	90%
Information Transmission, Computer Services, and Software	786.0	880.3	112%
Wholesale and Retail Trade	2,618.2	1,997.3	76%
Accommodation and Catering Services	661.6	277.2	42%
Finance	1,486.3	1,486.2	100%
Real Estate	1,473.9	853.7	58%
Education	888.7	943.7	106%
Public Administration and Social Organizations	1,378.4	n/a	n/a
*Sum of Eight Subsectors**	*10,929.4*	*7,917.3*	*72%*

* Revision of the last subsector is missing due to lack of source data.
Sources: NBS, *Economic Census* database, authors' calculations.

accommodation/catering and real estate also looked dubious to us. The recalculated accommodation/catering VA was less than half what NBS reported; real estate was about 60 percent of the official figure. It is unclear to what extent NBS used data from channels other than the *Economic Census* database to compute final tertiary VA. It is questionable whether NBS calculated tertiary VA in accordance with their stated national accounts manual methods, and the unusual degree of opacity raises big questions (Table 3.23).

A Gross Output and Value-Added Ratio Approach The second approach is more straightforward and similar to what we used for DRIEs in the secondary sector: because basic data are incomplete for most of the tertiary subsectors, we proceeded from the macro perspective. The idea is to multiply subsectors'—or industries'—gross output value in 2008 by respective VA ratios, depending on data availability, and compared the sum with official claims. To do that we took the VA ratios in China's benchmark *2007 Input Output Tables.*

China's input-output accounting is conducted once every five years, in years ending in 2 or 7, from which a set of "benchmark" input-output (IO) tables are produced. Between the benchmark years, a simpler set of "extended" input-output tables are produced in years ending in 5 or 0, where small-scale surveys are done and modest adjustments to some fundamental indices are carried out.[101] Unlike in advanced economies such as the United States, where the IO accounts serve as "building blocks" for other economic accounts, including those that produce estimates for GDP,[102] China's IO tables are published one full year after the second revision of GDP for the same measurement year, so they are not

101. Yong Wang, "中国投入产出核算: 回顾与展望 (China's Input-Output Accounting: Review and Prospect)," *Statistical Research* 29, no. 8 (August 2012): 65, http://www.npopss-cn.gov.cn/NMediaFile/2013/0626 /MAIN201306261355000282215289393.pdf.

102. U.S. Bureau of Economic Analysis, "Concepts and Methods of the U.S. Input-Output Accounts" (U.S. Department of Commerce, April 2009), chap.1, 1, http://www.bea.gov/papers/pdf/IOmanual_092906.pdf.

Textbox 3.3. Value-Added Ratios in China's Input-Output Tables

In 2007, the gap between China's national accounts-based and IO accounts-based GDP was virtually nonexistent, with the latter 0.1 percent larger than the former. At the industry level, however, the differences were more pronounced, as IO statisticians do not fully rely on national accounts data but also conduct their own surveys in making their best judgment. For example, the IO account-based financial value-added was 9 percent larger than that in the national accounts, wholesale/retail VA was 17 percent smaller, and accommodation/catering VA was basically the same.[1] Some of the differences were the result of the second economic census revisions, which the IO tables were not subject to, but some were due to different choices made by separate national accounts and IO accounts teams.

In the benchmark IO account "Use Tables," a breakdown of intermediate inputs and four income-approach value-added components for 42 categories—at the more detailed industry level for the secondary sector and the subsector level for the tertiary sector—as well as their gross output values are provided. The variance in the level of disaggregation is a legacy of China's past focus on material production accounting and the relative immaturity of its measuring services.

Although IO accounting is not exactly the same as GDP accounting—for instance, they treat tariff revenues, insurance services, and waste good processing services differently—the value-added ratios it provides are usable and valuable. NBS does not publish such ratio data elsewhere. Statistics for all the eight service subsectors we selected are available.

---

1. NBS, *2007 Input-Output Tables of China* (Beijing: China Statistics Press, 2009), 11, 46–47.

something statisticians would use as the basis to adjust GDP. On the contrary, the aggregate numbers in China's IO accounts, such as the overall GDP, are fit to comport with national accounts—the reverse of how the IO accounts are used in advanced economies. Therefore, one of the most valuable parts of the 2007 IO accounts is the implied economic structure, which is measured by the relative size between different industries (in the secondary sector's case) and subsectors (in tertiary sector's case), and each subsector's or industry's ratio of VA to gross output—rather than the absolute size of them—which is provided in the "Use Tables" (see Textbox 3.3).

In accordance with the NBS national accounts manual, we extrapolated gross output value for all the industries by using economic census data on operating revenue, costs, employment, and fiscal budget expenditures.[103]

---

103. For subsectors filled with small entities, such as wholesale/retail and accommodation/catering services, our extrapolated gross output value figures include gross output not just from enterprises but from

Table 3.24. Recalculations of Tertiary VA Based on IO Tables Data

Unit: RMB billion

2008	VA/GOV% in 2007 IO Tables	VA (Official)	VA (recl.)	Recl./Official %
Transport, Storage, and Postal Services	46.2%	1,636.3	1,511.9	92.4%
Information Transmission, Computer Services, and Software	60.0%	786.0	907.2	115.4%
Wholesale and Retail Trade	60.1%	2,618.2	3,195.2	122.0%
Accommodation and Catering Services	37.6%	661.6	779.8	117.9%
Finance	68.9%	1,486.3	1,487.5	100.1%
Real Estate	83.4%	1,473.9	976.7	66.3%
Education	56.0%	888.7	825.2	92.9%
Public Administration and Social Organizations	54.9%	1,378.4	1,583.7	114.9%
Sum of Eight Subsectors		*10,929.4*	*11,267.2*	*103.1%*

Sources: NBS, authors' calculations.

Table 3.24 summarizes our reestimates from this IO account value-added ratio approach. The sum of the recalculated VA was 3.1 percent bigger than official figures—a fairly small margin that could be explained by institutional differences between IO accounts and national accounts. Differentials at the subsector level are more pronounced. Because we relied heavily on national official data to compile these new figures, the results cannot effectively stress-test the quality of original VA data. The recalculations, consequently, are a comparator for reference, not a substitute.

A Value-Added and Proxy Growth Approach In this approach, we examined the relationship between national accounts data and real-economy indicators and the year-on-year consistency of these statistics. These techniques are also used by NBS. In general we used 2007 official VA data for the aforementioned eight service subsectors and multiplied them, subsector by subsector, by estimates of nominal VA growth rates extrapolated from a variety of real-economy indicators to see whether the derived results align with 2008 official VA figures. The resulting "proxy" calculations are not entirely "independent"

---

smaller entities including self-employed businesses as well as operations categorized into non-wholesale/retail or non-accommodation/catering subsectors. For subsectors such as transportation, storage, and postal services, the revenue data in the yearbook already cover the entire sector, so we did not need to extrapolate for the omitted entities. To be more specific, for certain industries such as information transmission, the revenue data in the NBS economic census yearbook cover enterprises only, excluding unincorporated entities; data on self-employed businesses do not allow us to extrapolate the gross output for them as we did for subsectors such as accommodation/catering. The impact of this decision is quantitatively unclear. On the one hand, leaving out self-employed business VA can understate the gross output value for a subsector, albeit by a small margin; on the other hand, our extrapolated VA for such small businesses in other subsectors may have been bigger than what NBS captured, because we used enterprises' revenue per capita as a substitute for output per capita at unincorporated businesses. The impact of these two factors would mitigate the effect of each other. Nevertheless, we think the net overall impact would be small, because such extrapolation involved unincorporated entities only.

because the base data are from official national accounts. However, this extrapolation offers important insights into NBS methods and data sourcing.

If our extrapolation of tertiary VA, starting with official statistics for the previous year and increased based on real-world indicators, does not comport with officially reported VA, then we have identified a reason for concern with this component of China's reported GDP. Conversely, if our imputed VA based on real-economy indictors is highly consistent with official VA, it suggests that officials may also be using these real-economy proxies, *rather than* (incomplete and likely flawed) *primary source data from firms* to calculate tertiary GDP. In the latter scenario, if past tertiary VA were understated, tertiary understatement going forward is likely to be systemic. If officials start with prior-year nominal VA and then use current-year real-economy proxies to extrapolate current-year VA, then any prior underestimation will just be carried forward (whereas if direct VA observations were made at the firm level, and the quality of measurement improved, this systemic bias would disappear). In fact, this is exactly what our recalculation model suggests.

Value-added data for 2007 in our eight subsectors were made public in the NBS statistical yearbook. Except for transportation, storage, and postal services, we used these official VA figures and conducted recalculations at the subsector level. For the transportation subsector we broke down the official VA figure by industry based on our bottom-up calculations for the share of each in total subsector activity. We then conducted the recalculation at the industry level and added them up to the subsector level. We did this because the broad transportation subsector includes nine industries, each with unique fundamental data profiles.[104]

The next step was to select real-economy value and volume measures that correlate well with subsector value-added. Some obvious choices are gross output and revenue; these are the essential figures from which value-added is derived. More narrow options focus on industry-specific data, like passenger transport turnover, or other flows among government, firms, and consumers such as household consumption expenditures, labor remuneration, insurance premiums, income taxes, and fiscal budget expenditures. We chose measures based on the suggestions in the NBS national accounts manual, which explains how the Bureau compiles and extrapolates VA in noncensus years. For some of the variables we chose, we tested statistical correlations with subsector VA and provide those details for the reader in the cross-country-comparison section. We selected variables understood to be reliable based on official and academic accounts; indicators seen as distorted, such as freight transport turnover, were avoided whenever possible.

The third step was to calculate nominal growth rates for selected real-economy indicators. Because such indicators describe different aspects of a sector's performance, for each service industry we took a simple average of growth rates across a set of proxies. For each subsector we took a weighted average of constituent industries' growth rates to compute

---

104. An underlying assumption here is that our bottom-up recalculations for 2008 reflect the proper share of each of the industries in the broader transportation subsector. Given that our bottom-up recalculation for transportation was 90 percent of the official figure, as described in the first approach, we believe that was a reasonable assumption.

Table 3.25. Real-Economy Proxies Used for Tertiary VA Growth Estimates

	Proxy 1	Proxy 2	Proxy 3	Proxy 4
Transport, Storage, and Postal Services				
Railway Transport	Industry Passenger Turnover*	National Railway: Sum of Operating Income and Net Income from Nonprincipal Business	Total Logistics Value	Industry Labor Remuneration
Road Transport	Industry Passenger Turnover	Total Logistics Value	Industrial Sales Value	Industry Labor Remuneration
Urban Public Transport	Industry Passenger Turnover	Shenyang: Urban Public Transport GOV	# of For-Hire Vehicles	Industry Labor Remuneration
Water Transport	Industry Passenger Turnover	Total Logistics Value	Total Freight Throughput (Coastal & River Ports)	Industry Labor Remuneration
Air Transport	Industry Passenger Turnover	Total Logistics Value	Air: Freight Turnover	Industry Labor Remuneration
Pipeline Transport	Pipeline Freight Volume	Pipeline Freight Turnover	Shenyang: Pipeline Transport GOV	Industry Labor Remuneration
Loading, Unloading and Other Transport Services	Industrial Sales Value	Total Logistics Value	Industry Value-Added†	Industry Labor Remuneration
Warehousing and Storage	Industry Value-Added†	Total Logistics Value	Total Freight Throughput (Coastal & River Ports)	Industry Labor Remuneration
Postal Service	Gross Value of Postal Services	Revenue Growth of Postal Services and Above-Threshold Delivery Enterprises‡	Total Logistics Value	Industry Labor Remuneration
Information Transmission, Computer Services, and Software				
Telecommunication and Other Information Transmission	Industry Business Revenue	Length of Long-Distance Calls (Fixed and Mobile Telephone)	Telecom Fixed Asset Investment	Industry Business Volume
Computer Services	Operating Revenue			
Software	Industry Sales Revenue	Industry # of Enterprises		
Wholesale and Retail Trade				
Wholesale Trade	Industrial Sales Value	Estimate of Gross Revenue Less COGS (Above-Threshold Firms)	Gross Value of Exports and Imports	Household Final Consumption
Retail Trade	Industrial Sales Value	Estimate of Gross Revenue Less COGS (Above-Threshold Firms)	Retail Sales of Consumer Goods	Household Final Consumption

(continued)

Table 3.25 (continued)

	Proxy 1	Proxy 2	Proxy 3	Proxy 4
Accommodation and Catering Services				
Accommodation Services	Industry Gross Operating Revenue	Consumption p.c. on Recreation, Edu, Cultural Service, Dining-Out (National Avg)	Disposable Income Per Capita (National Average)	Industry Labor Remuneration
Catering Services	Industry Gross Operating Revenue	Consumption p.c. on Recreation, Edu, Cultural Service, Dining-Out (National Avg)	Disposable Income Per Capita (National Average)	Industry Labor Remuneration
Finance				
Banking	Fin. Institution Total Loan	Banking Industry After-Tax Profit	Fin. Institution Total Deposits	M2 growth[§]
Securities	Industry Gross Revenue[l]	Turnover of Stock Trading	Turnover of Bond Trading	Turnover of Futures Trading
Insurance	Total Household Exp. on Insurance Services	Insurance Companies: Insurance Premium Less Indemnity	Insurance Companies: Balance of Fund Use	Total Insurance Company Assets
Real Estate	Estimate of Real Estate GOV			
Education	Total Educational Expenditures	Total # of Students Enrolled at Schools	Total Enrollment of Technical Schools	
Public Administration and Social Organizations	Final National Fiscal Expenditures[¶]	Extra-Budgetary Expenditures		

* Passenger turnover is measured in passenger-kilometer; freight turnover is in ton-kilometer.

[†] China Federation of Logistics & Purchasing.

[‡] China Post, 2009.

[§] 货币供应量与 GDP 总值的比例，应与银行中介服务的规模同向变动 (Goldsmith, 1983).

[l] China Securities Industry Association.

[¶] Ministry of Finance; 全国预算单位基本支出决算明细表及全国预算单位项目支出决算明细表中一般公共服务、外交、国防、公共安全、城乡社区事务等五项支出合计。

Sources: NBS, CEIC, authors' estimates based on official records, documents, and academic work.

Table 3.26. Recalculations of Tertiary VA Based on Real-Economy Proxy Growth

Unit: RMB billion

	2007 VA (Official)	2008 Nominal VA Growth (Imputed)	2008 VA (Official)	2008 VA (recl.)	2008 Recl./ Official %
Transport, Storage, and Postal Services	1,460.1	16.3%	1,636.3	1,697.6	103.7%
Information Transmission, Computer Services, and Software	670.6	28.7%	786.0	862.7	109.8%
Wholesale and Retail Trade	2,093.8	17.0%	2,618.2	2,450.1	93.6%
Accommodation and Catering Services	554.8	15.7%	661.6	642.1	97.1%
Finance	1,233.8	19.3%	1,486.3	1,471.9	99.0%
Real Estate	1,381.0	25.0%	1,473.9	1,726.2	117.1%
Education	769.3	9.3%	888.7	841.0	94.6%
Public Administration and Social Organizations	1,083.0	14.6%	1,378.4	1,241.4	90.1%
Sum of Eight Subsectors	*9,246.4*		*10,929.4*	*10,933*	*100.0%*

Sources: NBS, authors' calculations.

2008 overall growth, except in the cases of information transmission, computer services, and software; real estate; and public administration and social organizations, where reference weights were not available (see details in Appendix 3.1).

Table 3.25 summarizes the alternative value and volume measures we selected for each industry or subsector. The extrapolated nominal VA growth for each subsector and the subsequently computed 2008 VA—in comparison with the official 2008 figures—are listed in Table 3.26.

At the aggregate level, our VA estimate for these eight service subsectors is almost perfectly in line with the official figure, while the fit *within* the subsectors varies considerably. Our real estate VA estimate is much higher than official figures, presumably because the proxy we selected focused on real estate gross output value rather than the share of value-added. In the financial crisis trough year of 2008, the value-added ratio of property market activity likely took a severe hit. For the subsector of public administration and social organizations, we focused on budgetary and nonbudgetary expenditure numbers in the official records, without considering the expenditures and revenues from their side businesses—which could have grown faster than their principal business—so our approximation may not accurately capture the reality. Having said that, the similarity between our calculations and official VA at the aggregate level suggests a "systemic distortion" such as what we anticipated above: distortions in tertiary VA are likely not a single-year problem but a long-term one. If NBS had indeed used a set of proxies similar to our selection to compute and review year-on-year VA growth, the nominal VA numbers would appear compatible over the years because the previous year's number is the base to compute the next year's, and thus inaccuracy present in the previous year's figure would be carried over. The cross-year concordance we observed suggests a systemic distortion in tertiary VA and points to the need to employ methods independent of China's historical VA data to come up with meaningful alternative estimates. That is why we later used a cross-country comparison approach to impute VA for two important subsectors that lacked basic data: wholesale/retail and accommodation/catering services.

A Labor Wage and Productivity Approach The fourth approach to reestimating tertiary VA is based on labor productivity concepts. An assumption made for this approach is that in 2008, each service industry's wages per worker grew at the same pace as the industry's productivity—measured by value-added per capita. As a corollary to that, we assumed that labor remuneration as a share of each industry's VA remained unchanged from 2007 to 2008. With that leap, once we are able to compute the nominal growth of an industry's total wages—wage growth multiplied by employment growth—we can extrapolate its VA growth in 2008 (Textbox 3.4).

For urban and township entities (*chengzhen danwei*), employment data are broken down to the industry level; for private enterprises and self-employed businesses, data are only available at a subsector level that is less comprehensive than in national accounts. For the tertiary sector, only five subsectors have such private entity data: transportation, storage, and postal services; wholesale/retail; accommodation/catering; leasing and business services; and residential care and repair services. As an economic census measurement year, 2008 had richer employment data, but to calculate nominal VA growth we would need comparable data series for 2007 *and* 2008 that comport with the wage data categories described in Textbox 3.4, so we had to work with this incomplete set of subsector data.

For the first three subsectors that had employment data for both urban and township entities and private enterprises, we added up the two arrays of employment data and treated the aggregate as the total employment for the subsector; then we disaggregated the private enterprise and self-employed business data for the subsector to the industry level, according to the industries' respective shares in urban and township entity employment in that subsector. For the five other service subsectors we selected for VA recalculations that did not have employment data for private enterprises and self-employed businesses, we assumed that the growth of employment at urban and township entities represented the growth for the entire subsector.

We averaged urban private and nonprivate enterprise wages multiplied by subsector employment to compute total wages, and thus to extrapolate nominal VA growth. To continue on that path, we made two assumptions. First, for private enterprises, lacking 2007 per capita wage data, we used the 2008–2009 wage growth as a proxy to retrospectively extrapolate 2007 per capita wage; second, we assumed the growth of per capita cash wage was equal to that of total compensation, hence productivity and value-added per worker (Table 3.27).

Applying growth in value-added per worker to the employment growth in each subsector, we calculate nominal VA growth for the subsector. Table 3.28 summarizes VA

Textbox 3.4. China's Employment and Wage Data Publication

The employment and wage data that China publishes are not straightforward. For employment, China publishes by-industry figures for "urban and township entities" (*chengzhen danwei*), which do not include private enterprise and self-employed workers. The coverage of urban and township entities is quite broad: from an ownership perspective, it includes state-owned entities; urban and township collective–owned entities; "other" entities, such as shareholding entities, joint-owned entities, limited liability companies, and shareholding companies; and foreign-, Hong Kong–, Macau-, and Taiwan-invested entities.[1] Institutions covered include enterprises, public welfare organizations, and government offices.[2] The employment at urban and township entities is defined as those working and being paid by the entities, excluding those who have left the entities but still maintain a contracted employment relationship, such as pensioners or workers on paid furlough, interns, and outside workers whom the entities outsource to.[3]

China also publishes by-subsector data for private enterprises and self-employed businesses, which cover entities that locate in both urban and rural areas.[4] A separate data series on rural workers is not published; if rural residents work at an urban/township private enterprise or if they run their own businesses at or above the county capital level, then in theory their employment is included in the data described above.

For wage data, the series that corresponds to the employment data above is "average wage for employees at urban and township entities." Starting in 2008, NBS began releasing per capita wage data for urban private enterprises, which still did not include rural entities. NBS does not have composite wage data for all the urban entities including both the aforementioned urban and township entities as well as urban enterprises.[5] According to the NBS yearbook, the per capita wage here includes only cash wages, excluding benefits.

---

1. NBS, "Employment and Wages: Explanatory Notes on Main Statistical Indicators," in *2004 China Statistical Yearbook* (China Statistics Press, 2004), http://www.stats.gov.cn/tjsj/ndsj/yb2004-c/html/5i.htm.

2. NBS, 2009 *Statistical Yearbook*, http://www.stats.gov.cn/tjsj/ndsj/2009/indexch.htm.

3. NBS, "指标解释: 就业人员和工资 (Explanation of Terms: Employment and Wages)," October 29, 2013, http://www.stats.gov.cn/tjsj/zbjs/201310/t20131029_449543.html.

4. NBS publishes a separate series on urban and township private enterprises and self-employed businesses. See NBS's online database for details.

5. NBS, "常见问题解答: 人口和就业统计 (Frequently Asked Questions: Population and Employment Statistics)," January 13, 2015, http://www.stats.gov.cn/tjzs/cjwtjd/201308/t20130829_74322.html.

Table 3.27. Extrapolation for Nominal Growth of VA per Worker

Unit: RMB

	Average Wage per Worker		2008/2007 Ratio	Growth of VA per Worker
	2007	2008		
Transport, Storage, and Postal Services	22,005	24,912	1.13	13.2%
Information Transmission, Computer Services, and Software	36,171	40,626	1.12	12.3%
Wholesale and Retail Trade	18,489	21,316	1.15	15.3%
Accommodation and Catering Services	15,195	16,880	1.11	11.1%
Finance	30,387	38,245	1.26	25.9%
Real Estate	21,944	24,804	1.13	13.0%
Education	21,955	24,653	1.12	12.3%
Public Administration and Social Organizations	17,080	19,892	1.17	16.5%

Sources: NBS, CEIC, authors' calculations.

Table 3.28. Recalculations of Tertiary VA Based on Employment and Wage Data

Unit: RMB billion

	2007 VA (Official)	2008 Nominal VA Growth (Imputed)	2008 VA (Official)	2008 VA (recl.)	2008 Recl./ Official %
Transport, Storage, and Postal Services*	1,460.1	14.5%	1,636.3	1,710.9	104.6%
Information Transmission, Computer Services, and Software	670.6	19.3%	786.0	799.8	101.8%
Wholesale and Retail Trade	2,093.8	24.5%	2,618.2	2,605.8	99.5%
Accommodation and Catering Services	554.8	18.5%	661.6	657.7	99.4%
Finance	1,233.8	34.9%	1,486.3	1,664.0	112.0%
Real Estate	1,381.0	17.2%	1,473.9	1,619.0	109.8%
Education	769.3	13.3%	888.7	871.3	98.0%
Public Administration and Social Organizations	1,083.0	20.4%	1,378.4	1,304.1	94.6%
Sum of Eight Subsectors	9,246.4		10,929.4	11,232.6	102.8%

* For "transportation, storage, and postal services," because its aggregate VA was added up from the industry level, the result is slightly bigger than what is derived from directly multiplying 2007 official VA with our imputed 2008 subsector nominal growth. The difference is about +2.4 percent.

Sources: NBS, CEIC, authors' calculations.

reestimates for the eight subsectors based on this method. The aggregate VA we calculated for the eight subsectors turned out to be 2.8 percent higher than official claims, consistent with our estimates using the gross output and value-added ratio approaches.

A Census Labor Remuneration Approach The fifth and final approach we used to evaluate China's 2008 tertiary VA was to leverage 2004 *Economic Census* data, based on the assumption that the share of labor remuneration of GDP remained relatively constant in the subsectors of interest from 2004 to 2008 (Textbox 3.5).

As introduced in Textbox 3.5, the five subsectors' labor remuneration data in 2004 had to be adjusted before it could be used for our 2008 recalculation due to the definition change. Considering the significant distortion that change is likely to present for wholesale/retail/catering services—where unincorporated entities are most concentrated

---

Textbox 3.5. China's Labor Remuneration Data: Scope Changes and Our Adjustment

After the 2004 census, NBS retrospectively revised China's national accounts data and in 2007 published a comprehensive collection of historical national accounts information called the *Historical Materials for Chinese Gross Domestic Product Accounting 1952–2004*. In it, NBS included labor remuneration data, broken down by subsector, for all provincial and provincial-level regions, as well as for the entire country. With that information one can compute the share of labor remuneration in each subsector's value-added.

However, the way the tertiary labor remuneration data was disaggregated is not how NBS does it today. The classifications for the five available subsectors are transportation, storage, postal, and telecom services; wholesale/retail/catering services; financial and insurance;[1] real estate; and other services. Another factor that reduced the direct comparability of 2004 and 2008 data was that, after the 2004 census, NBS made a critical definitional change to labor remuneration.

Before the census, all "mixed income" for self-employed workers was counted as labor remuneration. Mixed income, according to 2008 SNA, describes the part of income for unincorporated enterprises in which labor remuneration to the business owner or the operating household cannot be identified separately from the operating return to the owner as entrepreneur.[2] After the 2004 census, in an effort to align China's national accounts practice with 1993 SNA, NBS started classifying mixed income into operating surplus, while only counting the explicit compensation to employees as self-employed businesses' labor remuneration.[3] However, during the 2008 census, to better reflect actual labor remuneration of self-employed businesses,

NBS decided to separate the labor remuneration portion of mixed income from the remaining operating surplus. To make that happen, NBS used the ratios of labor remuneration to operating surplus for similar-scale enterprises in the same industry for references in lieu of solid basic data. After that change, they went back to revise the historical data for 2004–2007 to make the data series comparable.[4]

Because the 1952–2004 historical accounts were published in 2007, prior to the 2008 change, the labor remuneration data still followed the old definition. That diminished the accounts' value to us because the labor remuneration shares of VA by subsector are not perfectly suited to what we wanted to impute. To make it more difficult, NBS has not published tertiary labor remuneration data *since* the 2008 change, so we did not have up-to-date compensation data. A workaround we came up with was to use the pre- and postchange national labor remuneration data and its respective shares of overall GDP to extrapolate the share change in the tertiary sector.

Based on the 1952–2004 historical accounts, we concluded that for the entire economy the share of labor remuneration in 2004 was 41.6 percent. This result was computed by summing regional data, rather than by relying on national data. We then used regional national accounts data to calculate the national labor remuneration share in 2008 and 2004, and computed the difference between 2004 national wage shares under the new and old definitions. Assuming that the 2008 definitional change affected the whole-economy and tertiary-sector labor remuneration proportionately, we retrospectively computed 2004 tertiary labor remuneration at 43.4 percent of tertiary VA, compared to 36.3 percent under the old definition. This is consistent with what NBS said about the update: classifying part of mixed income into labor remuneration should enhance the share of labor remuneration in both the tertiary sector and the overall economy. What our imputation suggests is that with a same-size service economy, the definitional change would enhance the 2004 labor remuneration level by about 1.2 times. We used this number as a "labor remuneration share adjuster" to complete our recalculation for 2008 tertiary value-added.

1. The original Chinese for this subsector was 金融保险业. It is unclear why insurance was separated from finance in the title for the subsector, especially because insurance was part of the financial subsector in the 2002 version of industrial classification.

2. UN, "Updated System of National Accounts (SNA): Chapter 7: The Distribution of Income Accounts" (United Nations, February 2008), 4, http://unstats.un.org/unsd/statcom/doc08/SNA-Chapter7.pdf.

3. Xu, "(Several Issues)."

4. Ibid.

Table 3.29. VA Revision for Transport, Storage, and Postal Services

Unit: RMB billion

Year	Labor Remuneration	Value-Added
	Official	
2004	221.60	930.44
2008		1,636.25
	Recalculations	
2008	686.87	2,403.34
	Recl./Official %	
2008		147%

Sources: NBS, *Economic Census* database, authors' calculations.

and our "adjuster" for the overall tertiary sector may not accurately reflect the impact to this specific subsector—as well as dramatic changes in the financial subsector from 2004 to 2008, we decided to apply this wage-based approach only to real estate and transportation, storage, and postal services.

For transportation, because labor remuneration data were mixed with telecoms in the 1995–2004 collection, we first used 2004 census data to separate them. Then, based on the 1.2 × labor remuneration share adjuster and our own calculation for subsector labor remuneration for 2008 from the *Economic Census* database, we extrapolated 2008 value-added (Table 3.29). Our revision of VA for the subsector came out at 1.5 times official estimates.

For the real estate subsector, the share of unincorporated entities was much lower than in other subsectors because property developers and property management companies contribute the majority of value-added. Considering the minimal scale of self-employed businesses in this subsector, we did not apply the 1.2 × "adjuster" when recalculating 2008 value-added (Table 3.30). Our revision wound up a quarter higher than the official reading.

There is a third subsector that this 2004 labor remuneration ratio approach could apply to: public administration and social organizations. Following the first economic census, NBS published financial data for administrative units (*xingzheng shiye danwei*) in each tertiary subsector, including gross revenue and gross expenditures, which included spending on wage and employee benefits. For most tertiary subsectors, the abundance of enterprises not counted as administrative units means that NBS's financial data cover only a small slice of the total. However, for public administration and social organizations—consisting of Communist Party organs, state government offices, organizations of other political parties

Table 3.30. VA Recalculation for Real Estate

Unit: RMB billion

Year	Labor Remuneration	Value-Added
	Official	
2004	80.16	717.41
2008		1,473.87
	Recalculations	
2008	206.22	1,845.56
	Recl./Official %	
2008		125%

Sources: NBS, *Economic Census* database, authors' calculations.

Table 3.31. VA Recalculation for Public Administration and Social Organizations

Unit: RMB billion

Year	Labor Remuneration	Value-Added
	Official	
2004	480.07	614.14
2008		1,378.37
	Recalculations	
2008	937.12	1,534.52
	Recl./Official %	
2008		111%

Sources: NBS, *Economic Census* database, Wang Xiaolu (2010), authors' calculations.

and the political consultative committee, social organizations, and "grassroots" public autonomous organizations—we believed an overwhelming majority of the value-added and labor remuneration was captured in NBS administrative-unit data. Based on the 2004 *Economic Census* accounting manual, we calculated the subsector's 2004 labor remuneration and extrapolated the 2008 VA shown in Table 3.31. Because unincorporated businesses were at most a trivial part of this subsector, we did not apply the 1.2 × labor remuneration share adjuster to our recalculation but rather factored in an approximate amount of "gray income" earned by employees at entities that were not accurately recorded by statistical authorities.

For well-known, if hard to talk about reasons, a sound estimate on the share of "gray income" for China's public officers and social workers is lacking. Our basis for extrapolation was the renowned study on Chinese gray income by scholar Wang Xiaolu. In his study for the year 2008, households categorized into seven income levels would earn gray income ranging from 0.9 to 218.7 percent of their officially reported income.[105] We took the scale of gray income for middle-ranked households as a proxy and thus inferred additional gray income equal to 28 percent of the officially recorded income. Multiplying this new total-to-reported-income adjuster of 1.28 by the subsector's labor remuneration value provided by the second economic census to compute "actual" total compensation, and then leveraging the 2004 labor remuneration ratio to extrapolate an alternative figure for 2008, we arrived at subsector VA 11 percent greater than officially reported for that year (see Table 3.31).

CROSS-COUNTRY COMPARISONS

Just as China's NBS uses different approaches for GDP estimates of primary and secondary sectors, for the tertiary sector we resorted to an alternative measure to supplement our previous reestimations relying on official aggregate data, due to the paucity of basic data needed for value-added calculations in the available database. Small and unincorporated self-employed businesses are particularly underreported in the wholesale/retail and accommodation/catering subsectors, despite playing a major role. We therefore turned to international growth patterns and applied a cross-country comparison approach to reevaluate portions of the Chinese economy. This approach refers to a group of countries with economic development levels and industrial structures comparable to China's to infer value-added for the two aforementioned Chinese subsectors.

Cross-country comparison is commonly used in a variety of areas for academic research and economic analysis. In international trade, both the European Union and the U.S. Department of Commerce use "surrogate" country data to determine tariffs imposed on imported goods deemed below market prices in antidumping investigations from countries perceived to offer inadequate production cost data. In finance, investment bankers often refer to known data for firms similar to an opaque enterprise they are evaluating. In the realm of GDP, enormous comparative studies have been done on Asian countries' rapid growth and their economic structures.

Analyses relying on cross-country comparisons of economies with questionable data are common in the international economic literature, including studies on China. Perkins grouped Asian economies and compared their growth trajectories to anticipate stable macroeconomic paths for China.[106] Jiang Xiaojuan and Li Hui, two economists from the Chinese Academy of Social Sciences (CASS), compared Chinese tertiary share of GDP and employment to a selection of lower-middle-income countries in 2002 and found China at the bottom tier of the lower-middle-income sample.[107] Another CASS working paper

---

105. Xiaolu Wang, "Gray Income and National Income Distribution," *Comparative Studies* 48, no. 3 (June 2010): 13, http://www.caing.com/upload/20100903/huiseshouru.pdf.

106. Dwight H. Perkins, "Rapid Growth and Changing Economic Structure: The Expenditure Side Story and Its Implications for China," *China Economic Review*, Special Issue: CES 2010 & Special Issue: SBICCI, 23, no. 3 (September 2012): 502–503, http://www.sciencedirect.com/science/article/pii/S1043951X10001008.

107. Xiaojuan Jiang and Hui Li, "服务业与中国经济: 相关性和加快增长的潜力 (Tertiary Sector and China's Economy: Correlation and Potential for Accelerating Growth)," *Economic Research Journal*, no. 1 (2004): 5, 9–10. China was categorized as a lower-income country by the World Bank in 1996–1997.

mentioned a cross-country comparison approach for estimating the tertiary sector share of GDP.[108] Using a world sample and a low-income country sample for 1996, they regressed the tertiary sector share of GDP on GDP per capita across countries. Based on the regression coefficients and China's GDP per capita in 1996, they estimated China's tertiary share of GDP to be 46 to 47 percent, depending on which sample was used,[109] 17 to 18 percentage points higher than official claims. Qian and Bai's essay that compared tertiary sector activity in China and India and Li Xin's study that restated China's tertiary GDP share by performing a regression using GDP data of more than 180 countries both fit into this school of studies.

While most previous studies have focused on the share of the tertiary sector as a whole, few have focused on the levels of specific subsectors' value-added. In light of the above studies, we decided to go with a more granular approach and apply this analysis just to subsectors with reasonable homogeneity across countries, as explained below. We also grouped countries in a more prudent manner to avoid the pitfalls of some previous efforts.

Summary of Methodology

The service subsectors we chose for cross-country comparison are wholesale/retail trade[110] and accommodation/catering services. We chose them for three reasons. First, both are major components of China's tertiary sector; according to official 2008 data—prior to 2013 census revisions—wholesale/retail trade accounted for 8.3 percent of GDP and 19.9 percent of total service VA, while accommodation/catering was 2.1 percent and 5 percent, respectively (Table 3.32). Second, these two subsectors are where China's self-employed businesses are predominantly concentrated. In 2008, of the 28.7 million licensed unincorporated operations across the country, 54 percent were wholesale/retail businesses, and 8 percent were in accommodation/catering.[111] In 2013, the third economic census found that the two shares declined only slightly to 50 percent and 7 percent, respectively.[112] With such a high concentration of self-employed businesses and a lack of basic noncensus year data, there is good reason for concern about various distortions in figures for these subsectors. Third, wholesale/retail and accommodation/catering are often considered "fundamental" economic activity. They grow in the early stages of economic development, serve the basic needs of consumers, are labor-intensive, require modest skills and technology, and

---

108. Shuguang Zhang et al., "核算性扭曲、结构性通缩与制度性障碍——当前中国宏观经济分析 (Distortion in National Accounts, Structural Deflation and Institutional Barriers: An Analysis of China's Current Macroeconomic Situation)," *Economic Research Journal*, no. 9 (2000): 12, http://jjyj.cbpt.cnki.net/WKB2/WebPublication /paperDigest.aspx?paperID=644BB304-FCB7-462D-9AE4-17C2F6DC68DE.

109. Ibid.

110. We use the terms *distributive trade* and *wholesale/retail trade* interchangeably. The OECD defines distributive trade to include motor vehicle sales, repair/maintenance, and retail sale of automotive fuel. In China's industrial classification, the wholesale/retail trade subsector includes motor vehicle trade, but it does not list it separately as an industry (rather, it is listed at a further disaggregated level). In some other countries, such as South Korea and Malaysia, motor vehicles are separated from wholesale trade and retail trade as a third subsector, due to variations in distribution channels across countries.

111. NBS, *2008 Census Yearbook*.

112. NBS, "Statistical Bulletin of Third National *Economic Census*," December 16, 2014, 8, http://www.stats .gov.cn/tjsj/zxfb/201412/P020141216347816258498.pdf.

Table 3.32. Composition of China's Service Economy in 2008

Unit: RMB billion

	GDP	% of GDP	% of Tertiary GDP
Tertiary Sector	*13,134.1*	*41.8%*	*100.0%*
Transport, Storage, and Postal Services	1,636.3	5.2%	12.5%
Information Transmission, Computer Services, and Software	786.0	2.5%	6.0%
Wholesale and Retail Trade	2,618.2	8.3%	19.9%
Accommodation and Catering Services	661.6	2.1%	5.0%
Finance	1,486.3	4.7%	11.3%
Real Estate	1,473.9	4.7%	11.2%
Leasing and Business Services	560.8	1.8%	4.3%
Scientific Research, Technical Services, and Geological Prospecting	399.3	1.3%	3.0%
Management of Water Conservancy, Environment, and Public Facilities	126.6	0.4%	1.0%
Services to Households and Other Services	462.8	1.5%	3.5%
Education	888.8	2.8%	6.8%
Health, Social Securities, and Welfare	462.9	1.5%	3.5%
Culture, Sports, and Entertainment	192.2	0.6%	1.5%
Public Administration and Social Organizations	1,378.4	4.4%	10.5%

Sources: NBS, authors' calculations.

need little government intervention. The development of such subsectors and the characteristics accompanying each development stage are often similar from country to country.

For example, of the countries we found most comparable to China in terms of development levels and general economic conditions, most reported a combined 2008 GDP share for wholesale/retail and accommodation/catering services within a narrow range: from 12.5 (South Korea) to 17.5 percent (Thailand). China's was 10.4 percent according to official accounts. Brazil, another comparator country, was the only outlier. With 79 percent of its economy attributed to consumption expenditures and a relatively small industrial subsector that accounted for less than 30 percent of GDP, Brazil's combined share from these two service subsectors was 20.3 percent in 2008.[113]

The international comparison approach is less helpful for service subsectors such as finance, education, public administration, and information transmission and computer services. In China, the financial subsector is heavily regulated by the central government, and banking is the overwhelmingly dominant constituent industry, quite different than in other countries. The education system, public administration, and social organizations that are subject to unique policies and serve political functions also vary tremendously across countries. For these industries, ownership composition plays a critical role in their development as well as economic scale, and thus their utility for cross-country comparison. In

---

113. UN, National Accounts Main Aggregates Database, http://unstats.un.org/unsd/snaama/selbasicFast.asp.

Table 3.33. State-Controlled Shares in China's Service Fixed Assets Investments

Unit: RMB billion, percentage

2008	Urban		
	Total	*State*	*State/Total %*
Transport, Storage, and Postal Services	*157.0*	138.0	87.9%
Information Transmission, Computer Services, and Software	*21.3*	13.3	62.2%
Wholesale and Retail Trade	*31.9*	4.7	14.6%
Accommodation and Catering Services	*17.4*	2.8	16.1%
Finance	*2.5*	1.8	71.9%
Real Estate	*359.1*	62.8	17.5%
Education	*23.6*	19.3	82.1%
Public Administration and Social Organizations	*32.4*	24.5	75.7%

Sources: NBS, Guo Tongxin (2010), authors' calculations.

China, fixed asset investment is dominated by state influence in certain service subsectors including transportation, finance, education, and public administration, reducing their direct comparability to other countries operated by a different political regime and with a varied market system (Table 3.33). While finance and certain transportation and telecommunication industries are controlled by state oligopolies in China, private investors dominate in the wholesale/retail and accommodation/catering subsectors. As shown in Table 3.33, the wholesale/retail and accommodation/catering subsectors had the lowest state-controlled shares in total fixed asset investment among all the service subsectors, which were 14.6 and 16.1 percent, respectively, in 2008, compared to more than 60 percent in telecoms and more than 70 percent in finance.

Transportation, for cross-country comparison purposes, is a peculiar case. On the one hand, it is considered a "fundamental" industry, as demand for transport services is universal; on the other hand, it is idiosyncratic across countries because geographical conditions and other natural endowments vary, especially for water transportation. This subsector's constituent industries—ground, railroad, air, water, pipeline transportation, and storage and logistics—vary drastically from one another, unlike other subsectors. All these factors complicated our initial attempt to reconstruct transportation VA using our cross-country comparison approach and generated distorted regression coefficients, which led to a negative VA value—an implausible result. We decided to drop this subsector and look only at wholesale/retail and accommodation/catering using this approach.

Our principal goal for this comparison methodology was to discern structural patterns in the comparator countries to make inferences about China accordingly. Toward that end, we started by selecting comparator countries and then employed the panel regression model to approximate subsector value-added for wholesale/retail and accommodation/catering.

To select comparator countries, we first considered the variety of fundamental economic indicators we would use to define *development level*—GDP per capita, catch-up

Table 3.34. Comparator Countries and Their Most Comparable Years to 2008's China

	GDP per Capita*	GDP Growth %	Start of Rapid Growth	Peak Decade Growth	I/C%, I/S%[†]	Antidumping Surrogate
China	**2008**	**2008**	**1978**	**2000–2008**	**2008**	
Brazil	2005	1969	1968	1970–1979	1975	Yes
Indonesia	2011	1973	1967	1970–1979	2012	Yes
Japan[‡]	1964	1962	1950	1961–1969	1961	Yes
Malaysia	1995	1991	1959	1970–1979	1995–1997	Yes
Philippines	2011	1973	1973	1970–1979	1976–1979	Yes
South Korea	1985	1991	1963	1970–1989	1991	No
Thailand	2004	1987	1957	1980–1989	1991–1996	Yes
Turkey	1988	1987	1981	1980–1989	1986–1988	No

* In PPP terms.

† I/C% is defined as gross capital formation/final consumption expenditures; I/S% is gross capital formation/tertiary VA.

‡ Because our initial screening covers a broad time span, Japan in the 1960s matches our criteria. Also, Japan is frequently used by both the EU and Latin American countries as China's surrogate in antidumping investigations. In addition, our regression results suggested that VA estimates for wholesale/retail and accommodation/catering and implied revisions to headline GDP, if excluding Japan from our sample, would not deviate significantly from using the full sample.

Sources: Penn World Table, World Bank, UN, Perkins (2012), U.S. Department of Commerce, EU Commission, authors' calculations.

growth patterns, and secondary and tertiary GDP share in the economy; we also looked at the comparator choices used in the U.S., European, and Latin American antidumping investigations aimed at China. Based on this review, we selected eight comparator economies for our assessment: Japan, South Korea, Malaysia, Indonesia, the Philippines, Thailand, Brazil, and Turkey (Table 3.34). Next, we selected 2006 to 2010 as the time series for our regression model, two years before and after 2008—our reconstruction year. For comparator economies that are at a more advanced development stage than China is today, using older period data would be more ideal; however, due to limited data availability and accounting methodology changes from previous years, we chose to focus on the same years for all eight comparator countries. Then, we performed our calculations using data aligned with both market exchange rates and purchasing power parity conversion rates, an essential step before running the regressions. After obtaining the final VA estimates for the two Chinese subsectors, we converted the values back to nominal RMB terms.

Results and Analysis

Our results suggest that value-added for China's wholesale/retail and accommodation/catering subsectors were higher than official claims in 2008. In our model, we computed VA figures based on both market exchange rates and PPP conversion rates, but we chose the PPP-based estimates for our final restatements because they offer an appropriate way to reduce distortions caused by exchange rate fluctuations and price differentials among countries, especially for nontradable services. The regression estimates here are directionally aligned with our previous recalculations based on Chinese national accounts data. More importantly, the reestimates from this approach are independent from China's previous-year national

Table 3.35. VA Recalculations for Two Service Subsectors

Unit: RMB trillion, percentage

2008	Wholesale/Retail	Accom/Catering
Value-Added (Official)	2.62	0.66
Value-Added (Recl.)	**3.04**	**0.70**
Market exchange rate-based		
Value-Added (Recl.)	5.00	0.80
Recl./Official %	190.8%	121.2%
PPP-based		
Value-Added (Recl.)	3.04	0.70
Recl./Official %	116.1%	105.7%

Sources: NBS, authors' calculations.

production/income accounts data. Hence, whatever bias there might be was not "carried over" in our 2008 restatements. Based on our PPP-based regression results, wholesale/retail value-added in 2008 was 16.1 percent higher than officially reported, while accommodation/catering VA was 5.7 percent larger (Table 3.35). In our final revisions to the entire Chinese economy, the combined GDP share for these two subsectors rose slightly.

Although we have constructed our regression model carefully, we treat these reestimates with caution. First, because our comparators are developing countries, the reliability of their data is less than ideal. Second, China's economic development patterns may be an outlier from global norms, making cross-country comparisons less valid. We discuss these points further below, and in Appendixes 3.3 and 3.4. Assuming the validity of our findings, there are two possible explanations for China's official VA being lower than cross-country regression estimates suggest it should be: China's official numbers may have understated the true size of the subsectors at hand, or value-added in China's wholesale/retail trade and accommodation/catering services may be inherently lower than elsewhere. Below we hypothesize why value-added levels in China would be low, taking wholesale/retail as an example to look at our results in depth. We also consider data issues as well as heterogeneous industry dynamics between China and comparator countries. We need to rule out these hypotheses if we are to embrace the view that China's statistics are understating the size of these two subsectors.

Wholesale/Retail Trade

For both subsectors, we extrapolated 2008 value-added using the observed relationships between subsector VA and real economy variables. Combing through subsector-specific variables, we established correlation tests, confirmed data availability in comparator countries, and finally settled on three indicators for each subsector examined.

The proxy variables we used for estimating wholesale/retail VA were the gross profits for the subsector, manufacturing GOV, and household consumption expenditures.

According to the NBS national accounts manual, the subsector's gross profit is defined as total sales revenue less cost of goods sold (COGS). For distributive trade services, it is important to note that "gross profits" is more relevant to the services' value-added than "sales revenue"; the latter is commonly used in secondary industries, as we have demonstrated earlier. The reason for this differentiation is that in distributive trade, value-added is generated through the transfer of ownership rather than through production and final sales of goods. This peculiarity means a large chunk of COGS for distributive services consists of goods purchased for resale, rather than regular business costs. Consequently, it renders gross profits inherently more relevant to value-added than gross revenue. As a corollary to that, the share of COGS in gross output for distributive trade services is generally higher than for other services such as accommodation/catering.

For example, according to South Korea's 2010 *Economic Census*, the ratio of COGS to sales revenue for wholesale/retail services was more than twice that for accommodation/catering (72 and 34 percent, respectively). Because value-added describes the newly created, incremental output from production activities, gross profits work better as a proxy for value-added in the case of wholesale/retail services. Further, gross profits, as the most comprehensive profit concept, includes a number of constituent items that are also captured in value-added, such as depreciation, labor remuneration, operating surplus, and taxes. That overlap increases the reference value of gross profits as one of the proxy variables we extrapolated value-added from. The other two proxy variables, manufacturing GOV and household final consumption, were selected because they represented the upstream (i.e., manufacturers) and the downstream (i.e., consumers) of the wholesale/retail trade subsector. All of the three proxy variables stood up to our correlation tests, meaning they have demonstrated significant correlation with wholesale/retail value-added in China's case and are appropriate to be used as proxies to construct the regression equation (see Appendix 3.2).

Accommodation/Catering Services

In official accounts published prior to—and hence not reflecting—the 2013 census revisions, accommodation/catering services accounted for 2.1 percent of China's GDP in 2008 and 5 percent of tertiary value-added. Like wholesale/retail trade, accommodation/catering consists of myriad individual proprietors of an even smaller scale, which are difficult to audit. We built a similar regression model to reestimate value-added based on the structural patterns in the comparable economies, and the final projection is based on the composition of three proxy variables shown to be highly correlated with the subsector's value-added: sales revenue for hotels and restaurants, internal tourism revenue (or expenditures),[114] and aggregate household disposable income.

---

114. OECD, "Glossary of Statistical Terms—Internal Tourism Definition," November 13, 2001, http://stats.oecd.org/glossary/detail.asp?ID=1396. Internal tourism, by definition, refers to tourism activities of both residents and nonresidents (i.e., domestic visitors and inbound foreign visitors) within the economic territory of a country. In China, tourism revenue and tourism expenditures are equal in value. Most tourism data for comparator countries are taken from their respective Tourism Satellite Accounts (TSA); if either tourism revenue or expenditures are not available, the other is used as a best proxy.

Our first proxy variable was sales revenue of hotels and restaurants. In China, the time series of this data point was not officially available, so we extrapolated based on earnings from subsector enterprises above and below the designated threshold, relevant production units classified into other subsectors, and self-employed businesses. We took internal tourism revenue as a second proxy variable for VA, given the close association between accommodation/catering services and the tourism industry; tourism is often considered a major source of income for the accommodation/catering subsector.[115] A higher demand for hotels and prepared food induced by more domestic travelers and a larger influx of foreigners would likely boost the prices charged on these services, the revenue, and possibly value-added (one VA component is service providers' operating surplus). The third proxy variable we chose was aggregate disposable income.[116] We chose household disposable income as a proxy because as residents' income grows, their consumption of hotel and food services would naturally grow, too, albeit not necessarily proportionally. Household consumption is service providers' revenue, so it describes the subsector's value-added picture from another dimension.

Finally, under the market exchange rate scenario, the regression model suggested a value-added 21 percent larger than the official figure for the subsector in 2008; under the PPP scenario, the restatement of accommodation/catering VA was 5.7 percent larger. In comparison, our previous approaches relying on Chinese national accounts data set the restatements at 75 to 118 percent of official figures. Of the four estimates—exclusive of bottom-up recalculations, due to the paucity of basic data—three were below the official level, possibly the result of a previous downward bias being carried over to the next year. In light of that, the cross-country comparison-based reestimates provide us a valuable reference largely independent from previous national accounts data pollution. For our qualifications of the accommodation/catering reestimation result, details are provided in Appendix 3.4.

DWELLING SERVICES AND RENT

When NBS announced its intention to transition to the 2014 *Chinese System of National Accounts*, one important element sure to impact headline nominal GDP was a change in counting value-added (VA) derived from the housing service that home owners provide for themselves—by residing in their own homes.[117] Some may wonder why the consumption of that housing service does not occur when residents *purchase* their dwellings; according to 1993 SNA, acquisitions of dwellings (and other buildings and structures) are counted as gross fixed capital formation, just like purchases of machinery and equipment, because both types of acquired assets are expected to *provide* services and generate value in the future.[118] For machinery and equipment, the VA from their future services is captured as

---

115. Due to inconsistencies in Brazil's tourism statistics, we excluded it from the set of comparable countries for the accommodation/catering subsector. In other words, our model for accommodation/catering included a total of seven countries and spans five years from 2006 to 2010.

116. At first, we wanted to use a subcategory of that disposable income: expenditure on recreation, education, and dining out. But that data series is not available in some comparator countries and is not statistically significant in the overall regression model.

117. NBS, "Reform of National Accounts System."

118. UN, *System of National Accounts 1993* (New York: United Nations, Department of Economic and Social Affairs, 1993), 283, http://unstats.un.org/unsd/nationalaccount/sna1993.asp.

fixed asset depreciation in the income-approach formula; likewise, the value derived from own-account dwelling services needs to be imputed. This is called "imputed rent."

Unlike most other services that households produce and consume themselves, imputed rent is within the production boundary defined by the SNA because otherwise a country's GDP would be distorted by differences in the ratio of tenants to home owner–occupiers, and the comparability of GDP statistics over time and across countries would be reduced.[119] As a result, of the rent recorded in national accounts, one is actual rent paid by tenants and the other is imputed to reflect what home owner–occupiers "pay" by "selling" themselves housing services. Measuring the latter is challenging and controversial, because money is not explicitly changing hands in an observable way.

According to 2008 SNA, in lieu of real transactions taking place, the valuation of such services has "to be imputed . . . using the appropriate prices of similar goods or services sold for cash on the market."[120] In the case of imputed rent, that "appropriate price" means rent actually paid for comparable housing in a similar part of the country.[121] Countries with a well-developed housing rental markets are able to collect information on rent paid for comparable dwellings. The way to calculate the value-added of imputed housing services is to subtract home owner–occupiers' intermediate inputs to maintain their dwellings, such as management and repair fees, from the gross imputed rent. The remainder, value-added, will all be counted as home owner–occupiers' operating surplus from an income-approach perspective.[122] One can think of this as a return earned (albeit from oneself) for the initial investment the home owners make in the property. The treatment for VA computation is the same as for rent arising from actual leasing activity; all are counted as operating surplus.[123] Meanwhile, from the expenditure- and production-approach perspectives, the value-added will be recorded as household final consumption and in the real estate subsector, respectively.

But not all countries are able to use the market rent approach for imputation. For countries with underdeveloped markets, rent data for dwellings comparable to those occupied by home owners are difficult to find. Either the rental market is small or nonexistent, especially in rural areas, or dwellings for lease are not representative of the overall housing stock. In some places, rental properties are primarily luxury dwellings for highly paid, white-collar domestic workers and expatriate managers; in others, they may be low-quality and subsidized housing for poorly paid migrant workers.[124] In circumstances where the standard market rent approach does not apply, the 1993 SNA recommended a "user cost approach" that estimates imputed rent by summing each of the costs that home-owners would need to price-in should they want to lease their dwellings and fix a market

119. UN, *2008 SNA*, 12.

120. Ibid., 185.

121. Lequiller and Blades, *Understanding National Accounts*, 125.

122. UN, *2008 SNA*, 187.

123. Ibid., 466.

124. World Bank, "Dwelling Services in ICP 2011" (World Bank, 2013), 3, http://siteresources.worldbank.org /ICPINT/Resources/270056-1255977254560/6483625-1273849421891/100702_ICP-OM_HousingServices_N.pdf.

rent. Such costs include consumption of fixed capital (namely, depreciation of the dwellings based on current market prices), net operating surplus, taxes on production, and other intermediate consumption such as repair fees.[125]

In China, where the rental housing market is nascent, NBS adopted the user cost approach based on current construction cost starting with the first economic census.[126] Prior to that, China used historical construction cost to depreciate and estimate the value of imputed rent,[127] which would obviously underestimate the value of housing services because original construction cost does not represent the current market prices—especially in China where the cost of real estate has increased so quickly from a low historical base. As of today, except for privately owned residential dwellings, China still computes depreciation of fixed assets at nonenterprise institutions based on historical construction costs (*guding zichan yuanzhi*), rather than on current prices, with NBS claiming China still lacks source data to reform the methodology.[128]

When it comes to housing service valuation, there is another Chinese idiosyncrasy to point out. In economies with better rent data coverage, VA from actual and imputed rental activities are calculated separately; the former comes from observable monetary transactions, whereas the latter is imputed from the market rent or user cost approach. In the former case, the housing service is produced by home owners and consumed by tenants; in the latter scenario, the service is produced by home owners for their own consumption. But in China, due to "limited source materials," according to NBS, both parts of VA are imputed from the user cost approach as if there was no for-profit rental activity.[129] This was noted by NBS deputy chief Xu Xianchun in a coauthored 2012 essay.[130] NBS vowed to fix this issue in their 2013 methodological transition announcement, but that plan has been deferred. Viewed in this light, when NBS mentions residential "own-account housing service" (*jumin ziyou zhufang fuwu*), it actually covers housing services to both home owner–occupiers and tenants, and the dwellings underlying such services include four types of privately owned residential property: original private housing, private housing obtained from housing reform, commercial housing, and leased private housing. In other words, when talking about "own-account housing" in the case of China's dominant GDP approach, NBS means privately owned housing.

That said, in China's household surveys and the expenditure-based national accounting, NBS does separate actual rent from imputed rent, as discussed at length in Chapter 2.

---

125. World Bank, "Owner Occupied Housing: User Cost for Rents of Dwellings in the West Balkan Countries" (World Bank, February 2010), 1, 4–5, http://siteresources.worldbank.org/ICPINT/Resources/270056 -1255977007108/6483550-1257349667891/6544465-1263333205953/01.12_ICP-TAG02_Housing -WestBalkanCountries.pdf.

126. NBS, "Reform of National Accounts System."

127. Hongyu Liu, Siqi Zheng, and Xianchun Xu, "房地产业所包含经济活动的分类体系和增加值估算 (Classification of Economic Activities of Real Estate Subsector and Their Added Values Estimation)," *Statistical Research*, no. 8 (2003): 26, http://tjyj.stats.gov.cn/CN/abstract/abstract348.shtml.

128. NBS, *Methods of Non-Economic Census Year, 2010 Ed.*, 8.

129. Ibid., 84.

130. Xianchun Xu et al., "居民住房租赁核算及对消费率的影响—国际比较与中国的实证研究 (On Residential Housing Rents and Its Impact on Consumption Ratio: An Empirical Study of China with International Comparisons)," *China Opening Journal*, no. 2 (2012): 13, http://www.cdi.com.cn/detail.aspx?cid=3612.

In this case, when NBS talks about "own-account housing," it includes only the first three types of private housing, exclusive of leased dwellings. To be specific, of the two types of residential consumption data NBS publishes now, the quarterly series of residential consumption expenditures on "residence" do not include imputed rent, only actual rent; however, the national accounting concept of household final consumption covers both.

This idiosyncrasy does not affect our own recount of the value-added from housing services, because—as will be demonstrated soon—our recalculation considers both actual and imputed rental activities, and the reestimate was added to the official headline GDP after deducting the total included VA arising from both types of rents (both were originally imputed by NBS based on the user cost approach). We now turn back to the problems with China's user cost approach and then explain our thought process in constructing the recalculation models. Bear in mind that by "imputed rent" we include both *de facto* imputed rent as well as actual rent treated as imputed rent by Chinese authorities.

In China, even with current construction cost being used for the user cost approach, a number of factors cause underestimation in VA of imputed rent. First, as China's real estate market has grown rapidly, construction costs have become increasingly less representative of both actual rents and market values—values that homeowners would obtain should they lease out their currently occupied dwellings. Second, in China's user cost approach, the derived VA includes fixed capital depreciation only and no other items indicated by SNA, such as net taxes on production and operating surplus.[131] Third, subsidized housing services provided by enterprises to their employees as benefits and by the government as social welfare were not clearly recorded within the production boundary of the real estate subsector until China replaced its 2002 version of industrial classification with a 2011 update. In the 2002 vintage—in use for national accounts in 2008—the real estate subsector was broken down into four industries: production activities of property developers, property management companies, (contract-based) property intermediary services, and "other."[132] There was no explanation whatsoever for "other," although it surely included housing leasing activities in both actual and imputed terms. But it was unclear whether subsidized leasing activity by enterprises and other institutions was counted; that point was made clear in the 2011 version. The 2011 classification added a fifth industry to real estate—"own-account real estate operating activities"—that explicitly includes institutional (except for real estate developers, management companies, and intermediaries) and residential purchase, sale, and leasing activities of their own property, for profit or not, with home owner–occupier services included.[133]

For many countries, it is critical to get imputed rent straight, because they are a substantial item in household final consumption. This is key information on residents' income and purchasing power, which in turn are important for policy and strategic decisionmaking. Underestimating imputed rent would result in an understated real estate subsector,

---

131. NBS, *Methods of Non-Economic Census Year, 2010 Ed.*, 88; World Bank, "Owner Occupied Housing," 2.
132. NBS, "(Industrial Classification of National Economy 2002)."
133. NBS, "(Industrial Classification of National Economy 2011)."

household consumption, revenue, and debt burden. The degree of underreporting is higher for countries with a high percentage of home owner–occupiers and will only grow as the property market becomes more developed. That is the situation China faces. Compared with advanced economies such as the United States, whose home ownership ratio remained in the 64 to 69 percent range over the last three decades,[134] China reports a particularly high share. In 2011, China's home ownership ratio reached 85 percent; this does not include ownership of leased property.[135] That soared to 89 percent in urban areas by March 2014 and to as high as 96.7 percent in rural areas, according to the China Household Finance Survey (CHFS) by the Sichuan-based Southwestern University of Finance and Economics.[136] With this home ownership ratio, the underlying underestimation in the construction cost method that NBS uses to impute value-added, and construction costs' widening departure from actual market value—thanks to China's investment frenzy and real estate boom— there is a remarkable downward bias against China's real estate VA, its share of the overall economy, and household consumption and income.

According to NBS, real estate accounted for 4.7 percent of China's GDP in 2008, 5.5 percent in 2009, and 5.7 percent in 2010. Prior to the 2013 *Economic Census* revisions, official records showed the subsector's GDP share stagnated at the 2010 level through 2013; after the revisions, the share was ticked up to about 6 percent for 2012 to 2014. In comparison, the U.S. property subsector—whose production boundary is largely defined the same as China's with imputed rent calculated in accordance with the market rent approach— constitutes about 12 percent since 2008 and about 11 percent during the decade earlier.[137] Other advanced economies, such as Canada and South Korea, report a similar level, if not higher. Developing economies, represented by the comparator countries we selected for the cross-country comparison approach for wholesale/retail and accommodation/service subsectors, also often register a higher level. For example, Turkey said its real estate subsector accounted for 11.4 percent of GDP in 2008, which, although gradually falling to 9.9 percent in 2013, was more than twice China's share in 2008.[138] Brazil reported a real

134. Paul Traub, "Economic Update" (Federal Reserve Bank of Chicago, November 5, 2014), 46, http://michiganeconomy.chicagofedblogs.org/wp-content/uploads/2012/12/MAS-Economic-Outlook.pdf.

135. Dongliang Wang, "China Human Development Report: National Housing Area Per Capita Reached 36 Square Meters," *Beijing Daily*, August 6, 2012, http://finance.eastday.com/eastday/finance1/economic/m1/20120806/u1a6761808.html; NBS, *Methods of Non-Economic Census Year, 2010 Ed.*, 159.

136. Survey and Research Center for China Household Finance, "Urban Housing Vacancy Rate and Development of the Housing Market" (Southwestern University of Finance and Economics, June 10, 2014), 29, http://chfs.swufe.edu.cn/upload/PPT-%E5%9F%8E%E9%95%87%E4%BD%8F%E6%88%BF%E7%A9%BA%E7%BD%AE%E7%8E%87%E5%8F%8A%E4%BD%8F%E6%88%BF%E5%B8%82%E5%9C%BA%E5%8F%91%E5%B1%95%E8%B6%8B%E5%8A%BF.pdf.

137. U.S. Bureau of Labor Statistics, "Industries at a Glance: Real Estate: NAICS 531," http://www.bls.gov/iag/tgs/iag531.htm.

138. Turkish Statistical Institute (TurkStat), "Gross Domestic Product in Current Prices by Kind of Economic Activity (NACE Rev.2)" (TurkStat, 2014), http://www.turkstat.gov.tr/PreTablo.do?alt_id=1045; Eurostat, "NACE Rev. 2: Statistical Classification of Economic Activities in the European Community" (European Commission, 2008), 80, https://www.lb.lt/n22873/nace_rev.2_2008-en.pdf. Turkey's real estate activities include buying and selling of own real estate, renting and operating of own or leased real estate, and real estate activities on a fee or contract basis (see NACE Rev. 2, p. 80). This is basically the same as how China defines its real estate activities in the 2011 version of industrial classification.

estate share of 8.1 percent in 2008.[139] The Philippines and Thailand, two Asian economies that do not separate real estate activities from leasing and business services, reported a combined share of 10.6 percent and 6.7 percent of GDP for 2008, respectively, whereas China's figure stood at 6.5 percent, lower than both much less-developed neighbors.[140] Admittedly, China's aggressive industrial expansion depresses the share of the real estate subsector and make it look smaller, as we explained in the beginning of this tertiary sector section, but both Chinese statistical officials and scholars have noted (publicly and privately) the understated share of real estate.

Xu Xianchun concluded in a 2003 coauthored essay that based on both market rent and construction cost approaches, the property subsector should have accounted for about 6.1 percent of GDP from 1996 to 2000. Using the market rent approach alone, the recalculated share would be 7.2 to 10.3 percent during that period.[141] In a 2012 coauthored essay, Xu recalculated the 2010 real estate VA of the southern city of Shenzhen based on actual rent and current housing prices and found that property should have accounted for 19.2 percent of GDP, rather than the 6.6 percent in official numbers based on the original construction cost approach. Shenzhen, the authors noted, was the first Chinese city that conducted household rent expenditure and income surveys, and it has the largest immigrant population—and thus the highest leasing percentage—among megacities of more than 10 million residents.[142] Given the maturity of its housing rental market and the floating housing prices, Shenzhen's actual real estate share of GDP was expected to be higher than the national average; still, the official national average of 5.7 percent in 2010 appears too low in comparison with the recalculated share for Shenzhen at 19.2 percent. During our interactions with NBS, a senior statistician said that recalculation of imputed rent based on market rent would augment the real estate share by at least 2 percentage points. That would mean about 7.5 to 8 percent of China's GDP, similar to Brazil's conditions. That, according to our own reestimates using the officially endorsed methodology, is still a conservative guess.

Finally, because imputed rent is part of both sides of the household income-consumption equation, both household incomes and expenses must be treated as understated. In Xu's 2012 essay, the recalculated GDP share of household final consumption in 2010 rose 5.1 percentage points from 33.8 to 38.9 percent.[143] That has two implications. First, the real picture of expenditure terms is likely more balanced than described by

139. Brazilian Institute of Geography and Statistics (IBGE), "System of National Accounts 2005–2009: Table 9—Gross Value Added" (IBGE, 2010), http://www.ibge.gov.br/home/estatistica/economia/contasnacionais/2009/tabelas_pdf/tab09.pdf; "Brazil: National Classification of Economic Activities (NCEA)," http://www2.dataprev.gov.br/pls/pradar/pkg_Baixa_Empr_CND.pr_Cons_Dominios?dominio=cnae&classif=d&Ender=27320353741.

140. The Philippines' numbers were accessed from CEIC; Thailand's were from its national statistics authority; see Office of the National Economic and Social Development Board (NESDB), "National Income of Thailand 2012: Table 4" (NESDB, 2014), http://www.nesdb.go.th/Portals/0/eco_datas/account/ni/cvm/2012/Tab.GDP-CVM2012.xls.

141. Liu, Zheng, and Xu, "(Real Estate Subsector)," 26–27.

142. Xu et al., "(On Residential Housing Rents)," 13–14.

143. The original 2010 GDP share of household final consumption was based on data in the 2011 NBS yearbook, according to the authors, which were not the final revised numbers for 2010 GDP. Calculating by

official figures because household consumption expenditures are statistically repressed by outdated methods. Second, as China continues urbanizing and growing, the housing rental market household incomes, purchasing power, and consumption expenditures should be expected to increase at a steeper rate. This is an important insight for policymakers and business executives. In addition to Xu and colleagues, Zhang Jun and Zhu Tian also found that China's household final consumption had been understated by 4 to 5 percentage points of GDP from 2004 to 2011 due to underreported imputed rent.[144] Morgan Stanley, in a 2013 report, also estimated China's actual household final consumption in 2012 was $1.6 trillion greater than officially stated, largely due to underestimates in modern, rapidly restructuring subsectors such as housing, auto, tourism, health care, and financial services. Their recalculations, based on a bottom-up approach and some bold assumptions—such as holding other expenditure items like gross capital formation constant at official values—suggested a household consumption share of GDP not at the official 34.8, but as high as 45.6 percent.[145]

We employ several approaches to reconstruct value-added for housing rental activities independently, including a market rent approach that counts both actual and imputed rents; a user cost approach based on current housing prices; and a user cost approach based on current construction costs, as well as some alternative routes using modified assumptions under the described scenarios. Because our study focuses on recalculating China's nominal GDP for 2008, we believe the market rent approach best represents the rental activity picture for that year.[146] But all these approaches point to the same conclusion: a greater real estate VA than officially stated. According to our market rent approach, China's actual real estate VA in 2008 was 2.3 times the official figure and accounted for about 9.5 percent of GDP—after accounting for all adjustments to other subsectors—instead of the official 4.7 percent. That would bring China on par with developing economy peers and closer to the bottom bracket among advanced economies.

A Market Rent Approach While NBS still does not publish systematic data on market rent, a method described in Xu's coauthored 2003 essay offers a workaround. The official statistics on household consumption expenditures and incomes, derived from NBS urban and rural household surveys, include an entry called "property income per capita" for urban residents. According to the official definition, such property income includes returns from household-owned movable property, such as bank deposits and securities, and returns from real estate, including actual rent. In other words, the rent that an average urban

---

final revised numbers, the official GDP share of household final consumption would be 34.9 percent, as documented in the 2012 NBS yearbook but still below the authors' reestimate.

144. Zhang and Zhu, "Underestimated Consumption," 12–13.

145. Jonathan Garner and Helen Qiao, "Asia Insight: China—Household Consumption: Bottom-Up Data Suggest US$1.6 Trillion Larger Than Officially Stated—Reiterate Chinese Consumer as Key Theme" (Morgan Stanley, February 28, 2013), 5, 7, 9.

146. If our study were about VA reconstruction over a period of time, we would settle on the current housing price approach because it would likely strengthen data comparability across historical periods, given that the housing price data are collected by officials and consistently released every year. But the market rent data in our study was imputed instead of directly accessed from official sources, and the market rent approach concerns urban rental activity recount only.

resident actually receives from tenants is part of the resident's property income, although what portion of total property income is not disclosed. Xu's 2003 essay cited internal official data indicating that actual rent was 35 percent of total property income—a fraction which allows us to extrapolate the value-added of housing leasing activity following the steps described in the 2003 essay:[147]

1. Multiply actual rental income per capita by total urban population to obtain the total actual rental income of urban residents.

2. Total actual rental income equals total actual rental expenditures; then find total tenant population and average urban residential floor area per capita to calculate total floor area of market rental housing, and thus obtain average actual annual rent per square meter in urban areas.

3. Because the housing rental market in China's rural areas is very limited, in both Xu's and our market rent approach, all rural dwellings are assumed to be occupied by homeowners. Given that and relatively slow appreciation in rural housing values, we assume (following Xu et al.) that the existing user cost approach still applies.

4. Because data on total urban residential floor area are available, under the assumption that annual imputed rent per square meter equals actual rent nationwide, we can extrapolate the total amount of rental income, including both actual and imputed rents: this is gross output of housing leasing activities concordant with SNA and CSNA definitions.

5. By multiplying that total rental output with a value-added ratio appropriately set for real estate activities, we can estimate value-added for leasing activity and then replace the old construction cost–based VA already included in the official GDP with this reestimate to obtain a new real estate VA figure.

We elaborate the choices we made for each of these steps and how we arrived at final real estate VA 2.3 times the official claim.

We first examined whether Xu and colleagues' estimate of 35 percent of urban residential property income from actual rent in 2000 still held for 2008. It appeared to, based on our review of various regional data: although market rent rose between 2000 and 2008, the channels for urban households to earn investment returns became more diverse as well. The growth of alternative investments, including securities, structured interest-bearing deposits, insurance products, and other types of assets, mitigated the expansion of the share of actual rent in property income. For Zhejiang, the share of actual rent in property income was 49.2 percent in 2008.[148] For Tianjin, the share was between 40 and 50 percent

147. Liu, Zheng, and Xu, "(Real Estate Subsector)," 26.
148. NBS Zhejiang Survey Team, "Property Income of Urban Households in Zhejiang Province: Research on Current Situation and Future Development" (Zhejiang Research Association of Regional Economy and Social Development, March 7, 2011), http://www.raresd.com/brownew.asp?n_ID=10153.

from 2005 to 2007.[149] For much less-developed county-level urban regions like Huanjiang county in the Guangxi Zhuang Autonomous Region, the share of actual rent constituted only 36.7 percent of property income in the first half of 2008.[150] In the similarly underdeveloped Henan city of Anyang, the portion only reached 34 percent in the first half of 2013.[151] Because China is so expansive and residential property income conditions vary drastically from region to region, we must take into consideration the 80 percent actual rental share in affluent areas such as Hunan's provincial capital of Changsha (in 2011)[152] and the Fujian city of Quanzhou (in 2008),[153] the 60 to 70 percent share in places like Anhui (in 2013)[154] and Guangdong (in 2006),[155] and the 10 to 20 percent share in the least-developed urban areas. We conservatively stuck with Xu and colleagues' 35 percent assumption in our study. If the actual rent share of property income were higher than 35 percent, then the market rent used to recalculate leasing activity VA would be *higher*, as would be final real estate VA.

Turning to the data on urban residential property income, there was some nuance to the statistic. Prior to 2013, the NBS household surveys were conducted separately for urban and rural households; in 2013, to enhance the comparability of urban and rural household data, NBS reformed the survey methodology and published a single set of household data for all Chinese households. The new methodology benefited from the 2010 *Population Census* and a more rigorous design, and its results better reflect reality than the old methods. For 2013, NBS still published separate urban and rural household data for comparison purposes, but the data series are expected to be suspended as early as 2016, according to NBS.[156] Because the composite household data under the new methodology are considered more accurate, we retrospectively extrapolated the part of urban residential property income per capita in 2008, based on the relationship between 2013 data from the old and new methodologies (Table 3.36).

The assumptions we made to derive adjusted urban residential property income in 2008 were as follows:

149. "Property Income of Urban Households in Tianjin: Current Situation and Development Strategies," People.com.cn, September 26, 2008, http://www.022net.com/2008/9-26/473844363096538.html.

150. "A Brief Analysis on Property Income of Urban Households in Huanjiang County" (Guangxi Zhuang Autonomous Region Bureau of Statistics, July 24, 2008), http://www.gxtj.gov.cn/tjxx/yjbg/sx_268/201208/t20120818_15063.html.

151. Anyang Bureau of Statistics, "Property Income of Urban Households in Anyang: Current Situation, Problems, and Suggestions," ed. Peng Fan (Henan Bureau of Statistics, August 16, 2013), http://www.ha.stats.gov.cn/hntj/tjfw/tjfx/sxsfx/ztfx/webinfo/2013/08/1376901173508965.htm.

152. Zhongwen Yuan, "Property Income of Households in Changsha Continues to Rise" (NBS Survey Office in Changsha, August 27, 2012), http://www.hndc.gov.cn/changsha/dybg/201208/t20120827_23030.html.

153. Yunzhong Zheng and Canfen Sun, "Property Income Boosted by a 130.9 Percent Increase in Actual Rent," *Quanzhou Evening News*, May 7, 2008, http://www.qzwb.com/gb/content/2008-05/07/content_2800686.htm.

154. "Actual Rent Accounted for 60 Percent of Urban Residential Property Income in Anhui Province," *Anhui News*, February 24, 2014, http://ah.anhuinews.com/system/2014/02/24/006323344.shtml.

155. Hubei Bureau of Statistics, "Per Capita Property Income of Urban Households in Guangdong Province Has Been Growing Rapidly" (Hubei Bureau of Statistics, December 24, 2007), http://www.stats-hb.gov.cn/wzlm/tjbs/swtjbs/1448.htm.

156. NBS, "NBS Press Conference: Director of Household Survey Office Wang Pingping Explains Methodological Reform and Relevant Statistics of Household Income" (NBS, February 24, 2014), http://www.stats.gov.cn/tjsj/sjjd/201402/t20140224_515109.html.

Table 3.36. Extrapolated Urban Residential Property Income under New Methodology

Unit: RMB

	Urban Residential Property Income per Capita (Old Method)	Rural Residential Property Income per Capita (Old Method)	Imputed Average Property Income per Capita (Old Method)	Average Net Property Income per Capita (New Method)	Imputed Urban Residential Property Income per Capita (New Method)
2007	348.5	128.2	229.3	571.8	869.1
2008	387.0	148.1	260.4	649.3	965.1
2009	431.8	167.2	295.1	736.0	1,076.8
2010	520.3	202.2	361.1	900.5	1,297.5
2011	649.0	228.6	444.1	1,107.6	1,618.5
2012	707.0	249.1	489.8	1,221.5	1,763.1
2013	809.9	293.0	570.7	1,423.3	2,019.7

Sources: NBS, authors' calculations.

1. Using official urban and rural residential property income, we calculated a weighted national average according to the ratio of urban to rural population.[157]

2. We assumed the ratio of new and old national average residential property income per capita in 2013 applies to recent years, including 2008.

3. We then assumed that the ratio in step 2 applies to the relationship between new and old urban residential property income per capita. An underlying assumption here was that the new methodology bumped up the level of urban *and* rural property income per capita by the same percentage.

Multiplying the assumed 35 percent actual-rent ratio by extrapolated urban property income per capita of RMB 965 in 2008 led us to a per capita actual rental income of RMB 338. With urban population data, we were able to obtain a value for total actual rental income

---

157. In NBS statistical yearbooks, the population data are year-end statistics. Ideally, to obtain the actual size of population for a year, one would need to average the measurement year's and the previous year's year-end data. However, in both of Xu et al.'s studies that we referred to in this section, the leveraged population data were unadjusted, year-end figures. Because we cited certain ratios and values from those two studies, to align with their methodology and assumptions, we needed to use year-end data as well. Hence, all population data in this imputed rent section are directly taken from NBS yearbooks without being averaged with the previous year's number. Further, after China conducted its 2010 *Population Census*, Beijing revised historical population data, including 2008's. Compared with prerevision data, the 2008 urban population number was revised up 2.86 percent, while the rural figure was cut by 2.4 percent, a change that better represented the pattern of rural-to-urban migration. In their 2013 study, Zhang and Zhu used postrevision population data to impute housing rent from 2004 to 2011. However, to render the comparison between our final reestimates and NBS 2008 data more meaningful, we decided to keep using prerevision population data, because that was what NBS had when they computed 2008 GDP. Postrevision population data are useful, but NBS did not possess that information back in 2008 and 2009. Using postrevision population data could reduce the comparability between our reestimates and NBS 2008 figures. One exception in population data was made, though, in the case of imputing property income, because we backwardly derived 2008 urban residential property income from 2013 statistics and the latter came after the 2010 *Population Census*. That said, this exception has *no* impact on the final extrapolated urban residential property income per capita (RMB 965.1), because the resulting changes in national average per capita property income under new and old methods offset each other.

of about RMB 205 billion. From official data on urban residential construction area per capita and urban population, we then computed the total urban residential usable floor area, assuming that usable floor area per capita is 70 percent of construction floor area, as Xu and colleagues described in their 2003 essay.[158] Then we estimated the size of the tenant population among urban residents. In the 2003 essay, the authors estimated that about 1.2 percent of the urban population were tenants in the period 1996–2000; we believed that was too low given the rapidly growing housing rental market, so we referred to a 2014 working paper based on the urban Chinese Family Panel Studies database (CFPS) maintained by statisticians at Peking University and extrapolated a tenant share of the urban population at 4.8 percent in 2010.[159] Based on this tenant share—which we assumed applicable to the year 2008—we calculated a total urban tenant population of 29 million and subsequently an average annual actual rent per square meter of RMB 356 in urban areas.

After obtaining that rent value, we cross-checked it with the 2000 market rent data used in Xu and colleagues' 2003 essay and China's official consumers' price index for market rent. The results appeared to comport closely: the average per-square-meter rent implied by the official rental CPI in 2008 was RMB 366, virtually the same as our own estimate of RMB 356, which was derived from a completely independent approach (Table 3.37).

We then applied this average unit rent of RMB 356 to the total urban residential usable floor area that we extrapolated earlier and obtained a value for total urban rental income of RMB 4.3 trillion, which includes both actual and imputed rents based on market rent in 2008. As noted earlier, the total rental income is equivalent to the gross output of housing leasing activity, so the next step is to derive value-added from that gross output. In Xu and colleagues' 2003 essay, they applied real estate developers' VA ratio of 51 percent to the urban housing rental activity; we did the same. Another reference ratio we could have leveraged was the VA ratio for the entire real estate subsector of 83 percent in China's 2007 *Input-Output Tables*. For simplicity, and because we adopted Xu and colleagues' other assumed ratios in this market rent approach, we decided to go with the 51 percent VA ratio. Thus, gross urban rental output of RMB 4.3 trillion translates to total urban rental VA of RMB 2.2 trillion.

---

158. Liu, Zheng, and Xu, "(Real Estate Subsector)," 26.

159. Fengjun Zhao, "Recalculating the Housing Consumption of Chinese Urban Households: Empirical Analysis from Chinese Family Panel Studies" (Working Paper 14-002, Peking University, 2014), 7–8, http://www .isss.edu.cn/cfps/d/file/p/2014-05-14/5365373a7585c8431370a78291676d23.pdf. To compute the tenant share of the urban population, we made the following assumptions: (1) the residential useable floor area per capita for urban home owner–occupiers and tenants was the same in the survey year of 2010; (2) for households that do not reside at their own dwellings or rent their property, such as households that live at enterprise-provided housing or relative-owned property, we assumed the average head count was the same as in households that occupy their own property. Based on the two assumptions above, our implied home ownership rate for China in 2010 was 84.3 percent, consistent with a number of official and academic accounts. For example, Xu and colleagues said in a 2012 essay that China's home ownership rate was above 80 percent; see Xu et al., "(On Residential Housing Rents)," 10. NBS said as of 2010, China's home ownership rate in urban areas was 89.3 percent; see Wenting Ma, "Home Ownership Rate of Urban Households Reached 89.3 Percent, Per Capita Living Area of Rural Households Reached 34.1 Square Meters," *Beijing Times*, March 8, 2011, http://epaper.jinghua.cn /html/2011-03/08/content_638164.htm.

Table 3.37. Imputed Urban Rental Price for Cross-Checking

Unit: RMB

	Annual Rent per Sqm (Xu 2003)*	Housing Rent CPI (PY = 100)	Imputed Annual Rent per Sqm
1996	189.7		
1997	219.3		
1998	244.2		
1999	245.4		
2000	251.3	109.2	268.0
2001		108.6	291.0
2002		104.4	303.8
2003		103.5	314.5
2004		103.0	323.9
2005		101.9	330.0
2006		102.7	339.0
2007		104.2	353.2
2008		*103.5*	*365.6*
2009		101.6	371.4

* Privately owned housing in urban areas.
Sources: NBS, Xu (2003), authors' calculations.

Our final step was to estimate the scale of urban rental VA that may already have been included in 2008 GDP. There is no official record of how much real estate VA came from urban property leasing activity, but the percentage implied in Xu and colleagues' 2003 essay was 18.8 to 18.9 percent from 1996 through 2000. This was a backward calculation based on final VA results, although the authors did not specifically state that they did so or that they adopted a constant ratio for those years.[160] The other semiofficial reference we found was in Xu's 2012 coauthored essay: this paper says *total* rental VA for Shenzhen in 2010 was RMB 20 billion. Because Shenzhen's real estate VA that year was RMB 62.8 billion, the implied percentage of *total* rental VA was 32 percent. Neither the authors nor Shenzhen authorities who oversaw the cited rent survey explicitly said that city-wide rental VA covered both urban and rural leasing activities, but, given that the survey "spanned all city residents," we believed its geographical coverage was at least as large as urban areas, which Xu and colleagues' 2003 essay and the 18.8 to 18.9 percent leasing share of total real estate VA concerned. Given that and the relatively developed property market and high construction costs in Shenzhen, as well as the fact that 2010 was two years into the global financial crisis following our accounting year, the 19 percent urban figure makes empirical sense to us.

After deducting already included imputed urban rental VA from our reconstructed figure, our net addition to China's 2008 real estate VA is RMB 1.9 trillion. Total real estate VA in 2008 (including rental VA adjustment only, not our earlier adjustment to nonleasing

---

160. Liu, Zheng, and Xu, "(Real Estate Subsector)," 26.

Table 3.38. Recalculated Real Estate Value-Added—A Market Rent Approach

Unit: RMB trillion (unless otherwise noted)

2008	Value
Property Income per Capita—Urban (RMB)	965.1
Market Rental Income per Capita—Urban (RMB)	337.8
Urban Population (million)*	606.7
Total Market Rental Income—Urban	0.2
Usable Floor Area per Capita—Urban (m²)	19.8
Total Usable Floor Area—Urban (billion m²)	12.0
Tenant Population—Urban (million)	29.1
Total Rental Housing Floor Area—Urban (million m²)	575.7
Average Market Rent per m² (RMB)	355.9
Total Market and Imputed Housing Rent (RMB trillion)	4.3
Urban Housing Rental Value-Added	**2.2**
Real Estate Value-Added (Official)	*1.5*
Urban Housing Rental VA Already Included[†]	0.3
Net Adjustment of Housing Rental VA	+1.9
Real Estate Value-Added (Recalculated)[‡]	**3.4**

* Population data in our recalculation are prior to 2010 *Population Census* revision so that our reestimates are more comparable to 2008 NBS figures.

[†] Extrapolated from data in Xu (2003); it considers urban housing rental activity only.

[‡] This approach does not include revision to rural housing rental VA.

Sources: NBS, Xu (2003, 2012), Zhao (2014), CEIC, authors' calculations.

real estate activity) increases from RMB 1.47 trillion to RMB 3.38 trillion. Including the revision to VA by property developers, management companies, and contract-based intermediaries, the total rises further to RMB 3.43 trillion. As a result, the real estate share of GDP would soar from the original 4.7 to about 9.5 percent of our recalculated Chinese GDP. Depending on our restatements of VA from China's research and development activities—explained in the following section—China's actual real estate share of GDP in 2008 should be between 9.4 and 9.7 percent (Table 3.38).

In Appendix 3.5, we discuss two alternative routes for calculating already included rental VA in China's 2008 GDP, which lead to alternative estimates for the final real estate VA. In the approach described above, we adopted the ratio that Xu and colleagues implied in their 2003 essay in lieu of a more authoritative figure; however, there are other workarounds based on household consumption expenditures and 2004 *Economic Census* data. For 2008, the final results derived from the two modified market rent approaches suggest a net addition of urban rental VA at RMB 2.26 trillion and RMB 1.9 trillion in comparison with our previous estimate of RMB 1.9 trillion. Because the differentials were minimal and the alternative estimates were less empirically grounded than the ones we described, we did not average them into our final estimates. They are provided here for the benefit of other scholars (see detailed discussion in Appendix 3.5).

A Current Housing Price Approach Because China still employs the user cost approach to impute rental VA, we explore this approach as well. But instead of basing depreciation on the dwellings' current construction cost as NBS does, we first chose to use the current housing price, which, according to SNA, better represents the market-based housing value. In fact, in NBS's national accounts manual, the formula to calculate imputed rental VA (which is equal to imputed depreciation, according to China's definition) is to multiply the "value" of urban or rural own-account housing by a designated depreciation ratio: 2 percent for urban dwellings and 3 percent for rural dwellings.[161]

Home values became increasingly divorced from construction costs as housing prices soared and profit margins for real estate developers widened. Based on 2007–2009 national real estate enterprise data, Xu and colleagues' 2012 essay applied a 25 percent profit margin to dwellings' current construction cost, which is called "value of dwellings completed" (*zhuzhai jungong jiazhi*) in China, to calculate a market value for leased housing.[162] Applying that profit margin to our model, we extrapolated an average current sale price of all urban own-account housing based on their construction cost, of which 80 percent was the value of construction cost and 20 percent was profit. Using official data for the urban population and urban residential construction floor area per capita, we calculated the total urban construction floor area and subsequently the value of that floor area based on the extrapolated sales price.

As previously noted, in China only privately owned housing stock counts toward own-account housing service, which means dwellings owned by residents (whether the owners occupy the residences themselves or lease them out), not by institutions. We already mentioned that the home ownership rate in 2008 was about 80 percent, but we have not discussed the share of privately owned housing, which is a broader concept than home owner–occupied housing. The share of privately owned housing is about 90 percent (the residual being owned by nonhousehold entities).[163] To calculate the portion of urban housing stock actually imputed for rental VA calculation, we needed to apply this ratio.

161. NBS, *Methods of Non-Economic Census Year, 2010 Ed.*, 85.
162. Xu et al., "(On Residential Housing Rents)," 13.
163. Zhao, "Recalculating the Housing Consumption," 6. This private ownership issue does not concern rural housing, because the officials assume all rural dwellings are occupied by home owners, hence privately owned. This issue does not concern the market rent approach either, because according to the Chinese industrial classification 2011, VA of all leasing activities, whether generated by household-owned property or non-household-entity-owned property, it invariably belongs to the industry of "own-account real estate operating activities" under the subsector of real estate. And the floor area for leased private dwellings and the market rate were computed from the tenant share of the urban population. In the user cost approach, it is necessary to separate publicly owned and privately owned real estate because if it is public property, then the depreciation should have been included in the public institutions' book already; counting it again as imputed housing depreciation will result in double accounting.

Table 3.39. Imputed Urban Housing Rental Value-Added

Unit: RMB trillion (unless otherwise noted)

2008*	Value
Urban Population (million)	606.7
Construction Floor Area per Capita (m²)	28.3
Total Construction Floor Area (billion m²)	17.2
Price of Residential Property (RMB per m²)	3,576.0
Total Value of Housing Stock	61.4
Total Value of Private Housing Stock	55.3
Depreciation Ratio for Housing	2%
Imputed Housing Rental Value-Added	**1.1**
Real Estate Value-Added (Official)	1.5
Urban Housing Rental VA Already Included	0.3
Net Adjustment of Housing Rental VA	**+0.8**

* All data above are urban-only.
Sources: NBS, Xu (2003, 2012), authors' calculations.

With the value of private urban housing stock, we multiplied the official depreciation ratio of 2 percent to obtain the value of imputed depreciation—the imputed rental VA based on current housing price—of RMB 1.11 trillion. Similar to the market rent approach, we deducted already included urban rental VA from 2008 real estate VA (RMB 0.28 trillion, same as in the market rent approach) and added this newly reconstructed imputed rental VA to get adjusted real estate VA of RMB 2.3 trillion, about 70 percent of our market rent approach result. This does not yet consider our recalculation of rural imputed rental VA (Table 3.39).

We next recalculated current housing price–based imputed rental VA for rural property. However, unlike urban property, a significant share of rural dwellings was constructed by rural residents on their own. Their market value is hard to measure and is not systemically published by NBS. The official data entry closest to the market-based housing value is called "value of newly constructed rural residential property" (*nongcun jumin jiating xinjian fangwu jiazhi*). But according to the NBS definition, that value includes only the cost of construction materials and labor remuneration—monetary and nonmonetary compensation combined—and is therefore still lower than the market rate, because no profit margin was accounted for.[164] According to NBS statistics, the value of newly constructed rural housing in 2008 was RMB 533.7 per square meter, but academic and press reports place the actual market value at least a couple of hundred yuan higher.

---

164. NBS National Data, "农村居民家庭新建房屋价值 (Value of Newly Constructed Rural Residential Property)," http://data.stats.gov.cn/workspace/index?m=hgnd.

Table 3.40. Recalculated Real Estate Value-Added— A Current Housing Price Approach

Unit: RMB trillion (unless otherwise noted)

2008	Value
Rural Population (million)	721.4
Residential Floor Area per Capita—Rural (m²)	32.4
Total Residential Floor Area—Rural (billion m²)	23.4
Current Housing Price of Rural Property (RMB per m²)	800.0
Total Value of Rural Housing Stock (RMB trillion)	18.7
Depreciation Ratio for Rural Housing	3%
Imputed Rural Housing Rental Value-Added	**0.6**
Real Estate Value-Added (Official)	1.5
Rural Housing Depreciation Already Included	0.2
Net Adjustment of Rural Housing Rental VA	**+0.3**
Net Adjustment of Urban Housing Rental VA	+0.8
Real Estate Value-Added (Recalculated)	**2.6**

Sources: NBS, Xu (2003, 2012), authors' calculations.

The state-backed *Securities Journal* reported in 2009 that the actual construction cost of rural dwellings in central China was about RMB 700 to 800 per square meter, and the total value of rural housing stock was about RMB 15.98 trillion.[165] Another academic, the executive director of the housing policy research center at Shanghai's Fudan University, said the 2011 market value for rural housing was RMB 1,600 per square meter.[166] Because 2008 was before China's recent real estate boom, we took a conservative approach in fixing the market value for rural housing at RMB 800 per square meter. For already included imputed rental VA, we extrapolated following the formula provided in the NBS national accounts manual and used official data on "rural residential property value" (*nongcun jumin jiating zhufang jiazhi*).

According to the NBS definition, "rural residential property value" represents the original construction or purchase value of the dwellings, and that value is reassessed at the end of the measurement period in accordance with the quality and conditions of the property.[167] In other words, it indicates the current value of the rural dwellings, exclusive of any development profit. In 2008, that value for rural property was RMB 332.8 per square meter.[168] The specific calculation process is as follows. First, multiplying the unit market

165. "国内住房总价值超 GDP 近两倍 (Total Value of Domestic Housing Stock Nearly Triples GDP)," *China Securities Journal*, September 15, 2009, http://finance.people.com.cn/GB/10052639.html.

166. Jie Chen, "中国居民资产之谜 (The Mystery of Chinese Household Assets)," September 14, 2012, http://www.ftchinese.com/story/001046537?full=y.

167. NBS National Data, "村居民家庭住房价 (Rural Residential Property Value)," http://data.stats.gov.cn/workspace/index?m=hgnd.

168. Ibid.

price of RMB 800 by the total rural residential housing stock[169] as well as official depreciation ratio, we obtained the adjusted value for rural rental VA. Then, to calculate rural rental VA that was already included in China's 2008 GDP, we leveraged the official current property value of RMB 332.8 per square meter, the total rural housing stock, and the depreciation ratio for computation. These steps gave us RMB 0.56 trillion and RMB 0.23 trillion, respectively. The differential, RMB 0.33 trillion, was the net addition of rural rental VA that our model suggested to add to 2008 GDP. Combining this rural reestimate with the previous urban restatement, the total rental VA adjustment in this current housing price approach would raise real estate VA to RMB 2.63 trillion (exclusive of impact from nonleasing activity adjustment for the purpose of this section), approximately 80 percent of our market rental approach result (Table 3.40).

A Current Construction Cost Approach The third and final approach we adopted to recalculate imputed rental VA basically followed official NBS practices. We used current construction cost in lieu of market-based housing prices to extrapolate the value of private urban and total rural housing stock. We considered only the newly constructed floor area from 1978 through 2008 as housing stock and added those up to obtain the total floor area in 2008 for urban and rural housing, respectively, rather than using the total population to multiply by per capita residential floor area, as we did in the two approaches above, modeling upon Xu and colleagues' 2003 exercise. Our reason for this choice is that this third approach emphasized "construction" more than "residential occupancy/purchase," so we should select a metric that best represents the incremental construction floor area during the measurement period. And because of massive housing demolitions in China in recent years to make room for new property and infrastructure, a significant amount of private housing built before the major reform year of 1978 was already gone by 2008. Consequently, we set the measurement period as 1978–2008. Adding up the newly constructed urban and rural housing during that period, the total urban and rural housing stock in 2008 would be 10.89 billion square meters and 21.25 billion square meters, respectively. Further, due to the ownership issue described previously, the private urban housing stock would be 90 percent of the urban total, or 9.8 billion square meters.

These two housing stock figures are smaller than what we came up with in the current housing price approach, but not by a significant margin. Private urban housing stock is 37 percent smaller, and rural housing stock is 9 percent lower. The differential could be attributed to the inflated housing stock in the current housing price approach—such as a result of outdated per capita floor area data that did not factor in extensive demolitions—the missing part in this current construction approach, or a combination of both. The actual level of housing stock is possibly somewhere in between.

We then multiplied these housing stock numbers with their respective construction cost—the value of buildings completed for urban housing (80 percent of the year's residential

---

169. Unlike urban dwellings, rural property does not have a construction to useable area conversion issue. In official data releases, the floor area is generally referred to as "residential area for rural dwellings," which is directly used in the imputed depreciation formula provided in the NBS national accounts manual.

Table 3.41. Recalculated Real Estate Value-Added—A Current Construction Cost Approach

Unit: RMB trillion (unless otherwise noted)

2008	Value
Urban	
Newly Constructed Residential Floor Area 1978–2008 (billion m^2)	10.9
Privately Owned (billion m^2)	9.8
Price of Residential Property (RMB per m^2)	3,576.0
Share of Construction Cost in Market Price	0.8
Current Construction Cost (RMB per m^2)	2,860.8
Total Value of Housing Stock	28.0
Imputed Housing Rental Value-Added	0.6
Rural	
Newly Constructed Residential Floor Area 1978–2008 (billion m^2)	21.3
Unit Value of New Rural Housing (RMB per m^2)	533.7
Total Value of Housing Stock	11.3
Imputed Housing Rental Value-Added	0.3
Total Imputed Housing Rental Value-Added	**0.9**
Real Estate Value-Added (Official)	1.5
Total Housing Depreciation Already Included	0.5
Net Adjustment of Housing Rental VA	+0.4
Real Estate Value-Added (Recalculated)	**1.9**

Sources: NBS, Xu (2003, 2012), authors' calculations.

property sales price) and the value of newly constructed rural housing—to compute the total value of housing stock. Finally, we depreciated the fixed capital to compute the imputed rental VA. Because this approach uses construction costs rather than current housing value and only counts the incremental private housing stock since 1978, the final real estate VA we obtained was the smallest thus far—RMB 1.86 trillion—yet still meaningfully higher than the officially stated RMB 1.47 trillion (Table 3.41).

Of the three different approaches, we believe the market rent approach best reflects the actual rental VA in China for 2008. That would mean the real estate subsector accounted for about 9.4 to 9.7 percent of that year's GDP, instead of the official estimate of 4.7 percent. Even in the most modest scenario based on current construction costs, the subsector's share of the overall economy would have risen about 1 percentage point. That would translate into hundreds of billions of dollars in missing value-added.[170] Seen through either a household income or asset lens, the missed book value due to antiquated statistical methods is even bigger. Considering the real estate subsector's "pillar industry" status in China, Beijing needs to get these data straight.

---

170. Our two user cost approaches have not yet considered rental value-added from publicly owned urban dwellings, which should have been re-evaluated and classified into the real estate subsector, rather than into the industry of the entities owning the property as fixed asset depreciation. If considered, the user cost-based results would have been larger.

However, Beijing chose not to upgrade the real estate accounting methodology as they said they would for the 2013 *Economic Census*. In light of that last-minute change, we can only imagine that their concerns were not statistical but political. Recalculating rental VA as we have done would significantly increase the structural weight of real estate in the Chinese economy, amplifying the criticism that China has over-relied on property as an engine of growth. In a society where those with real estate wealth are already viewed with envy by less moneyed citizens, and senior leaders claim to focus on promoting higher value-added sectors such as advanced manufacturing and information technology, the central government might be motivated to downplay the preponderance of the property subsector—even at the cost of data accuracy. This concern could have been compounded by Beijing's fear that if it announced a 2013 revision larger than 2004 and 2008 census revisions, observers at home and abroad might surmise things are getting worse not better. The methodological change for imputed rent, once implemented, would have a larger impact on headline GDP than any other revision.

It is unclear when NBS—and, perhaps more important, the central leaders above it—will finally upgrade the imputed rent accounting methodology. The answer depends on economic conditions down the road and leaders' appetite for getting large revisions out the door. Until then, the best the market can do is guess, and the closest China watchers can get is to reproduce the official methodology while applying adjusted values, as we have attempted here.

CONCLUSIONS FOR TERTIARY SECTOR

Imputed rent reestimation is the trickiest area of service sector revision. Where possible we have cross-checked national accounts data against real-economy indicators the same way officials claim to stress-test their figures. Using that methodology, we examined the eight largest service subsectors and applied those findings to proportionally extrapolate headline revisions—exclusive of housing rental VA adjustment due to its idiosyncrasy—to the remaining six service subsectors. This exercise in sum brings us to a 22.2 percent upward revision of official tertiary sector estimates. Because wholesale/retail and accommodation/catering are considered "fundamental" services across countries, we were able to apply cross-country comparisons to check Chinese data based on international development patterns. Using a purchasing power parity approach, we suggested a 16.1 percent upward revision for wholesale/retail and 5.7 percent for accommodation/catering. Wholesale/retail is a massive subsector characterized by a huge number of small, hard-to-count self-employed businesses and poorly documented invoices. Previously most researchers were left guesstimating how much VA was being missed. Our approach takes a step forward. Our real estate VA estimate is also arguably the first to specify an adjusted value under the internationally recommended methodology (Table 3.42).

Beyond the overall figures, there are three other implications from our tertiary revisions worth emphasizing. First, in light of our revisions, tertiary VA had almost reached parity with the secondary sector by 2008 and surpassed it in 2009. In official accounts prior

Table 3.42. Summary of Tertiary Sector Revisions

Unit: RMB trillion

2008	Official VA	Recalculated VA	Recl./ Official %	Recalculation Method
Tertiary Sector	**13.13**	**16.06**	**22.2%**	
Transport, Storage, and Postal Services	1.64	1.83	11.9%	Average of four estimates*
Info Transmission, Computer Services, and Software	0.79	0.86	9.7%	Average of four estimates
Wholesale and Retail Trade	2.62	3.04	16.1%	Cross-country comparison (PPP)
Accommodation and Catering Services	0.66	0.70	5.7%	Cross-country comparison (PPP)
Finance	1.49	1.53	2.8%	Average of four estimates
Real Estate	1.47	3.43	132.8%	Estimate from market rent approach, combined with nonleasing-activity VA adjustment[†]
Education	0.89	0.87	–2.1%	Average of four estimates
Public Administration and Social Organizations	1.38	1.42	2.7%	Average of four estimates
Other Six Service Subsectors	2.20	2.38	7.9%	Proportional adjustment[‡]

* "Average" denotes the arithmetic mean of the estimates from various recalculation approaches we applied to the subsector.

[†] The value of nonleasing activity VA adjustment is the arithmetic mean of the estimates we obtained for the rest of the real estate subsector.

[‡] Due to limited data availability, we were unable to make separate estimates for the remaining six service subsectors. Therefore, we assumed their combined level of VA distortion was equal to that of the eight largest subsectors (exclusive of the impact of housing rental VA adjustment, which is a real estate idiosyncrasy).

Sources: NBS, authors' calculations.

to 2013 census revisions, the 2008 secondary sector outsized tertiary by almost 6 percentage points in terms of nominal GDP contribution—overwhelmingly because NBS was missing service VA. By our recount, 2008 service activity accounted for 44 to 45.2 percent of Chinese GDP, versus 44.2 to 45.5 percent for the secondary sector, compared with the official picture of 41.8 versus 47.4 percent (the balance is primary activity, mostly agriculture). This means China's economy was significantly more balanced, structurally, than numbers suggest.

Second, real estate plays an even more important role in the Chinese economy than people already know. The growth of this subsector has much to do with Chinese households' revenue and expenditures and aggregate domestic demand, and the growth of household rental income has not been properly reflected in official numbers. This means households' purchasing power and assets are larger than generally stated, especially for higher-income households. Conversely, this means that when the property market runs into trouble and turns down—an acute concern today—the destructive impact on the overall economy would not just concern raw material suppliers, home appliance makers, and wealth management product holders but, to a greater extent than previously acknowledged, will directly punish household balance sheets. Today the implied purchasing power of China's households is outside observation, but the trauma felt in the event of a property market correction will be real and tangible, whether it is reflected in revenue numbers or not.

Third, from 2008 to today, more service subsectors have been liberalized and encouraged to pursue rapid growth: our accounting does not capture these most recent booms, especially in online services, for example. Still *more* value-added will "materialize" as accounting measures improve further. Without upgrading service accounting methods now, when possible, Beijing risks falling much further behind the ever-advancing credibility curve in the years immediately ahead. Upon announcing 2014 GDP numbers, NBS said they are dedicated to compiling more statistics this year to capture not only growth but structural shifts and growth quality. This is critical, because sound basic data are demonstrably more important to crafting effective policy at this new, middle-income phase of China's economic growth than they were in the initial takeoff.

Primary Sector

In mid-2013, shortly after the Central Commission for Discipline Inspection announced that the activities of the China Grain Reserves Corporation (CGRC) would be targeted for auditing, a major CGRC repository in Heilongjiang Province, ostensibly with some 47,000 tons of grain, caught fire. Two months later in Shanxi Province, state news reported that a supposed 25,000 tons of cotton were destroyed in another fire at a China National Cotton Reserves Corporation (CNCRC) storehouse. The incidents garnered public attention and fueled suspicions that the incidents were the result of arson to cover up empty granaries.[171] Beijing's subsidy policies for grain and cotton reserves have sometimes created a perverse incentive for local governments to inflate their reserves, which subsequently aggravated widespread doubts about the quality of agricultural data. In this section, we delve into the data reliability issues in the primary sector, which according to NBS accounted for 10.7 percent of China's GDP in 2008.

Under China's industrial classification in use until the 2013 *Economic Census* in 2014, the primary sector consisted of five industries: farming, forestry, animal husbandry, fishery, and agricultural services in support of the previous four industries.[172] Of the five,

---

171. Peng Liu, "中储粮到中储棉, 大火何以一烧再烧? (From China Grain Reserves Corporation to China National Cotton Reserves Corporation: Why the Fire Occurred Over and Over?)," *Xinhua News*, July 5, 2013, http://news .xinhuanet.com/comments/2013-07/05/c_116410023.htm.

172. During the third national economic census for 2013, services in support of farming, forestry, animal husbandry, and fishery were classified into the tertiary sector based on a 2013 update to China's industrial classification (2011) to better reflect the nature of the activity; see NBS, "三次产业划分规定 (Stipulation on Classification of Three Economic Sectors)," January 14, 2013, http://www.stats.gov.cn/tjsj/tjbz/201301/t20130114_8675

farming always has the largest gross output value (GOV), averaging 52 percent of the sector's total since 2000, followed by animal husbandry, fishery, and forestry. Of farming crops, grain (*liangshi*) is the largest component; in 2008, grain output volume (predominantly rice, wheat, and corn) was 59 percent of farming crops in official accounts.[173] For animal husbandry and fishery, the principal output is meat and seawater/freshwater aquatic products, respectively. So far, most studies on primary sector statistics have focused on the two largest industries, especially their main output—grain and meat (most often pork)—but not so much on fishery, forestry, and agricultural services. The main methodology used in this literature is a classic supply-demand analysis, which means that by comparing the volume of aggregate supply and demand of a certain product, one can obtain the differential and examine whether gaps can be reasonably explained. The underlying assumption of this methodology is that a country's total agricultural production, adjusted for net trade and spoilage, should equal consumption.[174]

Because agricultural data are lacking in both of our enterprise databases, we started constructing our recalculation model by reviewing literature and examining the existing models. Then, using data compiled on our own, we modified existing supply-demand models and produce alternative value-added estimates for the key agricultural industries. The bottom-up reestimate approach used for secondary and tertiary subsectors is not helpful here due to data limitations; therefore, we mainly relied on two enhanced supply-demand models, as well as China's own revisions after two primary-sector censuses (for 1996 and 2006), in our reestimates. Given data and literature availability, in this study we focus on the three largest primary industries—farming, animal husbandry, and fishery—which combined accounted for 93 percent of the sector's official GOV over the past decade.

Due to the Material Product System legacy, unaligned goals between regulators and national accountants, and capacity challenges in disaggregating data, China has more volume than value data for agriculture. For the primary sector, national and regional GOV data are available at industry and sector levels, and national value-added data are at the

---

.html. Also see NBS, Statistical Bulletin for *Third National Economic Census*, December 16, 2014, http://www .stats.gov.cn/tjsj/zxfb/201412/t20141216_653709.html. In 2008, however, the year we focused on in this study, the aforementioned service industry was still counted as part of the primary sector; see NBS, "Industrial Classification of National Economy 2002" and "Stipulation on Classification of Three Economic Sectors," May 14, 2003.

173. NBS, 2009 *Statistical Yearbook*, Table 12–15. For farming crops, NBS publishes volume data for the 10 main crops, while its GOV data covers the entire farming industry. Due to data limitations, we were unable to impute the aggregate volume of all farming crops. For the purpose of this study, we assumed the 10 main crops were equal to the total volume of farming crops. The 10 main crops are grain (cereal, beans, and tubers), cotton, oil-bearing crops, fiber crops, sugarcane, beetroots, tobacco, silkworm cocoons, tea, and fruits. Hence, in this section we refer to the aggregate of the 10 main crops as "farming crops" without specifying that a small amount of minor crops are not included. The underlying assumptions here are that the output of these minor farming crops is small enough not to affect grain's share of total farming crops, and the output has been accurately documented by authorities and requires no revision. We further elaborate on the second assumption in the next section. Such minor crops include vegetables, nuts, beverage and spice crops, and Chinese herbs.

174. Total uses refer to the sum of household consumption, industrial consumption, feed, seed consumption (if applicable), waste and spoilage, and inventory changes.

sector level only. In comparison, volume data are published for the main products of each industry except for agricultural services, permitting more granular assessment. Given this, we constructed our reestimates based on volume measures of the three select industries' respective principal product and then converted the findings into value terms. Hence, in the following section, unless otherwise noted, all output data are in volume terms. To enable our reestimates and volume-to-value conversion, three important assumptions were made.

Assumption one is that data distortion found in an industry's principal output cannot be applied to the rest of the industry. Previous literature and NBS output data focused on the industries' main output; but even within the same industry, products can widely vary from one another in nature, which reduces the applicability of one product's data misstatement to the rest of industry output. We are aware of this inapplicability. Given finite resources, we focused on adjusting estimates for the principal crop in each case. Unsure of even the direction of bias in the secondary crops, we stuck with official values rather than extrapolate. For instance, in the case of farming we identified accounting issues with grain, the largest farming crop, and adjusted accordingly, but settled for official cotton and fiber crops estimates. This qualification will likely have impact on our final reestimates, of which the direction is unknown, yet the scale appears tolerable. After all, grain accounted for nearly 60 percent of the farming industry's output, and meat, which we selected for animal husbandry, contributed 53 percent. In existing studies grain and meat are most often used as proxy variables for their entire industries. For fishery, we factored in total output by looking at both saltwater and freshwater aquatic products.

Our second assumption is that for the primary-sector national accounts, price data that *are* available are trustworthy, allowing us to transpose distortions from volume terms to value terms. We base this judgment on the grounds that NBS's vertically administered survey teams are directly in charge of collecting agricultural price data, including for farming, animal, and aquatic products. As many as 3,000 price surveyors are assigned to this endeavor, while the surveys span more than 550 cities and counties (nearly 50,000 survey locations) for 262 basic categories (600 kinds of goods and services in total).[175] We discussed the differences in central and local statistical authorities' capacities at length in Chapter 2. Price data, for political and business purposes, are one of the most intensely monitored indicators in China, improving accuracy, consistency, and serviceability. Compared with volume data either collected through sample-field surveys or submitted by local governments, prices data are considered more reliable.

Assumption three is that adjustments to primary-sector GOV can be converted proportionally to value-added. This means that the distortions in GOV are distributed proportionally across intermediate inputs and value-added, and as a result, the growth patterns of VA and GOV should be in lockstep when considered over time. This is exactly what we found when examining historical agricultural data: that the relationship between the sector's

175. Zheng Liu and Yingfeng Zhou, "撩起 CPI 的'面纱 (Unveiling the Consumer Price Index)," *Xinhua News*, June 8, 2009, http://news.xinhuanet.com/fortune/2009-06/08/content_11509173.htm.

Table 3.43. Ouput, GOV, and VA Revisions for Primary Sector

Unit: Million tons, percentage, RMB billion

| 2008 | Official | | | Recalculation | | | | | |
	Output (mn tons)	Output % of Industry	GOV	Output (mn tons)	Output % of Industry	GOV	% Adj. to Output Vol.	Adj. to GOV	% Adj. to GOV and VA
Farming	897.8		2,804	883.1		2,759		−45.8	
Grain	528.7	59%		514.0	58%		−2.8%		
Animal Husbandry	138.5		2,058	130.8		1,944		−114.2	
Meat	72.8	53%		65.1	50%		−10.6%		
Fishery	49.0		520	46.5		494		−26.4	
Aquatic Products	49.0	100%		46.5	100%		−5.1%		
Forestry	n/a		215	n/a		n/a	n/a	n/a	
Agri. Services	n/a		202	n/a		n/a	n/a	n/a	
Total			5,800			5,614		−186	**−3.2%**

Sources: NBS, authors' estimates.

value-added and GOV remained fairly stable over the last two decades, with VA averaging around 58 percent of GOV. This is likely a result of the overall input-output relationship being exempt from major shocks, such as a technological revolution or a persistent nationwide drought.

Given these three assumptions, our recalculation suggests that China's 2008 output volumes for grain, meat, and aquatic products were overstated. Our respective *downward* adjustments of output for these commodities are 2.8, 10.6, and 5.1 percent of their official levels. Converting these volume revisions to value terms, and assuming the remainder of output and the two unconsidered industries (forestry and agricultural services) were counted correctly, we concluded the *downward* VA revision to the entire primary sector is 3.2 percent of sector GDP in 2008, which translates into a 0.34 percent cut to the official headline, given the sector's GDP share (Table 3.43).

FARMING—GRAIN

Per NBS definition, China's major farming crops consist of 10 categories, including grain (cereal, beans, and tubers), oil-bearing crops (peanuts, rapeseeds, sesame, etc.), cotton, fiber crops, sugarcane, beetroots, tobacco, silkworm cocoons, tea, and fruits. NBS publishes separate output data for these farming crops but not for the rest, such as beverage and spice crops. In a typical Chinese diet, wheat flour–based products are the major staple food in northern regions, while rice is the staple in the south;[176] that diet preference is reflected in grain's high share in farming crops: approximately 60 percent over the last decade.

As noted, at the center of our recalculation model for this section is a supply-demand analysis, embodied in a balance sheet model, which is widely used in other academic work examining China's agricultural data. Two studies that we drew from are summarized below. Huanguang Qiu, from the Chinese Academy of Sciences' Center for Chinese Agricultural Policy (CCAP), and Wim van Veen, from the Center for World Food Studies at the Netherlands' VU University Amsterdam (SOW-VU), along with three other renowned agronomists[177] constructed a supply-demand balance sheet with which they compared China's total available grain—domestic grain production plus net grain imports—with its aggregate use of grain (including household consumption, feed, and authors' imputed "other use") from 2000 to 2012. After running the numbers for five types of grain crops, the researchers identified notable gaps.

Subtracting grain consumed as food and feed from the aggregate supply, the researchers obtained a discrepancy between official grain production and the observably consumed grain, which they marked as a residual "other use." From 2005 to 2012, the residual "other use" grew gradually from 7 to 21 percent of grain production, and in 2008, it was

---

176. Jacqueline M. Newman, *Food Culture in China*, Food Culture around the World (Westport, CT: Greenwood Press, 2004), 35–38.

177. The three other coauthors are Jikun Huang, Michiel Keyzer, and Scott Rozelle from CCAP, SOW-VU, and Stanford University, respectively.

about 12 percent.[178] There are some reasonable explanations, such as seed use, spoilage, and industrial consumption (e.g., maize being used to make ethanol); however, none could fully explain the large residual.[179] Their main argument was that seed and waste should only account for 5 percent of production and industrial use can only explain a smaller portion of the remaining "other use." Perplexed, the authors concluded they had underestimated the food and feed consumption of grain, implying official grain production figures were correct. However, we suspect the alternative hypothesis: that overstatement of production numbers is partly to blame.

The second study, published a few months later, sheds some light on the gap. Two Renmin University researchers, Zhun Xu and Wei Zhang, and Minqi Li at the University of Utah took a deeper look into the gap suggested by their supply-demand model. They estimated and combined known uses of grains, and compared the aggregate with reported production. Their results were in line with official numbers for 1981 to 2007, with divergences randomly distributed—a good sign. But starting from 2008 their estimates began to fall significantly below official output figures, by 10.1 percent in 2008 to 22.2 percent by 2012.[180] The close fit with official production data for 25 years prior to 2008, followed by divergence thereafter suggested a breakdown in statistical veracity and left them to conclude that official figures were likely overstated.[181]

In light of Xu and colleagues' methodology, we made new estimates for each grain use to construct our own supply-demand balance sheet. The total-use breakdown is the same as in Xu and colleagues', except we assigned exports and imports to total uses and supply separately, whereas they included *net* exports. First, we appraised 2008 food and feed uses based on official household food consumption and population data, leveraging a series of ratios that Xu and colleagues used to convert nongrain food and indirect feed use by residents to grain equivalent.[182] Our imputed per capita food and feed consumption of grain from this step is 336.2 kilograms for urban households and 356.5 kilograms for rural in 2008. In comparison, Xu and colleagues noted in their study that in 2012—the only year for which the researchers published their separate urban and rural estimates—the imputed per capita grain consumption for urban households was 485 kilograms, and 348 kilograms

178. Huanguang Qiu et al., "Matching China's Agricultural Supply and Demand Data," Presented at the Chinese Economist Society (CES) Business Meeting, Philadelphia, 2014, 23–24, https://www.aeaweb.org/aea/2014conference/program/retrieve.php?pdfid=833. The 12 percent was calculated using data from Table 4.2.

179. Ibid., 9.

180. Using official output data as the denominator, the gap between the authors' estimates and the official values in percentage terms would be reduced to 9.2 percent in 2008 and 18.2 percent in 2012 as a result of denominator augmentation. In our own recalculation, we used official output data as the denominator to measure the scale of the discrepancy; hence, when comparing our reestimates with Xu et al.'s, we referred to the 9.2 percent in 2008 instead of the original 10.1 percent. The discussion of comparing estimates is at the end of this farming section.

181. Zhun Xu, Wei Zhang, and Minqi Li, "China's Grain Production: A Decade of Consecutive Growth or Stagnation?," *Monthly Review*, 2014, http://monthlyreview.org/2014/05/01/chinas-grain-production/.

182. The coefficients converting nongrain food and indirect feed consumption to grain equivalents were imputed by two researchers at the Chinese Academy of Agricultural Sciences (CAAS); see Shumin Liang and Qingzhen Sun, "中国食物消费与供给中长期预测 (Mid- and Long-Term Forecast of China's Food Consumption and Supply)," *Food and Nutrition in China*, no. 2 (2006): 38, http://mall.cnki.net/magazine/Article/ZGWY200602013.htm.

for rural. Focusing on a year four years *after* what we measured, Xu and colleagues' urban estimate was 45 percent more than ours, while their rural figure proved slightly smaller. This divergence in urban and rural consumption patterns is largely a result of Xu and colleagues' adjustment to urban per capita consumption that we have not factored in: the inclusion of food consumed away from home (FAFH) into residential grain use.

In NBS household surveys, the officials do not take into account FAFH such as outside dining.[183] Hence, to compute the full aggregate residential food and feed consumption, researchers need to make extrapolations. For urban households, Xu and colleagues used NBS data on cash expenditure on outside dining to develop a grain equivalent of FAFH but assumed rural households have no such spending, and thus their rural estimate is closer to ours, which did not consider FAFH either. In Qiu and colleagues' work, the authors cited FAFH reestimates from a 2013 book draft on China's changing pattern of food consumption coauthored by Qiu, Junfei Bai, and Jikun Huang from CCAP, which factored in a wider range of indicators in recalculation than Xu and colleagues did.[184] Given its more sophisticated nature, we decided to reproduce Qiu and colleagues' FAFH estimation method in our model. The book draft that Qiu and colleagues cited noted that FAFH can result in a 25 to 30 percent increase in urban household grain consumption and a 15 to 20 percent addition for rural families.[185] We took the average of the two estimate-ranges as the new FAFH "adjusters"—namely, 27.5 percent for urban and 17.5 percent for rural households—and multiplied them by respective per capita grain consumption previously calculated. At last we arrived at two augmented consumption figures. Applying the proper population data, we computed the urban households' aggregate grain consumption in food and feed at 257.3 million tons, and rural households' at 303.4 million tons (Table 3.44). Comparing our 2008 FAFH-adjusted urban and rural total with Xu and colleagues', our 560.7 million tons is slightly larger than their 2010 figure of 553 million tons and a touch below their 2012 estimate of 569 million tons. The similarity of our results despite the difference in timeframe was mostly because we considered FAFH for rural residents, while they did not.[186]

We next turned to the industrial grain consumption estimate. Our main imputation method was to rely on data on China's ethanol production in 2008 and a grain-equivalent conversion ratio of 3.2, which we calculated based on the input-output relationship between grain feedstock use and fuel ethanol production in 2007.[187] For a third type of grain

183. Xiaohua Yu and David Abler, "Where Have All the Pigs Gone? Inconsistencies in Pork Statistics in China," *China Economic Review* 30 (September 2014): 479, http://www.sciencedirect.com/science/article/pii /S1043951X1400025X.

184. Xu, Zhang, and Li, "China's Grain Production"; Qiu et al., "Matching," 7; Junfei Bai, Huanguang Qiu, and Jikun Huang, *Changes of China's Food Consumption* (Beijing: China Academy of Sciences, 2013).

185. Qiu et al., "Matching," 7; Bai, Qiu, and Huang, *Changes of China's Food Consumption*.

186. Xu, Zhang, and Li, "China's Grain Production." We were not able to compare our estimates to those of Xu et al. in the same year (2008) because they only published data for separate years such as 2010 and 2012 in their study.

187. British Petroleum, *BP Statistical Review of World Energy*, June 2014, 39, http://www.bp.com/content /dam/bp/pdf/Energy-economics/statistical-review-2014/BP-statistical-review-of-world-energy-2014-renewables -section.pdf; International Institute for Sustainable Development (IISD), *Biofuels—At What Cost? Government Support for Ethanol and Biodiesel in China* (Geneva, Switzerland: IISD, November 2008), 16–17, http://www.iisd .org/gsi/sites/default/files/china_biofuels_subsidies.pdf. According to data on estimated consumption of maize,

Table 3.44. Grain Consumption as Food and Feed in 2008

Consumption pc (kg)	Urban	Rural	Conversion Ratio Urban*	Conversion Ratio Rural
Grain	63.6	199.1	1.1	1.0
Vegetable Oil	10.3	5.4	6.5	6.5
Animal Oil	n/a	0.9	4.6	4.6
Pork	19.3	12.7	4.6	4.6
Beef and Mutton	3.4	1.3	3.7	3.7
Poultry	8.5	4.4	3.2	3.2
Eggs	10.7	5.4	3.6	3.6
Aqua Products	11.9	5.2	2.0	2.0
Diary	15.2	3.4	0.2	1.2
Alcohol	7.7	9.7	0.7	0.7
Imputed Grain Consumption pc (kg)	336.2	356.5		
FAFH-Augmented Grain Consump. pc (kg)	428.7	418.9		
Population[†] (million)	600.2	724.4		
Aggregate Grain Consumption (mn tons)	*257.3*	*303.4*		

* The conversion ratio for urban households' grain consumption was given at 1.1. Without explicit explanation from the CAAS researchers, we assume it factors in the loss of grain in refining processes; the rural ratio does not.

[†] It denotes average population in 2008, calculated by averaging NBS's year-end population data for 2007 and 2008, prior to 2010 *Population Census* revisions.

Sources: Liang and Sun (2006), Bai et al. (2013), NBS, authors' calculations.

use—inventory changes—we calculated using grain stock estimates for China (including rice, wheat, and coarse grain) published by the U.S. Department of Agriculture (USDA),[188] because China does not publish food reserve levels, which are deemed state secrets.[189] Next, we moved on to appraise seed consumption and losses of grain, which turned out to be 4 percent of grain output.[190] Finally, we extracted exports and imports (including cereal—rice and wheat—soybean, and edible vegetable oil) data from the NBS statistical yearbook and converted nongrain commodity values into grain equivalent for the convenience of computations. Our final estimate for China's aggregate grain demand in 2008 came up at 605.9 million tons, 14.8 million tons short of official aggregate supply: we could discern no explanation for this discrepancy other than output overstatement. That translates into a 2.8 percent *downward* revision to the official grain output and equally proportionally to the grain portion of farming GOV and value-added (Table 3.45).[191]

---

wheat, and cassava used for fuel ethanol production in 2007 in the IISD report, we calculated the grain-ethanol conversion ratio for China at 3.2, and we assumed this ratio could be applied to 2008. Data on China's biofuel production were obtained from BP.

188. U.S. Department of Agriculture, "Grain: World Markets and Trade" (USDA, January 2015), 8, 13, 18, http://apps.fas.usda.gov/psdonline/circulars/grain.pdf.

189. U.S. International Trade Commission, *China's Agricultural Trade: Competitive Conditions and Effects on U.S. Exports* (Washington, D.C.: USITC, March 2011), 4–27, http://www.usitc.gov/publications/332/pub4219.pdf.

190. Xu, Zhang, and Li, "China's Grain Production."

191. Cereal and soybean are already grain crops by definition; edible vegetable oil is not and was converted to grain-equivalent using a ratio of 6.5 (as in Table 3.44).

Table 3.45. Supply-Demand Balance Sheet for Grain

Unit: Million tons

2008	Value
Aggregate Supply	*620.7*
Official Output	528.7
Imports	92.0
Aggregate Demand	*605.9*
Aggregate Grain Consumption as Food and Feed	560.7
Industrial Consumption	3.5
Seed Consumption and Losses	21.1
Inventory Changes	16.6
Exports	3.9
Supply-Demand Gap	*14.8*
Grain Output Revision as % of Official Output	**−2.8%**

Sources: NBS, authors' estimates.

Our 2.8 percent gap was smaller than the 9.2 percent discrepancy implied in Xu and colleagues' study (see Footnote 180 for details). Xu and colleagues' wider differential could result not only from official overstatement but also by the authors' underestimate of observable grain uses. In the conclusion section, Xu and colleagues did point out that the likelihood of official overreporting was higher than the other way around.[192] Given their assessment and our own reestimates, we believe the overall distortions in NBS grain output data are modest. NBS dispatches teams to collect grain output data directly, several times a year, and the households they survey produce more than 95 percent of national grain yield.[193] That regime design, along with other institutional improvements after two national agricultural censuses, has helped strengthen data soundness for grain and for the farming industry that takes up more than half of the primary-sector GOV. However, in two other industries we now turn to, the conditions appear less optimistic.

ANIMAL HUSBANDRY—MEAT

In China's animal husbandry industry, major products include meat (predominantly pork, beef, and mutton), milk, poultry and eggs, wool (sheep and goat), cashmere, and honey. Meat has always been the largest output, and its production has steadily grown over the last decade with population and wealth growth, except in 2007, when the outbreak of "blue ear disease" killed millions of hogs, resulting in a 7.8 percent drop in annual pork output and 3.2 percent fall in meat overall. Pork is the most consumed and produced meat in China, accounting for about 65 percent of total output. From 2001 to 2013 average growth

---

192. Xu, Zhang, and Li, "China's Grain Production."

193. NBS, "粮食产量 (Grain Yield)," 2014, http://www.stats.gov.cn/tjzs/tjbk/nsbzb/201402/P020140226558972787262.pdf.

rates both for pork and overall meat production were 2.6 percent. When pork output fluctuates, meat output mirrors the swing, regardless of how beef and mutton perform.

Official data on animal products output have long been suspected of overstatement, a view validated by findings from the two national agricultural censuses (for 1996 and 2006), both of which cut meat and pork output as well as animal husbandry GOV in general. Comparing NBS statistical yearbooks before and after these censuses, we found the first agricultural census erased 21.8 percent of pork output from the prerevision 1996 level and 22.3 percent for meat output in general. In value terms, 1996 animal husbandry GOV was revised down 15 percent, but only after a full year lag following the volume data revision. After the 2006 census, pork and meat output levels were again cut, by 10.5 percent and 12 percent respectively, and animal husbandry GOV was down by 11.4 percent. For meat output, unlike the first census that only revised back one year to 1995, the second census revision traced back to 2000. While providing a longer revised data series for independent researchers to assess, the fragmented revision left 1997–1999 in the dark, not subject to either census. For animal husbandry GOV, the restatements were even more selective: the first census adjusted 1996–1997 figures, published in NBS's 1999 *Statistical Yearbook*, whereas the second census revised 2006 GOV only, as reported in the 2008 *Statistical Yearbook* (Figure 3.2).[194] The inconsistency in time series, as was described in earlier sections, poses a great challenge for outside scholars, and erodes the credit Chinese statisticians should have earned for their efforts at improvement.

Suspicious about China's meat, and especially pork, data, Xiaohua Yu at University of Göttingen and David Abler at Penn State University used classic supply-demand analysis to delve into discrepancies they spotted between official pork supply and consumption statistics, and between official supply estimates and their own. With NBS supply figures significantly above both NBS consumption and the imputed pork supply data, the authors proposed hypotheses to explain the discrepancy, including production overreporting, loss and waste in the pork supply chain, and underestimated consumption.[195] After careful examination, the authors concluded that production overreporting was the main factor, accounting for about one-half of the gap in official accounts from 1996 to 2009.[196] Based on

194. Unlike the once-every-five-year economic census, the agricultural census does not revise historical data in a consistent manner. For both censuses, their revision years for meat output, animal husbandry and agricultural GOV, and primary-sector VA did not align. Besides what we have described about meat output and GOV changes in the main text, the second census resulted in *downward* revisions to primary sector value-added for 2005 and 2006, each by 2.8 percent, but not for other years; the first census did not entail any VA revision at all, based on our comparison of different years' NBS statistical yearbooks. There is no explicit explanation from NBS as to why the revisions were inconsistent, and we surmised it was a result of institutional incompetence and lack of basic materials to revise historical data. Beyond the two census revisions, there were other, more modest revisions to agricultural data over the last two decades, presumably due to routine GDP revisions and industrial reclassification.

195. Yu and Abler, "Inconsistencies in Pork Statistics," 469–484. Supply, in their definition, includes domestic production and net exports, wherein net exports of pork were negative in 2008 and 2010, indicating de facto net imports, and about zero in 2009.

196. Yu and Abler, "Inconsistencies in Pork Statistics," 472–482. Yu and Abler first estimated China's per capita pork supply in 2008 at 26.7 kg, using production data from the Ministry of Agriculture's National Fixed Point Survey and feed data from the China Feed Industry Association. They then compared their supply

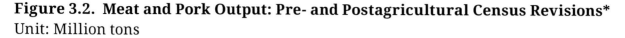

Figure 3.2. Meat and Pork Output: Pre- and Postagricultural Census Revisions*
Unit: Million tons

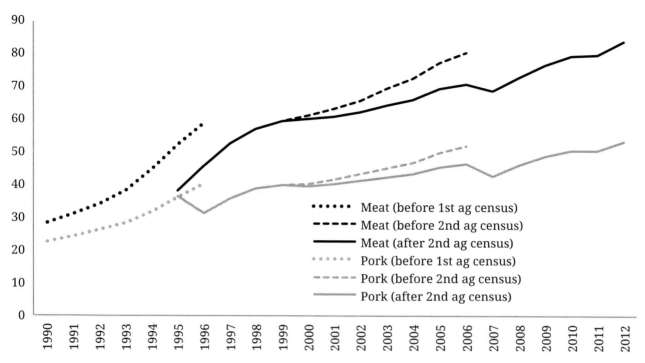

Legend:
- •••••• Meat (before 1st ag census)
- ‒ ‒ ‒ Meat (before 2nd ag census)
- —— Meat (after 2nd ag census)
- •••••• Pork (before 1st ag census)
- ‒ ‒ ‒ Pork (before 2nd ag census)
- —— Pork (after 2nd ag census)

* Besides first census revisions, 1996 data were also subject to modest, routine modifications over the decade prior to the second census.
Source: NBS.

the authors' findings we extrapolated implied distortion in meat statistics based just on pork (leaving other meat data unadjusted, as noted above): our results indicated that 2008 meat output should be adjusted down 15.1 percent.

Yu and Abler's pork supply-demand balance sheet is a valuable tool for stress-testing official statistics. However, one of their choices needed adjustment, in our view. The authors used the conversion ratio to impute hogs' live weight and applied a 70 percent dressing ratio—the share of carcass weight to live weight—to extrapolate pork output. The dressing percentage they cited was from a 1991 study by the UN Food and Agriculture Organization (FAO), which we considered outdated for a 2008 recalculation.[197] In a 1998 essay, a Peking University professor estimated an 80 percent dressing ratio for hogs, yet that was based on a single district's survey in Beijing and thus was unlikely representative

estimate with NBS's per capita production of 34.8 kg—adjusting the latter by adding per capita net imports of 0.2 kg—and argued the discrepancy of 8.3 kg was due to overreporting. In a second parallel comparison, they computed the gap between NBS's own per capita pork consumption in 2008 (15.7 kg) and production (34.8 kg)—similarly adjusting the latter by including the net imports of 0.2 kg—and found it was 19.3 kg. According to the authors' analysis, in 2008 production overreporting contributed 43 percent of the gap in the second approach, and the actual per capita pork production should be 23.9 percent lower than official claims.

197. Ibid., 473, 475–476. Food and Agriculture Organization of the United Nations (FAO), "Guidelines for Slaughtering, Meat Cutting and Further Processing," 1991, http://www.fao.org/docrep/004/T0279E/T0279E00.HTM.

of national conditions a decade later.[198] Given this, we set out to explore whether there is an alternative approach to appraise meat output distortion.

We turned to the two census revisions to meat output, the most authoritative acknowledgement of distortions in animal husbandry data. As noted earlier, the second agriculture census for 2006 entailed a much smaller *downward* revision to meat output than the first one—12 percent versus 22.3 percent in 1996—which implied that over the years, with improvements to China's agricultural data and statistical system, the scale of errors decreased.[199] Assuming that improvement in meat data were continuous and progressed at the same pace each year, we would be able to extrapolate the underlying level of distortion in 2008 data. With that leap we would conclude that the official 2008 meat output had been overstated by 11.8 percent—not a result from rigorous calculations but empirical extrapolations from limited official data—and the corresponding *downward* adjustment should be 10.6 percent of the official level.

In reality, the improvement in data distortions is unlikely to occur at a constant pace over the decade from 1996 to 2008. Yet, without sufficient data to construct an alternative model besides Yu and Abler's supply-demand balance sheet, the aforementioned reestimate provides a useful reference. It also comports with the 15.1 percent *downward* revision we extrapolated from Yu and Abler's work on pork data. In fact, when explaining the gap between NBS supply and their FAFH-adjusted official consumption data, the authors suggested that the actual FAFH, pork consumed away from home, could have been higher than the best estimate they brought into the final model. To be specific, the authors imputed FAFH under three scenarios in order to adjust official household consumption that do not consider FAFH, and they ended up with the midlevel estimate, meaning it was possible that a higher portion of China's pork supply-demand gap can be explained by FAFH underestimation and, correspondingly, a *smaller* portion by output overreporting.[200] In short, Yu and Abler's downward revisions to 2008 pork and meat output could have been smaller, and thus closer to our estimates.

FISHERY—AQUATIC PRODUCTS

Fishery is the third largest industry in China's primary sector. Since 1999, China has been the world's top fish-producing country, followed by Indonesia, the United States,

---

198. Feng Lu, "肉蛋水产品生产消费知多少? (How Much Do We Know About Production and Consumption of Meat, Eggs, and Aquatic Products?)" (China Center for Economic Research, 1998), 7, http://old.ccer.edu.cn/download/1282-2.pdf.

199. The revisions to 2000–2005 meat output data after the second census were not derived from direct reassessment of those years' data but from the 2006 census result. In China's statistical revision conventions, the revision to historical data would reduce in scale as it stretches back, as seen in 2004 and 2008 economic census restatements. Given this, we do not think the fact that 2000 meat output was revised less than 2006 data means the former was more solid than the latter; the former revision was not derived from a straightforward reevaluation but from the latter inversely through time at a progressively decreasing rate—the earlier the year of revision, the smaller the scale of revision. In this study we only consider the difference between revisions to 1996 and 2006, two census measurement years.

200. Yu and Abler, "Inconsistencies in Pork Statistics," 480.

and Peru.[201] In 2008 more than one-third of global fishery output, including capture and aquaculture, was from China.[202] Unlike the United States, which categorizes aquaculture as animal production, China includes aquaculture along with fishing in fishery and divides the industry's output, aquatic products, into seawater and freshwater categories. Of the two, seawater has always been the larger component, but its share of total domestic aquatic output has been declining for three decades, from more than 75 percent in 1978 to 51 percent in 2012, as capture fishery resources are being exhausted rapidly and aquaculture, more in freshwater than in seawater, is expanding with growing demand.

In China's fishery accounting regime, fishery statistics are submitted from the bottom up following two parallel lines of bureaucracy: fishery and statistical systems, a *kuai-kuai* structure as introduced in Chapter 2. Basic fishery data are first reported by fishermen and fishing companies to lowest-level fishery and statistical bureaucrats in villages and towns. The bureaucrats compile data for submission to county-level fishery and statistical authorities, which then hand data to the Ministry of Agriculture's Bureau of Fisheries and to the NBS. This kind of reporting hierarchy incentivizes local cadres to manipulate data in their own interest, such as to meet growth targets for political promotions. The reporting regime lacks key ingredients: close central supervision (such as in the case of grain surveying), alignment between industry regulators and state statisticians, and a consolidated Internet-based submission system (like that for secondary and tertiary subsectors). This invites considerable data problems.[203]

Besides bureaucrats, fishing companies massage data for various purposes, such as outranking competitors and qualifying for privileged access to funds. In a farcical October 2014 case, Zhangzidao Fishery Group Company—one of China's largest seafood producers and a listed company—announced a loss of nearly RMB 1 billion on its scallop stocks right *before* the harvest season, blaming severe cold water currents for the massacre. Shocked by the incident and the timing of the announcement, investors suspected Zhangzidao had faked inventory data in the first place, a hypothesis reinforced by a rapidly spreading rumor that Zhangzidao had made bad bets on real estate and was trying to hide losses through accounting manipulation. Such malfeasance, although rare at this scale, complicates national accounting for the industry.[204]

China's first agriculture census for 1996 did not cover fishery, so aquatic product data were not subject to major revisions like meat output until the second census. After three decades of operating in the dark, the 2006 census resulted in a 13.4 percent cut to official aquatic output estimates. The revisions were extended back to 1997, the first year after the

201. Food and Agriculture Organization of the United Nations (FAO), *Fishery and Aquaculture Statistics 2012* (Rome, 2014), xvi, http://www.fao.org/fishery/statistics/programme/publications/all/en.

202. Ibid.

203. Jiahua Le and Zhengyi Shao, "渔业统计制度的国际比较及对我国的启示 (A Comparative Study on Fishery Statistical System of Different Countries and Implication for China)," *Statistical Research*, no. 7 (2008): 91, http://tjyj.stats.gov.cn/CN/abstract/abstract888.shtml.

204. Jin Wang and Pengfei Li, "捕捞队员爆料: 獐子岛扇贝投苗掺沙子 (Fishing Crew Revealed Zhangzidao Group Casted Juvenile Scallops Mixed with Sand)," Yicai.com, November 5, 2014, http://www.yicai.com/news/2014/11/4036480.html.

Figure 3.3. Aquatic Products: Pre- and Post-2006 Census Revisions*
Unit: Million tons

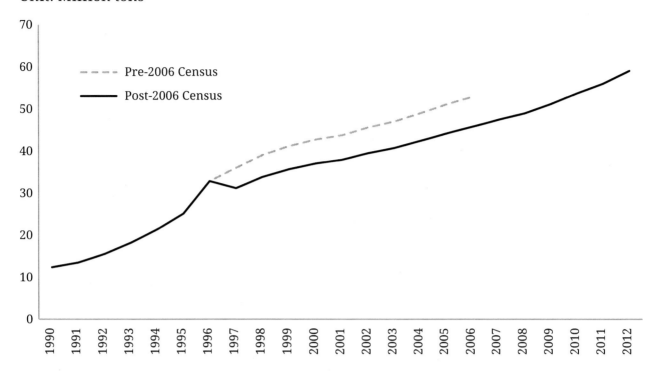

* The second census revisions covered the period of 1997–2006.
Source: NBS.

1996 census, with each year's level reduced roughly proportionately. Freshwater data were subject to a slightly deeper cut than seawater, by about 0.5 percentage points during the revision period (Figure 3.3).

With relatively abundant data for fishery, we decided to construct a supply-demand balance sheet like that for grain to stress-test official data. Aggregate aquatic supply should equal its aggregate demand (subject to net trade and other adjustments), but this does not hold for China. Based on the balance sheet models for farming and animal husbandry, we set the total supply and demand formulas as follows:

1. Aggregate supply of aquatic products = Total domestic output + Imports

2. Aggregate demand of aquatic products = Household consumption[205] + Food consumed away from home (FAFH) + Industrial consumption + Waste and losses + Exports + Inventory changes

Unlike in grain statistics, "industrial consumption" of aquatic products, which refers to final consumption of products in industrial activities, is not an officially established concept. Two terms akin to industrial consumption in official fishery accounts are "aquatic product input for processing" (*yongyu jiagong de shuichanpin zongliang*, "processing input")

---

205. Household consumption here refers strictly to the amount recorded in official NBS accounts.

and "total processed aquatic products" (*shuichan jiagongpin zongliang*, "processing output"). Processing input is a gross concept that is defined as total uses of aquatic products for processing purposes, and processing output includes a variety of processed fishery products, such as frozen products, minced fish, canned food, fish oil, and pearls. In lieu of an official definition, we defined industrial consumption in our balance sheet as equal to processing input less processing output. Because FAFH is not captured in NBS household surveys, and inventory change data are lacking, we cannot conveniently compute aggregate demand by summing up the different uses, as demonstrated in Table 3.46.

In this preliminary version of the supply-demand model, all data were either obtained directly from NBS yearbooks and China's fishery statistical yearbooks (overseen by the Ministry of Agriculture) or imputed from yearbook statistics. One exception is supply chain loss, data for which is missing from both yearbooks; but according to the National Development and Reform Commission's Development Plan for Agricultural Products Cold Chain Logistics in 2010, the loss should be 15 percent of total domestic output of aquatic products.[206] This means a 15 percent loss factor due to spoilage, waste, or other attrition.[207]

Given this, we revised our model. Among other changes, we substituted processing inputs for industrial consumption, inventory changes, and the portion of processed products in domestic consumption and exports. The underlying implication is that processing output is consumed domestically, exported, or added to inventories (of wholesalers, retailers, hotels, and restaurants). Because processing output is part of processing input and part of it flows to domestic dinner tables, there is an overlap between processing input and household consumption. USDA once noted in a fishery report that China's aquatic exports are mainly processed products,[208] which implies fresh aquatic products are largely for domestic uses. However, we do not yet know the exact share of unprocessed and processed products in either exports or residential consumption.

To compute the aggregate demand of aquatic products, we need to render all the components mutually exclusive of one another, so the overlap between residential

206. National Development and Reform Commission, "农产品冷链物流发展规划 (Development Plan for Agricultural Products Cold Chain Logistics)," June 2010, 5, http://zfxxgk.ndrc.gov.cn/Attachment/农产品冷链物流发展规划.pdf.

207. Here we used official figures for domestic fishery output and household consumption of aquatic products from NBS statistical yearbooks. Other data such as natural disaster loss, import, and export were obtained from the *China Fishery Statistical Yearbook 2010*. There is a discrepancy in aquatic export data between the NBS statistical yearbook and the fishery statistical yearbook: the NBS data are always smaller. This is because the coverage of export data in the fishery statistical yearbook is broader and includes not only general trade, as in the NBS yearbook, but also processing trade. The latter refers to goods imported for processing and then exported out. We chose the fishery yearbook data because it is more comprehensive, and such processing trade is counted toward GDP; see NBS, *Methods of Non-Economic Census Year, 2010 Ed.*, 175. Industrial consumption is calculated as processing input of aquatic products less processing output, with data from the fishery yearbook.

208. Chanda Beckman, Xinping Wu, and Angie Han, *China, Peoples Republic of: Fishery Products Annual Report*, GAIN Report (Beijing: U.S. Department of Agriculture, December 22, 2009), 7, http://gain.fas.usda.gov/Recent%20GAIN%20Publications/Fishery%20Products%20Annual_Beijing_China%20-%20Peoples%20Republic%20of_12-30-2010.pdf.

Table 3.46. Aquatic Product Supply-Demand Balance Sheet (Preliminary)

Unit: Million tons

2008	Value
Aggregate Supply	*52.85*
Output	48.96
Imports	3.89
Aggregate Demand	*n/a*
Household Consumption*	10.94
FAFH	n/a
Industrial Consumption†	2.70
Waste and Losses	9.40
Supply Chain Loss	7.34
Natural Disaster Loss	2.06
Exports	2.99
Inventory Changes	n/a

* Household consumption is computed based on official population and per capita aquatic product consumption data, exclusive of FAFH.

† Industrial consumption equals processing input less processing output, wherein processing input overlaps official household consumption, exports, and inventory changes.

Sources: NBS, Ministry of Agriculture, authors' estimates.

consumption—household consumption and FAFH (excluded in official consumption data)—and processing input must be addressed. The same is true for exports: because some of the processing output (and thus part of the processing input) is shipped outside China, we need to remove the double-counted part between official exports and processing input.[209] In light of these nuances, we revised the aggregate demand and supply formulas as follows:

1. Aggregate supply = Total domestic output + Imports

2. Aggregate demand = Household consumption (unprocessed only) + FAFH (unprocessed only) + Processing input + Waste and losses + Exports (unprocessed only)

Because all processed aquatic products—whether in household consumption, FAFH, exports, or other unspecified uses—are covered by processing input, data for which are available in official accounts, we only need to figure out the unprocessed portion in the aggregate demand formula. So three more estimates are needed: the portion of

---

209. According to China's fishery statistical yearbook, both live fish and iced fresh fish are not classified as processed aquatic products, while frozen fish is classified as a processed product.

unprocessed aquatic products in official household consumption, the unprocessed aquatic products in FAFH, and the unprocessed portion in total aquatic exports. Next we explain how we extrapolated each of these variables.

First, we tackled the overlap between household consumption and processing input. Because the NBS consumption data include both unprocessed and processed products, to separate the two, we used the ratio of processing input to aggregate supply for imputation. All aquatic products are either consumed without being processed or are processed first. Hence, we assumed that on Chinese diets, the share of unprocessed and processed foods (and indirectly consumed feeds) aligns with the national market structure. For specific computation, we relied on data in 2006, the year for the second agricultural census, for quality purposes. In 2006, of all aquatic product supply—official output plus imports—33.3 percent was used as processing input, and the remaining 66.7 percent was consumed as unprocessed, inside and outside China, or exhausted as waste and losses. We therefore assumed that of all household aquatic product consumption, 66.7 percent was unprocessed, and we applied this ratio to the 2008 analysis. Consequently, we computed households' consumption of unprocessed aquatic products in 2006 at 7.4 million tons and in 2008 at 7.3 million tons.

The second task is to impute the unprocessed portion of FAFH, aquatic products consumed away from home that are not included in official household figures. We reverted to the FAFH "adjusters" we previously referred to in the grain analysis based on Bai and colleagues' study. The three FAFH adjusters available are for grain, meat, and eggs, and each adjuster consists of a pair of indices for urban and rural households, respectively. In lieu of an ideal fishery product adjuster, we used that for meat. According to Bai and colleagues, FAFH can result in a 40 to 45 percent increase on top of official urban household meat consumption and a 20 to 30 percent increase for rural families.[210] We again averaged the two estimate-ranges, settling on a 42.5 percent adjuster for urban and 25 percent for rural households, and multiplied the adjusters by imputed, unprocessed household consumption to obtain the FAFH in unprocessed form. Assuming on the national level the ratio of unprocessed to processed aquatic consumption in urban and rural households is the same, we calculated the total FAFH of unprocessed aquatic products at 2.71 million tons in 2006 and at 2.66 million tons in 2008.

The third and last task we faced was to compute the portion of unprocessed export products. The process of extrapolation for this step is a bit complex, which we explain in detail in Appendix 3.6. To be brief, based on general customs and China's Ministry of Commerce (MOFCOM) data, we computed the unprocessed export products in the categories of fish, mollusks (such as scallops), and crustaceans (like crabs and lobsters) and added them up to compute the unprocessed portion of total exports. According to our calculations, in 2006, 6.48 percent of China's total aquatic exports were categorized as "unprocessed" under official definitions, whereas in 2008, the percentage slightly dropped to 6.02 percent.

---

210. Qiu et al., "Matching," 7; Bai, Qiu, and Huang, *Changes of China's Food Consumption*.

Table 3.47. Aquatic Product Supply-Demand Balance Sheet (Modified)

Unit: Million tons

	2006	2008
Aggregate Supply	*49.16*	*52.85*
Official Output	45.84	48.96
Imports	3.32	3.89
Aggregate Demand	*34.91*	*35.92*
Augmented Household Consumption*	10.12	9.97
Adjusted Official Household Consumption	7.40	7.30
FAFH	2.71	2.66
Processing Input†	16.35	16.37
Waste and Losses	8.25	9.40
Supply Chain Loss	6.88	7.34
Natural Disaster Loss	1.38	2.06
Exports (unprocessed only)	0.20	0.18
Gap = Aggregate Supply – Aggregate Demand	14.24	16.93
Gap as % of Official Output‡	31.1%	34.6%
Systemic Error in Demand as % of Actual Output	*31.1%*	*31.1%*
Recl. Actual Output	45.84	46.47
% of Overreporting in Official Output	0%	5.4%
Revision as % of Official Output	**0%**	**–5.1%**

* Augmented household consumption includes the portion of unprocessed aquatic products in official household consumption and imputed FAFH. That portion was decided based on 2006's ratio of unprocessed aquatic product demand to total supply; FAFH was imputed using ratios noted in Bai et al. (2013).

† Processing input includes industrial consumption and processing output (residential demand and exports of processed aquatic products, and all inventory changes).

‡ Here we assumed 2006 official output data were accurate in order to compute the systemic error in our model-based demand.

Sources: NBS, Ministry of Agriculture, MOFCOM, Bai et al. (2013), authors' estimates.

Leveraging these two ratios and general customs trade data, we calculated China's unprocessed export products in 2006 at 195,263 tons and in 2008 at 179,659 tons.

With all these new estimates and the modified formulas, we computed the gap between China's 2008 aggregate supply and demand of aquatic products at 16.93 million tons, or 34.6 percent of official domestic output. That is a large gap, yet we cannot attribute everything to output overreporting because there is one obvious factor still unaddressed: our potential understatement of aggregate demand due to underestimated FAFH,[211] undercounted supply chain losses due to lax logistics accounting, and other unaccounted uses. To test whether that systemic error exists and, if so, to gauge how large it is, we benchmarked our model against China's official data for 2006, the measurement year for the second

---

211. Although we factored FAFH into our model, the adjusters we used were for meat and thus can be inaccurate.

agricultural census. Based on our model, we believe a 5.1 percent cut to the 2008 official output is justified in order to reflect the reality; the erased part, needless to say, represents output overreporting suggested by our model (Table 3.47).[212]

Looking again at Table 3.43, which summarized our revisions to farming, animal husbandry, and fishery, all restatements are downward, thus illustrating the overstatement tendency of production-approach GDP that we described in Chapter 2. Primary sector is the only sector in China today whose preferred national accounting approach is solely based on production measures. With so many small farmers and unincorporated operations in this area, transitioning to an income approach is difficult. Statisticians have worked for 15 years to improve the primary sector statistical system, but their efforts are hampered. Current policy priorities emphasize rationalization and modernization for China's food production systems, but the statistical underpinnings of that reform have a long way to go.

Research and Development Expenditures

When NBS signaled in November 2013 that it intended to migrate to 2008 SNA by late 2014 or early 2015, some suspected an intention to overstate actual GDP or meet political goals set out in growth targets.[213] Such conspiracy theories are misguided. Advanced economies and the more capable developing nations worldwide are also in the process of comporting to 2008 SNA. This is not about accounting tricks but better statistical regimes. Moreover upward revisions to capture previously unrecognized activity make it harder to achieve higher growth results in the future, not easier. In the end, Beijing deferred stepping up to 2008 SNA when it released results of the third national economic census in December 2014—a reality NBS acknowledged in early 2015. In this section we assess what the transition would have done—and will at some point mean—for Chinese GDP, in particular the effect of counting research and development (R&D) expenditures as investment (a part of expenditure-based GDP), rather than just as an intermediate expense (which is not counted).

Based on other countries' experiences, the inclusion of R&D as capital formation is the most significant 2008 SNA revision. In the following sections we explain why counting R&D is important, discuss other national experiences, and look at China's current practice. Based on that foundation, we use available data to estimate a range of adjustments to China's 2008 GDP level from R&D inclusion.

---

212. For fishery data, 2006 is arguably the most accurately measured year thanks to the census. If we assume the postrevision output data in 2006 represented the actual domestic production level, the gap between our imputed aggregate supply and demand for 2006, when divided by 2006 official output, would represent the scale of systemic error in our model-based demand. Following the extrapolation steps above, we imputed 2006 aggregate demand data, which is 34.91 million tons, and 14.24 million tons short of the aggregate supply—officially reported output plus imports. That differential equals 31.1 percent of the official output (45.84 million tons) that year. Because we assumed that 2006 output data was accurate and the systemic error in our model applies to 2008, too, using that demand omission (as a share of actual output), we managed to impute the actual domestic output of aquatic products in 2008. It turned out to be 46.47 million tons, 5.1 percent *smaller* than the official reporting of 48.96 million tons.

213. Zhidong Qiao, "Experts: Thinking GDP Accounting Method Revision was to Window-Dress Growth is a Misreading," People.com.cn, July 4, 2014, http://finance.people.com.cn/n/2014/0704/c1004-25237404.html.

2008 SNA defines R&D as "creative work undertaken on a systematic basis to increase the stock of knowledge, and use of this stock of knowledge for the purpose of discovering or developing new products."[214] R&D spending and activities improve products and introduce efficiencies to production processes, while possessing the enduring value characteristics of fixed assets. R&D is closely tied to innovation, technology, and total factor productivity. R&D inputs can generate enormous economic benefits for a country. R&D assets, including patents, trademarks, and process knowhow, are continuously expanding. Neglecting to count them alongside factories and truck fleets obviously understates the productive capacity and growth potential of an increasingly knowledge-driven economy. Thus, 2008 SNA recommends expanding the asset boundary to include intangible R&D as a part of capital formation, except in cases where "it is clear that the activity does not entail any economic benefit for its owner, in which case it is treated as intermediate consumption."[215]

To measure R&D value, 2008 SNA recommends the summing of R&D expenditures when a market value for resultant R&D is not directly observable. In principle, it should be measured "in terms of the economic benefits it is expected to provide in the future."[216] China is capable of meeting this accounting burden, having systematically monitored science and technology (S&T) activities at the national level for two decades while gradually shifting its focus to R&D activities, an integral component of S&T activities by China's definition.[217] Better representation of the value derived from intangible assets is essential to an accurate understanding of China's allocation of investment and an assessment of whether the investment is still biased to already overcapacity industrial equipment in the face of growing intangible investment. From that increasing statistical need for capturing intangible assets, China has so far conducted two comprehensive national surveys for R&D resources—for 2000 and 2009, respectively—in a joint effort by several government agencies.[218] Based on results of the 2009 R&D census, NBS and other government agencies considerably amended the existing science and technology statistical framework, especially in emphasizing the role of innovation. Starting in 2010, both the *China Statistical*

214. UN, *2008 SNA*, 119.
215. Ibid., 122.
216. Ibid., 206.
217. NBS, *China's Main Statistical Concepts*, 439, 443–444. By definition, S&T activities include R&D activities, applications of R&D results, and related S&T services. R&D activities are the core and most innovative component of S&T activities. China established a national science and technology statistical reporting system (*keji zonghe tongji baobiao zhidu*) in 1992, when NBS also published total R&D expenditures for the first time. To supplement the previous annual reporting that only covered R&D institutions, higher educational institutions, and large and medium enterprises, in the mid-1990s, NBS established a science and technology survey system on a rolling basis (*keji tongji gundong diaocha zhidu*). The survey system includes a periodic survey on S&T activities conducted once every five years for small industrial enterprises and for a few S&T-intensive subsectors/industries; the system also includes an annual sampling survey for one or two subsectors, selected randomly.
218. Ministry of Science and Technology of the People's Republic of China, "Six Government Agencies to Launch the Second National R&D Census," July 6, 2009, http://www.most.gov.cn/kjbgz/200907/t20090703_71626 .htm. The supervising government agencies are the Ministry of Science and Technology (MoST), NBS, the National Development and Reform Commission (NDRC), the Ministry of Education (MoE), the Ministry of Finance (MoF), and the State Administration of Science, Technology and Industry for National Defense (SASTIND) under the Ministry of Industry and Information Technology (MoIIT).

Yearbook and *China Statistical Yearbook on Science and Technology* discontinued publishing S&T activity-related items.[219]

China needs to adjust its growth model. That reform mandate had been talked about for years and was forcefully underlined after the Party's Third Plenum in November 2013. This requires information on R&D returns—among other solid basic data—so that future investment can be allocated more efficiently. Better innovation outcomes was a clearly stated goal in the Third Plenum *Decision on Major Issues Concerning Comprehensively Deepening Reforms* (*Decisions*), which states that the government will "establish an innovation survey system and an innovation reporting system, while building an open and transparent mechanism for state scientific research resource management and project appraisal"[220] to disclose the research budgets of central government agencies. The aforementioned surveys for R&D activities have already included enormous information, such as number of personnel engaged in such activities, input and output relationships between R&D expenditures and funding sources, and relevant government policies. However, whether in annual reporting or two resource censuses, R&D expenditure data only explicitly cover enterprises, higher education, and government-affiliated R&D institutions but not necessarily government agencies per se.[221] It is unclear whether government's direct R&D expenditures have been considered and internally documented separately or have been assigned to administrative, educational, and R&D institutions, a large chunk of which are publicly (hence, government) owned in China.

In addition, the fact that the existing reporting scheme for R&D data starts from county- and city-level bureaus of science and technology and bureaus of statistics[222] fuels suspicion about local distortions of data and misgivings about central authorities' capability to cross-check information. To address the two data issues above, not only should the scheme be fundamentally reformed—as seen in the secondary sector and key tertiary subsectors—but statistical training should be reinforced for local staff. After all, R&D activities are a relatively alien concept to China's local statisticians compared with industrial output, and the definitions for different types of R&D activities are hard to strictly follow in practice.

In light of these problems with the existing R&D accounting regime, in March 2014, the State Council announced guidelines on improving transparency for government-led research grant allocation, a first step to address the systemic imbroglio.[223] Given this, the

---

219. NBS, *China's Main Statistical Concepts*, 442.

220. Daniel H. Rosen, *Avoiding the Blind Alley: China's Economic Overhaul and Its Global Implications* (New York: Asia Society, October 2014), 125, http://rhg.com/reports/avoiding-the-blind-alley-chinas-economic-overhaul-and-its-global-implications.

221. NBS, "Frequently Asked Questions: Science and Technology Statistics," November 5, 2013, http://www.stats.gov.cn/tjzs/cjwtjd/201311/t20131105_455938.html; Yutao Sun and Cong Cao, "Demystifying Central Government R&D Spending in China," *Science*, August 29, 2014, 1008, http://www.sciencemag.org/content/345/6200/1006.

222. NBS, *China's Main Statistical Concepts*, 445.

223. State Council, "国务院关于改进加强中央财政科研项目和资金管理的若干意见 (Several Opinions of the State Council on Improving Management of Central Government R&D Projects and Funds)" (Gov.cn, March 12, 2014), http://www.gov.cn/zhengce/content/2014-03/12/content_8711.htm.

previous Third Plenum *Decisions*, and NBS's earlier transition announcement, Beijing knows that accurately counting and capitalizing R&D into GDP is essential.

In late 2009, Australia became the first country to make its national accounts compliant with 2008 SNA, followed by Canada in 2012. In July 2013, the U.S. Bureau Economic Analysis (BEA) also took the step forward by comprehensively revamping the National Income and Product Accounts (NIPAs), including changing the treatment of R&D expenditures from intermediate consumption to investment in fixed assets, resulting in a net 2.5 percent upward revision to U.S. GDP in 2012.[224] South Korea converged to 2008 SNA in early 2014, the first nation in Asia to do so, with capitalization of R&D expenditures alone boosting its 2010 GDP by 3.6 percent.[225] Japan plans to fully implement 2008 SNA in 2016.[226] Other countries, including Israel and Mexico, have also recognized R&D as capital formation in their GDP. By September 2014, all EU member states had made the move.[227]

Among the countries that have converged to 2008 SNA and thus capitalize R&D expenditures, we selected six that published data on both R&D expenditures and final GDP change arising from R&D capitalization to estimate the conversion between R&D spending and value-added contribution. The six countries suggested that in 2008 (our recalculation year for China)—or another available year closest to 2008 if 2008 data were not available—an average of 88 percent of R&D expenditures passed through to headline GDP as value-added (Table 3.48).[228]

224. Stephanie H. McCulla, Alyssa E. Holdren, and Shelly Smith, "Improved Estimates of the National Income and Product Accounts: Results of the 2013 Comprehensive Revision," *Survey of Current Business* 93, no. 9 (September 2013): 17, 39, http://www.bea.gov/scb/pdf/2013/09%20September/0913_comprehensive_nipa _revision.pdf.

225. Goldman Sachs, "EM Macro Daily—Mind the Gap from New GDP Accounting Standards, Especially for Small Open Economies," September 17, 2014.

226. "全球GDP核算新变化对中国的启示 (The Implications of New GDP Accounting Method to China)," *China Economic Times*, May 23, 2014, http://www.cet.com.cn/ycpd/xbtj/1205017.shtml.

227. Eurostat, "Overview: About ESA 2010," http://ec.europa.eu/eurostat/web/esa-2010. Eurostat, "ESA 2010 Shifts Level of EU and Euro Area GDP Upward, Growth Rates Almost Unaffected," October 17, 2014, 1, http:// europa.eu/rapid/press-release_STAT-14-157_en.pdf.

228. The six countries have also been used as comparator countries in our model to estimate the impact of R&D capitalization on China's GDP in 2008, which we discuss at length in the following recalculation section. Some countries have upgraded R&D expenditure treatment to align with 2008 SNA but were not considered for this study due to one of the following reasons. First, because of timing differences between the countries' transition to 2008 SNA and the construction of our reestimate model, countries that had not made the leap by August 2014 were not considered. Second, among countries that made the transition early enough, Israel was excluded because official data on the R&D contribution to GDP were not available. Third, the Netherlands was not considered because its by-industry data on enterprise R&D expenditures, essential to our estimates for China, were incomplete. Fourth, the United Kingdom was dropped from our model because its economic structure was extravagantly different from China's. While the secondary sector played a dominant role in China's economy in 2008, the United Kingdom's tertiary sector was 3.5 times the secondary sector, and enterprise R&D expenditures of the tertiary sector were more than 50 percent larger than that of the secondary sector in the United Kingdom. Including the United Kingdom in our model was likely to distort our estimates for China. Consequently, we dropped it. Also, the 88 percent ratio does not represent a straightforward conversion relationship but a final result that considered new R&D expenditures, adjustments to source data in alignment with 2008 SNA definitions, and depreciation of the recalculated R&D asset stocks. We revisit this nuance with greater detail in the following recalculation section.

Table 3.48. Impact of R&D Capitalization on GDP (Select Countries)

	Year*	R&D Expenditures (% of GDP)	Resulting % Revision to GDP	% of R&D Exp. Converted to VA[†]
Australia[‡]	2007–2008	2.0 (2006–2007)	+1.4	66%
		2.25 (2008–2009)		
Canada	2008	1.7	+1.2	69%
United States	2008	2.8	+2.5	90%
South Korea	2010	3.7	+3.6	96%
France	2010	2.2	+2.2	96%
Singapore	2010	2.0	+2.2	108%
Average				**88%**

* For countries with data available for 2008, we selected 2008 in alignment with estimates for China; otherwise we chose the closest available year to 2008.

[†] The conversion ratio was calculated as a final, net value-added change to GDP divided by total R&D spending in the same period. The final change to GDP considered all adjustments related to R&D expenditure capitalization, including methodological changes to align source data with 2008 SNA concepts, removal of double-counting, and inclusion of asset depreciation. The presented conversion ratio is not a straightforward indication of how much R&D spending was effective and able to generate economic benefits.

[‡] The upward 1.4 percent revision to Australian GDP is for July 2007–June 2008. The Australian Bureau of Statistics publishes data in a form where the reference one-year period ends on June 30 each year; its GERD is produced every two years.

Sources: Eurostat, OECD, various state statistical authorities, Goldman Sachs, authors' calculations.

According to 2008 SNA, R&D undertaken by market producers on their own behalf should, in principle, be valued on the basis of the prices that would be paid if the research were subcontracted commercially, but in practice it is likely to have to be valued on the basis of total production costs (including the costs of fixed assets used in production).[229] Further, 2008 SNA dictates that "unless market value of the R&D is observed directly, it may, by convention, be valued at the sum of costs, including the cost of unsuccessful R&D."[230] In other words, because future benefits of R&D investment are not explicitly observable, per 2008 SNA's suggestion, such activities should be measured as the sum of R&D input costs, like R&D expenditures. While 2008 SNA does not provide a universal formula on how to capitalize R&D expenditures, according to the U.S. practice, the resulting addition to GDP equals the sum of total business R&D investment and depreciation of R&D assets built up by government and nonprofit institutions serving households (NPISHs), like trade unions.[231] For other countries, however, the implementation of the 2008 SNA ideal may vary, depending on whether part of R&D expenditures have already been counted in previous GDP; if they were, it depends in what form they were counted. That is the situation we faced when dealing with Chinese data.

229. UN, *2008 SNA*, 119.

230. Ibid., 206.

231. U.S. BEA, "Preview of the 2013 Comprehensive Revision of the National Income and Product Accounts: Changes in Definitions and Presentations," *Survey of Current Business* 93, no. 3 (March 2013): 15, http://www.bea.gov/scb/pdf/2013/03%20March/0313_nipa_comprehensive_revision_preview.pdf.

First of all, to gauge the impact of fully capitalizing R&D expenditures in China's GDP, we needed an accurate understanding of basic definitions and a clear picture of the current coverage of China's R&D statistics. According to the *2002 Frascati Manual,* a document of internationally recognized guidelines for collecting and using R&D statistics, "the main expenditure aggregate used for international comparison is gross domestic expenditure on R&D (GERD)," which by definition is total *intramural* expenditure on R&D performed on national territory during a given period.[232] Intramural expenditure means expenditure for R&D carried out within a statistical unit, regardless of funding sources; extramural R&D expenditures refer to payments made to R&D activity performed outside the statistical unit (e.g., contracted services).[233] Data on extramural R&D expenditures are usually collected in a separate survey. The guidelines separate the two expenses from a performer perspective to prevent double-counting R&D expenditures.[234]

Here is an illustration of how this regime works and the importance of separating self-conducted and contracted-out R&D activities in national accounting. When entity A contracts entity B to conduct R&D activity and makes a payment to B, that payment would be counted as entity A's extramural R&D expenditure, while entity B would report its expenses incurred while performing the R&D task as its intramural expenditure. Because the performer-based survey regime focuses on and captures only the latter, the *de facto* expenditure on R&D activity will not be counted twice. However, if the surveys do not separate intramural and extramural expenditures, then both entity A's and entity B's expenditures might be recorded (because both were actual spending, but only one is "final" expenditure), resulting in double-counting for the same R&D activity. According to the aforementioned guidelines, GERD is the sum of R&D expenditure data measured from a *de facto* performer perspective. Because performer-based R&D data are the primary expenditure statistics in the international standards, which our reestimation model relies on, in this section all our uses of "R&D expenditure" refer to performer-based expenditure data.

In China, there are three ways to categorize gross R&D expenditures: by performer, by source of funds, and by nature of research and development activity (Table 3.49). Of the three, performer-based data are directly collected through surveys, while the other two are derived from information that R&D performers provide. In 2008, China's GERD was RMB 461.6 billion, about 1.47 percent of the headline GDP. The performer-based GERD data are divided into four components: higher education, government-affiliated R&D institutions, enterprises, and others (mainly administrative institutions, *shiye danwei*).[235] In 2008, enterprise R&D expenditures were recorded as RMB 338.2 billion, of which 91 percent was spent by industrial enterprises above the designated size, or DRIEs, in performing R&D activities. R&D expenditures by government-affiliated R&D institutions and higher education accounted for 18 and 8 percent of GERD, respectively. In parallel to that performer-based classification, from a funding-source perspective, GERD consists of four parts: funds

232. OECD, *Frascati Manual 2002,* 6th ed. (OECD, 2002), 22, 121, http://www.oecd.org/science/inno/frascatimanualproposedstandardpracticeforsurveysonresearchandexperimentaldevelopment6thedition.htm.
233. Ibid., 21.
234. Ibid., 126.
235. NBS, *China's Main Statistical Concepts,* 444, 454.

Table 3.49. Chinese Categorization of Gross Expenditures on R&D

Unit: RMB billion

2008	Value	Share
GERD by nature of activity	*461.6*	*100%*
Basic Research	22.1	5%
Applied Research	57.5	12%
Experimental Development	382.0	83%
GERD by source of funds	*461.6*	*100%*
Government	108.9	24%
Enterprises	331.2	72%
Foreign	5.7	1%
Other	15.8	3%
GERD by performer	*461.6*	*100%*
Higher Education	39.0	8%
Research and Development Institutions*	81.1	18%
Enterprises	338.2	73%
DRIEs	307.3	67%
Large and Medium-Sized Enterprises	268.1	58%
Other	3.3	1%

* These are government-affiliated R&D institutions.
Sources: NBS, authors' calculations.

by government, enterprises, foreign entities, and other. Funding from government (central and local) and enterprises accounted for 24 and 72 percent, respectively. The remaining 4 percent came from administrative institutions, independent nonprofit organizations (e.g., civil societies and charities), individuals, and foreign sources.[236] A third way to classify GERD is by nature of activity, which includes basic research, applied research, and experimental development (*shiyan fazhan*).[237] It is important to note that in 2008, experimental development—application of existing research to real economy activities, mainly conducted by enterprises in China's case[238]—represented the lion's share of total R&D

236. NingBo Municipal Statistics Bureau, "科技工作统计手册 (Statistical Manual of Science and Technology)," n.d., 24, www.nbstats.gov.cn/softwares/File/1111.doc.

237. OECD, *Franscati Manual*, 30. According to the *Frascati Manual*, basic research is experimental or theoretical work undertaken for knowledge creation and to understand the fundamentals of some phenomena or observable facts, without any particular application or use in view. Applied research is also original investigation for acquiring new knowledge, but it is aimed primarily at a specific application or objective. Experimental development is systematic work, drawing on existing knowledge gained from research and/or practical experience, which is directed to producing new products, installing new systems, or to improving substantially those already produced or installed. For example, during the whole invention process of digital computers, the fundamental mathematical computing algorithms belong to basic research, research or experiments on the theoretical basis for a hypothetically executable machine would be applied research, and the buildup and testing of a real functioning machine are part of experimental development.

238. NBS, "Statistical Bulletin of Second National R&D Census," November 23, 2010, http://www.stats.gov.cn /ztjc/zdtjgz/decqgzyqc/ywjl/201011/t20101123_68914.htm.

expenditures at 83 percent, whereas basic research, the most innovative type of the three, only accounted for 5 percent.

Although China has not converged with 2008 SNA in terms of capitalizing R&D expenditures, part of the expenditures have already been counted toward GDP, which were (measured at a cost basis) mostly spending by government,[239] higher education institutions, government-affiliated R&D houses, and administrative institutions. That is because those not-for-profit entities often treat their expenditures as a proxy for gross output value in lieu of *de facto* "production" from which value-added is derived.[240] From an expenditure perspective, these previously included R&D expenditures would be counted as government consumption expenditures according to the 2010 NBS manual. From an industrial perspective, we surmise the value-added arising from those R&D activities would be assigned to the respective industries of the funders and/or owners of R&D results (not quite explicit from publicly available R&D survey data) or to the tertiary subsector of scientific research, technical services, and geological prospecting, but NBS never clarifies this issue.

Based on the previously described definition of R&D statistics and scope of R&D surveys, performer-based R&D activity serves as the foundation for estimating R&D investment. Per 2008 SNA's recommendation that R&D investment should be measured at cost of inputs when future economic benefits are not explicitly observable, we started our calculation of R&D capitalization with performer-based expenditure components of GERD because in China's case those are directly reported survey data and are presented with the greatest detail.

As previously noted, because we believed R&D expenditures by administrative and not-for-profit institutions such as higher education entities have already been counted toward Chinese GDP as government consumption expenditures, we decided to focus on enterprise expenditures only in our recalculation. We believe these are the main R&D elements left out of existing Chinese national accounts. In 2008, enterprise R&D expenditures accounted for nearly three-quarters of China's total performer-based R&D data, while the other three types in Table 3.49 took up the remaining one-quarter.[241] One caveat: although R&D expenditures by administrative and not-for-profit institutions have likely been included in Chinese GDP, the fact that they were recorded as consumption expenditures means there would be no depreciation derived from the accumulated R&D formation, because that formation is not counted as fixed assets. Therefore, our guiding assumption neglects the depreciation on the part of R&D assets initially documented as consumption expenditures. But because there is insufficient data for us to reestimate that portion of R&D assets and the resulting depreciation, we were left no option but to assume that part of R&D

239. Government R&D expenditures under national accounting refers to direct R&D expenditures (i.e., intramural expenditures), rather than extramural expenditures (e.g., grants to universities). However, R&D surveys in China do not cover the direct R&D expenditures of central or local government.

240. NBS, *Methods of Non-Economic Census Year, 2010 Ed.*, 128–129.

241. NBS, *Methods of Non-Economic Census Year, 2010 Ed.*, 162; U.S. BEA, "Comprehensive Revision," 15. The United States did not count NPISH R&D expenditures when transitioning to 2008 SNA because it was already included as consumption expenditure in previous GDP calculations.

asset depreciation in 2008 was zero.[242] Because we are not factoring in that depreciation, our final reestimates for R&D capitalization are likely on the low end.

Looking at enterprise R&D expenditures in China's official accounts, which are usually measured by cost rather than by market value, we suspect spending has been understated. A 2012 paper coauthored by Nie Huihua at Beijing's Renmin University and two other researchers found that in China's comprehensive industrial enterprise database, of 1.4 million entries on enterprise R&D expenditures from 2001 to 2007 (excluding 2004 because data that year were not available) about 90 percent recorded a value of zero. These zeroes indicate enterprises with no R&D expenses at all or those that chose to fill in zero for unknown reasons—such as lax corporate accounting practices, intentional underreporting of costs on intangible investment, or official statisticians using zero as dummy value for the cells left blank by the reporting companies. After cleaning up the data by removing export-driven enterprises and small- and medium-sized companies (with sales revenue below RMB 300 million), assuming those enterprises spent *de facto* nothing on R&D, the authors were still left with about 70 percent of entries recording a value of zero, which they found to be "clearly inaccurate."[243] Given that finding on industrial enterprise data and our experience in dealing with service sector numbers, we suspect the lack of R&D spending records was even more severe among service providers in 2008, and so was the understatement of R&D expenditures in the tertiary sector.

A second key assumption for our calculation arises from that important observation: in 2008, enterprise R&D expenditures—RMB 338.2 billion (73 percent of GERD)—covered industrial enterprises only. Here are the reasons for this assumption. First, according to performer-based data, 91 percent of all enterprise R&D expenditures were already contributed by DRIEs, as noted earlier. Second, that high share of DRIE spending appeared to be the result of Chinese authorities' tilted attention toward DRIEs in R&D accounting, demonstrated by the fact that in China, enterprise R&D expenditure data disaggregated by industry are only available for DRIEs. In the 2009 *China Statistical Yearbook on Science and Technology* (for reference year 2008), information was provided for DRIEs' R&D expenditures for 38 industries in the industrial subsectors but not for non-DRIEs.[244] This remained the case even after attention was shifted significantly from broader S&T data to R&D statistics after the 2009 R&D census. In addition, during our interactions with NBS, we were told in the context of China's R&D accounting, the "enterprises" include mainly state-owned

---

242. The estimation of a time series for R&D capital stock requires an initial R&D capital stock estimate, R&D prices, service lives of R&D by real sectors, and so on, which are all not available. Besides, NBS does not provide a reference for depreciation ratios in every industry or even every subsector; this makes it harder for researchers to impute depreciation and final capitalization, even when they manage to compile asset stock data. NBS only provides depreciation ratios for a few subsectors or certain industries under these subsectors in the 2010 manual: primary (excluding agricultural services); finance; real estate; scientific research, technical services, and geological prospecting; management of water conservancy, environment, and public facilities; education; health, social securities, and welfare; culture, sports, and entertainment; public administration; and social organizations.

243. Nie, Jiang, and Yang, "(Chinese Industrial Enterprise Database)," 154.

244. There is no enterprise R&D expenditure data for the Recycling and Disposal of Waste industry, not even in the 2009 R&D census.

enterprises (SOEs),[245] which have a natural concentration in industrial subsectors, given China's long-time status as a heavy-industry economy. This is not hard to understand; as outlined in Chapter 2, entities within the state-controlled "system" and with supervising regulators tend to have more solid data than otherwise, especially in the early periods after China converged with 1993 SNA. As a corollary to this third point, China's R&D accounting has also likely been biased toward the industrial subsectors, aligned with our other rationale.

To reach the aforementioned assumptions, one more issues remains: what about enterprise R&D expenditures in the primary sector and construction subsector? For the construction subsector, we first looked at the United States, whose published construction R&D data in 2008 was only 0.7 percent of that in the industrial subsector. Given that negligible level and the likelihood that China's construction business is less well organized and more labor, rather than technology, intensive, we assumed Chinese construction enterprises' spending on R&D in 2008 was zero. Similarly, for the primary sector, we assumed China's agricultural enterprises spent nothing on R&D in 2008. That assumption is grounded in our understanding that, according to the NBS manual, spending by nonenterprise institutions that service agricultural activities (farming, forestry, animal husbandry, and fishery) is part of government consumption expenditures,[246] and the enterprises that provide agricultural services, presumably including agricultural R&D support, are fairly small in size, contributing about 0.5 percent of China's GDP in 2008.[247] Considering that trivial share and Chinese agricultural businesses' development level, scale, and their nature, we were content to leave primary sector R&D spending at zero.

In summary, a second assumption enabling our recalculation of R&D capitalization is that China's official enterprise R&D expenditures data covered industrial enterprises only—within which 91 percent were DRIEs and the remaining 9 percent were smaller firms. That boils down the scope of our reestimates to industrial subsectors and the tertiary sector. This narrowing of recalculation coverage should also bias our reestimates slightly to the lower end.

With these two assumptions, we applied a two-step methodology for imputing R&D value-added. We first estimated the scale of enterprise R&D expenditures for all firms in industrial and service subsectors, and then used a two-scenario analysis to compute the net impact of the value-added arising from those expenditures on China's 2008 GDP. For the first step, we developed two parallel approaches.

A Tertiary-to-Industry Spending Ratio Approach With R&D expenditure data on China's industrial enterprises, if we could identify the general pattern between industrial and service firms R&D spending, we could extrapolate a value for the latter. To identify that

___

245. NBS, interview by authors, 2014.
246. NBS, *Methods of Non-Economic Census Year, 2010 Ed.*, 162.
247. This estimate for agricultural services' share of GDP was imputed assuming the industry's value-added ratio was the same as the rest of the primary sectors in 2008.

pattern without sufficient China tertiary data to work with, we resorted to the cross-country comparisons that we applied for the wholesale/retail and accommodation/catering subsectors. Of course, in the case of R&D accounting, the comparison would be in a more general and qualitative sense, because there is only a number of countries, all advanced economies, that have converted to 2008 SNA and made their R&D expenditure and final capitalization data available. That limited our choice of comparator countries and ways to conduct the comparison.

We resorted to the six countries that we referred to earlier when examining the conversion relationship between R&D expenditures and final impact on headline GDP—countries that have already adopted the SNA 2008 treatment of R&D expenditures and published their enterprise R&D data by sector. Based on their data, we calculated the ratio of R&D expenditures of all enterprises in the tertiary sector to that by industrial enterprises, which was an average of 15 percent. The six countries we chose here are Australia, Canada, the United States, South Korea, France, and Singapore. The final ratio of tertiary to industrial R&D expenditures we obtained factored in the differences between the scale of their two sectors and China's.[248] Given our assumption that all the enterprise R&D expenditures were industrial, the implied expenditures from service companies in our model would be 15 percent of the industrial firms' spending. As a result, of all the enterprise R&D expenditures in China in 2008, we conjectured that 87 percent were spent by industrial subsectors, with the remaining 13 percent by services. China's total estimated enterprise R&D expenditures for all firms in industrial and service subsectors under this approach were RMB 389.4 billion in 2008.

A Listed Company Approach In this second approach, we utilized listed Chinese companies' R&D spending and total asset data, and all industrial and service enterprises' asset figures to extrapolate total R&D expenditures for service firms, assuming that R&D spending relative to assets at listed enterprises (for which we have good data) is useful for predicting average service enterprises R&D spending. We exclude financial enterprises from this exercise because the huge (financial) assets on their books distort the picture. That said, excluding financial companies does not affect the final estimates much because the entire financial subsector, not just financial firms, accounted for just 0.02 percent of GERD in 2009.

The assumption that listed companies can be representative of the entire industrial and service economy in terms of R&D spending intensity is a bold one.[249] Listed companies

---

248. We adjusted the averaged T-to-I spending ratio of six countries using the averaged ratio of tertiary to industrial value-added ("T-to-I VA ratio") of the selected countries relative to China's. For example, if tertiary enterprises' R&D spending was 40.8 percent of the level of industrial enterprises in the United States in 2008, and the U.S. T-to-I VA ratio was 4.7 times that of China, then the T-to-I ratio in China would be adjusted down to 8.7 percent. Note that the selected small group of reference countries is consistent throughout this R&D section to ensure comparability and consistency. Data on business enterprise R&D expenditure by industry are from OECD's STAN Database; see http://stats.oecd.org/index.aspx?DatasetCode=ANBERD_REV4.

249. Listed companies here include Chinese enterprises listed in mainland China, Hong Kong, and U.S. stock exchanges.

usually have some characteristics that are different from those of typical Chinese firms. They tend to be larger and more developed. If the listed companies spend more on R&D than other firms per unit of assets, then this extrapolation will be biased to the high side. We therefore used this approach to define a ceiling of our reestimation interval—which later proved fortuitous.[250]

Based on these foundations we impute a value for total R&D spending by Chinese enterprises of RMB 1.22 trillion in 2008, significantly higher than the estimate from the first approach, RMB 389.4 billion. Using more official inputs produced a figure just 32 percent of this alternative reestimate; but we were concerned the latter was potentially overstating the upward revision. We surmised the actual expenditure value should fall somewhere in between.

The next step is to consider what portion of the estimated enterprise R&D expenditures should be capitalized and how to integrate that into the official GDP. As noted, part of the officially documented enterprise R&D *expenditures* may have already been included in the official GDP as fixed capital formation, required by the *Accounting Standards for Business Enterprises* issued by China's Ministry of Finance in February 2006 and implemented starting in 2007. The new accounting standards stipulate that enterprises, especially listed companies, should capitalize part of their R&D costs,[251] but we do not know exactly how much or how many firms have actually done so.[252] Consequently, how much R&D investment to deduct from the official GDP in order to add in our new estimates for all firms in industrial and service subsectors, while avoid double-counting, remains an uncertainty.

To address that, we applied an extreme case scenario approach. Under the maximum inclusion scenario, we assumed all the official reported enterprise R&D expenditures have been appropriately counted toward GDP as gross fixed capital formation. In that case, we

---

250. The listed company ratio approach is based on an assumption subject to a major qualification: that the company-recorded R&D expenditures include not only intramural R&D expenditures but also spending on purchased R&D services from other enterprises and research institutions. That can possibly result in double-counting in our final estimate for total enterprise R&D spending. A portion of that spending may be traded among enterprises and should be counted only once, but our model is unable to eliminate such repeating counting. In addition, there is always a risk that Chinese companies may have distorted their R&D spending for various purposes, such as in when planning for an IPO, to gain certain policy benefits. That can affect the soundness of our final estimate, too. The 2008 data we used on listed Chinese companies in mainland China, Hong Kong, and United States are sourced from Bloomberg.

251. Ministry of Finance of the People's Republic of China, "企业会计准则第6号 - 无形资产 (Enterprise Financial Accounting Standards No. 6—Intangible Assets)," 2006, http://kjs.mof.gov.cn/zhuantilanmu/kuaijizhuanzeshishi/200806/t20080618_46242.html.

252. We concluded that public data were insufficient to enable estimates for the already included R&D investment by enterprises for the following two reasons. First, before the second R&D census, disaggregated enterprise expenditure statistics (e.g., service fees, raw material expenditures, purchase or construction of fixed assets, etc.), which seemingly intimate the part of expenses that should be capitalized, were only available for S&T rather than R&D activities. Second, after the census, even though data breakdown became available for R&D activities (i.e., routine expenses and asset expenses), according to China's accounting standards, the actual accounting rule of corporate capitalizing R&D costs depends on the phase of R&D asset generation process—*research phase* (without ensuing economic benefits) versus *development phase* (with ensuing economic benefits). Hence, all costs (i.e., whether routine or asset expenses) associated with the development phase can be capitalized if they satisfy a few criteria. That said, we were unable to extrapolate the capitalized portion of enterprise R&D costs based on the breakdown of either S&T or R&D statistics.

would need to deduct all that included value-added and then add in our estimated industrial and service enterprise R&D value-added to obtain the final headline GDP statistic. Under the minimum inclusion scenario, we assumed none of those enterprise expenditures was counted toward fixed assets, and so were not included in GDP at all. Thus, we can directly add in our estimates without subtracting anything. The benefit of this dual-scenario approach is that because *some* of the enterprise's R&D expenditures must have been counted toward GDP, although we do not know exactly how much, extrapolating a range under the two extreme scenarios will capture the actual value somewhere in the middle.

Now that we know how to deal with the uncertainty in integrating our estimates into the official GDP, the only remaining issue is to decide what share of the enterprise R&D expenditures should be capitalized into GDP (i.e., the portion of expenditures that entails economic benefits in future production activities). As noted earlier, public R&D data on China and general accounting rules do not provide a definitive answer,[253] so we turn our attention to other countries again.

Looking at the same six countries we relied on in the T-to-I spending ratio approach, we compared their R&D expenditure data and respective GDP figures in the same year before and after the transition to 2008 SNA, and concluded that the net impact of R&D inclusion on their GDPs averaged 88 percent of R&D expenditures in the year.[254] We therefore applied that ratio to the recalculated enterprise R&D expenditures in China to obtain a final value-added number to add to official 2008 GDP.

With two reestimates for enterprise R&D expenditures and two maximum/minimum bounds for what had already been included in R&D value-added, we calculated that reformulated R&D inclusion would increase the official headline GDP by 0.14 percent (under the T-to-I spending ratio approach and the maximum inclusion scenario) to 3.41 percent (with the listed company approach and under the minimum inclusion scenario). That means an additional value-added of RMB 45 billion to RMB 1.1 trillion (Table 3.50). The actual headline impact should land somewhere in between, but exactly where is beyond our guessing.

---

253. Mingsheng Zhang, "中外汽车企业研发费用比较分析 (Comparative Analysis of R&D Cost in Chinese and Foreign Auto Companies)," *Shanghai Auto*, no. 8 (2013): 48–49, http://lib.cnki.net/cjfd/SHQC201308011.html. There is generally no universal ratio for how enterprises capitalize their R&D costs from an accounting perspective. We reviewed the United States' and China's general accounting principles, information on listed companies with reported capitalized R&D expenses, and some academic studies, and we found that the capitalized R&D costs of enterprises could be anywhere from zero to over 100 percent of their total R&D expenditures (including returns to capitalized R&D, which is mostly the case for listed Korean companies). The scale of the capitalized share is contingent on industry and the company's discretion. We therefore concluded that it is impossible to find an average ratio based on individual enterprises' data that we can use to estimate how much enterprise R&D expenditures should be capitalized.

254. The average R&D expenditure-to-VA ratio is 0.88, shown in Table 3.48. Note that this ratio merely reflects the net GDP addition after including adjustment of R&D expenditure data in each country's case, such as methodological changes like aligning expenditure data with 2008 SNA concepts, removal of double-counting, and addition of depreciation. Hence, the ratio does not tell how much R&D expenditure was effective or successful, or how much R&D expenditures directly contributed to GDP. In addition, this 88 percent ratio should be taken with a grain of salt; the rampant R&D grant embezzlement and academic corruption in China can reduce the conversion rate's applicability. Bad behavior in China's R&D activities can reduce the meaningful, value-added portion of overall R&D expenditures, as well as the assets' values in future production activities.

Table 3.50. Impact of R&D Capitalization on China's GDP

Unit: RMB billion

2008	Official	T-to-I Spending Ratio Approach		Listed Company Approach	
GERD by performer	*461.6*				
Higher Education	39.0				
Research and Development Institutions	81.1				
Enterprises	338.2	389.4		1,220.8	
Other	3.3				
GDP	31,404.5				
R&D Intensity	1.47%				
		max.	*min.*	*max.*	*min.*
Estimated Additional VA from R&D Capitalization*		45.0	341.8	774.7	1,071.6
Estimated % Impact on GDP		**0.14%**	**1.09%**	**2.47%**	**3.41%**

* Max. and min. indicate maximum and minimum inclusion scenarios, under which we deducted the already included enterprise R&D capitalization.
Sources: NBS, Bloomberg, authors' estimates.

Appendixes

APPENDIX 3.1. TECHNICAL NOTES FOR THE VALUE-ADDED AND PROXY GROWTH APPROACH

For the wholesale/retail subsector, the weighting of the wholesale and retail industries' growth rates in the composite subsector rate was decided based on the industries' gross output in 2008. For the accommodation/catering subsector, the weighting was computed according to the two industries' sales revenue. For the financial subsector, the weighting was calculated using PBoC researchers' industry-by-industry VA estimates for 2008.

The education subsector includes only one industry—education—so no weighting is required. For transportation, storage, and postal services, because we already calculated VA at the industry level, there was no need to calculate a nominal growth rate for the entire subsector (although we did extrapolate an implied growth rate for the subsector based on the added-up subsector VA and the original 2007 VA).

For information transmission, computer services, and software, we took the simple average of their nominal growth rates because the basic data did not support our weighting calculation. For real estate, we extrapolated the subsector's gross output according to the NBS formula using data on total sales revenue, land transfer revenue, and cost of sales and business revenue, and used the 2008 growth in gross output as the substitute for VA growth. For public administration and social organizations, lacking basic data, we resorted to 2008 fiscal budget expenditures and extra-budgetary spending as alternative figures to compute the growth and took the weighted average based on the two items' relative sizes in 2008.

APPENDIX 3.2. TECHNICAL EXPLANATIONS FOR CROSS-COUNTRY COMPARISON REGRESSION MODELS

In summary, our cross-country comparison approach followed these steps:

1. We used the following equation to estimate β coefficients of three proxies based on our eight comparator country sample from 2006 to 2010:

$$(Value\ Added)_{it} = \alpha + u_i + \lambda_t + \beta_1 (manufacturing\ gross\ output(t))_{it} + \beta_2 (gross\ profits)_{it} + \beta_2 (household\ consumption)_{it} + \varepsilon_{it}$$

where $(Value\ Added)_{it}$ is the value-added of the wholesale/retail subsector of country i in year t, μ_i and λ_t stand for country- and year-fixed effects,[255] and ε_{it} is the error term for unobserved factors.

2. We substituted China's 2008 official numbers into the above three proxies and came out with a VA estimate.

Based on market exchange rates, with all eight comparator countries incorporated into the equation, the regression model suggested China's 2008 wholesale/retail VA was 191 percent of the official 2008 number.[256] Under the PPP scenario, the reestimation range dropped significantly to 116 percent. While PPP rates have their shortcomings, for our purpose of ascertaining the level of activity in largely nontradable services, we believe they are better than the market rate–based results. With these preferred estimates, we concluded that China's wholesale/retail VA in 2008 should be 16.1 percent higher than official claims. By comparison, our recalculations relying on Chinese previous-year national accounts data ranged from 96 to 122 percent of the official value (exclusive of the reestimate from the bottom-up approach, because basic data in the database was obviously incomplete).

While the reestimation ranges from cross-country comparisons and the national accounts data approaches overlap, the uncertainty inherent in cross-country approaches should not be underestimated. We caution against overly confident interpretations of those results (see further discussion of our reservations in Appendix 3.3). Nonetheless, in the end we cannot identify a reasonable hypothesis for why China would generate lower value-added than our comparator country set. Our best guess from all the recalculations we have attempted is that China's 2008 official data understated the wholesale/retail service value-added.

---

255. Country-fixed effects refer to country-specific time-invariant confounding factors such as geography and culture; year-fixed effects refer to country-invariant period-specific shocks and development patterns.
256. All market exchange rate–based or PPP-based data inputs were deflated using a GDP deflator and price indices to control for within-country inflation across years.

APPENDIX 3.3. QUALIFICATIONS ABOUT CROSS-COUNTRY COMPARISONS, AND WHOLESALE/RETAIL VA RECALCULATIONS

A major concern is the reliability of comparator country statistics, which may affect our results in either direction. Developed economies like Japan and Korea have more abundant information and reliable data, but six out of eight countries we looked at are still developing economies, with data that can be just as questionable as China's. Due to conceptual issues (e.g., industrial classification, definitional boundary, and scope) and operational problems (e.g., mechanics of sampling, response errors), statistics across countries may not be reliable or comparable. With this in mind, we have endeavored to consolidate the most relevant set of data from a variety of sources, including national accounts, and business and household surveys.

Given differences in national accounting frameworks, substitutions were required in cases where ideal proxies were nonexistent. Take gross profits, the main concept we used in the wholesale/retail equation, for example. The Philippines has data directly available for this concept, called "gross margins"; some countries only have sales revenue and cost of sales, which we can use to derive gross profits. Indonesia and Malaysia have neither available. Fortunately, gross output is a similar concept to gross profits for the distributive trade sector because the sector acts as a middleman that channels goods from producers to consumers; thus, by definition, gross output for wholesale/retail trade does not include the cost of goods sold, unlike other industries. In such cases we use gross output to replace gross profits. Some countries' cost of sales includes other expenses in addition to the cost of goods purchased, resulting in smaller margins and changing our estimates.

Beyond reliability issues, we have comparability problems. We encountered these with another concept in the regression equation: manufacturing gross output. Indonesia does not provide data on gross output for its manufacturing industry, and we had to resort to third-party data. We found the World Input-Output Database (WIOD) and used that to fill the Indonesia gap, but a simple check on the consistency of gross output for the utilities sector—electricity, gas, and water supply—between WIOD and Indonesia's official numbers suggested that the discrepancy could vary from –0.8 to 31.5 percent. The discrepancy may result from output calculated based on different prices—producer's price versus basic price—or different approaches, such as income approach versus production approach. With larger manufacturing margins for the same amount of value-added, our predicted value may be underestimated. Overall, the combined effect on our estimates is ambiguous.

Despite data issues that we were unable to circumvent, certain idiosyncrasies in China's policy environment lie at the core of why we conclude China's value-added is significantly understated. We explore the causes further by looking at each of the three proxies we used in our regression equation. We noted that if China's 2008 official VA is *not* understated, then China's distributive trade sector must consequently generate less value-added than other nations, possibly due to lower average profit margins compared to other countries. Actual numbers seem to comport with this theory. The average gross profit-to-sales ratio for China's wholesale/retail subsector during 2006 to 2010 is 20.5 percent, smaller than that of South Korea, Malaysia, the Philippines, Thailand, Brazil, and Turkey, which range from 21.5 to 31.7 percent.[257]

There are two possible explanations for this. Either China's business environment embeds bad incentives for the underinvoicing of sales and overinvoicing of inputs (overstating costs to avoid tax liabilities) or China's tax policy has led to higher tax duties or larger operating expenses in the distributive sector that induces fraud. China has a turnover taxation system (*liuzhuan shuizhi*) that applies a value-added tax to the sale of goods. According to KPMG, the standard tax rate imposed on wholesale/retail enterprises in China is 17 percent, the same as Brazil and slightly less than Turkey, but much higher than other comparator countries (Table 3A.1).[258] With the input tax credit mechanism, VAT equals sales less COGS times the VAT rate. Thus, a VAT rate creates an incentive for enterprises to exaggerate their COGS to pay fewer taxes. Although there are incentives for Chinese enterprises to manipulate their financial data, these are still measurement issues that do not necessarily provide evidence for the distributive sector generating lower value-added than other countries.

Second, the structural divide of formal (i.e., large and medium enterprises and small businesses) and informal operations[259] (i.e., individual proprietorships) could largely affect the average profit margin of the distributive trade sector because gross profit rate depends on the size of operations. The profit margins of informal operations are generally higher than for formal business entities because informal operations have smaller scale, shorter operating cycles, and less overhead. Sageworks, a financial information company, published a report in which they showed that the net profit margins of private companies vary, depending on company size.[260] The smallest companies, with 0 to $1 million in revenue, have the highest net profit margin of around 7 percent, whereas firms with more than $1 million in revenue have an average of 4 to 4.5 percent net profit margin. China's gross profit rate for sole proprietorships was 21 and 26 percent in 2004 and 2008, respectively, larger than that of formal operations, which were 18 and 19 percent. It is difficult to tell whether China has more informal operations than other countries due to limited data availability. Self-employed businesses are not easy to track or capture in surveys, and even if they are recorded, many lack adequate resources to perform their own financial

257. Indonesia does not have data on total sales in the distributive sector, so we are not able to calculate the profit-to-sales ratio. Japan's cost of sales is equal to COGS for sole proprietorships, but for other businesses and enterprises, cost of sales equals COGS plus other expenses, which significantly lowers its profit-to-sales ratio.

258. KPMG, "Country VAT/GST Essentials," http://www.kpmg.com/Global/en/IssuesAndInsights /ArticlesPublications/vat-gst-essentials/Pages/default.aspx; Thailand Revenue Department, "Value Added Tax," March 13, 2014, http://www.rd.go.th/publish/6043.0.html.

259. UN, *System of National Accounts 2008* (New York: United Nations, Department of Economic and Social Affairs, 2009), 475–476, http://unstats.un.org/unsd/nationalaccount/docs/SNA2008.pdf. The informal sector refers to household unincorporated operations, such as self-employed businesses, that do not have employees or a limited size of employment.

260. Mary E. Biery, "Does Size Matter? Sales Growth, Margins by Company Size," *Sageworks*, April 30, 2012, http://www.sageworks.com/blog/post/2012/04/30/Does-size-matter-Sales-growth-margins-by-company-size .aspx.

Table 3A.1. Standard Value-Added Tax Rate Across Comparator Countries

Country	VAT Standard Rate
Turkey	18%
Brazil	17%
China	17%
Philippines	12%
Indonesia*	10%
Malaysia	10%
South Korea	10%
Thailand	7%
Japan	5%

* Indonesia's standard VAT rate is 10 percent with a lower bound of 5 percent and upper bound of 15 percent; even the upper bound is lower than China's VAT rate.
Sources: KPMG, Thailand Revenue Department.

accounting and report gross profits correctly. Thus, we lack evidence to definitively say whether China has more or less informal operations than other countries.

Manufacturing gross output—another proxy variable in our model—should also be factored in to see why China could be bucking the global trend. China's manufacturing GOV may generate less marginal increase in its wholesale/retail VA than comparator countries because a relatively larger portion of China's manufacturing gross output gets exported rather than entered into the domestic wholesale/retail market. However, based on export data, we did not observe an explicit pattern in support of that hypothesis. Using the World Input-Output Database, we derived the ratio of exports to manufacturing gross output. Surprisingly, China is near the bottom of that list. In 2008, China's export-to-output ratio for the manufacturing subsector was 17.8 percent—higher than Brazil (14.9 percent) but lower than Japan (20.4 percent), Turkey (27.2 percent), South Korea (34 percent), and Indonesia (42.5 percent). Even as China is considered the world's manufacturing hub, the export-to-output ratio of its manufacturing subsector is still low relative to other comparator countries.

Another explanation for inherently lower value-added was that China's household consumption—the third proxy in our model—may contribute less to the marginal increase in wholesale/retail VA because Chinese consumers purchase less goods than services compared to other countries. However, we found this intuitively unreasonable because the portion of consumption on services generally increases with per capita income. At its current level of development, in official accounts, the average consumer in China should be spending a larger portion of household income on goods over services. Revisiting the numbers, per capita consumption on goods is about twice the level of per capita consumption on services for both urban and rural households, suggesting that Chinese households are spending more on goods than services.[261] Comparing countries from 2006 to 2010, the share of total household consumption on food, beverages, tobacco, clothing, and footwear, on average, was 20 percent in Japan and South Korea, and between 28 and 40 percent in Malaysia, Turkey, and Thailand. In 2008, China spent 41 percent of total household consumption on the same goods. Only the Philippines and Indonesia, at 45 and 60 percent, respectively, spent more. Therefore, the hypothesis that China spends less on goods than comparator countries is not valid.

APPENDIX 3.4. QUALIFICATIONS ABOUT ACCOMMODATION/CATERING VA RECALCULATIONS

Similar to the analysis in wholesale/retail, we look at uncertainties for each proxy component of accommodation/catering. There are factors affecting our estimate in both directions. First, it is possible that the official reading had not understated the value-added of accommodation/food services because VA for this subsector is inherently lower than comparator countries, but the high savings ratio and fake invoices in China distorted our regression results. Although developing Asia has been known for a high savings rate, China has an even higher rate. According to World Development Indicators 2014, China's gross savings in 2008 reached 53 percent of GDP, the highest among comparator countries.[262] Based on our data collected from national statistics offices, household savings in China were also the highest in percentage of household disposable income among the same set of countries. Hence, using household disposable income as a proxy variable may have overestimated the residents' expenditures on accommodation and catering services. In the meantime, the notorious falsification of *fapiao* (or invoices) may inflate the actual spending on activities taking place in hotels and restaurants. The *New York Times*, for example, reported that forged travel receipts were being filed and reimbursed in China for large-scale conferences or events where not as many attendees showed up as were reported.[263] This could also lead to lower value-added in catering services.

However, our estimate could also possibly understate the actual value-added because of underreported sales revenue and issues with China's tourism statistics. First, it is pervasive for restaurants and hotels in China to use counterfeit receipts to hide revenue for tax evasion. Second, an economics professor from Northwest University in China pointed out several missing components in China's tourism numbers compared with the standards of the Tourism Satellite Account. The current official number on tourism expenditure is based on final cash outlets by travelers; it does not include expenses borne by companies on business trips, outbound pretrip and all posttrip tourism consumption,[264] consumption on luxury

---

261. According to the 2008 *Economic Census*, per capita consumption on goods includes food, clothing, and home appliances and household goods; per capita consumption on services includes health care, transportation, communication, and cultural/education/entertainment expenses.

262. The gross savings ratios for Japan, South Korea, Indonesia, Malaysia, the Philippines, Thailand, Brazil, and Turkey in 2008 were 26, 33, 26, 39, 52, 31, 19, and 17 percent, respectively (World Bank, WDI 2014).

263. Barboza, "Phony Receipts."

264. Outbound pretrip consumption refers to expenditures that occurred within China's borders before trips to foreign countries.

goods, and spending on travel agencies and guide services.[265] Thus, the current official number on tourism expenditure severely underestimated total inbound tourism revenue. Because our estimation equation uses both cross-country regression coefficients and official Chinese numbers for all three proxy variables to estimate the nominal level of accommodation/catering services value-added, the result could be downwardly biased. Overall, the averaged impact of all the above confounding factors remains unambiguous to us.

APPENDIX 3.5. TWO MODIFIED MARKET RENT-BASED ESTIMATES

When it comes to deciding how much rental VA was already included in China's official 2008 GDP—explicit or imputed; as noted earlier, China currently counts all rental VA using the construction cost approach intended for imputed VA[266]—there are two alternative methods.

The first method uses implied imputed rental expenditures in the official household final consumption data in China's national accounts and per capita household consumption expenditure statistics produced by NBS household surveys. According to official definitions, the former, which is a component of expenditure-based GDP, includes both imputed and actual rental expenditures in its "housing expenditure" subcategory; the latter, however, focuses on cash expenditure only, and so excludes imputed rental expenditure. This nuanced difference was explained at great length by Zhang Jun and Zhu Tian in their study of China's household consumption.[267] Therefore, subtracting total household consumption expenditures on "housing" from the household final consumption on "housing" will result in the approximate amount of imputed rental expenditures. Using 2008 official numbers, we derived an implied imputed urban rental expenditure of 2.3 percent of that year's GDP. Because China's home ownership rate was about 80 percent in 2008, using the existing NBS assumption that unit market rent can be represented by unit imputed rent, the scale of actual rental expenditure in 2008 would be one-quarter of the imputed rent; when combined, total urban rental expenditures equal 2.88 percent of official GDP. Based on a modified real estate VA ratio, which we explain in the next paragraph, that translates to RMB 606 billion of already included urban rental VA, more than twice the value computed based on the market rent approach described above.

In this case, because we factored in 2008 household expenditures to extrapolate already counted urban rental VA, we would need to reconsider the VA ratio we use to impute urban rental VA from total rental income. In the initial market rent approach, we used the Xu and colleagues–endorsed 51 percent, in alignment with our practice of adopting their implied ratio of urban rental VA to total real estate VA for 1996 through 2000. But in this modified method, because we incorporated 2008 conditions in computing the imputed urban rental VA, we would need to consider the change in the real estate subsector's VA ratio from 2000

265. Rong Kang and Yue Wu, "中国旅游消费统计与国际标准的差距及解决对策 (China's Tourism Expenditure Statistics and International Standard: Differences and Suggestions to Solutions)," *Statistical Research*, no. 12 (2009): 58, http://tjyj.stats.gov.cn/CN/abstract/abstract1636.shtml.

266. Xu et al., "(On Residential Housing Rents)," 13.

267. Zhang and Zhu, "Underestimated Consumption," 4.

Table 3A.2. An Alternative Estimate from the Market Rent Approach

Unit: RMB trillion (unless otherwise noted)

2008	Value
Property Income per Capita—Urban (RMB)	965.1
Market Rental Income per Capita—Urban (RMB)	337.8
Urban Population (million persons)	606.7
Total Market Rental Income—Urban	0.2
Usable Floor Area per Capita—Urban (m²)	19.8
Total Usable Floor Area—Urban (billion m²)	12.0
Tenant Population—Urban (million persons)	29.1
Total Rental Housing Floor Area—Urban (million m²)	575.7
Average Market Rent per m2 (RMB)	355.9
Total Market and Imputed Housing Rent (RMB trillion)	4.3
Urban Housing Rental Value-Added*	**2.9**
Real Estate Value-Added (Official)	*1.5*
Urban Housing Rental VA Already Included†	0.6
Net Adjustment of Housing Rental VA	+2.3
Real Estate Value-Added (Recalculated)‡	**3.7**

* Calculated based on value-added ratios in Xu (2003) and China's 2007 *Input-Output Tables.*

† Extrapolated from household consumption expenditure data; it considers urban housing rental activity only.

‡ This approach does not include revision to rural housing rental VA.

Sources: NBS, Xu (2003, 2012), Zhao (2014), CEIC, authors' calculations.

to 2008. Again we employed a simple and conservative estimate by taking the average of the Xu and colleagues' 51 percent for real estate developers in 2000 and the 83 percent for the entire subsector suggested in the 2007 *Input Output Tables* to arrive at 67 percent. Holding other factors from the market rent approach constant, such as total rental income at market rates, we arrived at a modestly different estimate. Considering the adjustment caused by rental VA recalculation alone, the new real estate VA is RMB 3.73 trillion, 10.6 percent bigger than our first estimate, but not too divergent (Table 3A.2). Considering the revision to non-leasing real estate activities as well, the reestimate increases to RMB 3.77 trillion.

The second modified method utilized the revisions NBS made to real estate VA during the 2004 census. According to NBS, current construction costs were used starting with the 2004 census.[268] Assuming the entire revision to 2004 census real estate VA was generated by this methodological change to urban dwellings—hence all real estate revision resulted from increased urban rental VA—we can obtain the level of newly added urban rental VA by comparing the pre- and postcensus real estate VA numbers. Xu and colleagues' 2003 essay provides a level for urban rental VA from 1996 to 2000, to which we added the new addition suggested by the 2004 census, and calculated the urban rent share of real estate

---

268. NBS, "Reform of National Accounts System"; Liu, Zheng, and Xu, "(Real Estate Subsector)," 26.

Table 3A.3. A Second Alternative Estimate from the Market Rent Approach

Unit: RMB trillion (unless otherwise noted)

2008	Value
Property Income per Capita—Urban (RMB)	965.1
Market Rental Income per Capita—Urban (RMB)	337.8
Urban Population (million persons)	606.7
Total Market Rental Income—Urban	0.2
Usable Floor Area per Capita—Urban (m²)	19.8
Total Usable Floor Area—Urban (billion m²)	12.0
Tenant Population—Urban (million persons)	29.1
Total Rental Housing Floor Area—Urban (million m²)	575.7
Average Market Rent per m² (RMB)	355.9
Total Market and Imputed Housing Rent (RMB trillion)	4.3
Urban Housing Rental Value-Added*	**2.9**
Real Estate Value-Added (Official)	*1.5*
Urban Housing Rental VA Already Included[†]	1.0
Net Adjustment of Housing Rental VA	+1.9
Real Estate Value-Added (Recalculated)[‡]	**3.4**

* Calculated based on value-added ratios in Xu (2003) and China's 2007 *Input-Output Tables*.

† Extrapolated from 2004 census revisions—assuming all revisions were urban restatement.

‡ This approach does not include revision to rural housing rental VA.

Sources: NBS, Xu (2003, 2012), Zhao (2014), CEIC, authors' calculations.

VA post the census. These assumptions suggest urban rental VA accounted for 65.8 percent of real estate VA on average during 1996–2000, on a construction cost basis. This appears to be too high, given Shenzhen's official 2010 *total* rent share of real estate VA at 32 percent. Nevertheless, we applied this share to the original 2008 real estate VA to obtain already included imputed urban rental VA, replaced that old value with our new estimate, and arrived at a new overall real estate VA practically equal to that in our original market rent approach: RMB 3.37 trillion (Table 3A.3).[269] Including the adjustment to nonleasing real estate activities, the overall VA will increase a bit more.

APPENDIX 3.6. EXTRAPOLATION OF CHINA'S UNPROCESSED AQUATIC EXPORTS

Official Chinese data do not break down processed and unprocessed export products conveniently. Therefore, to produce an unprocessed export statistic for 2008, we need to conduct

---

269. For this second alternative method, we again used the 67 percent VA ratio to calculate VA of urban housing rental activity instead of the 51 percent ratio mentioned in Xu et al.'s 2003 essay. The justification was that we included 2004 revisions in our model to compute already included imputed urban rental VA in official GDP, so we should factor in the change in real estate VA ratio from 2000 to 2004.

our own extrapolation. As noted earlier, China's fishery statistical yearbook provides more comprehensive export data than the regular NBS yearbook, because the former includes processing trade, while the latter does not.

According to the export product breakdown provided by MOFCOM (directly from the ministry's documents or from an academic source[270] that referred to the ministry), there are eight broad categories in China's fishery exports: further processed products, primarily processed frozen fish and fillet, primarily processed mollusks, primarily processed crustaceans, live fish, dried and salted fish, seaweed and related products, and iced fresh fish. According to Chinese official definitions for "processing" of aquatic products, live fish and iced fresh fish are undoubtedly unprocessed products, and of primarily processed mollusks and crustaceans, there are parts that are counted as unprocessed.[271] The rest are all processed products. Therefore, to compute the total unprocessed export products, we need to carve out the unprocessed portions in primarily processed mollusks and crustaceans.

Lacking ideal basic data for mollusks and crustaceans to work with, we assumed the unprocessed share in these two categories was the same as in fish products—namely, the percentage of live and iced fresh fish in all primarily processed fish products. Based on Chinese definitions and our interpretations, primarily processed fish include live fish, iced fresh fish, primarily processed frozen fish and fillet, and dried and salted fish. In 2006, the aggregate of primarily processed fish was 1.52 million tons, of which 10.2 percent was the unprocessed live and iced fresh fish. In 2008, primarily processed fish dropped slightly to 1.4 million tons, of which 10.3 percent was unprocessed fish products. In addition, the unprocessed share we estimated for 2007 based on official data was 10.1 percent; to us that ratio stayed fairly constant during that period of time. Applying the 2006 and 2008 shares to primarily processed mollusks and crustaceans to respective years, we obtained the levels for the unprocessed portions in the two. Combining that with unprocessed fish volume and dividing the sum by total aquatic product exports, we obtained the unprocessed share of all aquatic exports in 2006 (the second census year) and 2008, which was 6.48 percent and 6.02 percent, respectively. This again comports with the cited USDA report saying that China's aquatic exports are mainly processed products.[272]

---

270. Center for National Meat Quality and Safety Control, "2008 年全国水产品进出口贸易情况 (Status on Aquatic Imports and Exports in 2008)" (Nanjing Agricultural University, April 5, 2009), http://www.meat-food.com /newscontent.asp?d=217.

271. Mei Zhang, Zenghui Huo, and Fahai Yi, "中国水产品出口贸易结构的现状及其优化对策 (Aquatic Exports in China: Current Situation and Optimization Strategies)," *World Agriculture*, no. 11 (2006): 34, http://mall.cnki.net /magazine/Article/SJNY200611009.htm. According to the study by Zhang, Huo, and Yi, processing of aquatic products includes primary processing and further processing. Primary processing produces products that are live, chilled (in the case of iced fresh fish), frozen, dried, salted and marinated, and smoked, whereas further processed products include cans, fish meal and fish oil, and other products. However, in China's fishery yearbook, the definition for "processed aquatic products" is slightly different, which includes only frozen, dried, salted and marinated, smoked, and canned products, as well as fish meal, fish oil, and others. Based on the official definition, live and iced fresh aquatic products are categorized as "unprocessed" products.

272. Beckman, Wu, and Han, *Fishery Products Annual Report*, 7.

4 | Conclusions and Implications

We have reviewed what gross domestic product (GDP) is and why it is used as the principal yardstick for gauging national economic performance today. We have looked in depth at the past two decades of criticism, debate, and evolution of how China manages the task of producing a GDP estimate. On that foundation we analyzed in detail each major element of China's production-side national accounts that go into the nation's GDP calculation, explored the variety of adjustments researchers have proposed, made judgments about the most sensible revisions, and arrived at a well-grounded alternative estimate of 2008 GDP—the most recent year for which the National Bureau of Statistics (NBS) has made the data required for such an estimate available—in Chapter 3. Calling to mind the parable of blind monks and an elephant, we conclude the study by looking at our quantitative results in three different ways. First, we look at the implications of our results in appraising China's post-2008 economic performance through the eyes of a domestic China economist. Second, we consider China's economic position in the broader context as seen through the eyes of China's political leaders. Third, we look at our results through foreign eyes to understand the implications of an altered picture of Chinese GDP from the viewpoint of geoeconomics, geopolitics, and business interests overseas.

Our Headline Results and China's Official Revision

Before turning to those conclusions, a preliminary note is required. We are confident about our choices made to reappraise 2008 numbers, but debate on China's economic performance concerns not just that year but the entire period since. Extrapolating forward the patterns found in one year always presents some risk. This is true in an advanced economy, and even more so in an emerging nation like China that is prone to greater volatility and adjustment. Adding to the risk, 2008 was affected by the global financial crisis. The chance that our revised 2008 results do not carry through to the present cannot be ruled out, but we have three reasons to expect they do. First, thanks to its countercyclical stimulus efforts, China was less disrupted by the financial crisis than virtually any other major economy. This is why renowned economist Nicholas Lardy called China's response to the crisis the "gold standard."[1] Second, the impact of the crisis on advanced economy

---

1. Nicholas R. Lardy, *Testimony at the Hearing before the US-China Economic and Security Review Commission: China's Role in the Origins of and Response to the Global Recession* (Washington, D.C.: Peterson Institute for

consumption growth rates, which was in many ways the hardest pill for China to swallow, was not so much a one-year phenomenon but rather the start of a new normal. There has been continuity in the growth of Chinese consumption as a share of world consumption from 2008 to 2013, indicating that patterns that first drew heavy notice in 2008 continued. Finally, we have benefited from extensive informal interaction with China's statistical authorities, in the course of which we have stress-tested our broad findings for 2008 against Beijing's working hypotheses for the current period. While we are not privy to official results for the current period needed to empirically carry forward our 2008 estimates, we are comforted that our perspective is not fundamentally inapplicable to conditions in recent years.

Our conclusions must be understood in light of the extent to which Beijing is officially embracing a revised picture of both its GDP level and growth rate. In December 2014, Beijing released results from China's 2013 *Economic Census*, in which it updated data on 2013 GDP and value-added for three broad sectors. In February 2015, Beijing unveiled more detailed revised numbers, covering both 2013 and 2012, but this announcement was given much less publicity than the previous one—no press conference or even a straightforward declaration on NBS's website. The restatements were included in the first issue of China Monthly Economic Indicators for 2015 but not reflected in NBS's online database as of the end of the first quarter. In addition to improved estimates of activity as previously defined (the "old base") with the benefit of the comprehensive every-five-year census carried out in 2014 (for reference year 2013), this twice-a-decade moment was the typical occasion to introduce any methodological upgrades of China's national accounting ("new base" revisions). In other words, these revisions can reflect both a refined count using the old formula and changes based on an improvement in formula.

After the 2008 *System of National Accounts* (SNA) was launched internationally, China established a team to prepare for eventual concordance with it, led by NBS Deputy Chief Xu Xianchun, a leading government national accounts statistician. In November 2013, the preparatory team announced that China would step up to 2008 SNA and that the transition would accompany the 2013 *Economic Census*, with a new "2014 Chinese SNA" standard set to be published in 2015. The new methodology would adopt most advancements of the 2008 SNA, particularly treatment of research and development expenditures as fixed capital formation and an improved count of services, including—most important—a revision to "imputed rent" based on current value rather than construction cost.

When the time came to release census results in December 2014 NBS reported just a 3.4 percent upward restatement of 2013 GDP, compared to our estimate of 13.1 to 16.3 percent needed to correct old base undercounting and move to 2008 SNA standards as intended (Table 4.1). Furthermore, based on details released in February 2015, 40 percent of the official revision was attributed to an augmentation of financial service value-added. We suspect a large portion of that resulted from an expansion of value-added boundary in

---

International Economics, 2009), http://www.iie.com/publications/testimony/print.cfm?ResearchId=1165&doc=pub.

Table 4.1. A Reconstruction of China's 2008 GDP

Unit: RMB trillion

	Official VA	Recalculated VA	Recl./Official %
GDP*	31.40	35.51	13.1%
		36.53	16.3%
Primary Sector	3.37	3.26	−3.2%
Secondary Sector	14.90	16.14	8.3%
Industry	13.03	14.13	8.5%
Construction	1.87	2.01	7.3%
Tertiary Sector	13.13	16.06	22.2%
Research and Development	n/a	0.04	n/a
		1.07	

* The two values are derived from two scenarios of R&D inclusion's impact on GDP. The official data are not subject to 2013 census revisions.

Sources: NBS, authors' calculations.

light of China's updated 2011 industrial classification, which was first put into use during the 2013 *Economic Census* and hence was not part of our reestimate. It means that the missed financial value-added would be *added* to our underestimate projections for the current period. A detailed breakdown of NBS 2013 revisions and a comparison with our recalculations is shown in Table 4.2. While the basis of China's revisions are not yet explained, it is clear that they included only minor adaptation to 2008 SNA standards. They chose to stick with the old methodology, as indicated by their statement that "revisions were mainly due to changes in the basic materials from the economic census," and that they "strictly followed the NBS-sanctioned GDP accounting methodology for economic census years." That is, they stuck to the old approach.[2]

Clearly, this turn of events reflected a change of heart, given the preparations that had been made for transition to 2008 SNA. Thus, the census revisions raise more questions than they answer. The first question is, why? NBS would not have previously announced plans to converge with 2008 SNA without high-level consensus among central leaders. Both public statements and private communications pointed to transition. At the last minute, those intentions were shelved, to the surprise of many. The second question is, when *will* Beijing move forward to modernized standards? Later in 2015? By the start of the 13th Five Year Period (2016–2020) starting from next year? Or only by 2020, the completion date for the many reform pledges at the core of the Xi administration's economic plan? If, instead of being declared at once today, these augmentations to GDP level are to be slipped in gradually over the years to come in the name of smoothing the adjustment, without transparent explanation of the schedule (such as with the recent 2013 census roll-out), critics could reasonably argue that annual GDP growth were being made to look higher than it is. The unusual machinations around the December 2014 release leave us no choice but to at least

---

2. NBS, "NBS explains 2013 GDP Revisions."

Table 4.2. A Breakdown of Official Revisions to 2013 Chinese GDP

Unit: RMB billion, percentage

	Precensus (NBS)	Postcensus (NBS)	Scale of Census Rev.	Scale of Our 2008 GDP Reestimate
GDP	56,884.5	58,801.9	3.4%	[13.1%, 16.3%]
Primary Sector	5,695.7	5,532.2	–2.9%	–3.2%
Secondary Sector	24,968.4	25,681.0	2.9%	8.3%
Industry	21,068.9	21,726.4	3.1%	8.5%
Construction	3,899.5	4,080.7	4.6%	7.3%
Tertiary Sector	26,220.4	27,588.7	5.2%	22.2%
Transportation, Storage, and Postal Services	2,728.3	2,603.6	–4.6%	11.9%
Wholesale and Retail Trade	5,567.2	5,628.4	1.1%	16.1%
Accommodation and Catering Services	1,149.4	1,022.8	–11.0%	5.7%
Finance	3,353.5	4,119.0	22.8%	2.8%
Real Estate	3,329.5	3,598.8	8.1%	132.8%
Other*	10,092.5	10,616.0	5.2%	5.1%

* Our revision for "Other" here does not consider capitalization of R&D expenses for the convenience of comparison with official results.
Sources: NBS, authors' calculations.

consider that possibility. The third question is whether a still distorted picture of GDP would impact policymaking and business decisions. We delve into these questions in the following sections.

In addition to our headline conclusion that China's GDP was significantly understated in the most recent analyzable year, the takeaways from our analysis include the following. First, the output of employment-intensive subsectors in industry and construction, and the service subsectors of wholesale and retail trade and accommodation and catering, has been undercounted, due in large part to a high concentration of small-scale businesses and self-employed workers. Better data argue for leaders' priority on empowering private and small and medium enterprises as the proven foundation of job growth and dynamism. Second, the economy and, in particular, households are even more at risk to real estate shocks than official models suggest. As demonstrated by our reestimates, the property subsector is the greatest source of undervaluation, as a result of the outdated calculation methods Beijing continues to employ: its contribution to GDP could be twice what official figure suggest. Without a methodological update, that weight in output will remain obscured, and hence make the degree of pain in event of a property sector downturn feel oddly more wrenching than one would expect. Yet the other side of this real estate coin is our third takeaway: China's economic structure looks more balanced than previously believed. According to the NBS census revisions, the secondary sector—industry and construction—remained the largest GDP contributor right up until 2012. However our reestimates, with the most significant upward adjustments to real estate, wholesale and retail trade, and transportation, suggest that the service sector surpassed its secondary counterpart as early as 2009. In other words, services are already playing a dominant role in growing the Chinese economy: they are not so much failing to expand as they are underappreciated due to antiquated counting methodologies and practices.

Through Domestic Economic Eyes: Revisiting Debates

The period since 2008 has been a busy one for economists debating China's economic performance. Optimists and pessimists on the nation's outlook have been at odds. The growth of lending and liquidity has been a constant source of concern. Slow rebalancing from old-line industries to sunrise sectors like services has been a focus of criticism. The relationship between new credit and resulting growth has been a concern among development economists. A range of other relationships, including energy intensity, employment intensity, and resource intensity, have been perennial items for discussion. Many of these debates need revisiting in light of restated GDP.

REBALANCING

The extent to which a needed structural adjustment, or rebalancing, of China's economy is or is not taking place is hotly debated. Analysts disagree about whether rebalancing is needed, whether it is happening, what the consequences are, what the impediments are, whether leaders *intend* to rebalance, and seemingly endless variations on this theme. There is no standard definition of what rebalancing even means, but it generally concerns whether the sectoral sources of growth are sustainable and adjusting in a manner aligned with a nation's potential, rather than being distorted to defend existing beneficiaries at the cost of overall or future welfare. The principal concerns are the balance between domestic and external demand orientation, the balance between domestic investment and consumption, and the evolution from overreliance on heavy industry to a broader set of activities.

Viewed using official pre-2013 census revisions data, China's service sector finally achieved parity with the industry and construction sector only in early 2013. *The Economist* called this a rebalancing "milestone" but also noted that China remained 10 to 15 percentage points underweight in services compared to other countries at the same stage of development.[3] The years 2008–2012 were dominated by concerns about the rise of "state capitalism" and fears that the 1990s pruning back of statism had given way to government resurgence in the 2000s driven by the SOE giants of manufacturing and heavy industrial industries.

Our reestimation suggests that services had already pulled into the lead by 2009, and thus that this 2008–2013 debate was missing a key fact. China was more like similarly developed countries than previously thought. It was, in this sense, more "normal."

---

3. "Economic Rebalancing: Industrial Eclipse," *Economist*, April 15, 2013, http://www.economist.com /blogs/analects/2013/04/economic-rebalancing.

Table 4.3. Sectoral Composition of the Chinese Economy*

Unit: Percentage

2008	Official	Recl. (Low)	Recl. (High)
Primary Sector	10.7%	9.2%	8.9%
Secondary Sector	47.4%	45.5%	44.2%
Tertiary Sector	41.8%	45.2%	43.9%
Research and Development	n/a	0.1%	2.9%
GDP	100%	100%	100%

* The two recalculation scenarios depend on the scale of R&D expenditure inclusion. The official 2008 data are not subject to 2013 census revisions.

Sources: NBS, authors' calculations.

Table 4.3 presents our estimates indicating that the GDP share of the tertiary sector was 2.1 to 3.4 percentage points higher than official 2008 figures without even counting the increased contribution to services from research and development investment. And given the sectors' expansion in 2009, services rose to become China's biggest sector starting in 2009.

Does this mean that China has less to worry about in terms of rebalancing? That it is through the hardest part? Not really. While the rise of service sector activity is an indication of where China is in the development process—it has passed the industrialization peak, and that industry is regressing back to a more normal level of growth after a decade of hyper-expansion—the most difficult rebalancing challenges remain ahead. China remains far too dependent on the capital-intensive heavy industries as a target of fiscal stimulus to manage GDP growth expectations even today. Within domestic production—both secondary and tertiary—a shift toward consumer-oriented, higher-value-added output is urgent, instead of directing additional investment to already overcapacity industries as remains the instinct even today in 2015. Similarly, the temptation to stoke growth with larger external imbalances and rely on foreign demand rather than reforms to free up domestic demand is an ongoing concern, with a 2014 goods trade surplus approaching half a trillion dollars. Officials and Chinese think tank economists reflexively point to hopes of growing net exports contributions in 2015 despite already large imbalances, and the prime minister justifies subsidies for outbound direct investors as a means to support exports for overcapacity industries. While elements of rebalancing are further along than generally credited, key components of this reform process still need to be accelerated.

EMPLOYMENT AND HOUSEHOLD INCOME

While China's domestic policy debates and priorities are often framed in terms of the need to generate sufficient employment growth to satisfy the needs of the world's largest labor pool and thus maintain social stability, the bias toward directing growth capital toward heavy industry tells a different story. Heavy industry is not employment-intensive compared to light industry and services, which generate many times as much employment per unit of capital invested (Figure 4.1). Because official employment statistics are unreliable—reported urban unemployment has barely moved, staying between 4 and 4.3 percent since

Figure 4.1. Lower Heavy Industry Growth, More Job Creation*

Unit: Employment per million of RMB fixed asset investment, 2013

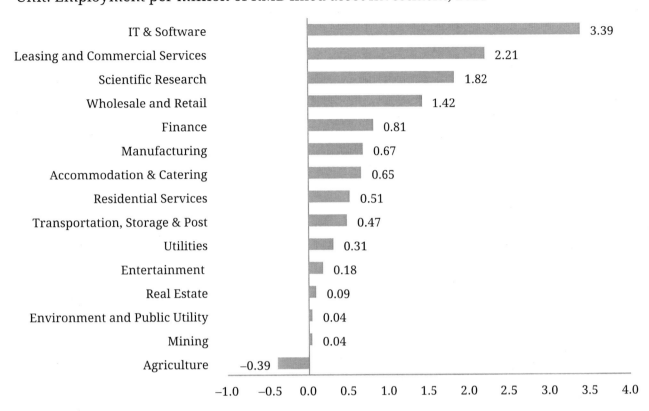

* Official employment data by industry include urban nonprivate entities only; fixed asset investment denotes investment of at least RMB 5 million and excludes those from rural households.
Sources: NBS, authors' calculations.

2002, a highly implausible immunity to economic conditions—analysts must consider circumstantial factors to evaluate the efforts of the central government on labor market slack.[4] Our revised picture of 2008 GDP suggests certain indirect implications about employment dynamics in China.

As noted above, our revisions suggest more rapid growth of the labor-intensive service subsectors than otherwise thought. In the absence of more reliable employment data,[5] and all other things being equal, this is a desirable outcome from an employment perspective. Nearly half of our upward revision to the old base estimate of China's GDP occurs in service subsectors, equal to $148 billion in additional service sector activity, which would be associated with something in the neighborhood of 1 million additional jobs at the observed employment-intensity of service sector investment. Keep in mind, however, that the

4. Premier Li Keqiang pledged to introduce improved employment statistics during the fall of 2014; see "李克强主持召开国务院常务会议 (Li Keqiang Convened the State Council Executive Meeting)," *People's Daily*, July 31, 2014, http://paper.people.com.cn/rmrb/html/2014-07/31/nw.D110000renmrb_20140731_3-01.htm.

5. In June 2013, China's National Development and Reform Commission started publishing an alternative unemployment rate data series based on surveys in 32 cities. That rate, published a total of five times as of this writing, only modestly fluctuated between 5 and 5.17 percent over the course of 18 months. Given this and the relatively short period of observations, one cannot be certain it is a reliable indicator of the actual employment conditions in China.

majority of increased income implied by our modeling results from imputed rent on residences and returns on capital for business owners. China's Gini coefficient—a measure of income distribution equality or inequality—is therefore likely to be even worse (more skewed toward the wealthiest segments of society) than generally thought.

ACCURACY IN NATIONAL ACCOUNTING

Domestic Chinese economists, not just foreign observers, fret over the reliability of China's national accounting data. Our reestimates contribute to this line of discussion in three ways worth pointing out here. First, we have demonstrated that a considerable share of doubt arises from the difficulty of parsing arcane accounting practices that have evolved over time with incomplete explanation. Rather than failures to accurately measure activity, or intentional distortion, these problems revolve around the presentation of Chinese data rather than accuracy per se. However, responsibility for that presentation falls entirely on Beijing's shoulders, and no one can argue that officials have done what is required to make Chinese statistics clear and accessible. Chinese statisticians, like those in many nations, will respond that they are severely resource-constrained; this may be the case, but it does not resolve the problem.

Second, our results add to the evidence that China's statistical practices do remain inadequate to give leaders the reliable picture of economic activity they increasingly need. About half of the 13.1 to 16.3 percent GDP upward adjustment we calculated results from refining the boundaries of what is counted, and not faulty execution. That means, however, that half of it does result from execution errors—a very considerable value in the world's second largest economy. Of the portion of adjustment that does not concern production boundaries, nearly 60 percent is not in the admittedly harder-to-measure service sector but in the secondary sector. It is fair to argue that adjustments of this magnitude are not atypical for middle-income countries undergoing rapid growth. But it is also true that given China's size, the errors and deviations in policymaking that could arise from such misestimation are likely to be consequential both at home and abroad.

Drilling down further into China's statistics, our results point to three serious shortcomings in accuracy. The first is failure to make time series data consistent, resulting in conceptual and quantitative breaks. China's economy is evolving and so is its national accounting system. But while statisticians are working to patch the system, suspicions caused by the data series breaks divert attention from the improvements. While we focus on point-in-time data in this study, we recognize the importance of historical data comparability. To assess a country's long-term trends and performance, consistent multiyear numbers are necessary. That need is often unmet in China, and researchers confront data fragmented by definitions, methodologies, and classifications over the course of more than six decades. Second, divergent goals of regulators and national accountants dent the availability and accuracy of data. As described in Chapter 3, NBS relies on industry regulators for information, and if regulators do not survey or share certain data NBS cannot get the national numbers right. Given bureaucratic competition and the fact that NBS is lower ranked than many regulators, resolving this problem requires leadership intervention.

Third, but not least, the entanglement of economic statistics and bureaucratic job promotion distorts data. To resolve this, Beijing must reform performance evaluation, as is widely understood. There are signs of change, but hurdles will remain as long as industrial policy is a favored government approach to achieving growth.

In the end, our independent assessment of China's nominal GDP permitted us to make a judgment regarding a third line of debate about China's statistics as well: whether results are prone to politicization. As we noted in a January 2015 preview of this study,[6] for some time analysts have questioned Chinese GDP in light of observable consumption of inputs like electricity. For years, real GDP growth and electricity consumption growth moved together around a one-to-one ratio. This has broken down in recent years: as of late 2014, industrial electricity consumption growth was below 3.8 percent, while official GDP growth stood at 7.4 percent, leading some to speculate that the latter was overstated. But recall the rise of services and the struggle of heavier industries. In our view, 3.8 percent electricity consumption growth is fairly consistent with reported GDP growth, given the rising weight of services.

But while changing input/output ratios do not demonstrate politicization to us, Beijing's decision not to upwardly revise China's GDP estimate according to new information and best practice following the 2013 census does. If Beijing were to have fully revised up existing GDP, the value of new marginal activity necessary to report a given rate of GDP growth would be even higher in the future. By keeping the base lower, a given rate of growth is easier to achieve. Further, if the revisions to the base are introduced in the near future without sufficient explanation, GDP would appear to have grown, rather than simply having swelled from a belated revision. Frankly, we did not initially expect to encounter this concern, because we expected—as had been pledged—that China's methodologies were to be upgraded with clear explication in December 2014, but the unusual last-minute change-of-heart decision not to upgrade the Chinese national accounts framework forced us to evaluate why.

CREDIT AND DEBT

Because our revisions suggest an upward adjustment to (most) components of Chinese output in GDP terms without a matching revision in more directly observed inputs such as raw materials and capital, the results suggest a different ratio for many of the equations used to describe the intensity of economic growth. The first that deserves attention is credit and debt to GDP. At issue is the investment intensity of China's growth. Gross fixed capital formation, such as investment in plants and equipment by firms, has long been the largest component of GDP in expenditure terms; in the production approach, it shows up by way of the increased demand for products produced to build that plant, equipment and property. If capital were infinite, then a nation and its firms could expand GDP at any rate, forever, simply by pumping in more capital. But it is not infinite: new investment must come either from existing wealth such as previous retained profits, or debt, both of which are finite.

6. Daniel H. Rosen and Beibei Bao, "China's GDP—2015 Target and Outlook," January 28, 2015, http://rhg .com/notes/chinas-gdp-2015-target-and-outlook.

The relationship between today's new financial capital, such as lending, or physical capital stock formation such as factory assets, and tomorrow's output growth is of great concern to economists, who assess the incremental capital output ratio, or ICOR, to see whether an economy is becoming more or less capital-intensive. When an economy becomes overly dependent on ever-greater levels of capital formation to maintain growth, alarm bells ring.

Alarm bells over China's dependence on investment-led growth have been ringing for a decade and a half—since state banks ran up double-digit levels of nonperforming loans (NPLs) in the course of enabling 1990s GDP growth. National asset management companies (AMCs) were created to absorb those bad loans in 1999 and keep the banking system solvent by creating promissory notes, many of which have been carried ever since and are simply extended by sovereign edict. In 2014, similar provincial-level "bad debt banks" were created to absorb NPLs from local government financial vehicles (LGFVs) in order to avoid a subcentral financial crisis. Not only has the volume of dubious lending undertaken to sustain growth rates in recent years been large, but the accuracy of data to describe the associated risks is suspect. By the second quarter of 2011, the China Development Bank, with RMB 5.5 trillion in LGFV loans outstanding (two-thirds of its total loan book), was claiming that just one-quarter of 1 percent were nonperforming.[7] By mid-2014 the broadest measures of all Chinese debt (the largest share has been nonfinancial corporate liabilities, and the government share was at around 45 percent) stood above 250 percent of GDP.[8]

Our revisions to the GDP denominator of these equations would lower the debt ratios somewhat. Under the official GDP prior to 2013 census revisions and the International Monetary Fund (IMF) debt data, the ratio of "augmented" government debt—government debt with direct liabilities plus off-budget activities such as those conducted through LGFVs—to GDP in 2013 was 55.4 percent. The modest official 3.4 percent upward revision presented in December 2014 lowers that slightly to 53.6 percent. Carrying our 2008 revisions forward to 2013 results in a further decrease, to 48 to 50 percent of GDP. In the meantime, instead of a 2013 credit growth to GDP ratio (using M2, a broad measure of monetary supply) of 23.3 percent, we get a range of 20 to 21 percent. These are marginal improvements, not changes of magnitude, but they do turn back the assumed state of affairs by several years.

China's 2008 ICOR, using official prerevision figures, was 4.44—meaning that in inflation-adjusted terms, RMB 4.44 of fixed capital formation took place for each RMB of GDP growth. That ratio is at the top of the range typical over a business cycle in China since the 1990s. Moreover, it is the start of an apparent worsening trend that continues to the present, thanks in large part to the massive stimulus that Beijing kick-started in late 2008 to salvage the economy from the financial crisis storm (Figure 4.2). Ever-larger build-out of the capital stock is occurring without the resultant output growth Beijing had come to expect. China is getting less "bang for the buck," or, in their case, for the RMB. The

---

7. Yuanyan S. Zhang and Steven Barnett, "Fiscal Vulnerabilities and Risks from Local Government Finance in China" (IMF Working Paper No. 1404, International Monetary Fund, 2014), 24, http://www.imf.org/external/pubs/ft/wp/2014/wp1404.pdf.

8. Gabriel Sterne and Alessandro Theiss, "China's Debt Time Bomb—the Fall Out," *Financial Times*, December 2, 2014, http://blogs.ft.com/beyond-brics/2014/12/02/guest-post-chinas-debt-time-bomb-the-fall-out/.

Figure 4.2. China's Capital Investment Contributes Increasingly Less to Growth*

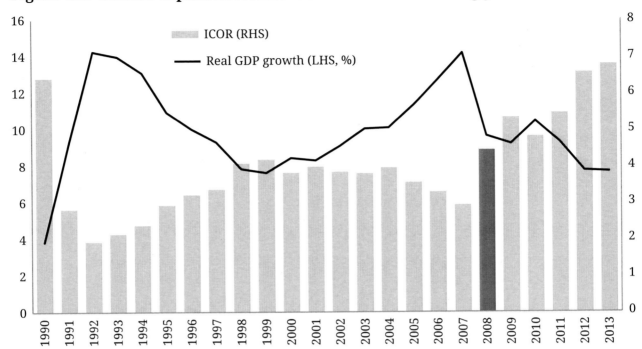

* 2005 is the base year for this chart. 2012 and 2013 GDP data are post-2013 census revisions.
Sources: NBS, authors' estimates.

relationship is far out of the historic range and in worrisome territory. Japan, South Korea, and Taiwan averaged ICORs of 2.7 to 3.2 at their heights.[9] If more financing is being deployed to build capital stock but less growth results, then the system is not working.

Our GDP revisions suggests a 4.19–4.38 ICOR for 2008, moderately less out of line with the historic range, though still very high. According to development economist William Easterly, the ICOR for countries at the height of GDP growth is usually between 3 and 4,[10] suggesting that ratios above 4 reflect dwindling investment efficiency. This diminishing marginal output return on capital is a part of the fall to today's 7 percent growth, a rate which is, however, still impressive. The restatements resulting from our GDP re-estimates suggest that whatever your degree of alarm over China's debt levels, it can be stepped down a few notches, because there is marginally more value-added activity occurring per unit of observed capital input than previously thought. And as noted above, the less capital-intensive service subsectors have already grown larger than previously credited. However, while China may have a few more years of wiggle room than commonly thought, the pace and direction of mounting debt concerns are just as alarming as before.

9. C. H. Kwan, "Improving Investment Efficiency in China through Privatization and Financial Reform," *Nomura Capital Market Review* 9, no. 2 (2006): 34, http://www.nicmr.com/nicmr/english/report/repo/2006/2006sum03.pdf.

10. Olivier Basdevant, "How Can Burundi Raise Its Growth Rate? The Impact of Civil Conflict and State Intervention on Burundi's Growth Performance" (IMF Working Paper No. 0911, International Monetary Fund, 2009), 5, https://www.imf.org/external/pubs/ft/wp/2009/wp0911.pdf.

ENERGY INTENSITY OF GDP

The "discovery" of a higher level of output in China relative to other inputs to the production process beyond capital and labor is important as well. Notable in this regard is China's use of energy and thus the energy intensity of GDP. The growing energy intensity of China's growth is concerning for a number of reasons. First, it reflects the overdeployment of resources into energy-intensive heavy industries such as steel, aluminum, cement, and petrochemical refinery. Because China is well beyond sufficient in meeting its own internal steel needs, for instance, and given that the negative environmental and energy security externalities of additional capital deepening in this industry are severe, this has been a clear-cut reason for concern. In short, vested interests benefiting from uneconomical investment in steel are perverting the national interest.

That remains the case, regardless of the GDP aggregates. Choking pollution is depleting the natural environment and poisoning the population, reducing the potential growth contribution of China's demographic in nontrivial ways, including diminished life expectancy, lost days of worker availability due to respiratory illness and other maladies, and an obvious exodus of many skilled, more mobile professionals from careers in China (and alongside them, new business investment chasing after skilled workers and a healthy working environment).

The overcapacity in many heavy industries is not changed by our GDP results, as volume measures of material goods output and aggregate demand for these basic materials are not significantly altered in our recount. However, our results do imply that the energy intensity of China's GDP is marginally lower than previously reported. As illustrated below, initial economic reform triggered a profound lightening of China's energy intensity that continued until the beginning of the 2000s. Thereafter, the so-called China supercycle of heavy industry build-out to support infrastructure and property construction commenced, and the downward pattern in energy intensity reversed for some years, sending projections of China's energy needs soaring, given the ever-expanding GDP base (Figure 4.3). In our reestimate, in 2008, China required 80 to 82 tons of coal or its equivalent (TCE) to produce RMB 1 million of nominal GDP output, rather than 93 TCE as the official statistics imply. Applied to today's case using the precensus revision 2013 GDP figure, that lowered intensity implies 7.6 to 9.3 fewer TCE per unit of nominal GDP output than would be the case based on the official ratio of 66 TCE. In short, the rise in services activity is improving China's energy profile—at least in terms of the ratio.

This has policy implications. First, recall that whatever revisions are made based on the 2013 census—whether the official 3.4 percent announced so far or our augmented 13.1 to 16.3 percent—NBS would extend adjustments back only to the first year after the previous census, 2009, but not further except in a few cases. Chinese commitments to reduce carbon intensity—which is related to energy intensity—are measured as a percentage reduction from the 2005 baseline. If 2005 GDP data were revised upward *proportionally* along with 2008-forward numbers, then these commitments would be intact. But that turned not to be the case as of this writing. With the 2005 commitment baseline on one side

Figure 4.3. China's Energy Intensity of GDP, 1954–2020*

Unit: Tons of coal equivalent (TCE) per RMB million of real GDP output

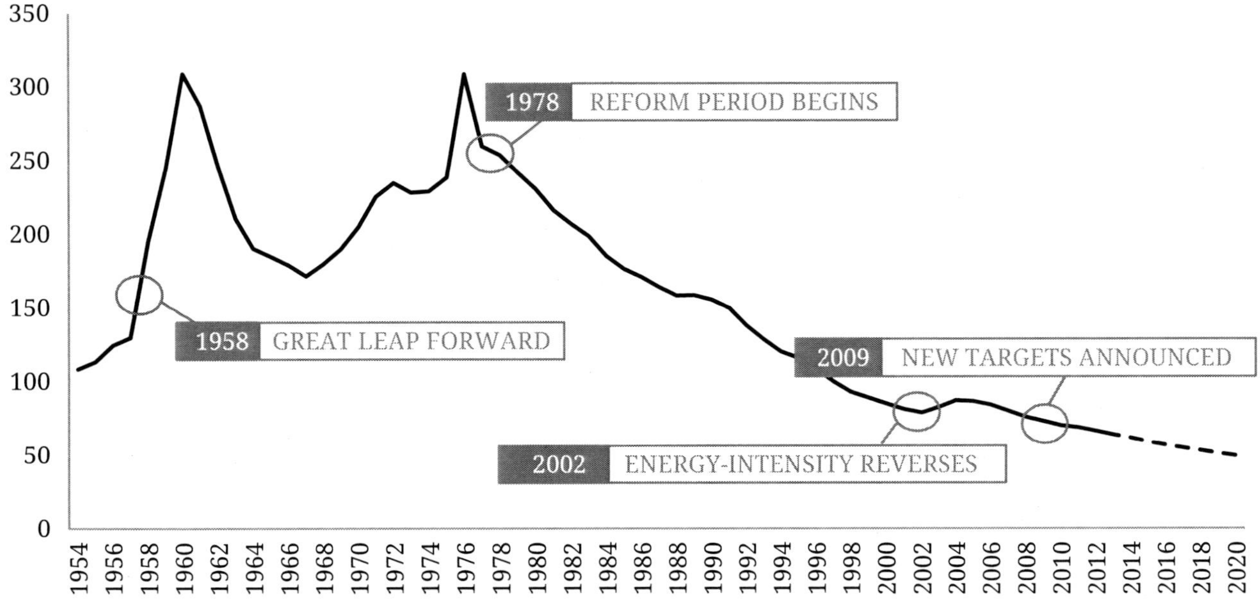

* 2013 is the base year for this chart. 2012 and 2013 GDP data are post-2013 census revisions. 2014–2020 energy intensity levels are Rhodium Group's forecasts.
Sources: NBS, Rhodium Group, authors' estimates.

of the revision-watershed, and current performance on the other, China will be misleadingly closer to its policy objectives than otherwise. Observers and analysts will need to take that into account, and Chinese energy and climate policy negotiators should assure that their policy commitments will not be diluted by statistical technicalities.

REAL ESTATE

Our revision from a better calculation of imputed rent alone adds 6 percent to China's 2008 GDP. This is almost twice the *total* revision NBS made following the 2013 census, so it is fairly obvious that China chose not to update its methodology for counting this component of GDP in 2014. It continued to use the complex mix of indicators such as housing stock, construction cost, and depreciation ratio—less accurate than the SNA-preferred comparable market rent—to attribute value-added to owner-occupied dwellings. In preparation for release of 2013 census revisions, Beijing indicated that it *would* update its imputed rent methodology, so this came as a surprise. The most logical explanation for this choice is that upgrading GDP accounts to better reflect market rent and thus the value of imputed rent would—in presenting a more accurate picture of the property subsector of the economy—show real estate to have been even more of a bubble than is commonly thought.

Official 2008 figures present the real estate subsector of services as 4.7 percent of total Chinese GDP for that year. Our reestimate suggests a real estate weight of between 9.4 and 9.7 percent of the augmented total GDP—more than double the official share. Chinese and foreign economists have warned about overreliance on property market investment to sustain high GDP growth and the underlying risks. The phenomena of "ghost towns," unsold or unoccupied property in places such as Ordos and Caofeidian, and the risks associated with so much household wealth and institutional financial assets locked into a potentially unstable store of value are serious problems. The GDP value attributable to imputed rent keyed to market rent is inherently regressive: it implies more income to the wealthiest categories of Chinese society—urban households owning newly built, rapidly appreciating property—contributing to the income inequality picture. And yet, that is the reality that a more up-to-date calculation of China's GDP presents. We conclude that China would be better off updating its GDP and dealing with the policy implications forthrightly rather than deferring adjustment, holding the reality back from the public, and putting off the necessary debates required for long-term Chinese prosperity.

Through China's Political Eyes: GDP in a Broader Context

China's GDP statistics have a political significance that goes well beyond economic concerns. As discussed in Chapter 1, the history of national accounting in the modern era includes a regular tug of war for control of growth statistics, with leaders often believing that the appearance of economic growth and stability is critical and self-fulfilling, and vice versa: an inability to report stable growth would procyclically accelerate a downturn. National statistics were a pawn in the Cold War contest between market and socialist economic systems. In modern China, the central government's monopoly on reporting the growth performance of the nation has been an essential political tool, because, as President Xi and his predecessors have explicitly asserted, the Party's mission and social stability in China depend on developing the economy and raising the people's living standards. Several of the conclusions from our assessment relate to the broader political tableau.

POLITICAL CHALLENGES OF SLOWDOWN—CLOSER AT HAND

A higher per capita GDP level means, all things being equal, that the growth moderation point is closer or already present. Among economists, this observation is obvious; trends *revert to the mean*, which is to say that China's atypical, continuously high-speed growth (relative to its own history and international comparisons) will give way to the more typical pattern of more moderate growth. This argument was recently made by economists Lant Pritchett and Larry Summers.[11] It is the long duration of China's high growth rates, rather than higher per capita income levels per se, that Pritchett and Summers found most strongly predictive of a forthcoming slowdown. They conclude:

> We have had a number of people suggest that China will not have a growth
> slowdown because a slowdown would be politically costly and hence Chinese

---

11. Lant Pritchett and Lawrence H. Summers, "Asiaphoria Meets Regression to the Mean" (Working Paper No. 20573, National Bureau of Economic Research, 2014), 2, http://www.nber.org/papers/w20573.

policymakers have every incentive to avoid that. Thus, they will act to prevent it—and a known "trap" should be easily avoidable. But acting to sustain an unsustainably high growth rate may lead subsequent adjustment to be much harsher. As our friend Ricardo Hausmann puts it, "The path from 8 percent growth to 4 percent growth often goes through negative 2 percent."

Other analysts, including those at China's powerful NDRC, also conclude that slowing growth (from high to "moderate to high" speed) is a "new normal," based on bottom-up estimations of growth potential. Our study suggests that China's past growth has been *even faster* than recognized by official data, adding to the risk of future regression to a more normal mean. That adjustment will be painful, and it will be more difficult the longer it is deferred. Our results suggest per capita GDP in China in 2014 would more accurately be stated at $8,300 to 8,550 in current dollars, rather than the $7,600 official post-2013 census revision data present. Our projections were under the assumption our restatements for 2008 GDP can be carried over to today and the 2013 census revision was not significant enough to present an accurate picture. One can read that as indicating that China is roughly one to two years deeper into the challenges of middle-income territory than standard data suggest.

This analysis implies that the option of taking additional policy measures in order to sustain GDP growth rates at previous levels, rather than permit a natural deceleration, is even more ill-advised than previously thought. Some influential Chinese policy economists argue to leaders that a 7 percent GDP growth is below potential and the leadership should avail itself of opportunities to stoke the fires of growing higher, to above 8 percent, for some time to come. In light of the unrecorded economic activity we identified, leaders have further reason to be mindful of the social instability that will be aggravated by further delays in economic adjustment and national accounting improvement.

GLOBAL PASSING POINT

Our revisions suggest that China is nearer to the number one ranking in global GDP tables on a nominal dollar basis. On a purchasing power parity (PPP) basis, the IMF announced that China was the world's largest economy in October 2014, but such calculations can be misleading because they reflect low prices in the typical consumer basket (and thus more buying power) that are not truly for comparable goods or reflect anomalously cheap labor costs for many services. In geopolitical terms, the nominal GDP comparison is more germane. Much attention is directed to the questions of if and when China will catch up to and pass the economic size of the United States. To a great extent that event is only symbolically important. On a per capita basis, and in many other critical regards, China will still lag behind advanced economies for many decades.

However, politicians—in Beijing, Washington, and elsewhere—would indeed treat China's arrival as the world's largest economy as a significant milestone. This will surely be regarded as a historical *return* to global preeminence for an economy thought to have been the world's largest for millennia until faltering in the early 1800s during the Qing

Dynasty (coincident with the expansion of European powers in East Asia). It will also precipitate deeper soul-searching on the part of other nations overshadowed by China's ascension and expectations that China should take greater responsibility for bearing the costs of the international system it stands atop in GDP terms, expect less recourse to arguments that it should be exempt from various obligations as a developing country, and invite further contemplation of the balance of power options in case China displays a tendency to throw its new geostrategic weight around.

Our results do not offer a straightforward answer to the question of when China could pass the United States. To answer that question, one must make multiple complex assumptions about U.S. and Chinese GDP growth rates for one to two decades to come, about inflation rates, and about exchange rates (because this comparison must be made in a common currency). Our work does not speak to all those variables, and thoughtful analysts can arrive at completely different projections for them that are equally reasonable. What our study *does* do is to provide a more accurate base-year value from which to apply those annual assumptions going forward. For instance, if using the baseline scenario growth projections we made for China in *Avoiding the Blind Alley*,[12] the U.S. Congressional Budget Office's forecasts for U.S. growth rates, and with the assumption that the RMB will gradually strengthen against the USD over the next 15 years at the average strengthening pace from 1995 to 2013, we found that if Beijing did not revise its preliminary 2013 GDP, China would pass the United States in 2022 (if the RMB-to-USD ratio remained at the 2013 level of 6.20, that parity year would come three years later in 2025). However, if applying our midpoint 2008 restatement level to China's prerevision 2013 GDP, the passing point arrives in 2020, two years earlier than the official numbers demonstrated, just due to the effect of a higher base. With bolder assumptions about growth rates and exchange rate adjustments, that passing point could be sooner, in which case our upward revision is even more important in terms of shortening the period until parity. Alternatively, one can push the crossing point much further back by assuming that Chinese growth will fail to achieve its potential due to sputtering economic policy reforms or that U.S. growth will outperform, among other contingencies.[13]

Chinese leaders remain sensitive to the political ramifications of this international economic ranking, as they have in the past and have with almost all other statistical representations. Deng Xiaoping famously advised in the early 1990s that China should bide its time and hide its capabilities so as not to invite external anxieties about or reactions to its reemergence, which he feared would be deleterious to the nation's interests. In the Xi Jinping era, Chinese leaders have parted with that dictum and shifted to unreserved displays of Chinese political and security power abroad. And yet, when it comes to trumpeting its *economic* power, China's leaders continue to pull their punches. In January 2014, not long after the Third Plenum, President Xi Jinping reiterated that China is still and will remain at the preliminary stage of socialism, emphasizing China's status as the world's

---

12. Rosen, *Avoiding the Blind Alley*, 143.
13. For a detailed analysis of what we consider to be reasonable scenarios for China's long-term growth, see Rosen, *Avoiding the Blind Alley*, 134–144.

most populous *developing* country with "backward social production" unaligned with "rising material and cultural needs among the masses."[14] In October 2014, Zhu Guangyao, Vice Minister of Finance, responded to the IMF's PPP-based GDP figure published in the same month, which identified China as the largest economy. At a conference held by the Peterson Institute for International Economics (PIIE) in Washington Zhu reiterated that China is still a developing country and that a huge gap exists between China and the United States in terms of the quality of economic growth.[15] An inclination to defer a little longer the change in international expectations that may well be triggered by China's arrival atop the global rankings is—we conjecture—one factor shaping China's GDP posture, including its decision not to converge with 2008 SNA just months, if not weeks (or even days), before announcing the 2013 census results.

STATISTICS AND STEERING THE SHIP OF STATE

As China's economy becomes more mature and normal, leaders face new challenges. The essential question about the nation's long-term growth potential is whether leaders can permit the market to play a decisive role in determining economic outcomes, while managing the myriad political and security challenges China will confront as a result. There is no simple answer: the outcome relies both on science and art. But for science to play its part, accurate and timely data to reflect the performance of the economy must be available to leaders. We have concluded that an ever-greater share of growth in China arises in the service industries but that these remain confounding to statisticians and senior-most policymakers. We find that overreliance on real estate is even greater than estimated, but the opportunity to upgrade accounting to capture that was declined. And we have determined that the benefits of drawing in skeptical investors by permitting greater data transparency are still overshadowed by the fear of losing the ability to control the official narrative about the state of growth, and thus the narrative of the central government's credibility in ruling the economy and society.

Which comes first—freedom to chart a policy course presumed to generate statistics satisfactory enough to publish? Or sufficient statistical transparency that policymakers are compelled to set priorities that maximize growth? Even if control over the statistical narrative was sometimes helpful to sustaining GDP growth in the past, it is reasonable to argue that transparency must play a more central role in the future. The comprehensive reform program presented at the November 2013 Party Third Plenum emphasized transparency and open registries for public expenditures, property rights, government fees, real estate property, financial securities, land rights, environmental impacts and pollution emissions, employment levels, and other information making up the statistical foundation of how the Chinese political system works. While the decision not to fully embrace the more modern 2008 SNA regime indicated hesitance over more accurate reporting, the sweeping reference

14. Jinping Xi, "切实把思想统一到党的十八届三中全会精神上来 (On Unifying Thoughts onto Spirits of the Third Plenary Session of 18th CPC Central Committee)," *People's Daily*, January 1, 2014, sec. 2, http://paper.people.com .cn/rmrb/html/2014-01/01/nw.D110000renmrb_20140101_1-02.htm.

15. Patrice Hill, "China Presses Congress for Action on Stalled IMF Reforms," *Washington Times*, October 8, 2014, http://www.washingtontimes.com/news/2014/oct/8/china-presses-congress-for-action-on-stalled-imf-r/.

to new roles for public access to information reporting is an important indication of what leaders think a fully functioning China of the future must look like.

Through Foreign Eyes: A Resized Rival

Viewed from abroad, our reassessment of China's GDP has implications as well. First of all, still licking their analytical wounds from a mixed experience estimating the size of the Soviet Union during the Cold War (which turned out to be smaller than thought), some western analysts are inclined to believe that the size of China's economy may be overstated. This study concludes that the bias is in the other direction. We can only speculate why Beijing would choose to understate GDP. One hypothesis is that it would permit a periodic "topping off" of annual growth rates over the coming years to project stronger performance, all the while moving national accounts marginally closer to an accurate count. Another motivation may be to dodge, for the time being, the international debate over the implications of China's ascension to the global number one position. In any case, our conclusion is that China's GDP is neither overstated nor out of line with an independent assessment by as much as some have believed, and also that its practices have generally converged with international best practice over time, despite the remaining material shortcomings and institutional constraints. Rather than being concerned with aggregate overstatement, four other implications should concern foreign observers.

THE PASSING POINT FROM THE FOREIGN PERSPECTIVE

As noted above, the point in time when China reaches parity with and then passes the United States as the world's largest economy will inevitably be assigned historical significance. As noted, our assessment does not offer a forecast for that date but rather a more solid initial value from which to make projections under whatever assumptions the ambitious analyst deems reasonable, which include both countries' growth rates, inflation levels, and exchange rates. Our adjustments imply that the date could move 2 years earlier, but the actual crossing point could be anywhere from 5 to 20 or more years into the future, depending on one's assumptions.

Besides the passing time dynamics, this study also sheds some light on the challenges Beijing will confront in trying to maximize growth rates over those years to come. Despite progress, officials still have a difficult time measuring and analyzing economic activity, especially in the less tangible and increasingly diverse service industries that are expected to produce the bulk of future growth. Much of future growth is reliant on total factor productivity (TFP) gains, which in turn rely on improving institutional conditions such as NBS's ability to collect and report accurate information on growth, alongside other bureaucracies responsible for basic data, without political or ideological interference. In the course of independently assessing China's GDP, we have not only come to a different estimate of economic activity, but we have also come to better appreciate the political and institutional hurdles impeding the productive flow of accurate, complete statistical information.

So while our results move forward the projected year for China-U.S. GDP parity, they also underscore the challenges China will face in achieving that convergence. And, most of all, we observe that a Chinese economy able to reach the point of GDP parity with the United States would necessarily be a different China—both politically and economically—than the one we know today. If China pursues a mercantile, illiberal economic path that would undermine the international economic norms which the U.S. and other advanced economies have worked to establish, then it is unlikely to sustain sufficient growth to reach parity with a United States averaging 2.3 percent growth over the next 15 years, according to the Congressional Budget Office (CBO). If Beijing succeeds in redoubling its reform and external opening strategy, it does have the prospect of parity, but as a far more liberal polity. The illiberal tack is a real possibility, but not in combination with high-trend potential growth.

It is also worth observing that just as the evolution of the GDP accounting boundary plays a part in our upward revision to China's economic size today, so too could shifting constructs for counting national economic activity change over the conceivable "passing time frame" in ways the alter a simple side-by-side accounting of China and the United States. As discussed in Chapter 1, there is considerable debate about the adequacy of GDP or other output measures as a benchmark for human welfare and national performance. While statisticians stress that GDP does not pretend to be more encompassing of human welfare than it is, the reality is that politicians and the public treat it as the most comprehensive indicator available today. But by the time China is at parity with the United States in terms of annual economic output, the weight of the hedonic, intangible quality-of-life value that citizens enjoy thanks to innovative new services may make GDP passé. The value of preserving the assets of the natural environment around us may become far more important than production value-added (as the present exodus of highly skilled professionals from heavily polluted but high-growth northern China reminds us). The security of institutions that ensure freedom of beliefs, speech, and association may be valued more highly than the growth rate of material output.

THE RELIABILITY QUESTION: RISK OF ECONOMIC BLINDSIDE?

The 2008/2009 global financial crisis demonstrated how misjudging economic strengths and systemic risks can have dramatic and even devastating consequences for the global economy. China has become one of the most systemically important countries for the global economy. No other country has had the potential to rival U.S. economic power for the past century. China has long since ceased to be buffered from the world by self-imposed self-sufficiency, and is deeply integrated with global markets. When China reported a 16.8 percent upward GDP revision for 2004, after its first national economic census, it was a bit less than 4.5 percent of the world economy. By 2013 that share almost tripled to 12.6 percent. As China has grown from a nonparty to international trade and investment in 1979 to a dominant force, the consequences of its economic performance have mushroomed as well (Figure 4.4). In the early 2000s, China's policymakers profoundly underestimated the extent of coming growth in demand for energy resources and basic materials, leading to a

Figure 4.4. China and the Global Economy: 2000 vs. 2012

Unit: Share of global total

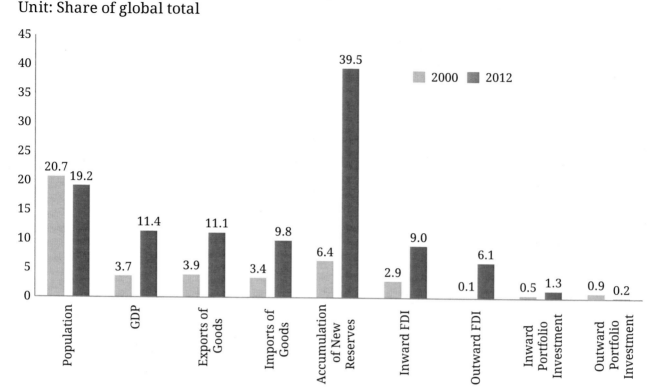

Sources: World Bank, IMF World Economic Outlook (WEO) database, United Nations Conference on Trade and Development (UNCTAD stat), authors' estimates.

demand shock in international markets that sent commodity prices to unanticipated levels. The change in global direct investment flows in pursuit of the resulting profit streams and global trade flows resulting from a boom in extractive sector exports was massive. It was large enough to change political dynamics and economic development patterns across broad swaths of Africa, Latin America, and Southeast Asia, and to alter exchange rates, employment, and fiscal balances in Australia, Korea, Brazil, and Canada as well.

Unlike more advanced economies, China—as a middle-income transitional economy still reliant on infrastructure and property booms for a large share of aggregate demand—is sure to present volatility in its profile as it works through rebalancing and structural adjustment in the years ahead. That means a high possibility for demand and supply shocks that, in combination with its enormous size, have seldom been experienced with a transitional economy before, posing risks to a global economy still recovering only weakly and wary of more geopolitical risks. There are great dangers of being blindsided by abrupt inflections in Chinese economic activity.

This study sheds light on the estimate of China's nominal GDP measures; it does not refine short-term growth estimates most connected to demand and supply shocks. But our analysis does have implications for efforts to manage the challenge of anticipating near-term impacts. First, our reestimates are a reminder that large restatements of China's economic size remain possible, and are indeed necessary. These should not be assumed to indicate trouble: instead, they would be a step toward greater reliability and accuracy, and it is important not to overreact to such moves. Second, the deferral in upward revision seen at the end of 2014 foreshadows the possibility that GDP growth will be overstated in the years ahead instead, adding to the apparent disconnect between reported growth and observed demand for both tangible and intangible inputs. Third, our results suggest that China is even further along into the era of services-intensive growth and has relied even more on a property bubble than generally assumed. The course correction from overde-ployment of resources (financial, physical, and otherwise) into heavy industries is more urgent and immediate than otherwise believed.

Fourth, a corollary to this course correction is that Beijing's ability to manage expecta-tions about the stability of future growth is rapidly eroding, so the prospect of a painful external shock from Chinese volatility is increased. In the previous era, China's external demand was concentrated in intermediate inputs for processing and reexport and for raw materials feeding into domestic infrastructure and property booms. As shown in our revision model and elsewhere, the contribution of these drivers to China's demand is flagging. There is vast potential for new activity in promising sunrise industries and in servicing household consumption, but Beijing has much less ability to command and control the cycles in these areas. Less and less of China's sustainable economic activity is suited to "the plan," because the plan has been made based on incomplete, less than satis-factory, data mixed with political imperatives rather than sane economic rationale.

INTERNATIONAL GOALS BENCHMARKED TO GDP

The impacts of revising China's GDP on internal debates about the labor, capital, and energy intensity of China's growth were discussed above. However, external considera-tions arise as well. Some important ongoing international negotiations are framed in terms of the factor-intensities of GDP; other issues are influenced by GDP size.

Voting shares in international organizations, in particular the IMF, have been a source of tension with China in recent years as its share of global GDP has swelled by more than three times over the course the last decade. The IMF periodically adjusts voting shares, derived from members' quotas, "to reflect changes in their relative positions in the world economy."[16] This reallocation is not automatic, and incumbents including the United States have resisted a rapid shift of voting power to China, but an upward revision of China's GDP further strengthens Beijing's argument that its position is underweight. Of course, other nations also make technical revisions to GDP: Italy and Britain recently did so by including prostitution and sales of illegal drugs in the GDP boundary; the United States did so by upgrading to 2008 SNA in 2013 and counting more intellectual property investment in GDP; and in early 2015 India changed its GDP methodology in ways that upped apparent growth but left the central bank head, finance minister, and private economists all unsure about

---

16. IMF, "Factsheet—IMF Quotas," October 3, 2014, http://www.imf.org/external/np/exr/facts/quotas.htm.

what was changed and what it meant.[17] So China's partial revision made in December 2014, or even the full revision we regard as necessary, could, unsurprisingly, be taken with a grain of salt and not translate immediately into a claim on more IMF voting rights.

Other negotiations could be impacted by a Chinese GDP revision as well, especially one that increases overall output without implying an upward adjustment of inputs. This would be most pronounced under our 13.1 to 16.3 percent revision scenario, but even the modest revision China announced in December 2014 has implications. In the 2013 *Economic Census*, for example, Beijing expanded the accounting boundary for the financial subsector, which resulted in 22.5 percent and 22.8 percent upward revisions for 2012 and 2013 in its value-added, respectively. The revisions, as far as we can tell, resulted from including financial activities that were not in China's old industrial classification and newly noted in the 2011 update. Despite the same value-added calculation method, the enlarged accounting boundary justifies a longer-than-usual retrospective revision by NBS, stretching back to 1978 rather than 2009, and these adjustments have changed financial value-added for each year.

With the increasing weight of financial value-added over time, the calculated energy intensity of China's growth, and thus the *carbon emission intensity* of China's output, is reduced. International efforts are underway to reduce greenhouse gas emissions. Some reduction goals are set in terms of reduced carbon intensity over time, and the sudden "discovery" of additional low-carbon economic activity reduces China's apparent carbon intensity.

As noted, unlike the financial subsector revisions, most of a prospective upward adjustment in China's GDP catalogued in this study will not be projected back all the way to 1978, but instead will only be revised back to 2009—the year after the previous national economic census. Important climate policy commitments, however, are benchmarked to China's 2005 carbon intensity. If 2005 data connected to carbon intensity are not revised or not revised *proportionally* to the adjustment to data for 2009 and after, the implied progress on carbon reduction will be exaggerated.

This does not suggest that China is wrong or irresponsible to revise its GDP measures. GDP revisions are normal and appropriate. However, it is important that the international community and Chinese policymakers assess whether China has met its energy- and carbon-intensity targets using a consistent GDP series. If Beijing continues past practice and does not extend nominal GDP revisions *proportionally* back to 2005, the base year for energy-intensity reduction tracking, then Beijing simply needs to estimate energy-intensity/carbon-intensity reductions using the previous GDP methodology alongside the revised GDP estimates.

---

17. Portia Crowe, "India Changed Its GDP Calculations and It's Confusing Everybody," *Business Insider*, February 10, 2015, http://www.businessinsider.com/india-changed-its-gdp-calculations-2015-2.

OPPORTUNITIES AND COMPETITIVENESS

Finally, policymakers and business decisionmakers abroad should not lose track of the most obvious, significant implication of this study: China's economy is even bigger than was thought, with consequent market opportunities and competitive implications as well.

The market size of China has been a beacon to global business for centuries, and since the modern reform era, investors have bet heavily on the nation's economic potential and consumption appetite. Our research demonstrates that China is realizing that potential, that Chinese consumers have more purchasing power than thought, and that output has reached levels even greater than reported. This is not a *Potemkin village* economy, built on fabricated reports.

There are myriad elements of misallocation, distortion, and risk to future growth in China, and we have discussed many of these. At the same time, a highly critical assessment of China's national accounting nonetheless concludes that value-added is at or meaningfully above the nominal reported level—about $10.4 trillion in 2014—or perhaps closer to $11.5 trillion, if fully revised. Advanced economies, not least the United States, should enjoy growing opportunities in this phase of China's development: the service industries where we identified the greatest unrecorded activity in China are often areas of comparative advantage for firms from advanced economies.

The magnitude of those opportunities of course comes with a flip side: competition. We believe China's rebalancing toward a more efficient allocation of resources is further along than believed. Services overtook industry and construction four years earlier than thought and continue to grow faster than the latter. China was able to achieve extraordinary productivity and global market share in the past, even without the next-generation elements of policy reform under discussion today, such as robust intellectual property rights protection, capital markets deepening, priority on human capital investment, and consumer welfare–oriented competition policy. Combining the structural adjustment inferred from our comprehensive review of the national accounts with the current reform agenda, one can imagine a still more competitive Chinese economy in the future.

About the Authors

Daniel H. Rosen is the founding partner of Rhodium Group (RHG) and leads the firm's work on China. Mr. Rosen is a senior associate of the CSIS Simon Chair and is affiliated with a number of other American think tanks focused on international economics. He is an adjunct associate professor at Columbia University and has taught graduate seminars on the Chinese economy at the School of International and Public Affairs (SIPA) since 2001. Mr. Rosen writes and speaks extensively on China and other emerging economy topics. From 2000–2001, Mr. Rosen was senior adviser for International Economic Policy at the White House National Economic Council and National Security Council, where he played a key role in completing China's accession to the World Trade Organization and accompanied the president to Asia for summits and state visits. He is a member of the Council on Foreign Relations and board member of the National Committee for U.S.-China Relations.

Beibei Bao is a research analyst at RHG, where she monitors and analyzes business, regulatory, and political developments in China. Her research has focused on Chinese economic statistics, financial markets, trade, Chinese society, and U.S.-China relations. She writes and comments regularly on trends in China's marketplace, and her work has appeared in publications by CSIS, Harvard University, the Aspen Institute Italia, and elsewhere. Prior to joining RHG, Ms. Bao worked as a researcher for the *New York Times* covering China's economy. A native of Beijing, she holds two bachelor's from Peking University in journalism and economics and two master's from Columbia University in international relations and journalism, where she graduated with honors.